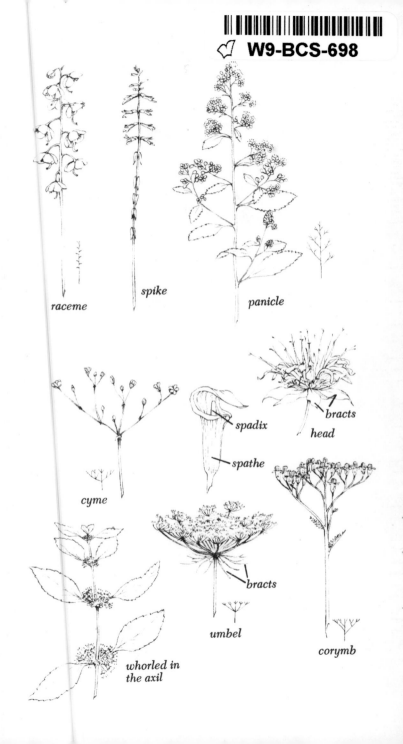

raceme

spike

panicle

cyme

spadix

spathe

bracts

head

umbel

bracts

corymb

whorled in
the axil

Newcomb's Wildflower Guide

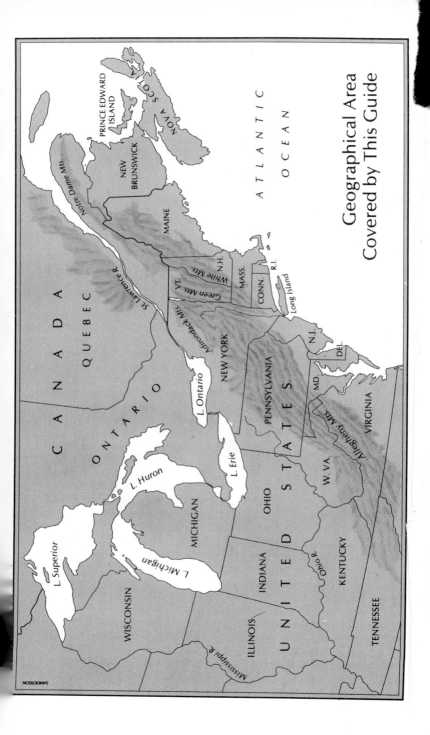

Geographical Area
Covered by This Guide

Newcomb's Wildflower Guide

An Ingenious New Key System for
Quick, Positive Field Identification of the
Wildflowers, Flowering Shrubs and Vines of
Northeastern and North-central North America

LAWRENCE NEWCOMB

Illustrated by Gordon Morrison

Foreword by Roland C. Clement
Vice President, National Audubon Society

Little, Brown and Company—Boston—Toronto—London

This book is dedicated to my wife, Betty,
for her inspiration and support

I am deeply grateful to Mrs. Earl C. Bourne, Mrs. Emily S. Parcher, Mr. Albert W. Bussewitz and Mr. Lewis E. Dickinson and other friends who located specimens of elusive plants for illustration and who were of help in many other ways. I especially thank Mr. Louis E. Hand of New Lisbon, New Jersey, for so generously guiding me to the unique flora of the pine barrens. I am also grateful to the New England Botanical Club for the use of its herbarium and to the Massachusetts Horticultural Society and the New England Wild Flower Society for the use of their libraries.

Dr. Richard E. Weaver, Jr., at the Arnold Arboretum of Harvard University was extremely helpful in reviewing the final draft and made many valuable suggestions for improvements in the text and illustrations. Mrs. Jean Whitnack and Miss Nancy Ellis of the editorial staff of Little, Brown and Company did a superb job of meticulously checking the entire book.

Finally, the book could not have been completed without the enthusiastic cooperation and the long hours of painstaking work of the artist, Mr. Gordon Morrison.

L.N.

AHS

LIBRARY OF CONGRESS CATALOG CARD NO. 77–47

10   9

Designed by Susan Windheim

Published simultaneously in Canada
by Little, Brown & Company (Canada) Limited

PRINTED IN THE UNITED STATES OF AMERICA

Foreword

Every generation needs its own introduction to the environment. For me it was F. Schuyler Matthew's delightful line drawings that made the northeastern flora come alive. For an even earlier generation, *Gray's Manual* had been helpful to eager amateurs because it was modest in its purview and also fitted neatly into one's field-jacket pocket. When M. L. Fernald's 1,500-page eighth edition of *Gray's Manual* appeared in 1950, however, it overwhelmed almost everyone and, in my opinion, actually gave field botany a setback. This was ironic because Fernald himself was a superlative field botanist and utterly fascinating in his erudition.

Several authors have tried to supply us with a workable wildflower guide since Fernald's day, but none of these guides "caught on," presumably because none of them quite filled the niche a field guide must fill. In addition to being compact, it must be reasonably representative of the complete regional flora, well illustrated, and helpful in clarifying what must even so remain a complex area of knowledge, simply because Nature's evolutionary processes are never simple, pigeon-hole systems.

But twenty-five years is nearly a generation, and it is time we went afield again for more than bird-watching. Lawrence Newcomb's exciting new book has all the earmarks of the practical wildflower guide we have been looking for. Its system of identification stresses the type of plant (wildflower, shrub or vine), leaf characteristics, and parts of the flower, and quickly gets one to an answer. These identification keys have been field-tested for several seasons by the staff and students of the Audubon Center of Greenwich, Connecticut, where both the experienced and the amateur have been enthusiastic about the clarity and dependability of the Newcomb method. This is a high recommendation, and it leads me to believe that this book has the potential for reintroducing a generation of new amateurs — young and old — to the pleasures of knowing the wildflowers.

The question of representation, or "coverage," is always a difficult one for an introductory book. Some experts contend that amateurs are frustrated if every plant they may attempt to track through the keys and pictures is not included. But the obverse is also true, because plants are so many and so varied that if too much detail is included, the beginner is overwhelmed and often turns away altogether. For example, the asters (with over fifty species in the East) and the goldenrods (with over seventy species) are genera that only the most persistent field botanist will attempt to master. In such large groups it suffices to know a few of the more conspicuous, most pleasing representatives. Mr. Newcomb seems to me to have struck a good balance by including all the major species of the Northeast, plus lesser-known species that are frequently seen once one learns to look. The amateur who is more ambitious can of course always go on to more technical works after having enjoyed a stimulating introduction to the subject.

Although all the wildflowers included in this book can be identified solely by use of the keys, the illustrations by Gordon Morrison are an important first step in recognizing species in the field almost as soon as you see them. You should of course always confirm your identifications by checking text against illustration, and illustration against text, to be sure you have not overlooked some important detail. It is this sort of discriminating interplay that builds one's critical faculties and speeds the process of learning one's way about. Time, experience, and a good memory are then the only things that stand between you and expert status.

Remember that your studies of the wildflowers will introduce you only to the showiest members of the plant communities of the Northeast. There are many others with inconspicuous flowers, and some with none at all. Trees, for example, run the gamut in this respect. Together, the plants of a region constitute its flora, its vegetation. Once started, you will find a whole new world opening before you. You will find that different communities of plants occur in recognizable environments. Broadly speaking, these are dune communities, fresh or salt-water marsh (dominated by grass-like plants), pasture (our temporary, eastern equivalent of prairie), swamp (which is wet forest), and upland forest of various types. All of these communities are dependent on soil and water relations, local climate, and on what man has done to these environments over the millennia. Such insights are the basis of ecological awareness.

Finally, your enjoyment of wildflowers and other plants should make an important contribution to your feeling at home on this planet. We are growing increasingly aware that our ability to function well as individuals, and as members of social groups, depends to a large extent on our sense of belonging. At a time when social changes are bewilderingly rapid and uncertain, familiarity with the natural environment — especially when enhanced by field work with plants — provides a valuable anchor in reality. In addition, of course, your field work can be a source of endless pleasure because it deals with the beauty of nature.

There are now so many of us that I cannot send you off with a cheery "Good Picking," but I do hope this new wildflower guide will facilitate your search for a meaningful grasp of the world around us.

ROLAND C. CLEMENT
Vice President
National Audubon Society

Introduction

The purpose of this guide is to take the guesswork out of wild-flower identification for the nature lover with no formal botanical training. By following a simple but precise and logical key system, he or she can identify quickly any of 1,375 wildflowers, shrubs and vines of the northeastern United States and neighboring Canada.

Many attempts have been made in the past to organize wild-flowers for the layman. Some authors have grouped the plants by the color of the flower; others, by the time of bloom or the habitat. Unfortunately, although color has popular appeal, it is not suffi-ciently precise to serve as the starting point for identification: many shades fall somewhere between two major color groups and the names of colors mean different things to different people. Also, the color groups are so large that, unless a key is provided, much page flipping and guessing are required. Time of bloom and habi-tat likewise have severe limitations in that blooming periods and most habitats merge gradually one into another. These groupings may be helpful when applied to a small number of distinctive plants, but they are unwieldy when used as the basis for classifying a comprehensive cross section of our flora.

Another, more professional approach, of course, is to separate the plants botanically by family and genus, a method that enjoys the advantage of keeping related plants together. But since it is based on the often hard-to-distinguish technical details of flower structure — number of styles and stamens, position of ovary, and so forth — rather than on more conspicuous features like the color of the flowers and the shape of the leaves, it is unsuited to anyone without botanical training. And there are enough exceptions to the rules even in this system to make it far from perfect; some of our best-known plants do not conform to their family specifications, and many others can easily deceive the uninitiated.

None of these systems leads the nonbotanist to a firm iden-tification in which he has confidence. And so the belief has be-come widespread that systematic and successful identification of wildflowers is a difficult process reserved for professionals. Typi-cally, the layman approaches it in a haphazard, illogical way, searching at random through his favorite wildflower book, hoping to stumble on a picture or description that matches his specimen. Success often depends on whether he already knows a closely related plant and can thus reduce the field of search to a reason-able size. Even when he has narrowed the possibilities down to two or three similar species, he still may have trouble determining what distinguishes them from one another. And always the uncomfortable suspicion lurks that somewhere else in the book he may have missed a flower that matches his specimen better.

To overcome his difficulties and frustration, this guide provides a new and eminently workable key system, which is based on the most easily seen features that make each species unique, features the untrained eye can distinguish. To the extent that botanical distinctions are readily recognizable, the system takes full advantage of them, and therefore closely related plants are usually found together. And it as readily makes use of artificial groupings — color of flower, shape of leaf, and so on — if they provide the easiest path to identification. For those who wish to use the time-honored visual means of identification, the guide is fully illustrated, but it is hoped that the convenience of the key system will persuade them to use this more dependable and logical method.

The area covered by the guide is shown on the map opposite the title page. Coverage is, of course, less comprehensive on the periphery. Limitations on the size of the book prevent its describing every one of the several thousand species growing in the area, but it has been the intention to include all the distinctive or frequently seen species and to describe many more flowering shrubs than most books of this kind do. For species that had to be omitted, the reader should consult a complete botany, such as *Gray's Manual of Botany* (eighth edition), from which the Latin names in this guide were taken.

Contents

ON THE ENDPAPERS

Front left: The Three Classifications
            Steps in Identification
Front right: Floral Arrangements
Back left: Leaf Shapes
Back right: Other Leaf Terms

The Key System and How It Works

Identification begins with answering five standard questions about your specimen. Your answers determine the plant group to which it belongs. You then refer to this plant group in the Locator Key, which in turn sends you to the page in the text where your plant and others similar to it are described. You complete your identification by matching your specimen to the pertinent description and, as a double-check, to the illustration on the facing page. A unique feature of the text is that *the first sentence of each description distinguishes that plant from all others in that group.*

THE FIVE QUESTIONS

Flower Type

- Is the flower regular (radially symmetrical) or irregular, or are the flower parts indistinguishable?
- If regular, how many petals or similar parts does it have?

Plant Type

- Is the plant a wildflower or a shrub or a vine?
- If a wildflower, is it without leaves, or if it has leaves, are they all at the base of the plant, or are they arranged singly on the stem (alternate), or are they opposite one another in pairs or whorls?

Leaf Type

- Are the leaves entire (with even and unbroken margins), or are they toothed or lobed or divided?

If you are a beginner, you no doubt will need further explanation before you are able to answer all the questions. Turn to page xiv, where the basic terms are explained and illustrated simply and nontechnically. Even if you are experienced at identification, you should review the basic terms to learn their specific definitions in this book.

DETERMINING THE PLANT GROUP AND THE GROUP NUMBER

Each plant is classified in three ways. The first is by Flower Type: the arrangement and number of the petals or similar flower parts. The second is by Plant Type — wildflower, shrub or vine — and, if the plant is a wildflower, by the arrangement of its leaves. The third is by Leaf Type. The combination of these three classifications determines the *plant group* to which your specimen belongs. The three classifications are as follows:

Flower Type

1. Irregular Flowers
2. Flowers with 2 Regular Parts
3. Flowers with 3 Regular Parts
4. Flowers with 4 Regular Parts
5. Flowers with 5 Regular Parts
6. Flowers with 6 Regular Parts
7. Flowers with 7 or more Regular Parts
8. Flower Parts Indistinguishable

Plant Type

1. Wildflowers with No Apparent Leaves
2. Wildflowers with Basal Leaves Only
3. Wildflowers with Alternate Leaves
4. Wildflowers with Opposite or Whorled Leaves
5. Shrubs
6. Vines

Leaf Type

1. No Apparent Leaves
2. Leaves Entire
3. Leaves Toothed or Lobed
4. Leaves Divided

Your answers to the first two of the Five Questions enable you to assign your specimen to one of the sections under Flower Type. Similarly, your answers to the third and fourth questions will send you to the appropriate section under Plant Type, and your answer to the fifth question will refer you to the proper section under Leaf Type.

You now utilize the three section numbers as a 3-digit *group number*. For instance, if your flower is irregular (section 1 under Flower Type), and is a wildflower with alternate leaves (section 3 under Plant Type), and has toothed leaves (section 3 under Leaf Type), your group number is **133**. Another example: roses will be found in plant group 554 because they have five regular petals (5--), and are shrubs (55-) with divided leaves (554).

USING THE LOCATOR KEY

Next, you find your group number in the Locator Key, which begins on page 1. There your search is narrowed further and you are sent to the page of the text where your plant and those similar to it are described and illustrated. You then identify your specimen either by comparing it with the illustration and confirming your identification with the description, or vice versa. Remember that the first sentence of each description distinguishes that plant from all others in its group.

Let us take a flower at random — Fireweed — and use the key system to identify it.

Step 1. *Answer the Five Questions.* The answers are:

- The flower is regular (radially symmetrical).
- It has 4 regular parts.
- The plant is a wildflower.
- The leaves are alternate on the stem.
- The leaves are entire. (Some leaves of the Fireweed may have a few minute teeth, so the key system has been set up to accommodate the answer "toothed" as well.)

Step 2. *Determine the group number by matching your answers to the classifications on page xi* (the classes are also given on the inside of the front cover):

    Regular flower with 4 parts: **4**
    Wildflower with alternate leaves: **3**
    Leaves entire: **2**

This gives us a group number of **432** for Fireweed.

Step 3. *Find group number 432 in the Locator Key.* Here is how the Locator Key looks at group number 432 (page 4):

		PAGE
432	Leaves entire	
	White, pink, magenta or purple flowers	
	Leaves under 1″ long and evergreen	128
	Leaves not evergreen	130
	Yellow or green flowers	132

The first question to decide is the color of the flowers — in this case, magenta. The second question is whether the leaves are small and evergreen, or not evergreen. Since the leaves of Fireweed are several inches long and are not evergreen, the plant will be found on page 130.

Step 4. *Turn to page 130,* where you will find four plants fully described and illustrated, and five others that have only brief descriptions and are cross-referenced to other pages. First, choose the illustration on the facing page that matches the plant. Then confirm your choice by reading the corresponding text description. Note that the first sentence of *only one* of the nine descriptions in this group of plants fits Fireweed: "Large (¾–1″ wide) magenta flowers in a long, spikelike raceme."

If your plant is not illustrated, read the first sentence of each description on the page. You will usually discover that you have arrived at a cross reference. Turn to the page specified and you will find both the illustration and the complete description. *Caution:* "Continued" at the bottom of a page indicates that the group of plants continues on the next two facing pages.

If none of the descriptions fit your plant, the chances are that you have made an error somewhere along the way. Go back and redo every single step very carefully. It is possible, of course, that your specimen is a rare species that had to be omitted from the guide for reasons of space; or it could differ from the norm in some fashion; or it might be a hybrid that a trained botanist would find difficult to pin down. But such cases are rare. The vast majority of wildflowers will be readily identified in these pages.

After you are experienced in wildflower identification, you will find that you can ignore the three-digit group numbers and use the Locator Key directly.

GOLDENRODS AND ASTERS: A SPECIAL NOTE

These two large genera of familiar fall wildflowers have been placed in a separate section at the end of the text, to avoid having to split them up among many plant groups. This special treatment does not affect the workings of the key system, but it does provide a shortcut. If you recognize, at the outset, that your specimen belongs to either of these genera, you can immediately refer to pages 13–14 in the Locator Key and follow it to the page on which your specimen is described.

Explanation of Basic Terms

In any book on wildflowers some botanical terms are unavoidable. In this guide they have been kept to a minimum. Some may already be familiar to you; the rest are nontechnical and should be easily grasped. The terms needed to answer the five questions are explained in detail and illustrated in the following paragraphs. Others, which you will come across in the Locator Key and in the text, are listed and defined in the Glossary, pages xix–xxii.

FLOWERS: REGULAR, IRREGULAR AND INDISTINGUISHABLE

Regular flowers are radially symmetrical, which means that their petals or petal-like parts (or rays in flowers like the Daisy) are arranged around the center like the spokes of a wheel. Each petal or petal-like part is similar in size, shape and color to all the others. If the petals or parts are united, as in bell-shaped flowers like the Lily-of-the-valley, then the lobes of the flower are likewise similar in size, shape and color. The majority of flowers are regular. Examples are Lilies, Roses, Buttercups and Asters. *Caution:* Some

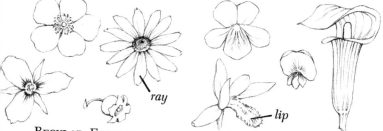

REGULAR FLOWERS

IRREGULAR FLOWERS

flowers grow closely grouped together in a spike or head; the familiar clover head is an example. In counting the flower parts or determining whether the flower is regular or not, you will need to isolate a single flower and examine that.

Irregular flowers are not radially symmetrical; that is, their petals or petal-like parts are not similar in size, shape or color. Usually, these flowers have upper and lower parts that are called *lips*. Familiar irregular flowers are Violets, Orchids and Peas.

Indistinguishable flowers either have no visible petal-like parts or the parts are so small that it is difficult to make out their number or arrangement. *Caution:* A flower may be very small and still

have parts that are quite discernible. If you cannot find your specimen after assigning it to the Indistinguishable section, you will
need to reexamine it, preferably with a small magnifying glass (5-
or 10-power), to make sure that it is, in fact, indistinguishable.

WILDFLOWERS, SHRUBS AND VINES

For the purposes of this guide, a *wildflower* is any flowering
plant that grows in a natural state and is not a tree, a shrub or a vine
as defined below.

A *tree* is a woody plant, generally with a single main stem that is
permanently above the ground. At maturity it is over ten feet high.

A *shrub* is also a plant with a woody stem permanently above
the ground, but at maturity it is usually under ten feet high. Char-
acteristically, shrubs are bushy and extensively branched, but so
are a few wildflowers, so the real point of distinction is the tough-
ness and woodiness of the shrubs' main stems.

Certain plants, among them Wintergreen and Trailing Arbutus,
are technically shrubs because they have woody stems, but since
the layman would not recognize them as shrubs, they have been
included among the wildflowers.

A *vine* is a plant with long trailing, twining or climbing stems
generally over two feet long. Trailing or creeping plants with
shorter stems, such as Partridgeberry and Myrtle, will be found
among the wildflowers.

Some shrubs are also vines; that is, their woody stems trail or
climb or twine. They will be found in the vines section.

ARRANGEMENT OF THE LEAVES: BASAL, ALTERNATE, OPPOSITE AND WHORLED

Leaves growing from the base of the plant are *basal leaves;*
those growing above the base are *stem leaves;* many plants have

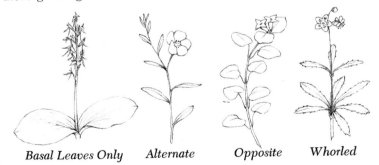

Basal Leaves Only   *Alternate*   *Opposite*   *Whorled*

both. When the stem leaves grow directly across from each other,
in pairs, the leaves are called *opposite;* when they grow in circles
of threes, fours, fives, and so on, they are termed *whorled.* If, on
the other hand, the leaves are arranged singly on the stem, first at
one point and then at another, they are *alternate.*

When determining whether leaves are opposite or alternate,

avoid if possible the tips of the stem where the leaves are crowded together. Instead, select a part of the main stem where the leaves are widely spaced and their arrangement is distinct. If there is only one stem leaf, it is considered alternate.

TYPES OF LEAVES: ENTIRE, TOOTHED, LOBED AND DIVIDED

If the margin of a leaf is even and unbroken, the leaf is said to be *entire*.

If the margin has more or less regular, shallow indentations, the leaf is *toothed*. Included are leaves with wavy and scalloped edges as well as those with pointed teeth.

The leaves of some plants have one or more deeper indentations, which separate the leaf into several sections known as *lobes*, as in the familiar oak leaf and maple leaf. EXCEPTION: by convention, leaves that are lobed only at the base, such as heart-shaped and arrow-shaped leaves, are considered entire or toothed depending upon their margins.

Often a leaf is actually *divided* into separate parts known as leaflets. The clover leaf, for example, is composed of three leaflets. For the purposes of this guide, if some of the leaf indentations go *almost* to the midrib, even though the divisions are not strictly leaflets, the leaf is considered to be divided. In borderline cases they will appear both ways in the Locator Key: under *lobed* and under *divided*.

Beginners sometimes mistake a divided leaf for a branch. The leaflets of a divided leaf all lie in the same plane, so that the whole leaf forms a flat surface; also, all the leaves look alike. Branches of the same plant, on the other hand, vary greatly in size and appearance; the leaves normally face in different directions and will therefore not lie flat. Branches also bear flower and leaf buds, which leaves never do.

Always select the largest or best-developed leaves, usually the lower leaves of the plant, when determining the leaf type. If two types of leaves are present, those with the deepest indentations determine the category in which it should be placed. For instance, if some of the leaves are lobed and others divided, the plant should be classified as having divided leaves.

The various shapes of leaves are illustrated and identified on the back endpapers.

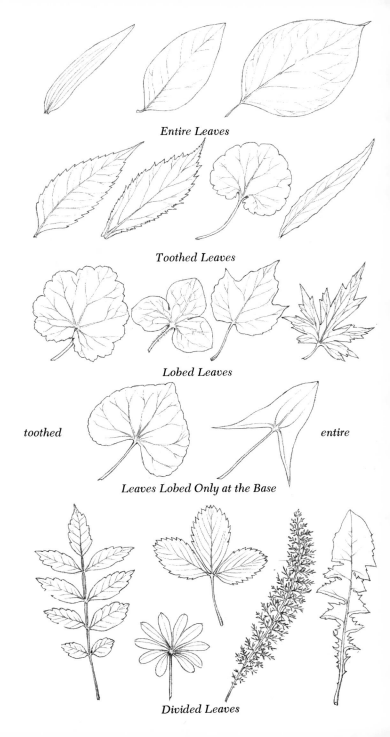

Entire Leaves

Toothed Leaves

Lobed Leaves

toothed   entire

Leaves Lobed Only at the Base

Divided Leaves

Floral Structure

The plant's reproductive organs occupy the center of the normal flower. The female part consists of one or more *pistils*, each containing an *ovary*, which after fertilization expands and forms the fruit. The top of a pistil may have one or more projections called *styles*, each bearing a *stigma* at the end. The male organs are the *stamens* and are made up of two parts — the *filament* or stalk, and the *anther* or pollen-bearing tip. Some species have flowers that are *unisexual*, that is, they have either stamens (*staminate flowers*) or pistils (*pistillate flowers*) but not both together in the same flower. Both types of unisexual flowers can be on the same plant or they can be on separate plants.

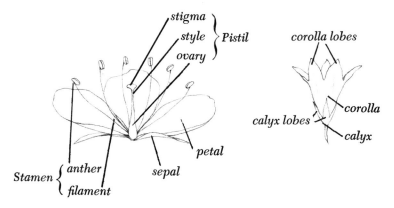

Surrounding the reproductive organs in most flowers, there are two sets of floral parts. The upper set is the *petals*, which may be of any color; the lower set is the *sepals*, which are usually green. However, if only one set is present they are considered to be sepals, even though they are brightly colored, as in the Marsh Marigold. The petals collectively are called the *corolla*. If the petals are joined together at the base, as in the Harebell, they are then more properly called *corolla lobes*. Similarly, all of the sepals comprise the *calyx*, and if they are joined at the base, they are known as *calyx lobes*.

Flowers grow in several different arrangements — heads, spikes, umbels, and the like. These are illustrated on the front endpapers.

Glossary

A page number or the abbreviation FE (front endpaper) or BE (back endpaper) following a definition refers to the place where the illustration of the term may be found.

alternate: borne singly along a stem; not opposite. XV

annual: living but one growing season, then dying.

anther: the pollen-bearing part of the stamen. XVIII

axil: the upper angle formed between the leaf and the stem. BE

axillary: situated in the axils.

basal: situated at the base of the stem. XV

beak: a prominent elongated tip.

biennial: a plant that completes its life cycle in two years and then dies.

blade: the flat, expanded part of the leaf.

bloom: a whitish waxy or powdery coating easily rubbed off.

bract: a very small or modified leaf, usually growing at the base of a flower or flower cluster. FE

bristly-toothed (leaves): having a short bristle at the tip of each tooth.

bulb: an underground bud with thick, fleshy scales.

bulblet: a small bulb, especially one growing in a flower cluster.

calyx: the outer circle of flower parts, made up of sepals. XVIII

capsule: a dry fruit that splits open at maturity into two or more sections.

clasping (leaf): partially surrounding the stem. BE

cleft: deeply cut.

corolla: the inner circle of flower parts, made up of petals. XVIII

corymb: a flat-topped or convex branched flower cluster in which the branching is typically alternate. FE

creeping: running along the ground and rooting as it goes.

crested: bearing conspicuous ridges or projections on the surface.

cyme: a more or less flat-topped, branched flower cluster in which the branching is typically opposite. FE

disk: in composite flowers like the Daisy, the central part of the flowering head; it is made up of numerous tiny, tubular flowers.

divided (leaf): cleft to, or almost to, the base or the midrib. A 2- to 3-times-divided leaf has each of its segments divided again and sometimes again. XVII

downy: covered with very fine, soft hairs.

egg-shaped: broader at one end than the other, like an egg; typically, 1½ to 2 times longer than wide. BE

elliptical: broadest in the middle and tapering equally toward both ends. BE

entire: with the margin unbroken by teeth, lobes or divisions. XVII

family: a group of related plants. Families are divided into genera, which are further divided into species.

filament: the anther-bearing stalk of a stamen. XVIII

fine-hairy: covered with fine hairs.

genus (plural: genera): a group of closely related species. The genus is designated by the first word in the Latin scientific name of a species and is always capitalized.

glands: minute protuberances, resembling swollen hairs, which secrete oils and other substances.

globular: round, like a globe.

halberd-shaped: arrow-shaped, but with the lobes at the base of the leaf pointing outward. BE

head: a group of flowers joined together in a short, dense, terminal cluster, as in the clovers and in all members of the Composite Family. FE

indistinguishable: said of flowers with no visible petal-like parts or with parts so small that it is difficult to make out their number or arrangement.

inflorescence: the flowering part of a plant.

introduced: not native to the region covered by this guide; introduced species are marked with an asterisk.

involucre: a circle of bracts below a flower or flower cluster.

irregular: said of flowers in which the parts are dissimilar in size, shape or arrangement. XIV

joint: (1) a point on a stem where two sections are visibly joined together, usually resulting in a slight swelling of the stem, as in grasses and members of the Buckwheat Family (BE); (2) a section of a pod separated from others by a constriction, as in the Tick Trefoils.

lance-shaped (leaf): broader toward one end and tapering to the other, like a lance; typically, 3 or more times longer than wide. BE

leaflet: one of the separate and similar parts of a divided leaf.

lip: the upper or lower part of many irregular flowers. XIV

lobe: one of the segments, usually rounded, of a leaf or flower. XVII, XVIII mealy: covered with small dustlike particles resembling cornmeal.

midrib: the central vein of a leaf or leaflet.

neutral (flower): without stamens or pistils.

oblong (leaf): longer than broad with parallel sides. BE

opposite: arranged in pairs on the stem. XV

oval: broadly elliptical. BE

ovary: the enlarged base of the pistil that produces the seeds. XVIII

palate: a projection on the lower lip of a flower.

palmate (leaf): with the leaflets radiating from a central point, like the fingers of a hand. BE

palmately lobed, cleft or divided (leaf): lobed, cleft or divided so as to give the leaf a palmate configuration.

panicle: an elongated branched flower cluster. FE

pappus: bristles, hairs and the like on top of the fruit of members of the Composite Family.

parasite: a plant that gets its food from another living plant.

perennial: a plant that normally lives more than two years.

petal: one of the segments of the corolla. XVIII

pinnate (leaf): divided in such a way that the leaflets are arranged on both sides of a common stalk, like the pinnae of a feather. In once-pinnate leaves, the stalk is unbranched; in 2- to 3-times-pinnate leaves, the stalk is branched once or twice, with each of the branches having leaflets. BE

pinnately lobed, cleft or divided (leaf): lobed, cleft or divided so as to give the leaf a featherlike configuration.

pistil: the central female reproductive part of a flower. XVIII

pistillate: having pistils but no stamens.

pith: the softer, central part of a twig or stem.

pod: a dry fruit, especially of the Pea Family.

pollen: the male spores produced by the anther.

prostrate: lying flat on the ground.

raceme: an elongated flower cluster with stalked flowers arranged along a central stem. FE

ray: (1) one of the stalks of an umbel; (2) in members of the Composite Family, the straplike or petal-like flowers encircling the disk flowers. XIV

recurved: curved downward or backward.

reflexed: abruptly turned downward or backward.

regular: having all of the parts alike in size and shape. XIV

rib: a prominent vein of a leaf.

rootstock: a horizontal, underground stem.

rosette: a circular cluster of leaves, usually at the base of a plant. BE

runner: a slender, prostrate branch.

saprophyte: a plant that gets its food from dead organic matter.

scale: a tiny colorless leaf found on some plant stems.

sepal: one of the segments of the calyx. XVIII

sheath: a thin membrane surrounding the stem. BE

shoot: a newly developed stem and its leaves.

soft-hairy: covered with soft hairs.

spadix: the fleshy spike of flowers in species of the Arum Family. FE

spathe: a large bract enclosing a flower cluster, as in the Arum Family. FE

species: a distinct kind of plant. Each species has a two-word scientific Latin name, of which the first word designates the genus and the second word the species. For example, the scientific name of the Three-lobed Violet is *Viola triloba*.

spike: an elongated flower cluster with stalkless flowers arranged along a central stem. FE

spur: a hollow, tubular projection of a flower, as in the Larkspur.

stalk: the stem of a leaf or a flower.

stamen: the male organ of a flower, consisting of a slender stalk (filament) and a knoblike, pollen-bearing tip (anther). XVIII

staminate: having stamens but no pistil.

stigma: the pollen-receiving tip of the pistil. XVIII

stipule: a small leaflike growth at the base of a leaf stalk. BE

style: the stalk of the pistil, connecting the ovary and the stigma. XVIII

tendril: a slender, coiling growth used for climbing or support. BE

terminal: at the end of a stem or branch.

toothed (leaf): having several to many small indentations along the margin. XVII

trailing: running along the ground, but not rooting.

tuber: a short, thick, underground stem with buds.

umbel: a flower cluster in which all the flower stalks radiate from the same point, like the ribs of an umbrella. FE

vein: one of a network of tiny channels in a leaf through which the plant's fluids flow.

whorled: arranged in a circle around a central point. XV

wing: a thin, narrow membrane extending along a stem, stalk or other part.

Locator Key

IRREGULAR FLOWERS (Cont.)

Group continued

IRREGULAR FLOWERS (Cont.)

Wildflowers with Opposite or Whorled Leaves (cont.)

FLOWERS WITH 2 REGULAR PARTS

FLOWERS WITH 3 REGULAR PARTS

Wildflowers with Basal Leaves Only

Wildflowers with Alternate Leaves

FLOWERS WITH 3 REGULAR PARTS (Cont.)
Wildflowers with Alternate Leaves (cont.)

FLOWERS WITH 4 REGULAR PARTS

Group continued

Group continued

FLOWERS WITH 5 REGULAR PARTS (Cont.)

Group continued

Group continued

FLOWERS WITH 5 REGULAR PARTS (Cont.)

Vines (cont.)

FLOWERS WITH 6 REGULAR PARTS

Wildflowers with Basal Leaves Only

Wildflowers with Alternate Leaves

Wildflowers with Opposite or Whorled Leaves

FLOWERS WITH 6 REGULAR PARTS (Cont.)

FLOWERS WITH 7 OR MORE REGULAR PARTS

FLOWER PARTS INDISTINGUISHABLE (Cont.)

GOLDENRODS (Solidago)

*A distinctive genus of yellow flowers, typical of the
fall, although some species begin blooming in July.
The flower heads are small and numerous, composed
of 3–16 tiny rays surrounding a group of yellow disk
flowers. Leaves entire or toothed. Silverrod (p. 382) is
the only white-flowered member of the genus. There
are about 70 species in our area. Composite Family.*

Group continued

GOLDENRODS (Solidago) *(Cont.)*

ASTERS (Aster)

*A large genus of white, blue, purple or violet flowers,
blooming in late summer and fall; flower rays 7–40
(40–50 in the New England Aster). The Fleabanes*
(Erigeron) *have over 40, very narrow rays, while the
White-topped Asters* (Sericocarpus) *have 4–6 rays.
There are about 60 species of asters in our area, of
which the more representative are covered in this
manual. Some species hybridize freely, producing
offspring with characters intermediate between the
two parents. Composite Family*

Descriptions of Species

SYMBOLS AND ABBREVIATIONS APPEARING IN THE TEXT

An asterisk (*) following the name of a plant means that the plant is not native to the area but has been brought in by one means or another and has become established.

A dagger (†) following the name of a plant means that the plant is not illustrated.

In describing the range of a plant, the following abbreviations are used: *e.* = eastern; *w.* = western; *n.* = northern; *s.* = southern; *c.* = central. Similarly, *se.* = southeastern, and so on. As is customary in giving the limits of a plant's range — "south to Va.," for example — the *to* means "to and including," not "as far as." If a description says nothing about range, you can assume that the plant grows generally throughout the area covered by the guide.

THE ILLUSTRATIONS: COLOR DESIGNATIONS AND SCALE

If a flower or fruit can occur in more than one color, only the commonest color is given on the illustration page (all the colors are given in the text).

The scale of the drawings is given on each illustration page. For example, × ½ = half life size; × 1 = life size; × 2 = twice life size.

WILDFLOWERS WITH NO APPARENT LEAVES AT FLOWERING TIME

Aquatic Plants of Ponds and Wet Shores

Bladderworts (*Utricularia*) The finely divided underwater leaves bear tiny bladders that entrap minute water life. The 2-lipped flowers grow singly or in a small cluster at the top of the stalk. There are 7 other species in our area. Ponds and streams. Summer. Bladderwort Family.

1. PURPLE FLOWERS

Purple Bladderwort (*U. purpurea*) Flowers about ½″ long, with a 3-lobed lower lip.

2. YELLOW FLOWERS

Horned Bladderwort (*U. cornuta*) Stalk erect, not floating or creeping; flowers with a conspicuous spur projecting downward from their base. Flowers ¾″ long. The tiny leaves grow beneath the soil. Wet shores.

Inflated Bladderwort (*U. inflata*) Leaves with inflated stalks, in a whorl beneath the surface and serving as a float. Flowers about ⅔″ long. Near the coast.

Common or **Greater Bladderwort** (*U. vulgaris*) Leaves finely divided; flowers ¾″ long, with lower lip about as long as the upper. Plant floating. The commonest species.

Flat-leaved Bladderwort (*U. intermedia*) Leaves finely divided; flowers about ½″ long, with lower lip twice as long as the upper. Plant creeping on the bottom.

Humped Bladderwort (*U. gibba*) Flowers small (about ¼″ long), with the upper and lower lips nearly equal. Leaf divisions and bladders few.

Not Aquatic; Plants with a Single Flower

Arethusa or **Dragon's Mouth** (*Arethusa bulbosa*) Magenta-pink flower, 1–2″ long, with the lower lip purple-spotted and crested with yellow hairs. The grasslike leaf develops after the plant blooms. 5–10″ high. Sphagnum bogs; rare. Spring. Orchis Family.

Skunk Cabbage (*Symplocarpus foetidus*) Flowers in a knob-shaped cluster (spadix) inside a purple-brown and green mottled hood (spathe) 2–5″ long. The large egg-shaped leaves have a heart-shaped base, unfold after the plant blooms, and have a disagreeable odor when crushed. Swamps. Early spring. Arum Family.

One-flowered Cancerroot or **Ghost Pipe** (*Orobanche uniflora*) Pale-lavender or whitish, tube-shaped flower. See p. 172.

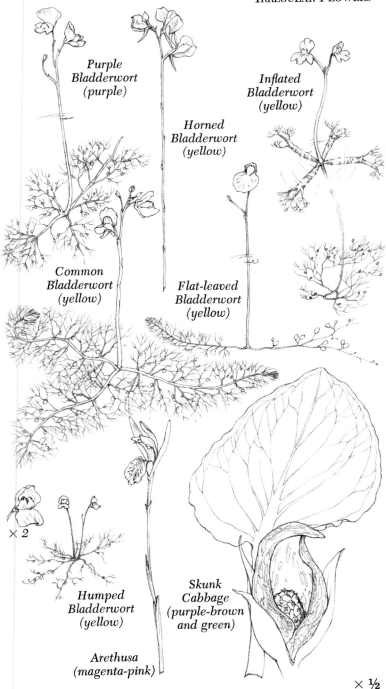

Purple
Bladderwort
(purple)

Inflated
Bladderwort
(yellow)

Horned
Bladderwort
(yellow)

Common
Bladderwort
(yellow)

Flat-leaved
Bladderwort
(yellow)

× 2

Humped
Bladderwort
(yellow)

Skunk
Cabbage
(purple-brown
and green)

Arethusa
(magenta-pink)

× ½

Not Aquatic; Flowers in Spikes or Racemes

Beechdrops (*Epifagus virginiana*) Plant branches from near the base; found in beech woods. Flowers whitish with purple-brown blotches, 4-lobed and somewhat 2-lipped, and scattered along the stems. Parasite on the roots of beech trees. Fall. Broomrape Family.

Squawroot (*Conopholis americana*) Covered with overlapping, brown scales and resembling a pine cone. The yellowish flowers grow between the scales. Parasite on tree roots, especially oaks. Late spring. Broomrape Family.

Puttyroot or **Adam-and-Eve** (*Aplectrum hyemale*) Purplish or yellowish-brown flowers, with a white, magenta-spotted lip, not spurred; blooms in late spring. Rootstock bears 2–4 roundish tubers. In the fall an oval, wrinkled leaf appears, but usually disappears before the plant blooms the following spring. Woods. Orchis Family.

Cranefly Orchis (*Tipularia discolor*) Greenish-purple flowers, with a long, slender spur; blooms in summer. Raceme long and loosely flowered. An egg-shaped leaf grows up in the fall, withers in the spring. Rich woods, s. Mass. to s. Ind. south; rare in the n. part of the range. Orchis Family.

Coralroots (*Corallorhiza*) Purplish or yellow-green flowers, with a white or purple-spotted lip; stems purplish, brownish or yellowish. Saprophytic plants with a short, stubby-branched root resembling coral. Orchis Family.

Early Coralroot (*C. trifida*) Stem yellowish; yellowish-green flowers with a white, usually unspotted lip; spring and early summer. 4–12″ high. Damp woods and swamps.

Large Coralroot (*C. maculata*) Stem brownish or purplish; lip white, purple-spotted, 3-lobed; flowers ½–¾″ long; blooms in summer. Yellowish forms are occasionally found. 8–20″ high. Woods.

Late Coralroot (*C. odontorhiza*) Stem brownish or purplish; lip purple-spotted, not lobed; flowers ¼″ long; blooms in late summer and fall. 4–7″ high. Woods.

Wister's Coralroot (*C. wisteriana*) Stem purplish; lip purple-spotted, notched at the tip; blooms in spring. 8–16″ high. Woods, Pa. to S.D. south.

Ladies' Tresses (*Spiranthes*) White flowers in a spike. See p. 26.

Naked-flowered Tick Trefoil (*Desmodium nudiflorum*) Rose-purple, pea-shaped flowers. See p. 36.

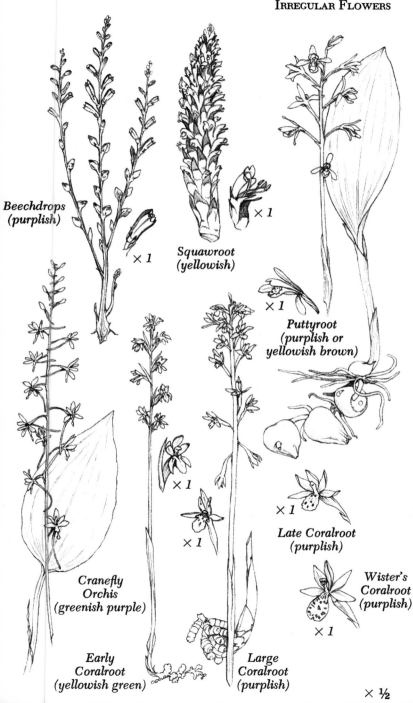

Beechdrops
(purplish)

× 1

Squawroot
(yellowish)

× 1

Puttyroot
(purplish or
yellowish brown)

× 1

Late Coralroot
(purplish)

× 1

Wister's
Coralroot
(purplish)

× 1

Cranefly
Orchis
(greenish purple)

× 1

× 1

Early
Coralroot
(yellowish green)

Large
Coralroot
(purplish)

× ½

Leaves with a Heart- or Arrow-shaped Base

Water Arum or **Wild Calla** (*Calla palustris*) Leaves heart-shaped, long-stalked, 2–6″ long. The inflorescence resembles the florist's Calla Lily, having a large, white spathe with a dense, knob-shaped spadix of greenish flowers at the base. Bogs. Late spring to summer. Arum Family.

Arrow Arum (*Peltandra virginica*) Leaves arrow-shaped, long-stalked, like those of the Arrowhead. Inflorescence a pointed, green, leaflike envelope 4–8″ long, enclosing a slender, club-shaped spadix. Shallow water. Late spring. Arum Family.

Skunk Cabbage (*Symplocarpus foetidus*) Leaves short-stalked, unfolding after the plant blooms. See p. 16.

Leaf Solitary, Not Heart- or Arrow-shaped

Grass Pink (*Calopogon pulchellus*) Magenta-pink flowers in a short raceme; leaf grasslike, 8–12″ long. Flowers showy, 1″ wide, with an erect, yellow-crested lip at the top of the flower. Bogs and wet meadows. Summer. Orchis Family.

White Adder's Mouth (*Malaxis brachypoda*) Numerous, greenish-white flowers; leaf oval, 1–2″ long, its base sheathing the stem. Green Adder's Mouth (p. 46) is similar, but the flowers are greenish and the leaf clasps halfway up the stem. Bogs and damp woods. Summer. Orchis Family.

Blunt-leaved Orchis (*Habenaria obtusata*) Greenish-white, spurred flowers in a loose raceme; leaf egg-shaped, blunt at tip, 2–5″ long. Lip long and narrow. Mossy woods, n. and w. N.Eng. to Minn. north. Summer. Orchis Family.

Small Round-leaved Orchis (*Orchis rotundifolia*) Rose-colored flowers with a white, purple-spotted lip, in a short raceme; leaf oval or round, 1½–3″ long. Lip 3-lobed. Mossy woods, n. N.Eng. to Wis. north; very rare. Early summer. Orchis Family.

Calypso or **Fairy Slipper** (*Calypso bulbosa*) Flower solitary, about 1″ long, with a scoop-shaped lip crested with yellow hairs and marked with purple. Leaf roundly egg-shaped, 1–2″ long. Cold woods, n. N.Eng. to Wis. north and west; very rare. Spring. Orchis Family.

Arethusa or **Dragon's Mouth** (*Arethusa bulbosa*) Flower solitary, magenta-pink, 1–2″ long; leaf grasslike. See p. 16.

Puttyroot (*Aplectrum hyemale*) Purplish or yellowish-brown flowers; leaf oval, 4–6″ long. See p. 18.

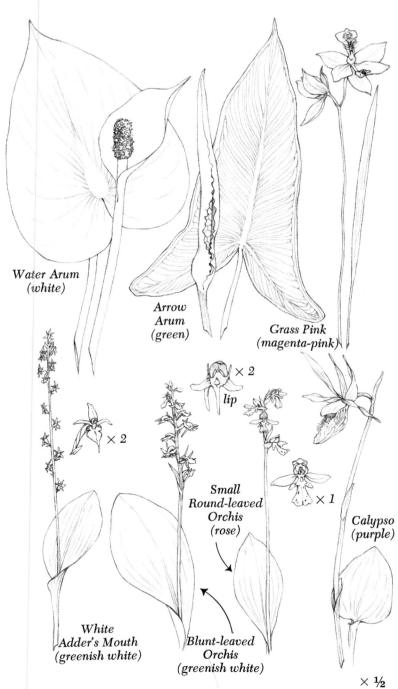

Water Arum
(white)

Arrow
Arum
(green)

Grass Pink
(magenta-pink)

× 2
lip

× 2

Small
Round-leaved
Orchis
(rose)

× 1

Calypso
(purple)

White
Adder's Mouth
(greenish white)

Blunt-leaved
Orchis
(greenish white)

× ½

Leaves 2, Large and Broad

Pink Lady's Slipper or **Moccasin Flower** (*Cypripedium acaule*)
Flower solitary, the lip 1–2″ long, hollow-pouch–shaped and cleft
in the center. Color ranges from deep rose to white, the latter form
becoming more common in the n. parts of the range. Our only
Lady's Slipper without stem leaves. Dry or moist woods, usually
under oaks or pines. Spring. Orchis Family.

Showy Orchis (*Orchis spectabilis*) Magenta flowers, about 1″ long,
with a white lip, in a loose 3- to 8-flowered spike. Leaves egg-
shaped and shining, 4–8″ long. Rich woods, mostly in limestone
regions. Spring. Orchis Family.

Rein Orchids (*Habenaria*) Greenish-white or green flowers in racemes; leaves round and lying flat on the ground. Each flower has
a long, slender spur beneath the lip. For other species, see pp. 20,
42, 44, 48. Rich woods. Orchis Family.

> **Large Round-leaved Orchis** (*H. orbiculata*) Stem bearing 1 or
> more small bracts. Greenish-white flowers, 1″ long. Leaves shin-
> ing, 3–8″ in diameter. 1–2′ high. Summer. Another species (*H.
> macrophylla*) with somewhat larger leaves and flowers twice as
> large is found in N.Y. and N.Eng. north.

> **Hooker's Orchis** (*H. hookeri*) A smaller species with a naked
> stem and yellow-green flowers ¾″ long. Leaves thick and fleshy,
> 2½–6″ long. 8–15″ high. Early summer.

Twayblades (*Liparis*) Purplish-brown or yellowish-green flowers
in racemes; leaves elliptical or egg-shaped, shining. Plants of the
genus *Listera* are also called Twayblades (see p. 74). Late spring
and early summer. Orchis Family.

> **Large Twayblade** (*L. lilifolia*) Purplish-brown flowers, ½″ long,
> with a broad, rounded lip. Rich woods, s. N.Eng. to Minn. south.

> **Loesel's** or **Bog Twayblade,** or **Fen Orchis** (*L. loeselii*) Yellow-
> ish-green flowers, ¼″ long, with an oblong lip. Bogs and damp
> woods.

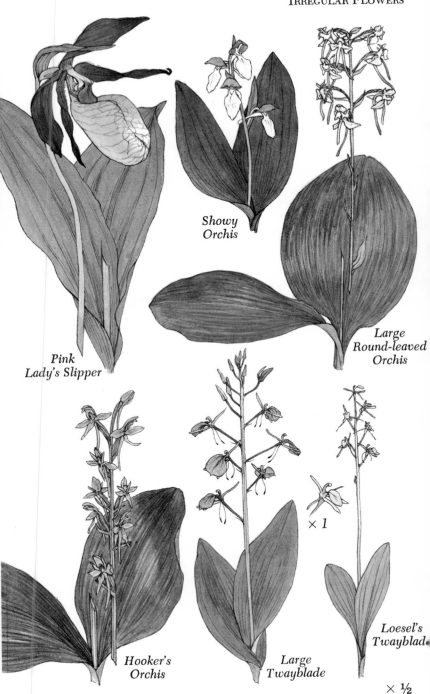

Showy Orchis

Large Round-leaved Orchis

Pink Lady's Slipper

Hooker's Orchis

Large Twayblade

× 1

Loesel's Twayblade

× ½

Leaves More Than 2 (Normally), Not Heart- or Arrow-shaped, in a Basal Rosette

Rattlesnake Plantains (*Goodyera*) Leaves dark green, veined with white. Woodland plants with a rosette of distinctively marked, egg-shaped leaves. The small, whitish flowers grow in a spike at the top of a bracted stalk. Summer. Orchis Family.

Downy Rattlesnake Plantain (*G. pubescens*) Flowers in a dense cylindrical spike (neither one-sided nor spiral); leaves 1–2″ long with many fine, white veins. 6–20″ high. The commonest species.

Dwarf or **Lesser Rattlesnake Plantain** (*G. repens*) Spike one-sided; leaves only ½–1″ long, with broad white veins. Lip pouch-shaped with a recurved tip. 4–10″ high. Cold, deep woods, mostly in the mountains.

Checkered Rattlesnake Plantain (*G. tesselata*) Flowers in a loose spiral; leaves, 1–2″ long, dull green, and criss-crossed with a network of paler lines. Lip not as pouch-shaped as that of the Dwarf Rattlesnake Plantain, and tip only slightly recurved. 5–12″ high. Dry or moist woods, N.Eng. to Wis. north.

Green-leaved Rattlesnake Plantain (*G. oblongifolia*) Spike one-sided or in a loose spiral; leaves 2–4″ long, usually with a light stripe down the center but without conspicuous white cross-veins. 6–20″ high. N. Me. and e. Can. west to the Rockies.

Water Lobelia (*Lobelia dortmanna*) Leaves narrow, hollow. Found along sandy shores of ponds, usually with its rosette of cylindrical leaves under water. Pale-violet or white flowers, ½″ long, in a loose raceme. Summer and fall. Lobelia Family.

Butterwort (*Pinguicula vulgaris*) Leaves yellow-green, greasy to the touch, with inrolled edges, ½–1½″ long. The violet flowers grow singly, ¾″ long, with a straight spur, and resemble a violet. An insectivorous plant which digests the small insects that stick to its greasy leaf surfaces. 1–6″ high. Damp rocks, n. N.Eng. and N.Y. north; rare and local in the s. part of its range. Early summer. Bladderwort Family.

Continued

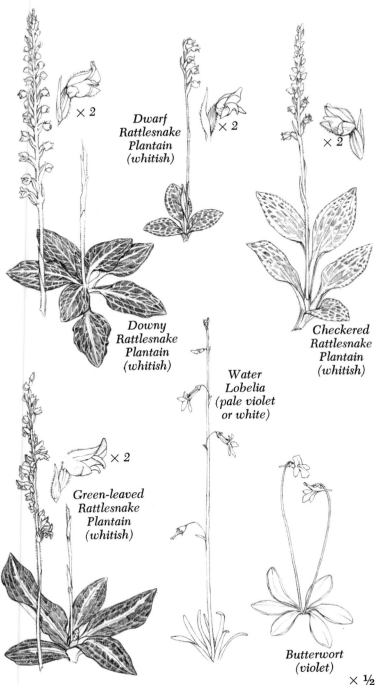

× 2

*Dwarf
Rattlesnake
Plantain
(whitish)*

× 2

× 2

*Downy
Rattlesnake
Plantain
(whitish)*

*Water
Lobelia
(pale violet
or white)*

*Checkered
Rattlesnake
Plantain
(whitish)*

× 2

*Green-leaved
Rattlesnake
Plantain
(whitish)*

*Butterwort
(violet)*

× ½

Leaves More Than 2 (Normally),
Not Heart- or Arrow-shaped, in a Basal Rosette (cont.)

Ladies' Tresses (*Spiranthes*) Leaves either grasslike or short and egg-shaped. Flowers small and white, in a slender, often spirally twisted spike. The leaves grow mainly from the base of the plant, although there may be a few small stem leaves or all of the leaves may have disappeared by flowering time. Orchis Family.

1. FLOWERS IN A ONE-SIDED, OFTEN SPIRALLY TWISTED, SPIKE

Slender Ladies' Tresses (*S. gracilis*) Basal leaves egg-shaped or absent; lip with a green center and white margins. 4–24" high. Dry fields and open woods. Summer.

Little Ladies' Tresses (*S. tuberosa*) Basal leaves egg-shaped, usually absent at flowering time; lip white. 4–8" high. Dry fields and open woods, Mass. to Ind. south. Summer.

Grass-leaved or **Spring Ladies' Tresses** (*S. vernalis*) Basal leaves narrow, grasslike and present at flowering time. Lip with yellow center or entirely white; base of flowers downy. 6–30" high. Dry or moist places, s. N.Eng. to s. Ohio and Mo. south. Summer.

2. FLOWER SPIKE NOT ONE-SIDED

Wide-leaved Ladies' Tresses (*S. lucida*) Blooms in spring and early summer; lip yellow. Leaves shining, lance-shaped. 4–10" high. Moist places.

Nodding Ladies' Tresses (*S. cernua*) Blooms in late summer and fall; lip white or whitish, not narrowed in the center; flowers horizontal or slightly nodding. Leaves long and narrow. 4–24" high. Moist meadows, swamps and open woods. The commonest species in most parts of our range.

Hooded Ladies' Tresses (*S. romanzoffiana*) Blooms in midsummer and early fall; lip white, fiddle-shaped (narrowed in the middle); flowers not nodding. 4–16" high. Bogs and meadows; more frequent northward.

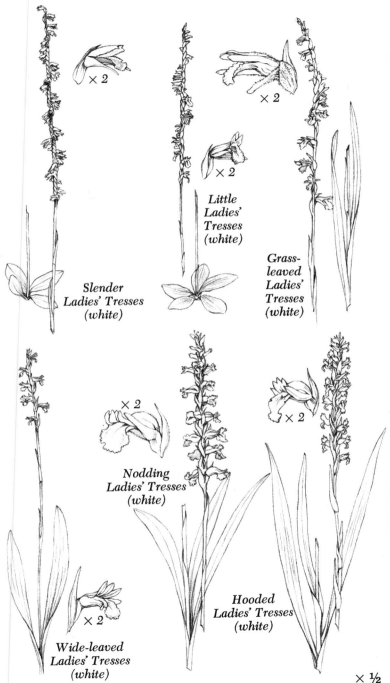

× 2

× 2

× 2

Little
Ladies'
Tresses
(white)

Grass-
leaved
Ladies'
Tresses
(white)

Slender
Ladies'
Tresses
(white)

× 2

× 2

Nodding
Ladies' Tresses
(white)

Wide-leaved
Ladies'
Tresses
(white)

Hooded
Ladies' Tresses
(white)

× ½

White or Yellow Flowers

Violets (*Viola*) A familiar group of spring wildflowers found in
various habitats. The flowers have 5 nearly equal petals, the lower
one usually larger than the rest and spurred at the base. Violets are
divided into two groups: those with basal leaves only, and those
with stem leaves (for the latter, see pp. 54 and 56). Those with
basal leaves only are numerous and difficult to identify; the following are the ones most widely distributed. Violet Family.

1. WHITE FLOWERS (WHITE FORMS OF BLUE VIOLETS ALSO
   OCCUR)

a. Leaves heart-shaped, rounded or blunt at the tip

Northern White Violet (*V. pallens*) Leaves about as wide as
long, with a blunt tip, smooth. Flowers fragrant, under ½"
long. Spreads by slender runners. Beside brooks and springs;
common.

Kidney-leaved Violet (*V. renifolia*) Largest leaves wider than
long, rounded at the tip, and usually with downy stems and
undersurfaces. Without runners. Cool woods, n. and w. N.Eng.
to n. Minn. and Colo. north.

b. Leaves heart-shaped, short-pointed at the tip

Sweet White Violet (*V. blanda*) Leaf stalks and flower stalks
reddish and smooth; 2 upper petals narrow and bent backwards.
Flowers ½" long. Often confused with the Northern White Violet above, but grows in rich woods rather than wet places and
begins to bloom about two weeks later.

Large-leaved White Violet (*V. incognita*) Leaf stalks and flower
stalks usually downy; upper petals egg-shaped, not reflexed.
Leaves larger and held more erect than those of the Sweet
White Violet. Moist woods.

c. Leaves lance-shaped, egg-shaped or oblong

Lance-leaved Violet (*V. lanceolata*) Leaves lance-shaped, tapering to the stalk. Damp meadows and shores.

Primrose-leaved Violet (*V. primulifolia*) Leaves egg-shaped or
oblong, abruptly narrowing to the stalk. Moist soil of meadows
and open woods.

2. YELLOW FLOWERS

Round-leaved Violet (*V. rotundifolia*) Flowers expand with the
leaves in early spring. Leaves heart-shaped, with scalloped
teeth, and at flowering time only about 1" long; by summer they
are 2–4" long. Rich woods.

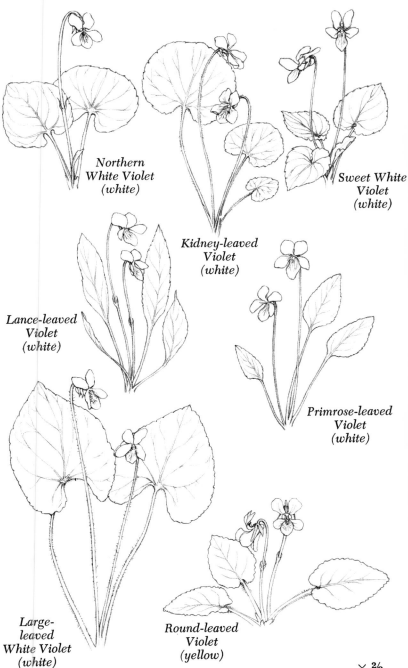

Northern
White Violet
(white)

Sweet White
Violet
(white)

Kidney-leaved
Violet
(white)

Lance-leaved
Violet
(white)

Primrose-leaved
Violet
(white)

Large-
leaved
White Violet
(white)

Round-leaved
Violet
(yellow)

× ⅔

Blue, Violet or Purple Flowers

Blue Violets (*Viola*) Spring wildflowers with spurred lower lip. Some species have albino forms. For a discussion of the genus, see p. 28. Violet Family.

LEAVES HEART-SHAPED AND NOT DEEPLY LOBED

1. LEAVES SOMEWHAT POINTED AND LONG-STALKED, THE
STALKS DISTINCTLY LONGER THAN THE LEAF BLADES

a. Flower stalks soft-hairy or downy

Northern Blue Violet (*V. septentrionalis*) Lower petal soft-hairy on the inside at the base. Leaf stalks and undersurfaces of the leaves slightly hairy. Woods and clearings.

Woolly Blue Violet (*V. sororia*) † Lower (spurred) petal smooth-ish on the inside. The leaf stalks and the undersurfaces of the leaves are more hairy than those of the Northern Blue Violet. Moist woods and meadows.

b. Flower stalks smoothish

Marsh Blue Violet (*V. cucullata*) Plant of wet places; flowers darker toward the center. Flowers long-stalked, usually growing higher than the leaves. A distinctive feature is the hairs on the inside of the side petals, which are short and thick (actually swollen at the tip, which can be seen with a magnifying glass). Common.

Common Blue Violet (*V. papilionacea*) A common violet of meadows and moist woods, often found in dooryards; lower (spurred) petal smooth on the inside. Hairs of the side petals long and slender. The cultivated Confederate Violet is a pale, variegated form of this species.

Broad-leaved Wood Violet (*V. latiuscula*) Plant of dry woods; lower petal with a tuft of hairs at the base. The early leaves are generally tinged with purple beneath, while the mature leaves are mostly wider than long. Vt. and N.Y. south.

LeConte's or **Pale Early Violet** (*V. affinis*) Plant of moist woods and meadows; lower petal tufted on inside at the base. Flowers with conspicuous white throat. Leaves more narrowly heart-shaped than the Broad-leaved Wood Violet. Vt. to Wis. south.

Continued

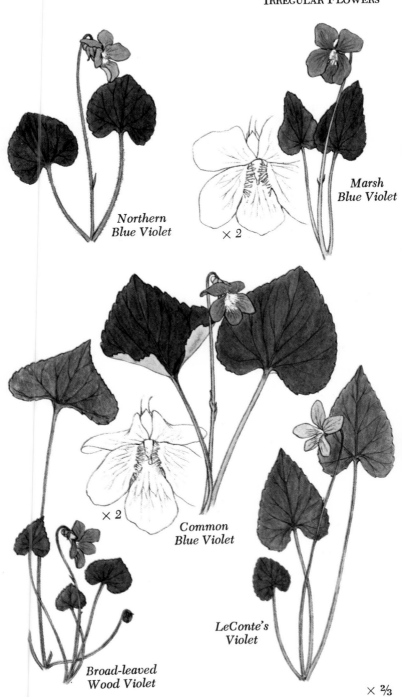

Northern
Blue Violet

Marsh
Blue Violet

× 2

× 2

Common
Blue Violet

LeConte's
Violet

Broad-leaved
Wood Violet

× ⅔

Blue, Violet or Purple Flowers (cont.)

Blue Violets (*Viola*) (cont.)

LEAVES HEART-SHAPED AND NOT DEEPLY LOBED (CONT.)

2. SMALL VIOLETS WITH LEAVES MOSTLY BLUNT AND
SHORT-STALKED (THE STALK IS NOT MUCH, IF AT ALL,
LONGER THAN THE LEAF BLADE)

Southern Wood Violet (*V. hirsutula*) Grows in rich woods;
reddish-purple flowers; stalks of leaves and flowers smooth.
Leaves blunt at the tip, usually purplish beneath and often
purple-veined, spreading on the ground. Conn. to Ind. south.

Selkirk's or **Great-spurred Violet** (*V. selkirkii*) Grows in cool
woods; pale-violet flowers, the lower petal bearing a prominent
spur ¼" long at the back. The rounded bases of the leaves are
close together and sometimes overlapping; upper surface of
leaves slightly hairy. South to Pa., Mich. and Wis.

Alpine Marsh Violet (*V. palustris*) Grows along alpine brooks;
light-violet to nearly white flowers, with a short, rounded spur
⅛" long. Leaves smooth. Spreads by underground runners. Mts.
of N.Eng. north.

Ovate-leaved Violet (*V. fimbriatula*) Grows in dry open places;
plant conspicuously downy. See below.

*LEAVES HEART-SHAPED IN OUTLINE, BUT SOME LOBED (FOR
VIOLETS WITH DIVIDED LEAVES, SEE P. 34); PLANTS HAIRY*

Three-lobed Violet (*V. triloba*) Leaves essentially cleft into 3–5
lobes, the central lobe widest, but some of the leaves may be
heart-shaped and unlobed. Some forms approach the Early Blue
Violet below. Rich woods, s. and w. N.Eng. to Ill. south.

Early Blue or **Palmate Violet** (*V. palmata*) Leaves deeply cleft
into 5–11 lobes, which are mostly narrower than those of the
Three-lobed Violet. S. N.H. to Minn. south.

*LEAVES LANCE-, ARROW- OR EGG-SHAPED, SOMETIMES
LOBED AT THE BASE*

Ovate-leaved Violet (*V. fimbriatula*) Leaves egg-shaped or oblong; whole plant conspicuously downy. Sepals with fine hairs
along the margins. Dry open places; common.

Arrow-leaved Violet (*V. sagittata*) Plant (including the sepals)
smooth, or in some forms slightly downy. Blooms later than the
Ovate-leaved Violet, and is usually found in moister places.
Leaves broadly lance-shaped and often deeply lobed at the base.

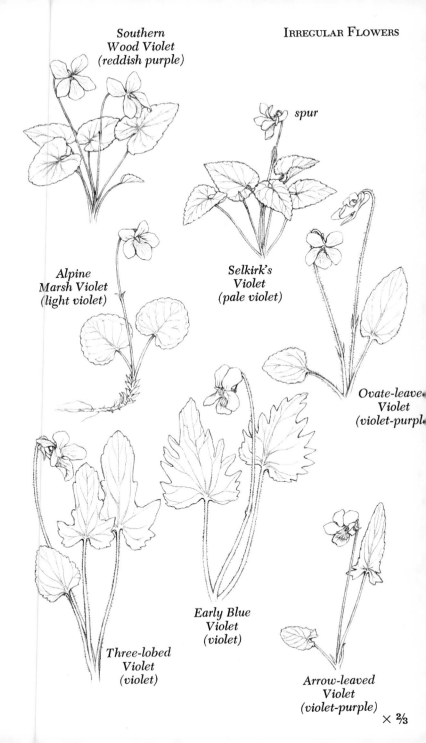

Southern
Wood Violet
(reddish purple)

spur

Alpine
Marsh Violet
(light violet)

Selkirk's
Violet
(pale violet)

Ovate-leave
Violet
(violet-purpl

Three-lobed
Violet
(violet)

Early Blue
Violet
(violet)

Arrow-leaved
Violet
(violet-purple)

× **⅔**

Leaves Divided into Narrow Segments

Violets (*Viola*) Violet, purple, or lilac flowers. The following species have the leaves palmately divided into 5 or more narrow, irregularly lobed leaflets. Spring. Violet Family.

Birdfoot Violet (*V. pedata*) All of the petals pale lilac-purple or the two upper petals dark violet (more frequent southward). Flowers ¾″ or more wide, with orange stamens conspicuously visible in the throat. Fields and dry open woods. Occasionally blooms again in the fall.

Coast Violet (*V. brittoniana*) Rich-violet flowers, 1–1½″ wide, with a conspicuous white throat. Leaf stalks and underside of leaves smooth. The early leaves may be toothed rather than cleft. Sandy or peaty soil, s. Me. south along the coast.

Early Blue or **Palmate Violet** (*V. palmata*) Violet-purple flowers; leaf stalks and underside of leaves hairy. A species with variable leaves, some more deeply cleft than others. See p. 32.

Dutchman's Breeches, Squirrel Corn and **Wild Bleeding Heart** (*Dicentra*) Delicate woodland plants with racemes of dangling white or pink flowers. Flowers ½–¾″ long and composed of 4 petals, the outer pair large and spurred, the inner pair narrow. Rich woods and shaded ledges. Poppy Family.

1. WHITE FLOWERS, IN UNBRANCHED RACEMES

Dutchman's Breeches (*D. cucullaria*) Spurs (at top of flower) widely spreading and as long as the flower stalk. The quaint flowers appear like pairs of pantaloons hung up to dry. Tubers white, clustered, resembling a scaly bulb. Spring.

Squirrel Corn (*D. canadensis*) Spurs short and rounded, shorter than the flower stalk. Tubers resembling kernels of corn or yellow peas. Spring.

2. PINK FLOWERS, IN BRANCHING RACEMES

Wild Bleeding Heart (*D. eximia*) Flowers with rounded spurs like the Squirrel Corn, but pink. Plant somewhat larger than the 2 preceding species. S. N.Y., Pa. and W.Va. south; often cultivated. Spring to fall.

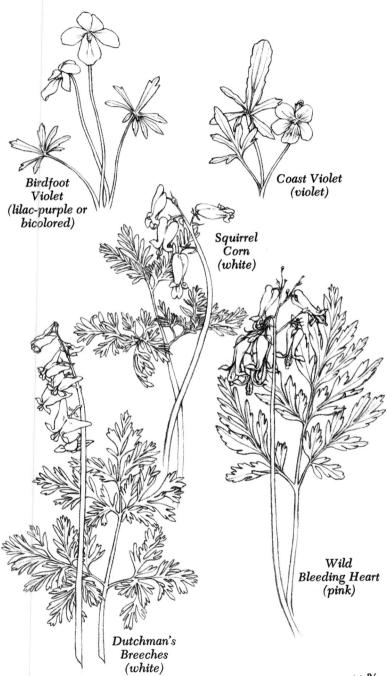

Birdfoot
Violet
(lilac-purple or
bicolored)

Coast Violet
(violet)

Squirrel
Corn
(white)

Wild
Bleeding Heart
(pink)

Dutchman's
Breeches
(white)

× ⅔

Leaves Divided into 3 or More Leaflets

White Clover (*Trifolium repens*) * White or pale-pink flowers in a dense, round head. Leaflets 3, finely toothed. Stem creeps along the ground. Very common weed of grassy places. Spring to fall. Pea Family.

Naked-flowered Tick Trefoil (*Desmodium nudiflorum*) Rose-purple flowers in a loose raceme. A leaf stalk rises from near the base of the flower stalk, bearing at its top a cluster of leaves, each having 3 broad, entire leaflets. Occasionally the flower stalk bears a few similar leaves. 1–3′ high. Dry woods. Summer. Pea Family.

Jack-in-the-pulpits (*Arisaema*) Inflorescence solitary, growing beneath the leaves (usually 2) and consisting of a striped green-and-purple canopy (spathe) over a club-shaped spadix (the "Jack"); leaflets 3. The fruit is a dense cluster of scarlet berries. 1–3′ high. Well-known plants of moist woods, combined by some authorities into a single species. Spring and early summer. Arum Family.

Jack-in-the-pulpit or **Indian Turnip** (*A. atrorubens*) Leaflets usually pale beneath; hood arches downward over the spadix; tube of spathe slightly ridged on the outside, but not deeply furrowed. Our commonest and earliest species.

Northern Jack-in-the-pulpit (*A. stewardsonii*) Leaflets green and shining beneath; tube of spathe deeply furrowed on the outside, forming conspicuous white ridges. South to N.J. and Pa. and in the mountains to N.C.

Small Jack-in-the-pulpit (*A. triphyllum*) A smaller species with a narrower, more or less horizontal hood which is often nearly black beneath; leaflets green beneath; tube of spathe not deeply furrowed. The plant frequently has only a single leaf. North to s. N.Eng., Pa. and Ky.

Green Dragon or **Dragon Arum** (*Arisaema dracontium*) Inflorescence solitary, green; leaf usually solitary and divided into 5–15 leaflets. Similar to the related Jack-in-the-pulpit, except that the long, tail-like spadix protrudes several inches beyond the hood. 1–4′ high. Low woods and along streams. Late spring. Arum Family.

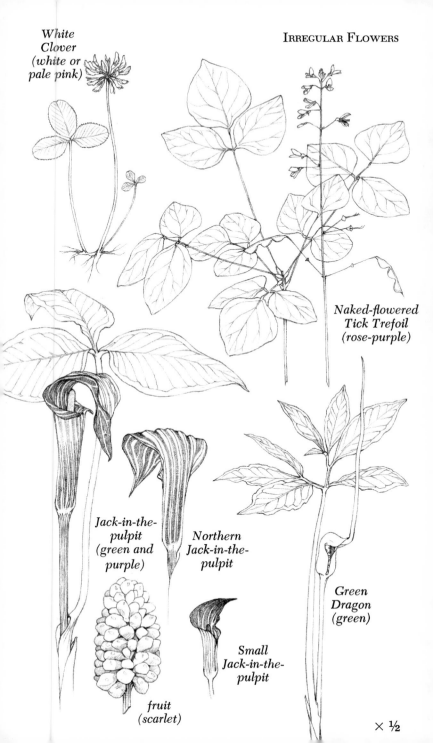

White Clover (white or pale pink)

Naked-flowered Tick Trefoil (rose-purple)

Jack-in-the-pulpit (green and purple)

Northern Jack-in-the-pulpit

Green Dragon (green)

Small Jack-in-the-pulpit

fruit (scarlet)

× ½

One- to Three-flowered; Orchids with Crested or Pouched Lip

Lady's Slippers (*Cypripedium*) Lip enlarged into a hollow, inflated pouch. A distinctive group of Orchids with mostly large, solitary flowers, or sometimes a pair of flowers. The leaves are broad with prominent veins. The Pink Lady's Slipper (p. 22) is the only one of our species with basal leaves. Orchis Family.

Yellow Lady's Slipper (*C. calceolus*) Yellow flower. This species occurs in two forms. The **Larger Yellow Lady's Slipper** (var. *pubescens*) is found in woods, and is 1–2' high, with a flower over 1″ long with yellow-green, twisted petals. The **Smaller Yellow Lady's Slipper** (var. *parviflorum*) is found in boggy places and is not as tall; the flower is less than 1″ long and has purple petals. Late spring.

Showy Lady's Slipper (*C. reginae*) White flower, suffused with pink, 1–2″ long. 1–2½' high. A beautiful but disappearing Orchid of swamps and bogs. Early summer.

Ram's-head Lady's Slipper (*C. arietinum*) Flower veined with crimson on the outside, ½–¾″ long. The flower pouch tapers to a point, giving the flower a grotesque look. 6–15″ high. Cold woods and bogs; very rare. Mass. to Minn. north. Late spring.

Small White Lady's Slipper (*C. candidum*) White flower, faintly striped with purple on the inside, ¾″ long. 6–15″ high. Marly bogs and low meadows; very rare. C. N.Y. to N.D. south. Late spring.

Rose Pogonia or **Snakemouth** (*Pogonia ophioglossoides*) Rose-pink flower, ¾″ long, with a yellow-bearded lip, usually solitary. The pink sepals and petals are about the same size. A single lance-shaped or oblong leaf clasps the middle of the stem and a leaflike bract grows below the flower. 8–12″ high. Bogs and wet shores. Late spring and early summer. Orchis Family.

Spreading Pogonia or **Rosebud Orchis** (*Cleistes divaricata*) Pink flower, 1–2″ long, with the petals and the narrow concave lip forming a tube. The 3 brownish sepals are long and narrow and extend above the flower. As in the Rose Pogonia, a single leaf clasps the middle of the stem and a bract grows beneath the flower. 1–2' high. Moist pinelands, bogs and sandy woods, s. N.J. (very rare) south. Early summer. Orchis Family.

Continued

Smaller
Yellow
Lady's Slipper

Larger
Yellow
Lady's Slipper

Ram's-head
Lady's Slipper

Showy
Lady's Slipper

Small White
Lady's Slipper

Rose
Pogonia

Spreading
Pogonia

× ½

One- to Three-flowered; Orchids with Crested or Pouched Lip (cont.)

Nodding Pogonia or **Three Birds** (*Triphora trianthophora*) Pale pink or whitish flowers, ½–¾" long, usually in 3's. Flowers nodding from the upper axils. Leaves very small, egg-shaped, clasping the stem. 3–8" high. Rich woods, s. Me. to Wis. south; rare and not appearing above the ground every year. Late summer and early fall. Orchis Family.

Flowers Growing Singly or 2–4 in a Cluster; not Orchids

Fringed Polygala, Flowering Wintergreen or **Gaywings** (*Polygala paucifolia*) Rose-purple flowers, fringed at the tip, ¾" long. Flowers few, growing in the leaf axils. Leaves egg-shaped, mostly clustered at the top of the stem. 3–6" high. Moist woods. Late spring and early summer. Milkwort Family.

Asiatic Dayflower (*Commelina communis*) * Blue flowers, ½–1" wide, with 2 large blue petals above and 1 very small white petal below, growing singly or in small clusters. Leaves lance-shaped and tapering. The similar Virginia Dayflower (p. 120) has 3 blue petals. Weak-stemmed plant, 6–15" long, rooting at the joints. Moist, shaded places, often around dwellings. Summer and fall. Spiderwort Family.

Rattlebox (*Crotalaria sagittalis*) Yellow, pea-shaped flowers, ½" long, in short clusters from the axils. The hairy stem bears prominent arrow-shaped stipules that point down. The seeds in the inflated pods rattle. 8–16" high. Dry sandy places, Mass. to S.D. south. Summer. Pea Family.

Green Violet (*Hybanthus concolor*) Greenish-white flowers, about ¼" long, hanging from the axils, 1–3 in a cluster. One of the petals is larger than the others and spurred. Leaves elliptical, long-pointed, sometimes with a few small teeth. 1–2' high. Rich woods, w. N.Eng. to Wis. south. Spring. Violet Family.

Dwarf Snapdragon (*Chaenorrhinum minus*) * Small, blue or lilac flowers, ¼" long, growing on long stalks from the axils. The flowers have a short spur at the base. Leaves narrow, about 1" long. A low plant of waste places, especially along railroad tracks. Summer. Figwort Family.

Virginia Snakeroot (*Aristolochia serpentaria*) Greenish or brownish-purple flowers, at the base of the plant. See p. 122.

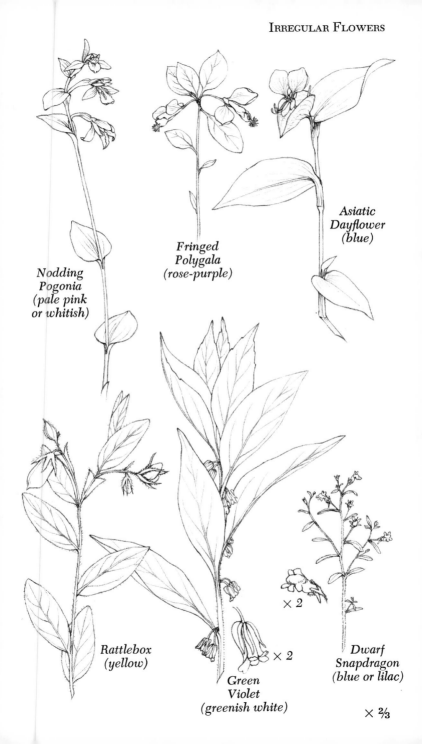

Nodding Pogonia (pale pink or whitish)

Fringed Polygala (rose-purple)

Asiatic Dayflower (blue)

Rattlebox (yellow)

Green Violet (greenish white) × 2

× 2

Dwarf Snapdragon (blue or lilac)

× 2/3

White, Green or Purple Flowers, with Spurs, in Spikes or Racemes

Showy Orchis (*Orchis spectabilis*) Plant with two large basal leaves; magenta, white-lipped flowers. See p. 22.

Rein Orchids (*Habenaria*) Plants without basal leaves or with a single basal leaf. A large group of Orchids having a long or short spur projecting from beneath the lip. For species with basal leaves, see pp. 20 and 22. Orchis Family.

1. LIP FRINGED

a. Magenta or purple flowers

Smaller Purple Fringed Orchis (*H. psycodes*) Flower spike 1–1½" in diameter; flowers about ¾" long, fragrant; lip ¼–⅔" wide. 1–3' high. Wet woods and meadows. Summer.

Larger Purple Fringed Orchis (*H. fimbriata*) Flower spike 2–2½" in diameter; flowers about 1" long; lip ¾–1" wide. Intergrades with the Smaller Purple Fringed Orchis and is often considered an earlier blooming, large variety of it. 2–4' high. Cool moist woods and swamp margins. Late spring and summer.

b. White or green flowers

Ragged Fringed or **Green Fringed Orchis** (*H. lacera*) Lip divided into 3 lobes, the central one narrow and longer than wide; greenish-white flowers, about ¾" long. The deep and threadlike fringe gives the flower a very tattered appearance. 1–2' high. Fields and wet meadows. Summer.

Prairie Fringed Orchis (*H. leucophaea*) Lip divided into 3 lobes, the central one broadly wedge-shaped and about as wide as long; creamy-white flowers, about 1" long. Flowers fragrant. 2–3' high. Moist prairies and bogs; rare and local in the East. Early summer.

White Fringed Orchis (*H. blephariglottis*) Lip not divided, oblong, fringed with short hairs. Flowers usually pure white, although sometimes creamy. 1–2' high. Bogs. Summer.

Continued

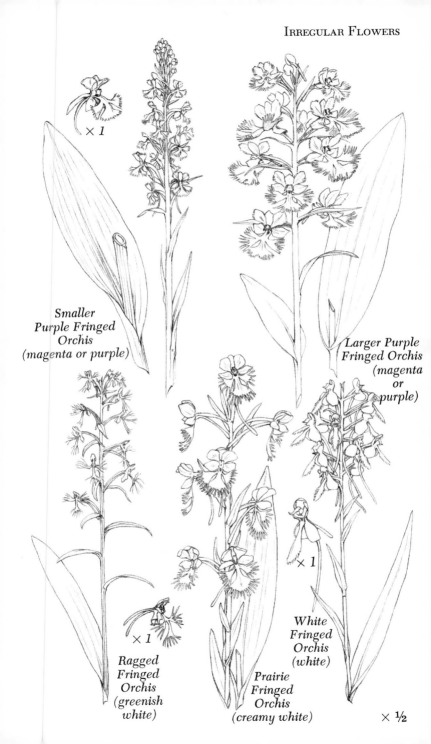

× 1

Smaller
Purple Fringed
Orchis
(magenta or purple)

Larger Purple
Fringed Orchis
(magenta
or
purple)

× 1

Ragged
Fringed
Orchis
(greenish
white)

Prairie
Fringed
Orchis
(creamy white)

White
Fringed
Orchis
(white)

× ½

White, Green or Purple Flowers, with Spurs, in Spikes or Racemes (cont.)

Rein Orchids (*Habenaria*) (cont.)

2. LIP NOT FRINGED

a. Purple flowers

Purple Fringeless Orchis (*H. peramoena*) Lip divided into 3 lobes, with toothed edges. Rose-purple flowers. 1–3' high. Moist meadows and thickets, w. N.J. and s. Pa. south. Summer.

b. Green, yellow-green or greenish-white flowers

Tubercled or **Pale Green Orchis** (*H. flava*) Flower spike slender, with long bracts, the *lower* ones more than twice as long as the flowers; the spur is longer than the oblong lip. The lip has a small protuberance (tubercle) in the center. Well-developed stem leaves 2 or more. 1–2' high. Moist meadows. Late spring and summer.

Long-bracted Orchis (*H. viridis* var. *bracteata*) All the bracts of the flower spike are 2–6 times longer than the flowers; spur very short and inconspicuous. Lower leaves broad and blunt. 6–20" high. Rich woods and meadows. Late spring and summer.

Green Wood Orchis (*H. clavellata*) Flower spike short and broad, the greenish-white flowers often twisted to one side; spur very long, slender and curved. There is one well-developed leaf near the base of the stem; the other leaves are much smaller. 8–18" high. Wet woods. Summer.

Northern Green Orchis (*H. hyperborea*) Green or yellow-green flowers in a slender spike; the spur about equals the lance-shaped lip. 6–36" high. Bogs and woods. Summer.

c. White flowers

White Bog Orchis (*H. dilatata*) Flowers in a long, slender spike, fragrant; the spur about equals the lip in length. 1½–2½' high. Cold bogs and wet meadows, mostly in the mts. Summer.

Snowy Orchis (*H. nivea*) Spur long and slender, often twisted to the side. Lip situated at the top of the flower, rather than at the base as in the other species of this genus. Leaves narrow. Bogs in pine barrens, s. N.J. south. Late summer.

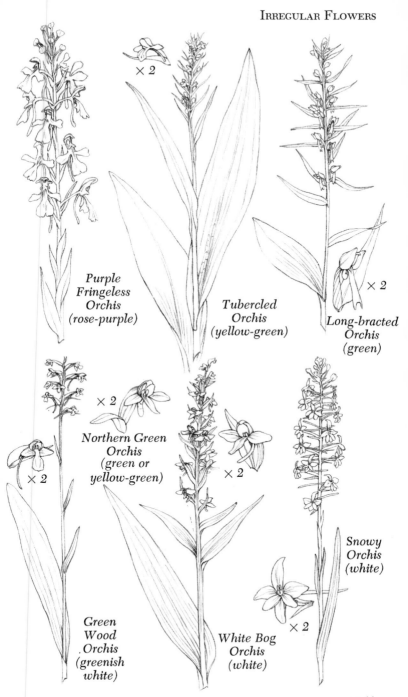

Purple
Fringeless
Orchis
(rose-purple)

× 2

Tubercled
Orchis
(yellow-green)

× 2

Long-bracted
Orchis
(green)

× 2

Northern Green
Orchis
(green or
yellow-green)

× 2

× 2

Snowy
Orchis
(white)

Green
Wood
Orchis
(greenish
white)

× 2

White Bog
Orchis
(white)

× ½

White, Green or Purple Flowers, without Spurs, in Spikes, Racemes or Heads

LEAF SOLITARY, IN THE MIDDLE OF THE STEM

Green Adder's Mouth (*Malaxis unifolia*) Greenish flowers in a short, thick raceme, the raceme 1–3″ long. The lip is 3-toothed at the tip. 4–10″ high. Open woods, bogs. Summer. Orchis Family.

LEAVES 2 OR MORE, THE LOWER LEAVES NOT OVER 1½″ LONG

Milkworts (*Polygala*) Plants with small (¼″ or less long) flowers in spikes, racemes or cloverlike heads. Juice not milky. For other species, see pp. 40, 48 and 72. 4–20″ high. Milkwort Family.

1. PLANTS WITH SEVERAL STEMS FROM THE SAME ROOT, THE STEMS UNBRANCHED AND BEARING A SINGLE RACEME OR SPIKE

Racemed Milkwort (*P. polygama*) Rose-purple (rarely white) flowers, ¼″ long, in a raceme 1–4″ long. Leaves numerous, lance-shaped, about 1″ long. Dry woods and clearings. Summer.

Seneca Snakeroot (*P. senega*) White or greenish-white flowers in a spike, the flowers about ⅛″ long. Leaves gradually become smaller toward the base of the plant. Dry woods and rocky slopes. Late spring and early summer.

2. STEM SOLITARY, USUALLY BRANCHED AND BEARING MORE THAN 1 FLOWER CLUSTER; BLOOMS IN SUMMER AND FALL

a. Flower clusters ⅓–½″ thick

Purple Milkwort (*P. sanguinea*) Flowers rose-purple to green, in a very dense head. Moist meadows.

Curtiss' Milkwort (*P. curtissii*) † Flower head not as dense as that of Purple Milkwort; flowers bright pink or rose-purple with yellow tip. Dry or moist soil, Del. to W.Va. south.

b. Flower clusters ⅛–¼″ thick

Whorled Milkwort (*P. verticillata*) Flower cluster tapering to the tip; lower leaves usually opposite or whorled. See p. 72.

Nuttall's Milkwort (*P. nuttallii*) Cluster blunt or short-pointed; all leaves alternate. Tiny, purplish or greenish-white flowers. Dry sandy soil, Mass. south.

Chaffseed (*Schwalbea americana*) Yellowish-purple flowers, 1–1½″ long, in a leafy-bracted, spikelike raceme. Lower leaves 3-veined, egg-shaped or oblong. 1–2′ high. Moist sandy soil, Mass. and e. N.Y. south; local. Late spring and early summer. Figwort Family.   Continued

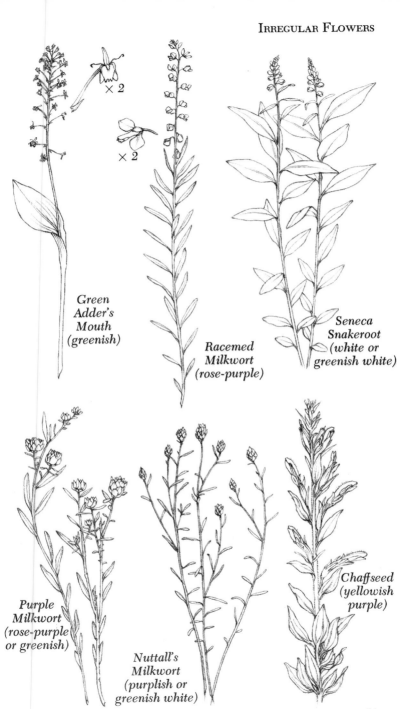

Green
Adder's
Mouth
(greenish)

× 2

× 2

Racemed
Milkwort
(rose-purple)

Seneca
Snakeroot
(white or
greenish white)

Purple
Milkwort
(rose-purple
or greenish)

Nuttall's
Milkwort
(purplish or
greenish white)

Chaffseed
(yellowish
purple)

× ½

White, Green or Purple Flowers, without Spurs, in Spikes, Racemes or Heads (cont.)

LEAVES 2 OR MORE, THE LOWER LEAVES OVER 1½" LONG

Helleborine (*Epipactis helleborine*) * Flowers purple or green tinged with purple, in a raceme, which is often one-sided. Leaves egg-shaped or lance-shaped, clasping the stem. 1–2' high. Woods and thickets. Summer. Orchis Family.

Pale Painted Cup (*Castilleja septentrionalis*) Two-lipped, yellowish flowers in a spike surrounded by cream or purplish bracts. Upper leaves lance-shaped with 3–5 parallel veins; lower leaves narrower. 6–24" high. Gravelly soil on higher mts. of N.Eng. north and west. Summer. Figwort Family.

Ladies' Tresses (*Spiranthes*) White flowers in a spike; leaves grasslike, near the base of the plant. See p. 26.

Long-bracted Orchis (*Habenaria viridis* var. *bracteata*) Greenish flowers in a leafy-bracted spike. See p. 44.

Yellow or Orange Flowers in Spikes, Racemes or Heads

Butter-and-eggs (*Linaria vulgaris*) * Yellow, spurred flowers with an orange palate, 1" long, in a raceme. Leaves very narrow and numerous, ½–1½" long. 1–3' high. Roadsides and waste places; common. Summer. Figwort Family.

Rein Orchids (*Habenaria*) Yellow or orange, spurred flowers in spikes; lower leaves lance-shaped. 8–24" high. Late summer. Orchis Family.

> **Yellow Fringed Orchis** (*H. ciliaris*) Lip fringed; spur about 1" long, somewhat longer than the flower. Spike 1½–3" wide. Bogs, sandy woods, s. N.Eng. to Wis. south.

> **Crested Yellow Orchis** (*H. cristata*) Lip fringed; spur under ½" long. Spike less than 1½" wide. Bogs and moist meadows, N.J. south.

> **Southern Yellow Orchis** (*H. integra*) Lip toothed or sometimes entire. Spike 1–1½" wide. Wet pine barrens, s. N.J. (rare); N.C. to Tenn. south.

Orange Milkwort (*Polygala lutea*) Small, orange-yellow flowers in a dense head. Leaves lance-shaped, ½–1½" long. 6–12" high. Low ground in pine barrens, Long I. south. Late spring to fall. Milkwort Family.

Dyer's Greenweed (*Genista tinctoria*) Yellow, pea-shaped flowers, ½" long, in loose racemes. See p. 104.   Continued

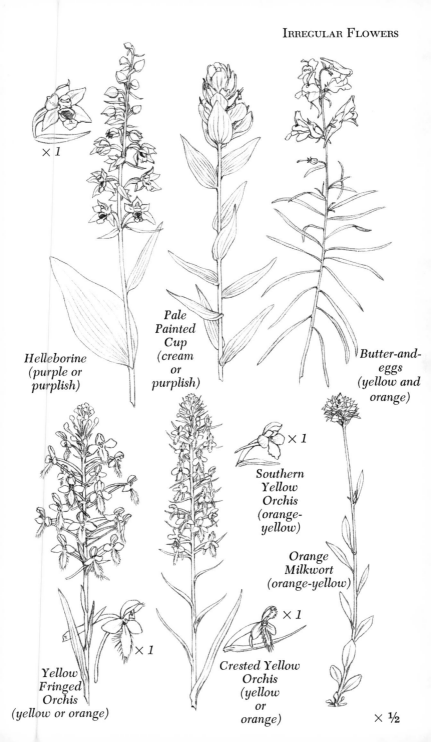

× 1

Helleborine (purple or purplish)

Pale Painted Cup (cream or purplish)

Butter-and-eggs (yellow and orange)

× 1

Southern Yellow Orchis (orange-yellow)

Orange Milkwort (orange-yellow)

× 1

Yellow Fringed Orchis (yellow or orange)

Crested Yellow Orchis (yellow or orange)

× ½

Blue Flowers in Spikes or Racemes

Pickerelweed (*Pontederia cordata*) Leaves heart-shaped at the base, long-stalked. The individual flowers are 2-lipped, with each of the lips 3-lobed, and grow in spikes 3–4″ long. 1–3′ high. Common on margins of rivers and ponds. Summer and fall. Pickerelweed Family.

Viper's Bugloss or **Blueweed** (*Echium vulgare*) * Stem bristly-hairy. The flowers are bright blue, ¾–1″ long, opening one at a time in a series of short, one-sided spikes, which together form a long, terminal cluster. Stamens protruding. 1–3′ high. Locally abundant weed of fields and waste places, usually in limestone regions. Summer. Borage Family.

Blue Toadflax (*Linaria canadensis*) Blue flowers, ¼″ long, with conspicuous white palate and long slender spur projecting beneath, in a slender raceme. The narrow leaves are ½–1½″ long. 4–24″ high. Sandy soil. Spring to fall. Figwort Family.

Lobelias (*Lobelia*) Flowers light blue, ¼–⅓″ long, and 2-lipped, the upper lip with 2 lobes and the lower lip with 3 lobes, growing in spikes or in loose racemes. In the following 3 species the leaves are entire or sparingly toothed. For other species, see pp. 24 and 52. Summer and fall. Lobelia Family.

Kalm's or **Brook Lobelia** (*L. kalmii*) Flowers in loose racemes; grows in wet or springy places in limestone regions. Flowers ⅓–½″ long, with white throat, long-stalked. Stem 6–18″ high and usually branched. Leaves narrow, entire or indistinctly toothed. N. N.J. to Iowa north.

Nuttall's Lobelia (*L. nuttallii*) Similar to the Kalm's Lobelia, but grows in sandy soil along the coast, north to Long I., and inland to Ky. Flowers smaller, about ⅓″ long.

Spiked Lobelia (*L. spicata*) Flowers in a slender, spikelike raceme; grows in fields and woods; stem leaves lance-shaped. See p. 52.

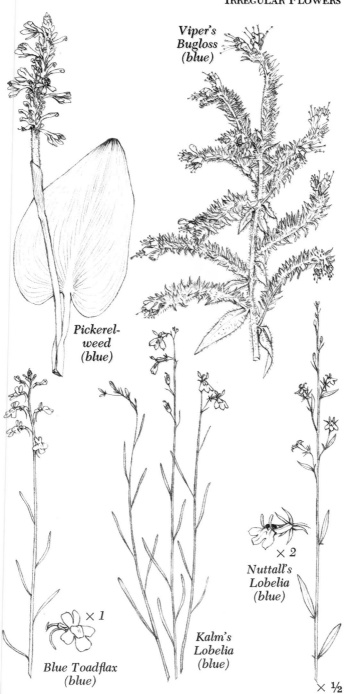

Viper's
Bugloss
(blue)

*Pickerel-
weed
(blue)*

× 1

*Blue Toadflax
(blue)*

*Kalm's
Lobelia
(blue)*

× 2

*Nuttall's
Lobelia
(blue)*

× ½

Flowers Short-stalked or Stalkless

Lobelias (*Lobelia*) Flowers 2-lipped, the upper lip with 2 lobes, the lower lip with 3 lobes. The flower tube is split down the middle between the upper lobes. Several kinds have spikes of showy flowers. For other species, see pp. 24 and 50. Lobelia Family.

1. FLOWERS LARGE, OVER ½" LONG

Cardinal Flower (*L. cardinalis*) Scarlet flowers, 1–1½" long. The long stamens project through a split in the upper lip. 2–5′ high. A striking plant of stream banks and damp meadows. Late summer and fall.

Great Lobelia (*L. siphilitica*) Blue flowers, about 1″ long, with the inflated tube striped underneath. Leaves 2–4″ long, pointed. 1–3′ high. Moist thickets and swamps. Late summer and fall.

Downy Lobelia (*L. puberula*) Blue flowers, about ¾" long, with white center. The flower spike is often one-sided. Leaves soft-hairy, 1–2″ long. 1–3′ high. Woods and clearings, N.J. to Ill. south. Late summer and fall.

2. FLOWERS ¼–½″ LONG

Spiked Lobelia (*L. spicata*) Light-blue to white flowers in a slender, leafless, spikelike raceme. The leaves are slightly toothed to entire, with some in a basal rosette. 1–3′ high. Fields and woods. Summer.

Indian Tobacco (*L. inflata*) Light-blue flowers, ¼" long, in leafy racemes. The calyx becomes inflated in fruit. Stem usually branched, 6–36″ high. Waste places, open woods and fields; common. Summer and fall.

Louseworts (*Pedicularis*) Yellow or reddish flowers, ¾" long, in a short spike or head; leaves fernlike.

Wood Betony or **Lousewort** (*P. canadensis*) Lower stem leaves long-stalked. See p. 70.

Swamp Lousewort (*P. lanceolata*) Stem leaves stalkless or very short-stalked, with some growing nearly opposite each other. See p. 82.

Painted Cup or **Indian Paintbrush** (*Castilleja coccinea*) Bracts surrounding the flowers bright red at the end and with 3–5 lobes. See p. 70.

Biennial Gaura (*Gaura biennis*) White or pink flowers with 4 petals and long, drooping stamens. See p. 138.

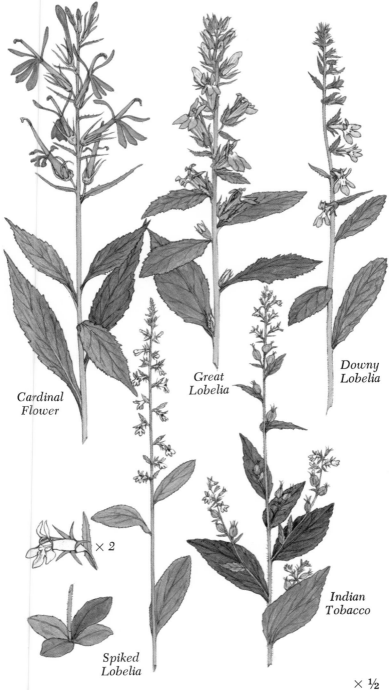

Cardinal
Flower

Great
Lobelia

Downy
Lobelia

× 2

Spiked
Lobelia

Indian
Tobacco

× ½

Flowers Long-stalked, the Stalks Nearly as Long as or Longer Than the Flowers

Touch-me-nots or **Jewelweeds** (*Impatiens*) Flowers about 1″ long, dangling from a long stalk. The flowers have a short inward-curved spur at the back. The leaves are egg-shaped, coarsely toothed. Fruit a plump pod that explodes when ripe. Stem succulent, 2–5′ high. Moist places. Summer and early fall. Touch-me-not Family.

Spotted Touch-me-not (*I. capensis*) Orange flowers, spotted with red-brown, longer than broad. Spur bent underneath and parallel to the flower. Common.

Pale Touch-me-not (*I. pallida*) Yellow flowers, less spotted than those of the Spotted Touch-me-not, and about as broad as long. Spur short, at right angle to the flower. Mostly in limestone regions.

Violets (*Viola*) Flowers with 5 petals, the lower petal veined with violet and spurred at the base. A group of woodland plants. The following species have heart-shaped leaves (except the Field Pansy). For violets with basal leaves only, see pp. 28–34. Spring (occasionally again in the fall). Violet Family.

1. YELLOW FLOWERS

Downy Yellow Violet (*V. pubescens*) Stem leaves about as broad as long; stem soft-hairy. The leaves are very broad, prominently veined, and hairy beneath, especially along the veins. Occasionally there is one basal leaf, but usually none. 4–12″ high. Dry woods.

Smooth Yellow Violet (*V. pensylvanica*) Similar to the Downy Yellow Violet, but the stem and leaves are nearly smooth and the plant has one or more basal leaves. Also, the leaves are not so wide or veiny. Moist woods.

Halberd-leaved Violet (*V. hastata*) Stem leaves about twice as long as wide, triangular or arrow-shaped. The backs of the petals are tinged with violet. Rich woods, Pa. and Ohio south.

Continued

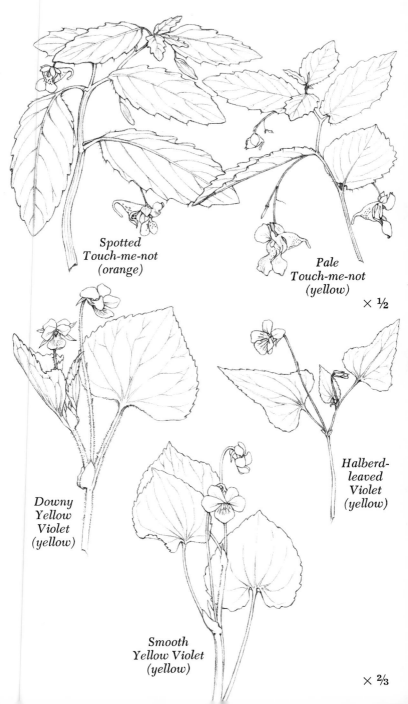

Spotted
Touch-me-not
(orange)

Pale
Touch-me-not
(yellow)

× ½

Downy
Yellow
Violet
(yellow)

Halberd-
leaved
Violet
(yellow)

Smooth
Yellow Violet
(yellow)

× ⅔

Flowers Long-stalked, the Stalks Nearly as Long as or Longer Than the Flowers (cont.)

Violets (*Viola*) (cont.)

2. WHITE OR CREAM-COLORED FLOWERS

Canada Violet (*V. canadensis*) Leaves heart-shaped; white flowers with a yellow throat. The backs of the petals are usually tinged with violet. Rich woods. Spring and early summer, and often again in the fall.

Pale or **Cream Violet** (*V. striata*) Leaves heart-shaped; cream-colored to milk-white flowers. The stipules are large and sharply toothed. Low woods and moist meadows, N.Y. to Wis. south.

Field Pansy (*V. kitaibeliana*) * Leaves small and roundish or tapering to the base; small, bluish-white to cream-colored flowers. The leaflike stipules are deeply lobed. An annual species, found in fields and along roadsides from N.Y. to Iowa south.

3. VIOLET OR LILAC FLOWERS

Long-spurred Violet (*V. rostrata*) Spur of lower petal ½″ long, slender. The flowers are pale lilac with a darker center. Rich woods.

Dog Violet (*V. conspersa*) Spur of lower petal about ¼″ long, blunt; pale-violet flowers; upper leaves broadly heart-shaped, blunt; stipules sharply toothed. Low woods and meadows.

Sand or **Hooked Violet** (*V. adunca*) Spur as in the Dog Violet; flowers darker violet; upper leaves somewhat pointed; stipules with few teeth or without teeth. Dry sandy or rocky soil, and alpine ravines, Can. south to N.Eng., N.Y., Mich., Wis. and west.

Green Violet (*Hybanthus concolor*) Greenish-white flowers, about ¼″ long, hanging from the axils. See p. 40.

Lobelias (*Lobelia*) Light-blue flowers, ¼–⅓″ long, with a white throat. See p. 50.

Monkshoods (*Aconitum*) Blue, helmet-shaped flowers, ¾″ long. See p. 68.

Speedwells (*Veronica*) Small, blue or white flowers with 4 lobes. See p. 96.

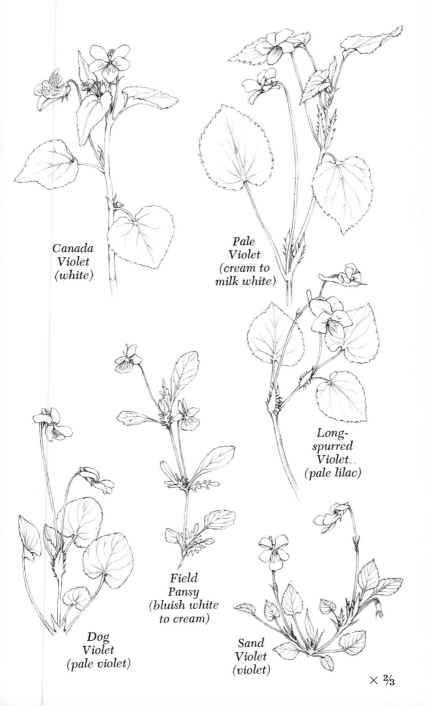

Canada
Violet
(white)

Pale
Violet
(cream to
milk white)

Long-
spurred
Violet
(pale lilac)

Field
Pansy
(bluish white
to cream)

Dog
Violet
(pale violet)

Sand
Violet
(violet)

× ⅔

Leaflets 3, Entire or Finely Toothed; Yellow Flowers

Black Medick (*Medicago lupulina*) * Flowers in small heads; leaflets tipped with a short bristle. A sprawling plant resembling the Hop Clovers. The fruiting cluster of small, black, spirally coiled pods is distinctive. Roadsides and waste places. Early spring to late fall. Pea Family.

Hop or **Yellow Clovers** (*Trifolium*) Flowers in heads; leaflets not bristle-tipped. Leaflets finely toothed. Low plants of fields and roadsides. Summer and fall. Pea Family.

Hop or **Yellow Clover** (*T. agrarium*) * The largest and commonest species, with flower heads and leaflets ½–¾" long; middle leaflets stalkless or nearly so. Plant more or less erect, up to 15" high.

Low Hop Clover (*T. procumbens*) * Flower heads and leaflets ⅓–½" long; the middle leaflet distinctly stalked. Heads normally with more than 15 flowers. Usually prostrate on the ground.

Least Hop Clover (*T. dubium*) * Similar to the Low Hop Clover, but the flowers are in very small heads (about ¼" long) of 3–15 flowers.

Yellow Sweet Clover (*Melilotus officinalis*) * Flowers in racemes 2–4" long; leaflets finely toothed. The foliage gives off the fragrance of new-mown hay when crushed or dried. Except for its color, very similar to White Sweet Clover (p. 60). 3–8' high. Roadsides and waste places. Late spring to fall. Pea Family.

Wild Indigo (*Baptisia tinctoria*) Yellow pealike flowers, ½" long, in few-flowered racemes at the ends of the branches; leaflets small, entire, broad and blunt at the tip. Plant bluish when young; foliage turns black when dried. Bushy-branched, 1–3' high. Dry open places. Summer and occasionally fall. Pea Family.

Pencil Flower (*Stylosanthes biflora*) Flowers about ¼" long, growing singly or in small clusters at the ends of the branches; leaflets narrowly lance-shaped or elliptical and bristle-tipped. Stems wiry. 6–20" high. Dry woods and fields, s. N.Y. to Kan. south. Summer. Pea Family.

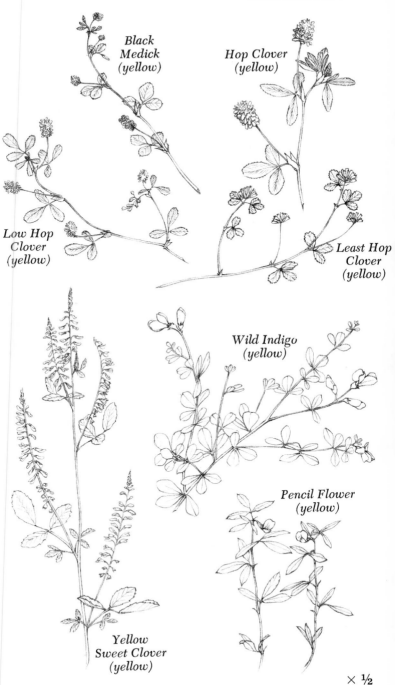

Black
Medick
(yellow)

Hop Clover
(yellow)

Low Hop
Clover
(yellow)

Least Hop
Clover
(yellow)

Wild Indigo
(yellow)

Pencil Flower
(yellow)

Yellow
Sweet Clover
(yellow)

× ½

Leaflets 3, Entire or Finely Toothed, the Middle One Stalkless or Nearly So; Flowers Not Yellow

Clovers (*Trifolium*) White, pink or purple flowers in dense heads. These familiar plants are found in fields, roadsides and waste places. Pea Family.

Red Clover (*T. pratense*) * Magenta or purple flowers in stalkless heads. The blunt, oval leaflets are usually blotched with a white V. 6–24" high. Fields and meadows; very common. Spring to fall.

Rabbit-foot Clover (*T. arvense*) * Flower heads grayish pink or grayish white, oblong, furry. The leaflets are rather narrow and silky-hairy. 4–10" high. Dry fields and roadsides. Summer to fall.

Alsike or **Alsatian Clover** (*T. hybridum*) * Pink or pinkish flowers in a round head, turning brown with age; stem erect or ascending. The heads are long-stalked, and the flowers are sweetly fragrant. 10–24" high. Fields and roadsides. Summer to fall.

White Clover (*T. repens*) White or pale-pink flowers in a round head; plant creeping at the base. See p. 36.

False Indigos (*Baptisia*) Blue or white flowers, about 1" long, in loose racemes. Leaflets 3, entire. Wild Indigo (p. 58) has yellow flowers. 2–5' high. Rich woods and thickets. Late spring and early summer. Pea Family.

Blue False Indigo (*B. australis*) Indigo-blue flowers. W. Pa. to s. Ind. south; escaped east to N.Eng.

White False Indigo (*B. leucantha*) † White flowers. S. Ont. and Ohio to Minn. south.

Jack-in-the-pulpits (*Arisaema*) Brown or green flowers, growing beneath the leaves. See p. 36.

Leaflets 3, Finely Toothed, the Middle One Distinctly Stalked; Flowers Not Yellow

White Sweet Clover (*Melilotus alba*) * White flowers in 2–4" racemes. Leaves fragrant when dried. 3–8' high. Roadsides and waste places. Late spring to fall. Pea Family.

Alfalfa or **Lucerne** (*Medicago sativa*) * Purple or blue-violet flowers in a short raceme. The leaflets are toothed toward the tip; the stalk of the middle leaflet is turned upward. Plant bushy, 1–3' high. Cultivated for fodder and escaped to roadsides and waste places. Summer. Pea Family.

Rabbit-foot
Clover
(grayish pink)

Red Clover
*(magenta or
purple)*

Alsike
Clover
(pink)

Blue
False Indigo
(indigo-blue)

White
Sweet
Clover
(white)

Alfalfa
*(purple or
blue-violet)*

× ½

Leaflets 3, Entire, the Middle One Distinctly Stalked; Flowers Not Yellow

Tick Trefoils (*Desmodium*) Purple or pinkish flowers, mostly in loose racemes or branched clusters; pods usually with more than 1 joint and covered with hooked hairs that cling to clothing. The Bush Clovers (p. 64) have single-jointed, nonadhesive pods, and usually a more compact flower cluster. Summer. Pea Family.

1. TERMINAL LEAFLET NARROW (4 TIMES LONGER THAN WIDE)

Panicled Tick Trefoil (*D. paniculatum*) Leaf stalks ½″ or more long; flowers ¼″ or more long. Flower cluster widely branched. 2–4′ high. Dry woods.

Sessile-leaved Tick Trefoil (*D. sessilifolium*) Leaf stalks ⅛″ or less long; flowers under ¼″ long. Pods with 1–3 joints. Sandy soil, Mass. to Kan. south.

2. PROSTRATE, TRAILING PLANT WITH ROUND LEAFLETS

Prostrate Tick Trefoil (*D. rotundifolium*) See p. 110.

3. NOT TRAILING, LEAFLETS 1–3 TIMES LONGER THAN WIDE

a. *Flowers about ½″ long, in close clusters*

Showy Tick Trefoil (*D. canadense*) Large rose-purple flowers in dense racemes. Stem downy. 2–6′ high. Pods with 3–5 joints, very sticky when mature. Banks and borders of woods.

b. *Flowers ¼–½″ long, in loose clusters*

Naked-flowered Tick Trefoil (*D. nudiflorum*) Stem smooth, with 1–3 scattered leaves. See p. 36.

Large-bracted Tick Trefoil (*D. cuspidatum*) Stem leafy, smooth or nearly so; terminal leaflet gradually narrows to a point; stipules lance-shaped; joints of pods almost twice as long as wide. 2–6′ high. Woods and banks, s. N.Eng. to Wis. south.

Dillen's Tick Trefoil (*D. glabellum*) Stem leaves 4 or more; leaves blunt or with a broad point; stipules minute or none; joints of pods about as wide as long. Dry woods and borders.

Hoary Tick Trefoil (*D. canescens*) Stem hairy, branching; stipules egg-shaped, prominent; joints of pods longer than wide. Pink flowers, turning green. 2–5′ high. Dry woods, clearings, Mass. to Neb. south.

c. *Flowers under ¼″ long; leaflets under 1½″ long*

Hairy Small-leaved Tick Trefoil (*D. ciliare*) Leaf stalks under ½″ long, hairy. Stem usually hairy. 1–3′ high. Dry woods, s. N.Eng. to Mich. south. *D. marilandicum* has longer leaf stalks and is smoothish.   Continued

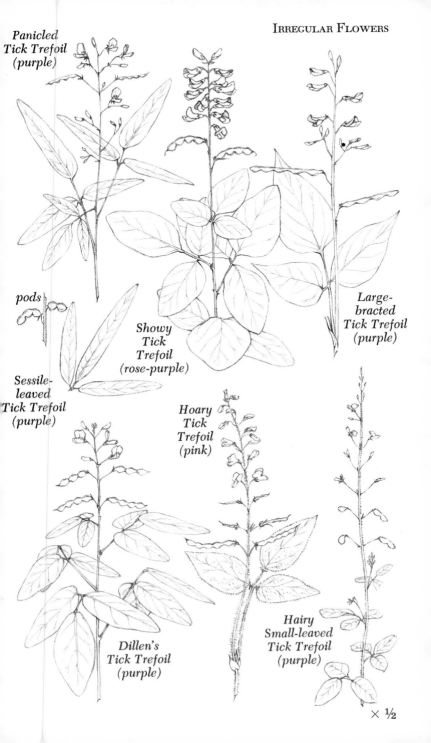

Panicled Tick Trefoil (purple)

pods

Sessile-leaved Tick Trefoil (purple)

Showy Tick Trefoil (rose-purple)

Large-bracted Tick Trefoil (purple)

Hoary Tick Trefoil (pink)

Dillen's Tick Trefoil (purple)

Hairy Small-leaved Tick Trefoil (purple)

× ½

Leaflets 3, Entire, the Middle One Distinctly Stalked; Flowers Not Yellow (cont.)

Bush Clovers (*Lespedeza*) White, purple or pink flowers, in axillary clusters, spikes or heads; pods with a single oval or roundish joint. The pods of the Tick Trefoils (p. 62) have usually more than 1 joint and adhere to clothing. Some of the flowers are self-pollinated and do not open. Dry woods and fields, c. N.Eng. to Wis. south. Summer and fall. Pea Family.

1. TRAILING PLANTS

Trailing Bush Clover (*L. procumbens*) Stems soft-hairy. Trailing plant with short side branches. Purple or pink flowers, ¼" long. Leaves oval, ½–1" long. Sandy soil.

Creeping Bush Clover (*L. repens*) † Similar to the Trailing Bush Clover, but stems smoothish.

2. ERECT PLANTS WITH WHITE FLOWERS

Round-headed Bush Clover (*L. capitata*) Leaves short-stalked, the leaflets 3 times longer than wide. Flowers creamy-white and purple-spotted, in dense clusters at the top of the stem or in the upper axils. Leaflets elliptical, 1–1½" long, silvery beneath. 2–5' high.

Hairy Bush Clover (*L. hirta*) Leaves long-stalked, the leaflets egg-shaped or roundish. Flowers in dense, spikelike clusters. 2–5' high.

3. ERECT PLANTS WITH PURPLE FLOWERS

Slender Bush Clover (*L. virginica*) Leaflets narrow, 4 times longer than wide. The flowers are found in short clusters in the upper axils. 1–3' high.

Violet Bush Clover (*L. violacea*) Leaflets oval, 1–2" long; flowering branches long-stalked, much longer than the leaves. This plant has a branching, loose-flowered appearance compared to the next species.

Wandlike Bush Clover (*L. intermedia*) Leaflets oval; flowering branches short-stalked, shorter or not much longer than the leaves. Most of the flowers are densely clustered at the top of the plant, with a few, short axillary clusters below. 1–3' high.

Butterfly Pea (*Clitoria mariana*) Pale-blue, showy flowers, 2" long; plant usually trailing or twining. See p. 110.

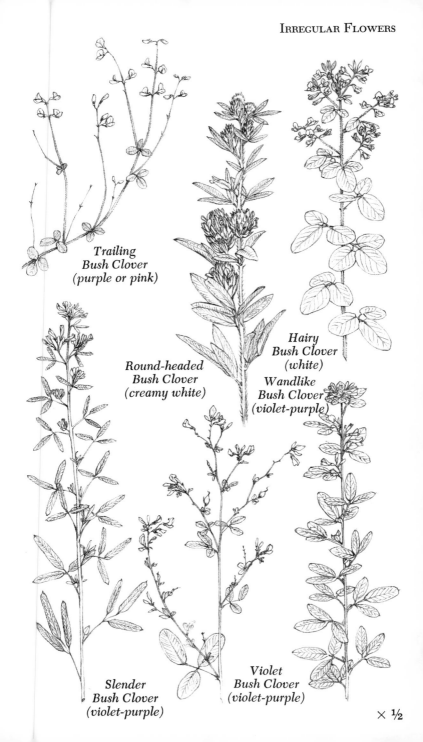

*Trailing
Bush Clover
(purple or pink)*

*Round-headed
Bush Clover
(creamy white)*

*Hairy
Bush Clover
(white)*

*Wandlike
Bush Clover
(violet-purple)*

*Slender
Bush Clover
(violet-purple)*

*Violet
Bush Clover
(violet-purple)*

× ½

Leaflets 4 or More, Entire or Finely Toothed

Birdsfoot Trefoil (*Lotus corniculatus*) * Bright-yellow flowers; leaflets 5, the lower 2 at the base of the leaf stalk. The flowers grow in small umbels at the ends of the branches. A low, cloverlike plant of fields and roadsides. Summer. Pea Family.

Lupines (*Lupinus*) Blue or blue-violet flowers (sometimes white); leaflets palmate. The pea-shaped flowers grow in showy racemes. Pea Family.

Wild Lupine (*L. perennis*) Lower leaves with 7–11 leaflets 1–2″ long; 8–24″ high. Racemes 4–10″ long. Dry sandy woods and banks, Me. to Minn. south. Late spring and early summer.

Garden Lupine (*L. polyphyllus*) * Lower leaves with 12–18 leaflets; 2–4′ high. Racemes 6–18″ long. Cultivated and escaped to roadsides and fields, n. N.Eng. and e. Can. Summer.

Goat's Rue (*Tephrosia virginiana*) Pale yellow and pinkish flowers with purple markings; plant silky-hairy. Leaflets 17–25, oblong. The ½–¾″ flowers occur in one or more dense racemes. Dry sandy soil, s. N.Eng. to Minn. south. Early summer. Pea Family.

Crown Vetch or **Axseed** (*Coronilla varia*) * Pink and white flowers in a cloverlike cluster (umbel), growing from the axils. Leaflets 11–25, oblong. A sprawling plant of roadsides, extensively planted as a ground cover for steep banks. Summer. Pea Family.

Canadian Milk Vetch (*Astragalus canadensis*) Cream-colored or yellowish flowers, ½–¾″ long, in a dense, thick spike; leaflets 15–31, oblong. Stem smooth or slightly downy. 1–4′ high. Shores and rocky banks, w. Vt. to B.C. south. Summer. Pea Family.

Sennas (*Cassia*) Yellow flowers composed of 5 separate petals. See p. 236.

Wild Peas or **Vetchlings** (*Lathyrus*) and **Vetches** (*Vicia*) Leaves bear a tendril at the end. See p. 112.

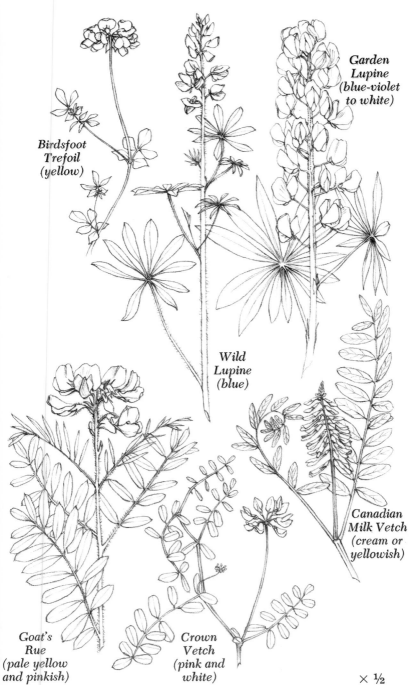

Birdsfoot
Trefoil
(yellow)

Garden
Lupine
(blue-violet
to white)

Wild
Lupine
(blue)

Canadian
Milk Vetch
(cream or
yellowish)

Goat's
Rue
(pale yellow
and pinkish)

Crown
Vetch
(pink and
white)

× ½

Leaves Deeply Cleft into Irregularly Lobed or Very Narrow Segments; Blue or White Flowers

Monkshoods (*Aconitum*) Blue flowers, with an enlarged, helmet-shaped upper sepal. The distinctive flowers are about ¾″ long and are borne in short clusters. Leaves very deeply cleft into 3–5 irregularly lobed segments. Woods and ravines. Buttercup Family.

> **Wild Monkshood** (*A. uncinatum*) Stem weak and leaning; upper part of stem smooth. 2–4′ long. S. Pa. to Ind. south. Midsummer to fall.

> **New York Monkshood** (*A. noveboracense*) † Similar to Wild Monkshood but stem mostly erect and upper part of stem hairy. 2–3′ high. Local, Catskill Mts., N.Y.; ne. Ohio; Iowa and Wis. Early summer.

Larkspurs (*Delphinium*) Blue (or occasionally white) flowers with the back sepal prolonged into a slender spur. Leaves deeply lobed into irregular segments. Buttercup Family.

> **Dwarf Larkspur** (*D. tricorne*) Leaves mostly at the base of the plant; flowers 1–1½″ long; blooms in spring. The flowers are in a few-flowered, loose raceme, and are sometimes variegated blue and white. Stem unbranched. 8–30″ high. Woods and rocky slopes, Pa. to Minn. south.

> **Tall Larkspur** (*D. exaltatum*) Stem leafy; flowers about ¾″ long, in an elongated raceme; leaves deeply cleft into 3–5 lance-shaped segments; blooms in summer. 2–6′ high. Rich woods and rocky slopes, s. Pa. and Ohio south.

> **Rocket Larkspur** (*D. ajacis*) * Flowers 1–1½″ long; upper leaves stemless, finely dissected into very narrow segments; blooms late spring to fall. Flowers in a loose, many-flowered raceme. 1–3′ high. Cultivated and escaped to roadsides and waste places. Summer.

Parsley Family (Umbelliferae) Small and numerous white flowers in broad clusters. See pp. 218–224.

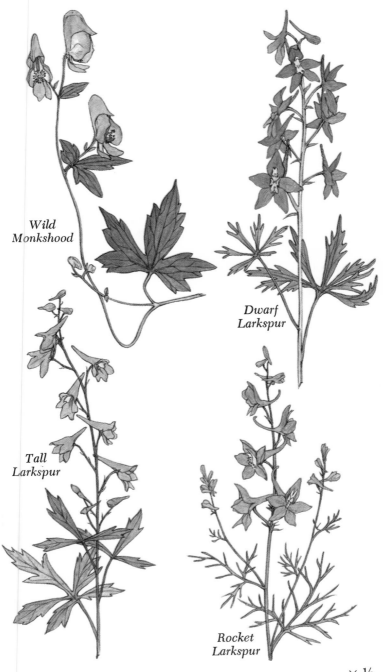

Wild Monkshood

Dwarf Larkspur

Tall Larkspur

Rocket Larkspur

× ½

Leaves Deeply Cleft into Irregularly Lobed or Very Narrow Segments; Yellow, Red or Pink Flowers

Wood Betony or **Lousewort** (*Pedicularis canadensis*) Yellow or reddish flowers in a short, dense spike; leaves deeply lobed, fernlike. The upper lip of the flower is arched over the 3-lobed lower lip. Plant hairy, 6–15″ high. The Swamp Lousewort (p.82) is smooth and has less deeply cut leaves. Dry woods and borders. Spring and early summer. Figwort Family.

Painted Cup or **Indian Paintbrush** (*Castilleja coccinea*) Flowers surrounded by leafy, 3-lobed, scarlet-tipped bracts, in a terminal spike. The true flowers are yellowish in color, tubular and 2-lipped. The stem leaves have 3–5 deep lobes; the basal leaves are entire and grow in a rosette. Stem hairy. 8–20″ high. Moist meadows, s. N.Eng. to Man. south. Late spring and summer. Figwort Family.

Corydalises (*Corydalis*) Flowers long and narrow, in short racemes, pink with yellow tip or yellow. Leaves finely divided, pale green or with a whitish bloom. The pods are long and slender. Poppy Family.

Pale or **Pink Corydalis** (*C. sempervirens*) Pink flowers with a yellow tip, about ½″ long. Stem erect, usually branched. 6–24″ high. Rocky places. Spring to fall.

Yellow Corydalis (*C. flavula*) Pale-yellow flowers, about ¼″ long. The spur at the rear of the flower is less than ¼ the length of the flower, and the upper lip is flaring and toothed. Stem spreading. 6–15″ high. Rocky slopes and open woods, Conn. to Minn. south. Spring.

Golden Corydalis (*C. aurea*) Golden-yellow flowers, ½″ long. Spur nearly ⅓ the length of the flower; upper lip not crested. Spreading, 6–24″ high. Rocky or sandy soil, Can. south to Vt., N.Y., W.Va. and west. Summer.

Fumitory (*Fumaria officinalis*) * Pinkish flowers with a crimson tip, in a long raceme. The leaves are light green and finely divided. Flowers about ⅓″ long. Stem reclining or partially erect, widely branched. 6–36″ long. Waste places or near old gardens. Summer. Poppy Family.

Bladderworts (*Utricularia*) Aquatic plants with finely divided leaves. See p. 16.

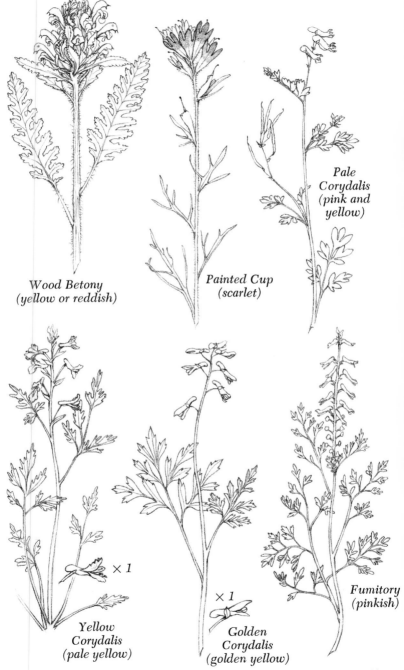

Wood Betony
(yellow or reddish)

Painted Cup
(scarlet)

Pale
Corydalis
(pink and
yellow)

Yellow
Corydalis
(pale yellow)

× 1

Golden
Corydalis
(golden yellow)

× 1

Fumitory
(pinkish)

× ½

Whorled Pogonias (*Isotria*) Flower solitary (sometimes 2), long-stalked, yellowish or greenish. The flower has a 3-lobed, crested lip and 3 narrow sepals. Leaves elliptical, in a single whorl of 5 at the top of the stem. Dry or moist woods. Late spring or early summer. Orchis Family.

Whorled Pogonia (*I. verticillata*) Sepals 1½–2″ long, much longer than the petals. When the flower is absent, the plant strongly resembles the Indian Cucumber Root (p. 352).

Small Whorled Pogonia (*I. medeoloides*) Sepals ¾–1″ long, little if at all longer than the petals. The leaves are gray-green and droop downward. Extremely rare and local, sometimes remaining dormant underground 10 or more years between blooming periods. N.Eng. south to N.C.

Milkworts (*Polygala*) Flowers large and rose-purple, or else small and numerous in heads, spikes or racemes. Juice not milky. For species with alternate leaves, see pp. 46, 48. Milkwort Family.

1. FLOWERS LARGE (¾″ LONG), 1–4 IN A LOOSE CLUSTER; LEAVES EGG-SHAPED

Fringed Polygala (*P. paucifolia*) Rose-purple flowers. See p. 40.

2. SMALL, GREENISH, PURPLE OR WHITE FLOWERS, IN DENSE HEADS OR SPIKES; LEAVES NARRTOW OR LANCE-SHAPED, ½–1½″ LONG

Cross-leaved or **Marsh Milkwort** (*P. cruciata*) Flower heads blunt and on very short stalks; side petals about as wide as long. Purplish to greenish flowers. The leaves are usually in whorls of 4. Low meadows and borders of swamps, Me. south along the coast, and from Ohio to Minn. south. Summer and fall.

Short-leaved Milkwort (*P. brevifolia*) Similar to the Cross-leaved Milkwort, but heads stalked and side petals longer than wide. Rose-purple flowers. Leaves in whorls of 4 or 5. Sandy swamps, N.J.; also on Gulf Coast.

Whorled Milkwort (*P. verticillata*) Flower spikes on long stalks and tapering at the tip. In one variety the leaves are mostly alternate instead of whorled. Fields and meadows. Summer and fall.

Spurges (*Euphorbia*) Yellowish or greenish flowers in a broad, terminal cluster. See p. 408.

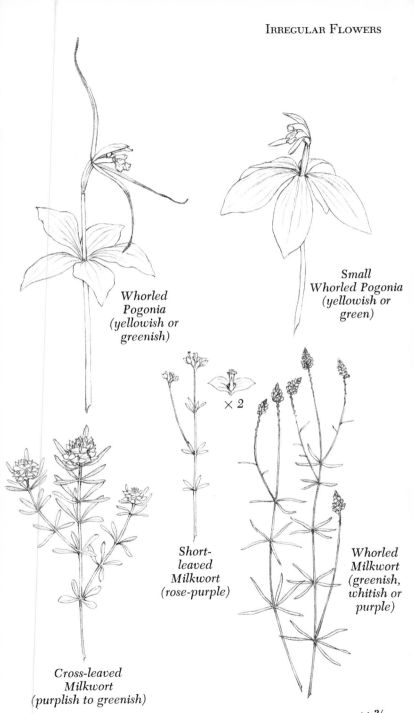

Whorled
Pogonia
*(yellowish or
greenish)*

Small
Whorled Pogonia
*(yellowish or
green)*

× 2

Short-
leaved
Milkwort
(rose-purple)

Whorled
Milkwort
*(greenish,
whitish or
purple)*

Cross-leaved
Milkwort
(purplish to greenish)

× ⅔

Leaves 2, in the Middle of the Stem

Twayblades (*Listera*) Low orchids, 4–10" high, with small, green-ish or purplish flowers in a raceme, and 2 broadly egg-shaped leaves midway up the stem. Another group of Orchids called Twayblades (*Liparis*) has 2 leaves at the base of the plant (p. 22). Moist woods and bogs. Late spring and summer. Orchis Family.

Heart-leaved Twayblade (*L. cordata*) Lip deeply cleft and about twice as long as the petals. Distance between the lower flowers and the leaves greater than the length of the leaves. Can. and n. U.S., south in mts. to N.C.

Southern Twayblade (*L. australis*) Lip as deeply cleft as in the Heart-leaved Twayblade, but the lip is at least 4 times as long as the petals. N.Y. south; rare in the n. part of its range.

Broad-lipped Twayblade (*L. convallarioides*) Lip broad, merely notched at the tip. Distance between raceme and leaves shorter than the length of the leaves. N. N.Eng. to Wis. north and west, and in mts. to N.C.

Leaves in Pairs; White or Blue Flowers, 4-lobed and Stalked, Growing Singly, or in Pairs or Racemes

Speedwells (*Veronica*) Flowers 4-lobed, 1 lobe smaller than the others. Low plants with small flowers in more or less leafy ra-cemes. The following species have entire or obscurely toothed leaves; the upper leaves are commonly alternate. For other species, see p. 96. Figwort Family.

Thyme-leaved Speedwell (*V. serpyllifolia*) * Creeping plant of grassy places or damp soil, forming mats. The leaves are ¼–½" long, egg-shaped or roundish. Flowers white or pale blue with darker stripes, ⅛–¼" wide, in small racemes. Spring to fall.

Marsh Speedwell (*V. scutellata*) Weak-stemmed plant of swamps. Leaves 1–3" long, entire or with a few tiny teeth. Blue flowers, ¼" wide, on long stalks. Late spring and summer.

Purslane Speedwell or **Neckweed** (*V. peregrina*) Erect or semi-erect plant of gardens and moist places. Lower leaves oblong, ½–1" long, entire or obscurely toothed. The tiny, whitish flowers grow in the upper axils. 3–12" high. Spring and summer.

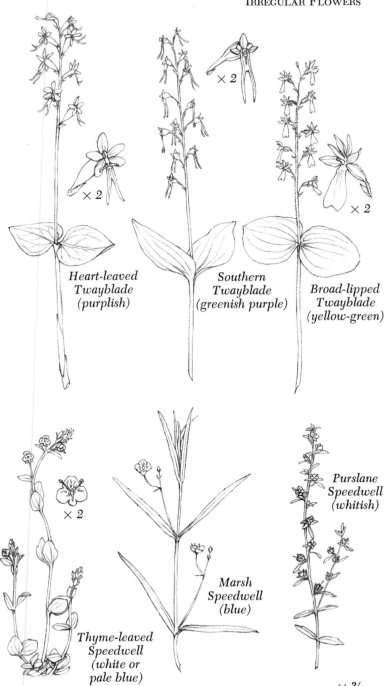

× 2

Heart-leaved
Twayblade
(purplish)

× 2

Southern
Twayblade
(greenish purple)

Broad-lipped
Twayblade
(yellow-green)

× 2

× 2

Purslane
Speedwell
(whitish)

Marsh
Speedwell
(blue)

Thyme-leaved
Speedwell
(white or
pale blue)

× ⅔

Leaves in Pairs; Flowers with 2 Lips or 6 Petals, Stalked, Growing Singly or in Pairs or Racemes

FLOWERS YELLOW OR WITH A YELLOW TIP

Golden Hedge Hyssop (*Gratiola aurea*) Yellow flowers; grows on wet, sandy shores. Flowers ½″ long, long-stalked in the axils; appear 4-lobed (actually 2-lipped with lower lip 3-lobed). Low and creeping. Summer and fall. Figwort Family.

Cowwheat (*Melampyrum lineare*) Whitish flowers with a yellow tip; grows in dry woods. Flowers about ½″ long, short-stalked in the upper axils. Lower leaves lance-shaped and entire; the upper have a few, pointed teeth at the base. 4–12″ high. Summer. Figwort Family.

BLUE, PURPLE OR WHITE FLOWERS

Clammy Cuphea or **Blue Waxweed** (*Cuphea petiolata*) Purple flowers with 6 unequal petals, 2 above and 4 smaller ones beneath. Leaves broadly lance-shaped. The flowers are ¼″ wide and grow in the axils. Plant sticky-hairy. 6–20″ high. Fields. Summer and fall. Loosestrife Family.

Blue Curls (*Trichostema dichotomum*) Blue flowers, ½–¾″ long, with long, coiling, blue or violet stamens. Leaves oblong or lance-shaped. Narrow-leaved Blue Curls (*T. setaceum*) of Conn. to s. Ohio south, has very narrow leaves. 6–24″ high. Plant of dry soil, often found along railroad tracks. Late summer and fall. Mint Family.

Hyssop Skullcap (*Scutellaria integrifolia*) Blue flowers, about 1″ long, with arched upper lip and flaring lower lip. Flowers in 1 or more short racemes. The lance-shaped leaves are 1–2″ long, the lower ones broader and slightly toothed. 1–2′ high. Borders of woods and clearings, Mass. to Ohio south. Late spring and summer. Mint Family.

Small Skullcap (*Scutellaria parvula*) Blue flowers, ¼″ long, nestled in the upper axils. Leaves egg-shaped, ½–1″ long, entire or slightly toothed. 3–12″ high. Sandy soil, usually in limestone areas. Spring and summer. Mint Family.

False Pimpernel (*Lindernia dubia*) Pale-purple or white flowers, ¼–½″ long, growing on long stalks from the axils; leaves egg-shaped; grows in wet places. Leaves ½–1½″ long, often obscurely toothed. Low, branching near the base. Summer and fall. Figwort Family.

Gerardias (*Gerardia*) Purple flowers; leaves very narrow. See p. 254.

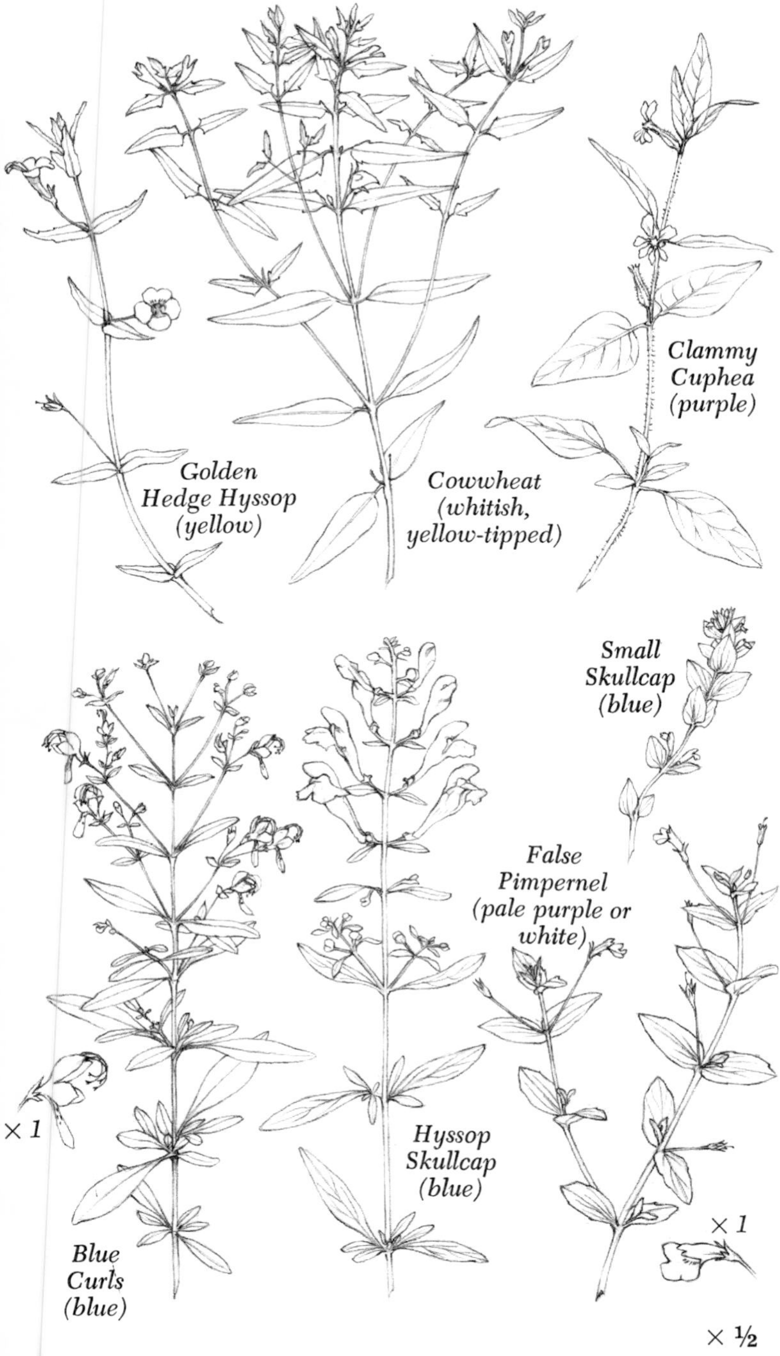

Clammy
Cuphea
(purple)

Golden
Hedge Hyssop
(yellow)

Cowwheat
(whitish,
yellow-tipped)

Small
Skullcap
(blue)

False
Pimpernel
(pale purple or
white)

× 1

Hyssop
Skullcap
(blue)

Blue
Curls
(blue)

× 1

× ½

Leaves in Pairs; Flowers Stalkless, Growing in 1 or More Whorls, Heads or Dense Clusters

LONGER LEAVES OVER 4" LONG

Water Willow (*Justicia americana*) Purple-spotted violet or white flowers in small heads, growing on long stalks from the axils. Leaves narrowly lance-shaped, 3–6" long. 1–3' high. Borders of lakes and streams, w. Vt. and sw. Que. to Wis. south. Summer. Acanthus Family.

Orange-fruited Horse Gentian (*Triosteum aurantiacum*) Dull purplish-red flowers, stalkless in the axils. Leaves egg-shaped, 5–10" long. Stem stout. 2–4' high. Fruit a conspicuous, red-orange berry. For a related species, see p. 256. Rich woods. Late spring. Honeysuckle Family.

LEAVES UNDER 4" LONG

Mint Family (Labiatae) A family of aromatic plants with square stems and opposite leaves. The flowers are generally 2-lipped, the lower lip 3-lobed. Most species have toothed leaves; in some of the following the leaves may be obscurely toothed.

1. WHITE, USUALLY PURPLE-DOTTED, FLOWERS IN SMALL HEADS

   Mountain Mints (*Pycnanthemum*) Plants with a pleasant minty odor, having small flowers in numerous, roundish heads. Two species have toothed leaves (pp. 84 and 92). 1–3' high. Dry woods, meadows, fields and thickets. Summer and fall.

   Narrow-leaved Mountain Mint (*P. tenuifolium*) Leaves very narrow, 1–2" long.

   Virginia Mountain Mint (*P. virginianum*) Leaves lance-shaped, stalkless and rounded at the base.

   Torrey's Mountain Mint (*P. verticillatum*) Leaves lance-shaped, tapering at the base, nearly smooth beneath. The leaves are often short-stalked and slightly toothed. W. N.Eng. to Mich. south.

   Hairy Mountain Mint (*P. pilosum*) Similar to the Torrey's Mountain Mint, but leaves and stem hairy. S. Ont. and s. Mich. south; also Mass. to e. Pa.

2. VIOLET OR PURPLISH FLOWERS, IN DENSE UNINTERRUPTED SPIKES OR HEADS, WHICH ARE LONGER THAN WIDE

   Selfheal or **Heal-all** (*Prunella vulgaris*) Leaves lance-shaped or egg-shaped, entire or obscurely toothed, the lower long-stalked. Sprawling or erect, usually under 1' high. Very common weed of lawns, fields and roadsides. Late spring to fall.   Continued

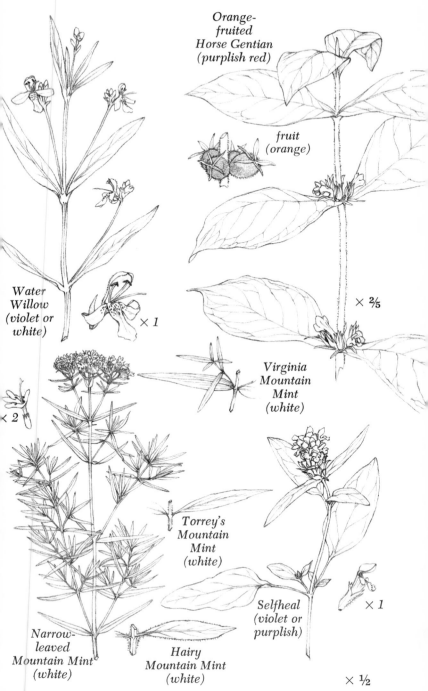

Orange-
fruited
Horse Gentian
(purplish red)

fruit
(orange)

Water
Willow
(violet or
white)

× 1

× ²⁄₅

Virginia
Mountain
Mint
(white)

× 2

Torrey's
Mountain
Mint
(white)

Selfheal
(violet or
purplish)

× 1

Narrow-
leaved
Mountain Mint
(white)

Hairy
Mountain Mint
(white)

× ½

Leaves in Pairs; Flowers Stalkless, Growing in 1 or More Whorls, Heads or Dense Clusters (cont.)

Mint Family (Labiatae) (cont.)

3. PURPLE, PINK OR BLUISH FLOWERS, IN WHORLS OR IN DENSE TERMINAL CLUSTERS

a. Stem creeping at the base

Wild Thyme (*Thymus serpyllum*) * Leaves oblong or egg-shaped, ¼–½" long. Flowers purple, in dense terminal clusters. Plant prostrate, in dense mats. Very aromatic. Locally established in fields and along roads. Summer.

Bugle (*Ajuga reptans*) Leaves egg-shaped, 1–3" long. See p. 84.

b. Larger leaves egg-shaped; stem erect and downy or hairy

Wild Basil (*Satureja vulgaris*) Pinkish or lilac flowers (sometimes nearly white), ¼–½" long, growing from dense, *bristly* clusters or whorls. The flower cluster has numerous stiff-pointed bracts. Woods and borders. Summer and fall.

Wild Marjoram (*Origanum vulgare*) * Pink or purplish flowers, ¼" long, in branching, terminal clusters; leaves long-stalked, rounded at the base. The dense flower clusters contain purple bracts. Stamens protrude. 1–2½' high. Roadsides and fields. Summer and fall.

American Pennyroyal (*Hedeoma pulegioides*) Very small, bluish flowers in a series of clusters in the axils; leaves very strongly scented with oil of pennyroyal. 4–18" high. Fields and dry woods. Summer and fall.

Downy Wood Mint (*Blephilia ciliata*) Purple flowers, about ½" long, in one or more dense whorls; leaves whitish beneath. See p. 84.

c. Leaves lance-shaped or narrow; stem erect and smooth

Hyssop Hedge Nettle (*Stachys hyssopifolia*) Stamens not protruding. Pale-purple flowers, ½" long, in one or more whorls. Leaves narrow. 8–20" high. Sandy shores and swamps, s. N.Eng. to s. Mich. south. Summer.

Hyssop (*Hyssopus officinalis*) * Stamens conspicuously protruding. Blue-purple flowers in a more or less interrupted spike. The leaves are lance-shaped or narrower. 1–3' high. Fields and roadsides. Summer and fall.

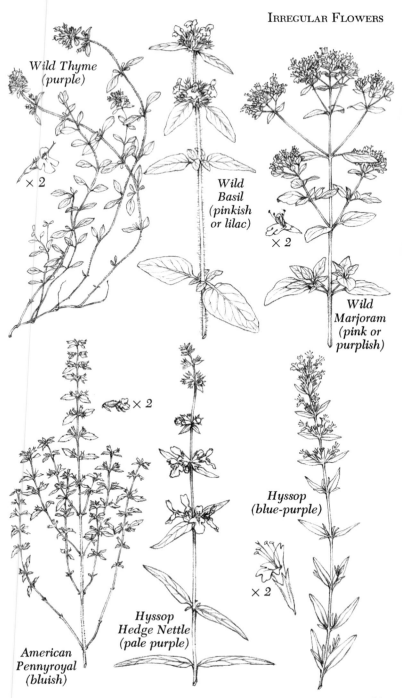

Wild Thyme (purple)

× 2

Wild Basil (pinkish or lilac)

Wild Marjoram (pink or purplish)

× 2

× 2

American Pennyroyal (bluish)

Hyssop Hedge Nettle (pale purple)

Hyssop (blue-purple)

× 2

× ½

Yellow, Yellowish or Straw-colored Flowers

FLOWERS NOTICEABLY STALKED

Horse Balm, Richweed or **Stoneroot** (*Collinsonia canadensis*)
Light-yellow, lemon-scented flowers, ½″ long, with protruding stamens. Lower lip of flower very long and fringed at the tip. Flowers
in a loose, branching cluster. The coarsely toothed leaves have a
strong odor of citronella when crushed. 2–5′ high. Rich woods, s.
and w. N.Eng. to Wis. south. Summer and fall. Mint Family.

Clammy Hedge Hyssop (*Gratiola neglecta*) Yellowish or cream-
colored, tubular flowers, ⅓–½″ long, with white lobes. Leaves
lance-shaped, slightly toothed. Stem low and usually branched.
3–12″ high. Wet or muddy places. Late spring to fall. Figwort
Family.

Yellow Violets (*Viola*) Yellow flowers, the lower petal veined with
violet; leaves heart-shaped at base. See p. 54.

FLOWERS STALKLESS OR NEARLY SO

Swamp Lousewort (*Pedicularis lanceolata*) Pale-yellow flowers,
¾″ long, in short spikes; leaves many-lobed, fernlike. Leaves less
deeply cut than Wood Betony (p. 70) and stalkless; stem nearly
smooth. Some of the leaves may be alternate. 1–3′ high. Low
meadows and swamps, Mass. to Man. south. Late summer and fall.
Figwort Family.

Yellow Rattle (*Rhinanthus crista-galli*) Yellow flowers, ½″ long,
with a bladderlike calyx becoming inflated in fruit; leaves coarsely
toothed. Flowers grow in one-sided spikes. 6–24″ high. Dry fields,
Can. south to N.Eng. and N.Y. Late spring to early fall. Figwort
Family.

Horsemint (*Monarda punctata*) Yellowish, purple-spotted
flowers, ¾–1″ long, in dense whorls; leaves lance-shaped, shallowly toothed. Flowers surrounded with conspicuous whitish or
lilac bracts. 1–3′ high. Dry fields and roadsides, w. Vt. to Minn.
south. Summer and fall. Mint Family.

Yellow Giant Hyssop (*Agastache nepetoides*) Pale greenish-
yellow flowers, ⅓″ long, in dense spikes; leaves egg-shaped,
coarsely toothed. Stamens protruding. 2–5′ high. Woods and
thickets, sw. Que. and Vt. to S.D. south. Summer. Mint Family.

Cowwheat (*Melampyrum lineare*) Straw-colored flowers with a
yellow tip; upper leaves with a few teeth. See p. 76.

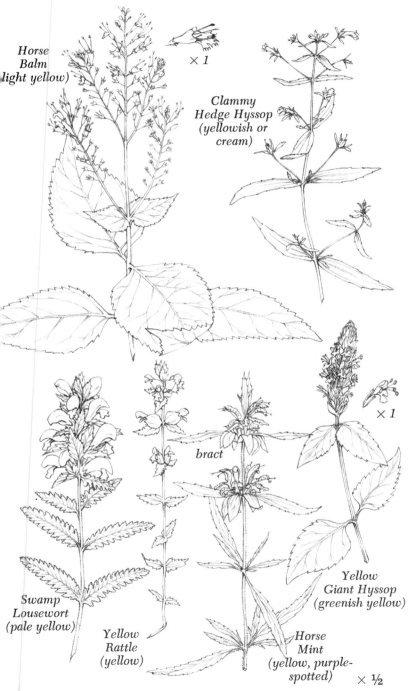

Horse Balm (light yellow)

× 1

Clammy Hedge Hyssop (yellowish or cream)

Swamp Lousewort (pale yellow)

Yellow Rattle (yellow)

bract

Horse Mint (yellow, purple-spotted)

Yellow Giant Hyssop (greenish yellow)

× 1

× ½

Flowers Medium-sized (¼–¾" Long), in Heads, Spikes or Whorls; Not Yellow; Stamens Protruding

Bugle (*Ajuga reptans*) * Blue flowers, ½" long, in leafy spikes. Leaves egg-shaped and bluntly toothed. The stamens project beyond the very short upper lip. 6–12" high, creeping at the base. Escaped from cultivation to lawns and roadsides. Spring and early summer. Mint Family.

American Germander or **Wood Sage** (*Teucrium canadense*) Purplish flowers in spikes; stamens protruding upward from the base of the flower. Upper lip apparently absent; lower lip prominent, broad. Leaves lance- or egg-shaped. 1–4' high. Shores and moist thickets. Summer. Mint Family.

Purple Giant Hyssop (*Agastache scrophulariaefolia*) Purplish flowers, ½" long, in close spikes; stamens protruding from the end of the flower tube. Leaves large and coarsely toothed. 2–5' high. Woods and thickets, s. and w. N.Eng. to Minn. south. Summer. Mint Family.

Hoary Mountain Mint (*Pycnanthemum incanum*) White or pale-lilac flowers with purple spots, ⅓" long, in heads or whorls; bracts, upper leaves and underside of lower leaves whitish. 1–3' high. Dry woods and hillsides, s. N.Eng. to s. Ill. south. Summer and fall. Mint Family.

Wood Mints (*Blephilia*) Light-purple flowers, ⅓–½" long, in heads or dense whorls; floral bracts colored, fringed. 1–3' high. Summer. Mint Family.

Hairy Wood Mint (*B. hirsuta*) Leaves egg-shaped, long-stalked, sharply toothed. Flowers spotted with darker purple. Stem hairy. Moist woods, Vt. to Minn. south.

Downy Wood Mint (*B. ciliata*) † Similar to Hairy Wood Mint but leaves stalkless or short-stalked, obscurely toothed. Leaves whitish beneath; stem downy. Dry woods, s. N.Eng. to Wis. south.

Field Scabious (*Knautia arvensis*) * Lilac-purple flowers in long-stalked heads; stem leaves usually deeply lobed. Basal leaves large, lance-shaped, toothed or lobed. 1–3' high. Dry fields. Summer and fall. Teasel Family.

Dittany (*Cunila origanoides*) Purplish flowers, ⅓" long, in rather loose clusters at the ends of the branches or in the upper axils. Leaves egg-shaped, 1–1½" long, nearly stalkless. Stem stiff and branching. 6–18" high. Dry woods, s. N.Y. to Ill. south. Summer and fall. Mint Family.

Continued

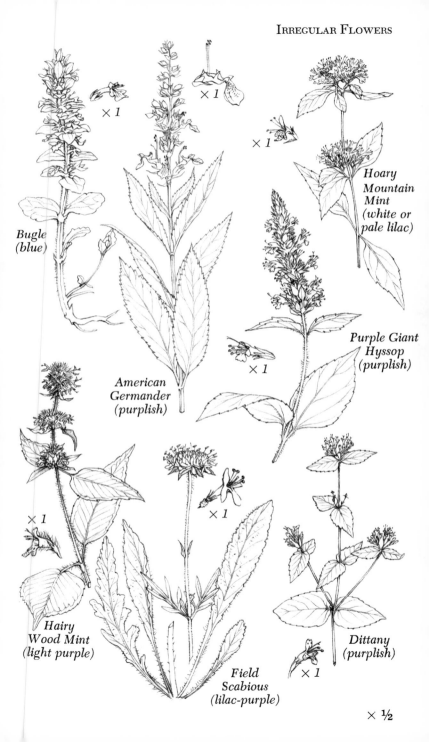

Bugle
(blue)

× 1

× 1

Hoary
Mountain
Mint
(white or
pale lilac)

× 1

Purple Giant
Hyssop
(purplish)

× 1

American
Germander
(purplish)

× 1

Hairy
Wood Mint
(light purple)

× 1

Dittany
(purplish)

× 1

Field
Scabious
(lilac-purple)

× ½

Flowers Medium-sized (¼–¾″ Long), in Heads, Spikes or Whorls; Not Yellow; Stamens Protruding (cont.)

Basil Balm (*Monarda clinopodia*) Whitish or pinkish flowers with dark spots, ¾–1″ long, in dense heads. See p. 92.

Flowers Medium-sized (¼–¾″ Long), in Heads, Spikes or Whorls; Not Yellow; Stamens Not Protruding

LEAVES ROUNDISH, ABOUT AS WIDE AS LONG

Ground Ivy or **Gill-over-the-ground** (*Glechoma hederacea*) * Blue or violet flowers, ⅓–½″ long; stem creeping at the base. Leaves long-stalked, bluntly toothed. A common weed of moist waste places. Spring and early summer. Mint Family.

Dead Nettles or **Henbits** (*Lamium*) Purplish or reddish flowers, ⅓–¾″ long; stems sprawling, not creeping. Leaves broad and the lower leaves long-stalked. Roadsides and waste places. Spring to fall. Mint Family.

> **Henbit** (*L. amplexicaule*) * Uppermost leaves clasping the stem and bluntly toothed. Calyx lobes not spreading.

> **Purple Dead Nettle** (*L. purpureum*) * Uppermost leaves short-stalked with blunt teeth and purple-tinged. Calyx lobes spread outward.

> **Cut-leaved Henbit** (*L. hybridum*) *† Similar to Henbit, but the uppermost leaves sharply toothed. Local, N.Eng. south.

Horehound (*Marrubium vulgare*) * White flowers, ¼″ long; leaves 1–2″ long. Whole plant white-woolly. Leaves deeply veined, bluntly toothed, the lower leaves long-stalked. 1–2′ high. Waste places. Summer. Mint Family.

Eyebright (*Euphrasia americana*) White flowers, with purple lines, about ⅓″ long; leaves ⅛–½″ long. The lobes of the flaring lower lip are notched in the center. Leaves coarsely toothed. 3–15″ high. Fields and roadsides, n. N.Eng. and N.Y. north. Six other species occur locally in n. N.Eng. north. Summer. Figwort Family.

SOME OF THE LEAVES DEEPLY LOBED

Motherwort (*Leonurus cardiaca*) * Lilac or pale-purple flowers in the upper axils of the long-stalked leaves. Stem leaves mostly with 3 pointed lobes; lower leaves deeply cleft into 3–5 lobes. 2–5′ high. Waste places. Summer. Mint Family.

Lyre-leaved Sage (*Salvia lyrata*) Violet flowers in several whorls; basal leaves forming a rosette. See p. 94.

Continued

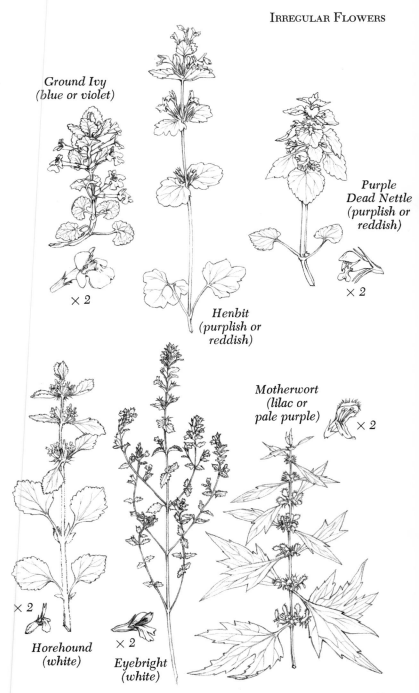

Ground Ivy
(blue or violet)

× 2

Henbit
(purplish or
reddish)

Purple
Dead Nettle
(purplish or
reddish)

× 2

Motherwort
(lilac or
pale purple)

× 2

Horehound
(white)

× 2

Eyebright
(white)

× ½

Flowers Medium-sized (¼–¾″ Long), in Heads, Spikes or Whorls; Not Yellow; Stamens Not Protruding (cont.)

LEAVES LONGER THAN WIDE, PROMINENTLY TOOTHED

Catnip (*Nepeta cataria*) * Whitish or pale-lilac flowers, purple-spotted, ½″ long, in short spikes; leaves somewhat heart-shaped at base, coarsely toothed. The aromatic foliage attracts cats. Stem grayish-downy. 1–3′ high. Waste places. Summer and fall. Mint Family.

Hemp Nettle (*Galeopsis tetrahit*) * White or purple flowers, often purple-striped, ½–¾″ long, in dense whorls; stem bristly-hairy and swollen below the joints. Leaves egg-shaped, coarsely toothed, long-stalked. 1–3′ high. Roadsides and waste places; common. Summer to fall. Mint Family.

Lopseed (*Phryma leptostachya*) Lavender or purplish flowers, ¼″ long, arranged in pairs in long, slender, leafless spikes. The faded flowers hang down oddly against the flower stalk. Leaves egg-shaped, coarsely toothed. 1–3′ high. Rich woods. Summer. Lopseed Family.

Hedge Nettles (*Stachys*) Rose-purple flowers, about ½″ long, in whorls forming an interrupted spike. 1–3′ high. Low meadows, swamps, shores. Summer and fall. Mint Family.

> **Common Hedge Nettle** (*S. tenuifolia*) Lower leaves with definite stalks (¼″ or more long). A very variable species with rough or smooth stem, and lance-shaped, oblong or egg-shaped leaves.

> **Marsh Hedge Nettle** or **Woundwort** (*S. palustris*) Similar to the Common Hedge Nettle, but lower leaves very short-stalked (⅛″ or less long). Spike more interrupted.

Red Bartsia (*Odontites serotina*) * Pink or rose flowers, ⅓″ long, in a leafy spike. Leaves lance-shaped with a few coarse teeth. 4–15″ high. Dry fields, Mass. to n. N.Y. north. Summer. Figwort Family.

False Dragonhead or **Obedient Plant** (*Physostegia virginiana*) Purple or rose flowers, ¾–1″ long, in spikes. See p. 94.

LEAVES DISTINCTLY LONGER THAN WIDE, OBSCURELY TOOTHED

Selfheal or **Heal-all** (*Prunella vulgaris*) Violet or purple flowers, ½″ long, in short spikes. See p. 78.

Wild Basil (*Satureja vulgaris*) Pinkish or lilac flowers (sometimes nearly white), ¼–½″ long, in dense, bristly clusters or whorls. See p. 80.

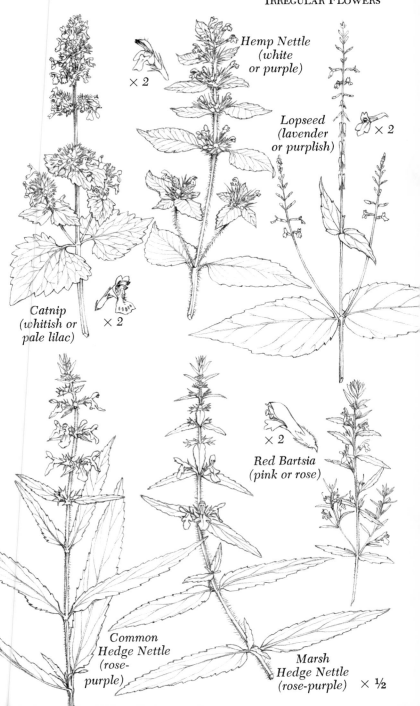

Hemp Nettle
(white
or purple)

× 2

Lopseed
(lavender
or purplish)

× 2

Catnip
(whitish or
pale lilac)

× 2

Red Bartsia
(pink or rose)

× 2

Common
Hedge
Nettle
(rose-
purple)

Marsh
Hedge Nettle
(rose-purple)   × ½

Flowers Very Small (under ¼″ Long), in Dense Heads, Spikes or Whorls

ALL OF THE FLOWERS WHORLED IN THE AXILS

Wild Mint (*Mentha arvensis*) Lilac (rarely white) flowers; leaves 1½–3″ long, strongly smelling of mint. Leaves egg-shaped or oblong; stem usually more or less hairy. 6–24″ high. Fairly common in moist or wet open places; occasionally in dry soil. Summer and fall. Mint Family.

Bugleweeds (*Lycopus*) Tiny white flowers; leaves not strongly mint-scented. Leaves sharply toothed or lobed. 6–24″ high. Common plants of moist and wet places. Several other species occur in our area. Summer and fall. Mint Family.

> **Northern Bugleweed** (*L. uniflorus*) Lower leaves coarsely toothed, but not lobed, light green, tapering gradually at both ends. The flowers have flaring lobes.

> **Virginia Bugleweed** (*L. virginicus*) Leaves similar to those of the Northern Bugleweed, but dark green or purple, rather abruptly narrowed at both ends. The flowers have erect lobes. Moist soil, s. Me. to Minn. south.

> **Water Horehound** (*L. americanus*) Lower leaves deeply lobed at the base; the upper leaves merely toothed.

> **Sessile-leaved Water Horehound** (*L. amplectens*) Leaves broad or rounded at the base, stalkless, shallowly toothed. Se. Mass. south along the coast; nw. Ind.

American Pennyroyal (*Hedeoma pulegioides*) Very small, bluish flowers; leaves ½–1½″ long, very strongly scented with oil of pennyroyal. See p. 80.

SOME OF THE FLOWERS IN TERMINAL SPIKES OR HEADS

Mints (*Mentha*) Purplish or pinkish flowers in spikes or in whorls forming an interrupted spike; leaves strongly mint-scented. Eight other species (or hybrids) are of local occurrence. All introduced except the native Wild Mint (above). Wet places. Summer and fall. Mint Family.

> **Spearmint** (*M. spicata*) * Leaves stalkless or nearly so; spike slender and interrupted. 8–20″ high.

> **Peppermint** (*M. piperita*) * Larger leaves distinctly stalked; spike thicker and more compact than that of Spearmint. Smells strongly of peppermint. 1–3′ high.

Continued

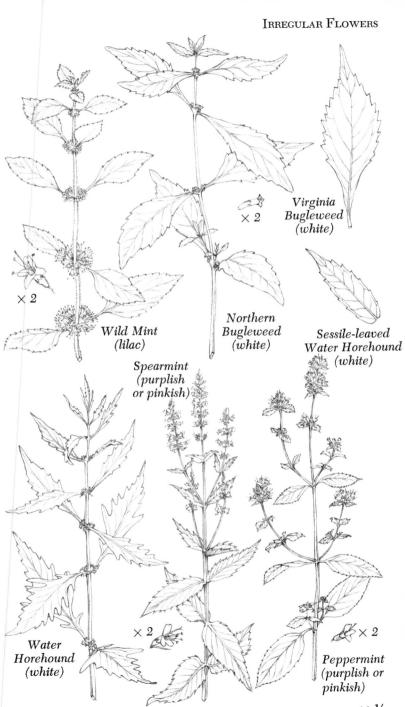

Virginia
Bugleweed
(white)

× 2

× 2

Wild Mint
(lilac)

Northern
Bugleweed
(white)

Sessile-leaved
Water Horehound
(white)

Spearmint
(purplish
or pinkish)

Water
Horehound
(white)

× 2

Peppermint
(purplish or
pinkish)

× 2

× ½

Flowers Very Small (under ¼″ Long), in Dense Heads, Spikes or Whorls (cont.)

SOME OF THE FLOWERS IN TERMINAL SPIKES OR HEADS (CONT.)

Mountain Mints (*Pycnanthemum*) White flowers in buttonlike heads. Leaves pleasantly fragrant. 1–3′ high. Woods and clearings. Summer and fall. Mint Family.

1. LEAVES OBSCURELY TOOTHED (SEE P. 78)

2. LEAVES SHARPLY TOOTHED

   Short-toothed Mountain Mint (*P. muticum*) Leaves egg-shaped, prominently veined. Dry to moist soil, s. Me. to Mich. south.

Teasel (*Dipsacus sylvestris*) Lilac flowers in a large, thistlelike head; stem prickly. See p. 160.

Common Speedwell (*Veronica officinalis*) Stem trailing along the ground; lilac or lavender flowers. See p. 96.

Flowers Large (1″ or More Long), in Heads, Spikes or Whorls; Not Yellow

Monardas or **Bergamots** (*Monarda*) Flowers in dense heads or whorls; stamens protrude beyond the narrow upper lip. Colored bracts grow at the base of the flower-head. Horsemint (*M. punctata*) has yellowish, purple-spotted flowers (p. 82). 1–5′ high. Summer and fall. Mint Family.

   Oswego Tea or **Bee Balm** (*M. didyma*) Scarlet flowers. Bracts of the flower-head reddish. An old-fashioned garden plant, favorite of hummingbirds. N.Y. to Minn. south; escaped from cultivation in N.Eng. Rich moist soil.

   Purple Bergamot (*M. media*) Deep red-purple flowers. Bracts dark purple, conspicuous. Range and habitat the same as those of the Oswego Tea.

   Basil Balm (*M. clinopodia*) Whitish or pinkish flowers with dark spots. The bracts of the flower-head are whitish. Woods and thickets, N.Y. to Ill. south; escaped from cultivation in N.Eng.

   Wild Bergamot (*M. fistulosa*) Lilac or pink flowers, unspotted. Floral bracts often pink-tinged. Leaves grayish, triangular or lance-shaped. 2–3′ high. Dry hillsides and margins of woods, s. and w. N.Eng. to Minn. south.

Continued

Short-toothed
Mountain Mint

× 2

Oswego
Tea

Purple
Bergamot

Basil
Balm

Wild
Bergamot

× ½

Flowers Large (1″ or More Long), in Heads, Spikes or Whorls; Not Yellow (cont.)

Turtleheads (*Chelone*) White or rose-pink flowers, 1″ long, in a short spike. The upper lip of the flower arches over the lower lip, giving a striking resemblance to a turtle's head. Leaves finely toothed, 3–6″ long. 1–3′ high. Late summer and fall. Figwort Family.

Turtlehead (*C. glabra*) Flowers white, or pink-tinged on top. Leaves lance-shaped. Swamps and stream banks.

Pink Turtlehead (*C. lyoni*) * Rose-pink flowers; leaves egg-shaped. Leaf stalks ½–1″ long. Moist thickets. Escaped from cultivation; native to the southern states.

Red Turtlehead (*C. obliqua*) † Similar to Pink Turtlehead but leaves lance-shaped. Flowers rose-pink. Leaf stalks ¼–½″ long. Swamps, Md. to s. Minn. south.

False Dragonhead or **Obedient Plant** (*Physostegia virginiana*) Pale-purple or rose flowers, ¾–1″ long, in spikes; leaves lance-shaped, sharply toothed. The flowers stay obediently for a time in whatever position they are placed. 1–5′ high. Moist thickets and banks. Summer and fall. Mint Family.

Lyre-leaved Sage (*Salvia lyrata*) Violet flowers, about 1″ long, in several whorls forming an interrupted spike. Basal leaves usually deeply lobed and long-stalked, forming a rosette; stem leaves few and are entire, wavy-toothed or lobed. Stem hairy. 1–2′ high. Dry open woods, s. Conn. to Ill. south. Spring and early summer. Mint Family.

Meehania (*Meehania cordata*) Light-purple flowers, 1–1½″ long, in one-sided spikes. Leaves heart-shaped and long-stalked, bluntly toothed. The stem is creeping, with short, erect flowering stems. Rich woods, w. Pa. to Ill. south. Late spring and early summer. Mint Family.

White Dead Nettle (*Lamium album*) * White flowers, about 1″ long, in the upper axils. The egg-shaped leaves are coarsely toothed. Escaped from cultivation to roadsides and waste places. Spring to fall. Mint Family.

Turtlehead

False
Dragonhead

Pink
Turtlehead

White -
Dead Nettle

Lyre-leaved
Sage

Meehania

× ½

Flowers 4-lobed, the Lower Lobe Smaller Than the Others

Speedwells (*Veronica*) Plants with small flowers (⅛–½" wide) growing in racemes or singly in the axils. Flowers often striped with purple. Eleven other species are found locally in our area. Figwort Family.

1. IN SWAMPS AND BROOKS

Water Speedwell (*V. anagallis-aquatica*) Leaves egg-shaped or lance-shaped, slightly toothed or entire, with the upper ones stalkless and clasping the stem. Blue or violet flowers. Stem erect or spreading, 1–3′ long. Late spring to early fall.

American Brooklime (*V. americana*) Similar to the Water Speedwell, but the leaves are sharply toothed and short-stalked, not clasping. The commoner of the two species. Late spring and summer.

Marsh Speedwell (*V. scutellata*) Leaves narrow and minutely toothed or entire. See p. 74.

2. IN WOODS, FIELDS, LAWNS OR GARDENS

a. Flowers in long-stalked racemes from the axils

Common Speedwell (*V. officinalis*) Lilac or lavender flowers, about ¼" wide. Leaves elliptical, ¾–2" long, sharply toothed and short-stalked. Stem hairy, trailing along the ground. Common. Late spring and early summer, and sporadically until fall.

Bird's-eye Speedwell or **Germander Speedwell** (*V. chamaedrys*) * Blue flowers, almost ½" wide. The leaves are egg-shaped and very coarsely toothed. Stems rise from a trailing base. Spring and summer.

b. Flowers growing singly in the axils

Persian Speedwell or **Bird's Eye** (*V. persica*) * Blue flowers, ⅓–½" wide, long-stalked; leaves with coarse teeth. Prostrate or ascending. Spring to fall.

Corn Speedwell (*V. arvensis*) * Tiny, blue or whitish, nearly stalkless flowers; stem and leaves hairy; lower leaves with distinct teeth. 2–10" high. Fields, open woods, rocky places. Spring to fall.

Thyme-leaved Speedwell (*V. serpyllifolia*) Pale-blue or white flowers, with darker stripes; plant creeping at base; leaves obscurely toothed. See p. 74.

Purslane Speedwell or **Neckweed** (*V. peregrina*) Whitish flowers; stem more or less erect; leaves obscurely toothed. See p. 74.

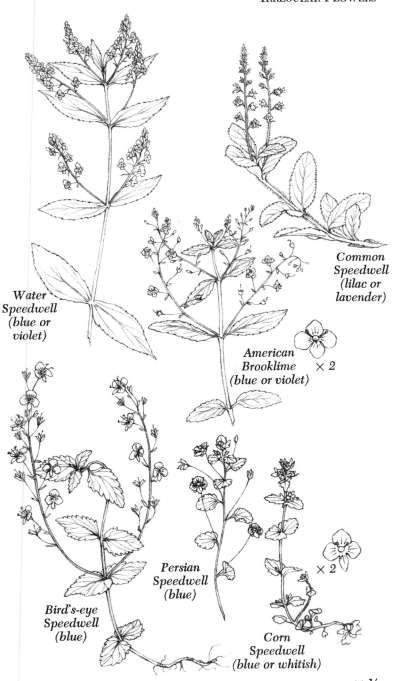

Water
Speedwell
(blue or
violet)

Common
Speedwell
(lilac or
lavender)

American
Brooklime
(blue or violet)   × 2

Bird's-eye
Speedwell
(blue)

Persian
Speedwell
(blue)

Corn
Speedwell
(blue or whitish)   × 2

× ½

Flowers Not Yellow, 2-lipped, Growing Singly or in Pairs, Racemes or Loose Clusters; Stem Square

Skullcaps (*Scutellaria*) Blue or violet flowers, with an arching, hooded upper lip and flaring lower lip, generally growing in pairs. The common name comes from the small hump on the top of the calyx. Summer and fall unless otherwise noted. Mint Family.

1. FLOWERS GROWING FROM THE AXILS

Mad-dog Skullcap (*S. lateriflora*) Flowers under ½" long, in one-sided racemes growing from the axils. Leaves egg-shaped, coarsely toothed, 1–5" long. Wet or moist woods and thickets. 6–30" high.

Marsh Skullcap (*S. epilobiifolia*) Flowers ⅔–1" long; grows in swamps and on shores. Leaves stalkless or nearly so, lance-shaped or oblong. 6–30" high.

Veined Skullcap (*S. nervosa*) Flowers ⅓" long, single or paired in the axils of well-developed leaves; leaves 1–2" long, egg-shaped, bluntly toothed. 8–20" high. Woods and thickets, N.J. to s. Ont. south.

Small Skullcap (*S. parvula*) Flowers ¼" long, in the upper axils; leaves under 1" long, nearly entire. See p. 76.

2. FLOWERS IN TERMINAL RACEMES

a. Leaves heart-shaped at the base

Heart-leaved Skullcap (*S. ovata*) Flowers about ¾" long, the lower lip whitish. Stem hairy. 1–3' high. Woods, Md. to Minn. south.

b. Middle leaves not heart-shaped at the base, toothed

Showy Skullcap (*S. serrata*) Flowers 1" long; stem smooth; leaves coarsely toothed and pointed. Flowers in a single raceme. 1–2' high. Woods, s. N.Y. to W.Va. south. Spring and early summer.

Downy Skullcap (*S. incana*) Flowers ¾–1" long; stem covered with fine down; leaves long-stalked, coarsely toothed and pointed. Racemes numerous. 2–4' high. Dry woods, N.J. and sw. N.Y. to Iowa south.

Hairy Skullcap (*S. elliptica*) Flowers ½–¾" long; stem hairy; leaves blunt, with rounded teeth, short-stalked. Dry woods, s. N.Y. to s. Mich. south. 1–2' high. Late spring and early summer.

c. Middle leaves oblong and entire

Hyssop Skullcap (*S. integrifolia*) Flowers about 1" long. See p. 76.

Continued

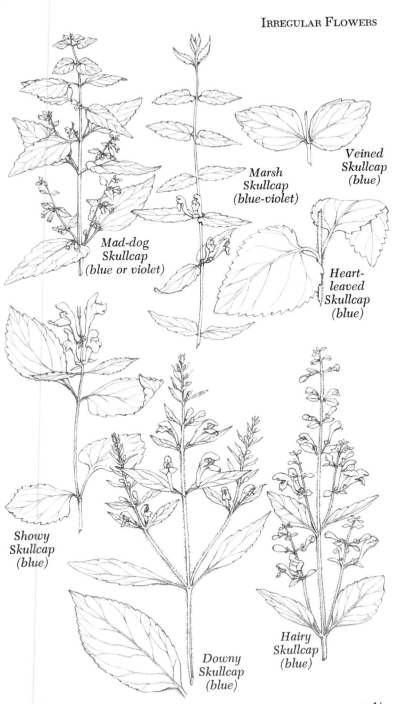

Mad-dog
Skullcap
(blue or violet)

Marsh
Skullcap
(blue-violet)

Veined
Skullcap
(blue)

Heart-
leaved
Skullcap
(blue)

Showy
Skullcap
(blue)

Downy
Skullcap
(blue)

Hairy
Skullcap
(blue)

× ½

Flowers Not Yellow, 2-lipped, Growing Singly, or in Pairs, Racemes or Loose Clusters; Stem Square (cont.)

Monkey Flowers (*Mimulus*) Violet or pinkish (rarely white) flowers, 1″ long, the lower lip with 3 wide-spreading lobes. The throat is partially closed with a yellow-ridged palate, so that the flower somewhat resembles a grinning face. Flowers in the upper axils. 1–3′ high. Wet places. Summer and early fall. Figwort Family.

Monkey Flower (*M. ringens*) Leaves stalkless; flower stalk longer than the calyx. The commoner species in most parts of our area.

Winged Monkey Flower (*M. alatus*) Leaves short-stalked; flower stalk shorter than the calyx. The stem is slightly winged. Conn. to s. Ont. and s. Mich. south.

Figworts (*Scrophularia*) Green or brown flowers, ¼–⅜″ long, in a loose, branching cluster. Flowers with an erect, 2-lobed upper lip; the middle lobe of the lower lip is bent downward. The broad undeveloped stamen under the upper lip does not bear pollen. Leaves egg-shaped, coarsely toothed, long-stalked. 3–8′ high. Woods and thickets. Figwort Family.

Carpenter's Square or **Maryland Figwort** (*S. marilandica*) Flowers dull on the outside: undeveloped stamen purple or brown. Leaves not as coarsely toothed as the next species. Summer and fall.

Hare Figwort (*S. lanceolata*) Flowers shining on the outside; undeveloped stamen greenish-yellow. Leaves very coarsely toothed. Late spring and early summer and sporadically to fall.

Ground Ivy, Gill-over-the-ground (*Glechoma hederacea*) Blue or violet flowers; leaves roundish, long-stalked. See p. 86.

False Pimpernel (*Lindernia dubia*) Pale-purple or white flowers, ¼–½″ long, on long stalks from the axils. See p. 76.

Lopseed (*Phryma leptostachya*) Lavender or purplish flowers, ¼″ long, arranged in pairs in leafless spikes. See p. 88.

Dittany (*Cunila origanoides*) Purplish flowers, ⅓″ long, in rather loose clusters at the ends of the branches or in the upper axils. See p. 84.

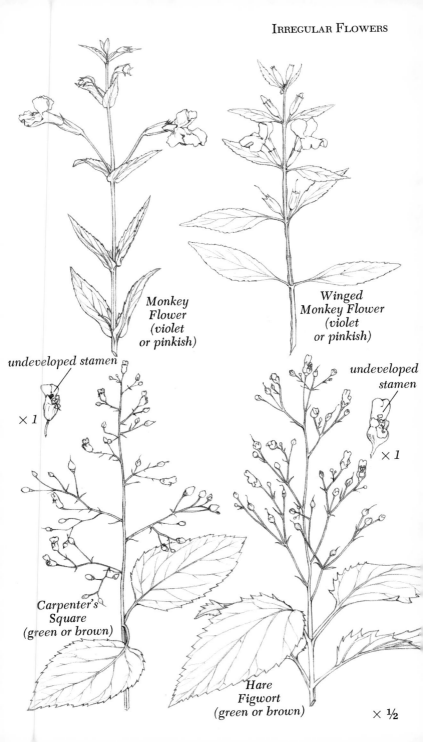

Monkey
Flower
(violet
or pinkish)

Winged
Monkey Flower
(violet
or pinkish)

undeveloped stamen

× 1

undeveloped
stamen

× 1

Carpenter's
Square
(green or brown)

Hare
Figwort
(green or brown)

× ½

White, Purple, Blue or Violet, 2-lipped Flowers Growing Singly, or in Pairs, Racemes or Loose Clusters; Stem Round

Beardtongues (*Penstemon*) Flowers ¾–1" long, trumpet-shaped, in a terminal cluster. The leaves are oblong or lance-shaped and finely toothed. 1–4' high. Late spring and early summer. Figwort Family.

Hairy Beardtongue (*P. hirsutus*) Stem covered with whitish hairs; flowers slender, with nearly closed throat, purplish or violet with white lips. Stem leaves lance-shaped. Dry woods or rocky hillsides.

Gray Beardtongue (*P. canescens*) Stem downy or hairy; flowers pale purple or violet, striped inside, enlarged and open at the throat, about 1" long. Stem leaves egg-shaped or oblong. Upland woods, Pa. to Ind. south.

White or **Foxglove Beardtongue** (*P. digitalis*) Stem smooth; white or purple-tinged flowers, about 1" long. Flower tube abruptly swollen in the middle. Fields and borders of woods.

Smooth Beardtongue (*P. laevigatus*) † Stem smoothish; pale-purple or violet flowers, ¾" long. Tube as in White Beardtongue. Rich woods, meadows, N.J., Pa. and W.Va. south.

Blue-eyed Mary (*Collinsia verna*) Bicolored flowers with white upper lip and blue lower lip, ½–¾" long. Center lobe of lower lip folded over stamens, so flower appears 4-lobed. Flowers in several whorls. Leaves egg-shaped, the middle stalkless and somewhat clasping. 6–18" high. Moist open woods, w. N.Y. to Wis. south. Spring. Figwort Family.

WILDFLOWERS WITH OPPOSITE OR WHORLED LEAVES / Leaves Divided

Pointed-leaved Tick Trefoil (*Desmodium glutinosum*) Purple flowers in a raceme. Leaves in a whorl at the base of the flower stalk; leaflets broad, the middle leaflet abruptly pointed. 1–4' high. Dry woods. Summer. Pea Family.

Bladderworts (*Utricularia*) Aquatic plants with yellow or purple flowers. See p. 16.

Jack-in-the-pulpits (*Arisaema*) Solitary, greenish flower growing beneath the leaves. See p. 36.

Field Scabious (*Knautia arvensis*) Lilac-purple flowers in long-stalked heads. See p. 84.

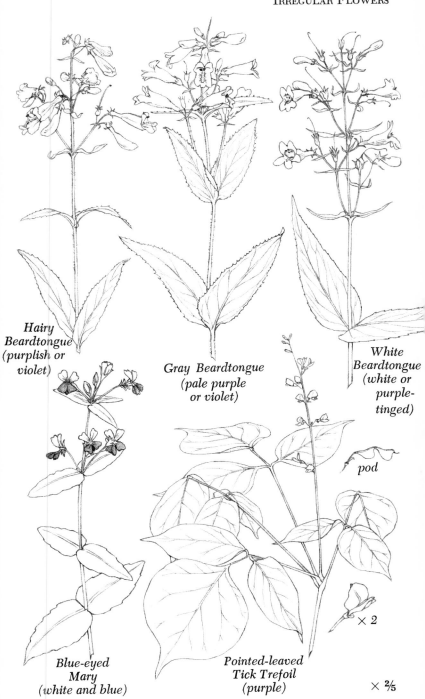

Hairy Beardtongue (purplish or violet)

Gray Beardtongue (pale purple or violet)

White Beardtongue (white or purple-tinged)

pod

Blue-eyed Mary (white and blue)

Pointed-leaved Tick Trefoil (purple)

× 2

× ⅖

SHRUBS /
Leaves Entire or with No Apparent Leaves at Flowering Time

Honeysuckles (*Lonicera*) Leaves growing in pairs. The flowers are tubular and 2-lipped in the shrubby species described below. Most of the members of this genus are vines (p. 108) or are shrubs with nearly regular flowers (p. 294). Honeysuckle Family.

1. FLOWERS INDISTINCTLY 2-LIPPED (SEE P. 294)

2. FLOWERS OBVIOUSLY 2-LIPPED

Swamp Fly Honeysuckle (*L. oblongifolia*) Flowers in pairs, growing from the axils; found in swamps and bogs. Yellowish flowers, ½–⅔" long. Leaves oblong. Berries orange to red. 2–5' high. N. N.Eng., n. and w. N.Y., w. Pa. to Wis. north. Late spring.

European Fly Honeysuckle (*L. xylosteum*) * Flowers in pairs, growing from the axils; found in thickets and on roadsides. Flowers whitish or yellowish, ¼–½" long. Leaves broad-oval. 3–10' high. Spring.

Glaucous, Smooth-leaved or **Limber Honeysuckle** (*L. dioica*) Flowers in a terminal cluster; uppermost leaves joined at the base. See p. 108.

Azaleas (*Rhododendron*) Leaves clustered at the ends of the branches or undeveloped at flowering time; flowers large and showy, 1" or more wide. Heath Family.

1. FLOWERS SLIGHTLY IRREGULAR (SEE P. 300)

2. FLOWERS DEEPLY 2-LIPPED, ROSE-PURPLE

Rhodora (*R. canadense*) Upper lip 3-lobed; lower lip divided into two narrow petals. Leaves oblong, gray-green, developing after the flowers. 1–3' high. Bogs and wet slopes, n. N.J. and ne. Pa. north. Early spring.

Redbud (*Cercis canadensis*) Leaves undeveloped at flowering time; rose-purple, pea-shaped flowers, ⅓" long. Flowers growing in small umbels along the branches. Leaves roundly heart-shaped, 2–6" long. A large shrub or small tree. Rich woods, s. Conn. and Pa. to Wis. south. Spring. Pea Family.

Dyer's Greenweed (*Genista tinctoria*) * Leaves lance-shaped or elliptical, alternate; yellow, pea-shaped flowers, ½" long. Flowers in short racemes. Leaves ½–1½" long. Low and branching, 1–2' high. Dry soil, locally from Me. to D.C., west to Mich. Summer. Pea Family.

Gorse or **Furze** (*Ulex europaeus*) * Leaves stiff and spinelike; yellow, pea-shaped flowers, ½–¾" long. Dense, spiny shrub, 2–6' high. Sandy soil, se. Mass. south to Va. and W.Va. Spring to fall. Pea Family.

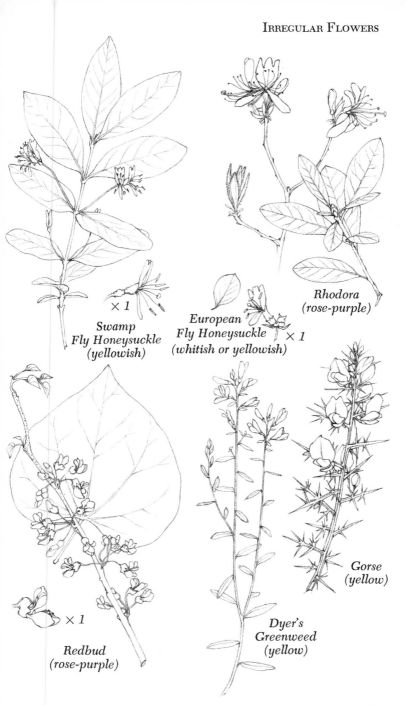

× 1

Swamp
Fly Honeysuckle
(yellowish)

European
Fly Honeysuckle
(whitish or yellowish)   × 1

Rhodora
(rose-purple)

Redbud
(rose-purple)

× 1

Dyer's
Greenweed
(yellow)

Gorse
(yellow)

× ½

SHRUBS /
Leaves Toothed

Bush Honeysuckle (*Diervilla lonicera*) Yellow flowers, about ¾″ long, usually growing in 3's. See p. 304.

SHRUBS /
Leaves Divided

Scotch Broom (*Cytisus scoparius*) * Yellow, pea-shaped flowers, 1″ long, in racemes. The lower leaves have 3 very small, entire leaflets; the upper leaves are often reduced to a single leaflet. A stiffly branched shrub, 3–5′ high. Sandy soil, mostly along the coast. Spring and early summer. Pea Family.

Bristly Locust or **Rose Acacia** (*Robinia hispida*) Rose-purple, pea-shaped flowers, ¾–1″ long, in short racemes. Leaves divided into 7–13 oblong leaflets. The twigs, leaf stalks and flower stalks are covered with bristly hairs. 2–9′ high. Native of Va. south, but cultivated northward and escaped to open woods and roadsides. Late spring and early summer. Pea Family.

False Indigo or **Indigobush** (*Amorpha fruticosa*) Violet-purple flowers, ¼″ long, in one or more spikelike racemes 3–6″ long. Each leaf has 11–27 oval, entire leaflets. Stamens protruding. 5–20′ high. Riverbanks and rich woods, s. Pa. to Wis. south; cultivated and locally escaped northward. Late spring and early summer. Pea Family.

Scotch Broom (yellow)

Bristly Locust (rose-purple)

False Indigo (violet-purple)

× ½

Honeysuckles (*Lonicera*) Woody trailing or twining vines, with tube-shaped, 2-lipped or nearly regular flowers. Leaves opposite, broad, egg-shaped or oblong, and 1–3″ long. Some of the species are shrubs (see pp. 104 and 294). Honeysuckle Family.

1. UPPERMOST PAIR OF LEAVES JOINED AT THE BASE; FLOWERS IN TERMINAL CLUSTERS

Hairy Honeysuckle (*L. hirsuta*) Yellow to orange flowers, 1″ long; leaves hairy beneath. Flowers sticky-hairy. Fruit a cluster of red berries. Moist woods and shores, w. N.Eng. to Neb. north. Late spring and early summer.

Glaucous, Smooth-leaved or **Limber Honeysuckle** (*L. dioica*) Greenish-yellow, orange or purplish flowers, ½–¾″ long; leaves whitened beneath. Berries red. Rocky woods and thickets. Spring and early summer.

Trumpet or **Coral Honeysuckle** (*L. sempervirens*) Red (rarely yellow) flowers, 1–2″ long, the flower lobes much shorter than the tube. See p. 326.

2. NONE OF THE LEAVES JOINED AT THE BASE; FLOWERS IN PAIRS IN THE UPPER AXILS

Japanese Honeysuckle (*L. japonica*) * White flowers, turning yellow when they fade, very fragrant. Some of the lower leaves may be lobed like those of the White Oak. Berries black. Roadsides and thickets, Mass. to Kan. south; an introduced weed, smothering out other plants by its rank growth. Late spring to fall.

VINES /
Leaves Divided

Leaves without Tendrils; Leaflets 5 or More

Groundnut or **Wild Bean** (*Apios americana*) Leaflets 5–7; brownish-purple flowers in short racemes. Flowers pea-shaped, ½″ long, with a distinctive, sweetish odor. Leaflets egg-shaped and pointed. Root a roundish, edible tuber. Moist thickets. Summer. Pea Family.

Climbing Fumitory, Mountain Fringe or **Allegheny Vine** (*Adlumia fungosa*) White or pinkish flowers, ½″ long, drooping in loose clusters from the axils. The flowers have 4 petals joined together, 2 large and 2 small. Leaves 3-times-pinnate; the leaf stalks twine around other plants; leaflets mostly 3-lobed. Moist ledges and wooded slopes, mainly in the mts. southward. Summer and fall. Poppy Family.

Glaucous
Honeysuckle

Hairy
Honeysuckle

Japanese
Honeysuckle

Groundnut

Climbing
Fumitory

× ½

Leaves without Tendrils; Leaflets 3

Prostrate Tick Trefoil (*Desmodium rotundifolium*) Leaflets nearly round, 1–2″ in diameter. Purple flowers, ⅓″ long, in loose racemes Plant soft-hairy. 2–6′ long. Trailing plant of dry woods, c. N.Eng to Mich. south. Late summer and fall. Pea Family.

Milk Pea (*Galactia regularis*) Leaflets elliptical, rounded at both ends, 1–1½″ long; reddish-purple flowers, ½–¾″ long, in racemes shorter or not much longer than the leaves. Prostrate. 1–3′ long. Sandy soil, se. N.Y. and e. Pa. south. Summer. Pea Family.

Hog Peanut (*Amphicarpa bracteata*) Leaflets egg-shaped, short-pointed; narrow, pale-lilac, pale-purple or white flowers, ½″ long, in racemes. There are also small, petal-less flowers near the base of the plant that produce a 1-seeded pod. Climbs on other plants Moist thickets; common. Summer and early fall. Pea Family.

Wild Kidney Bean (*Phaseolus polystachios*) Leaflets broadly egg-shaped, short-pointed; purple flowers, ⅓″ long, in slender racemes 2–6″ long. Climbing or trailing. Dry woods and thickets, s. Conn. to Ill. south. Summer. Pea Family.

Wild Beans (*Strophostyles*) Leaflets egg-shaped or oblong, 1–2″ long; greenish-purple or pink flowers, about ½″ long, in umbels or headlike clusters at the end of a long stalk. Summer and fall. Pea Family.

    Trailing Wild Bean (*S. helvola*) Leaflets egg-shaped or pear-shaped, often with 3 blunt lobes. Damp thickets and shores, Mass., s. Ont. to Minn. south.

    Pink Wild Bean (*S. umbellata*) Leaflets oblong or narrowly egg-shaped, rarely lobed. Sandy woods and fields, Long I. to Ill. south.

Butterfly Pea (*Clitoria mariana*) Leaflets broadly lance-shaped, bluntly pointed; pale-blue, showy flowers, 2″ long, usually solitary. Trailing or twining. 1–3′ long, sometimes erect. Dry open woods and thickets, s. N.Y. to s. Ohio and Ill. south. Summer. Pea Family.

Trailing or **Creeping Bush Clovers** (*Lespedeza*) Leaflets elliptical, ¼–¾″ long; purple flowers, ¼″ long, in clusters on stalks much longer than the leaves. See p. 64.

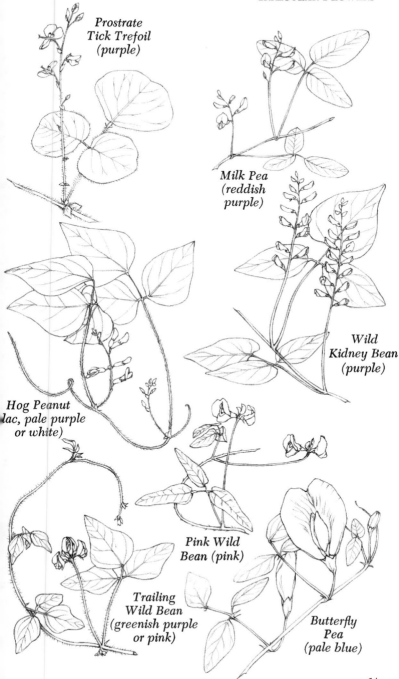

Prostrate
Tick Trefoil
(purple)

Milk Pea
(reddish
purple)

Wild
Kidney Bean
(purple)

Hog Peanut
lac, pale purple
or white)

Pink Wild
Bean (pink)

Trailing
Wild Bean
(greenish purple
or pink)

Butterfly
Pea
(pale blue)

× ½

Leaves with a Tendril at the End

Wild Peas or **Vetchlings** (*Lathyrus*) and **Vetches** (*Vicia*) Two closely related genera of trailing or climbing vines with pea shaped flowers and tendrils at the tips of the leaves. The Wild Peas are technically separated from the Vetches by having hairs along one side of the style instead of at the tip. Generally speaking, the Wild Peas have larger flowers and larger and fewer leaflets than the Vetches and have large stipules. Pea Family.

WHITE, YELLOWISH-WHITE OR YELLOW FLOWERS

Wood or **Carolina Vetch** (*V. caroliniana*) Flowers white or white with a bluish tip, under ½″ long; leaflets oblong, under 1″ long, mostly 10 or more. Woods and thickets, N.Y. to Minn. south. Spring.

Cream-colored or **Pale Vetchling** (*L. ochroleucus*) Yellowish-white flowers, ½–¾″ long; leaflets egg-shaped or elliptical, 1–2″ long, mostly 6. A pair of large stipules, heart-shaped on one side, at the base of the leaf stalk. Woods and rocky slopes, w. Vt., Pa., Iowa to Ore. north. Late spring and early summer.

Yellow Vetchling or **Meadow Pea** (*L. pratensis*) * Bright-yellow flowers, ½–¾″ long. The two leaflets are lance-shaped, and at the base of the leaf stalk is a pair of stipules that resemble the leaves. Fields and roadsides; local. Summer.

BLUISH, PURPLE OR PINK FLOWERS

1. STIPULES ¼″ OR LESS LONG AND INCONSPICUOUS; LARGEST LEAFLETS USUALLY NOT OVER 1″ LONG

a. Flowers more than 2 in a cluster

Cow or **Tufted Vetch** (*V. cracca*) * Violet-blue flowers, ½″ long, in dense, one-sided racemes; leaflets narrow; stipules entire; hairs pressed closely to stem. Fields and roadsides. Late spring and summer.

Hairy Vetch (*V. villosa*) *† Similar to the Cow Vetch, but stem has spreading hairs. Flowers large (over ½″ long) and bicolored (blue and white). Late spring to fall.

American or **Purple Vetch** (*V. americana*) Bluish-purple flowers ½–¾″ long, in a loose, few-flowered raceme; leaflets elliptical or oblong. Stipules sharply toothed. Moist thickets and meadows, w. Que. and N.Y. to Alaska south. Late spring and summer.

Continued

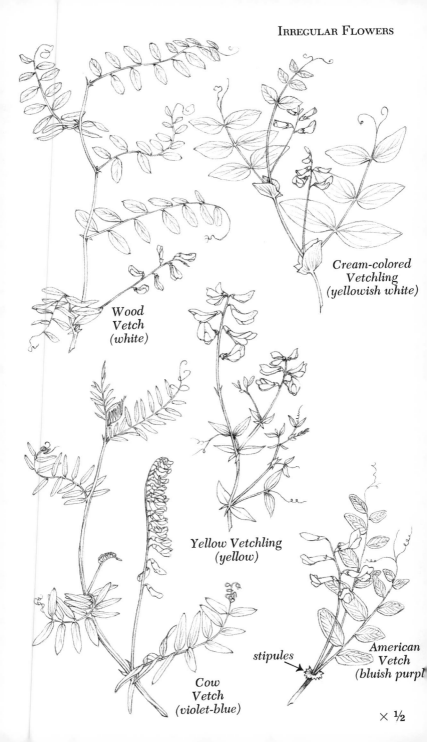

*Cream-colored
Vetchling
(yellowish white)*

*Wood
Vetch
(white)*

*Yellow Vetchling
(yellow)*

*American
Vetch
(bluish purpl)*

stipules

*Cow
Vetch
(violet-blue)*

× ½

Leaves with a Tendril at the End (cont.)

Wild Peas (*Lathyrus*) and **Vetches** (*Vicia*) (cont.)

BLUISH, PURPLE OR PINK FLOWERS (CONT.)

1. STIPULES ¼″ OR LESS LONG AND INCONSPICUOUS;
   LARGEST LEAFLETS USUALLY NOT OVER 1″ LONG (CONT.)

b. Flowers growing singly or 2 in a cluster

Slender Vetch (*V. tetrasperma*) * Pale-blue flowers, ¼″ long (including calyx), at the end of a long stalk. Leaflets narrow. Weak-stemmed, slender vine, 6–24″ long. Fields and waste places. Late spring and summer.

Narrow-leaved Vetch (*V. angustifolia*) * Purple flowers, ½–¾″ long, almost stalkless and growing in the axils. Leaflets variable, usually narrow. Fields and waste places. Spring to fall.

Spring Vetch (*V. sativa*) * Similar to the Narrow-leaved Vetch, but flowers ¾–1″ long, bicolored (purple and pink). Leaflets variable, usually broad at the tip. Fields and roadsides. Spring to fall.

2. STIPULES CONSPICUOUS (OVER ¼″ LONG); LARGEST LEAFLETS
   USUALLY OVER 1½″ LONG

Beach Pea (*L. japonicus*) Stipules broadly arrow-shaped, about as large as the leaflets. Flowers ¾–1″ long, 6–10 in a cluster. Leaflets broad and blunt. Fleshy plant of seabeaches and sandy or gravelly shores of the Great Lakes, Oneida Lake and Lake Champlain. Summer and occasionally fall.

Marsh Vetchling (*L. palustris*) Leaflets 4–10, usually 6; stipules half-arrow–shaped; flowers 2–9 in a *long-stalked* cluster. Leaflets varying from narrow to broad and stems winged or wingless. Moist meadows and shores. Summer.

Veiny Pea (*L. venosus*) Leaflets broad, usually 10 or 12; stipules half-arrow–shaped; flowers usually over 10 in a cluster. Stems square. 2–6′ long. Rich woods and thickets, w. N.J., Pa. and s. Ont. to Wis. south. Late spring and early summer.

Everlasting or **Perennial Pea** (*L. latifolius*) * Leaflets 2, lance-shaped or oblong. Purple or pink (rarely white) flowers, 1″ long, in long-stalked racemes. Stipules lance-shaped. Stems broadly winged. Escaped from cultivation to roadsides and waste places. Summer.

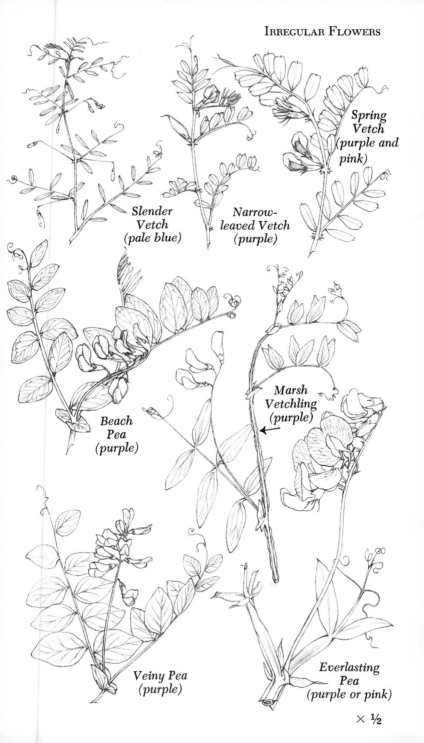

*Slender
Vetch
(pale blue)*

*Narrow-
leaved Vetch
(purple)*

*Spring
Vetch
(purple and
pink)*

*Beach
Pea
(purple)*

*Marsh
Vetchling
(purple)*

*Veiny Pea
(purple)*

*Everlasting
Pea
(purple or pink)*

× ½

WILDFLOWERS OR VINES
(with 2 regular parts)

Enchanter's Nightshades (*Circaea*) Small, white flowers in short racemes. Petals deeply 2-lobed. Leaves egg-shaped and long-stalked, opposite. Summer. Evening Primrose Family.

> **Enchanter's Nightshade** (*C. quadrisulcata*) Plant 1–2′ high. Leaves shallowly toothed, 2–4″ long. Woods and thickets.

> **Dwarf Enchanter's Nightshade** (*C. alpina*) Plant 3–10″ high. Leaves coarsely toothed, 1–2″ long. Moist woods and springy places, southward mostly in the mts.

Spurges (*Euphorbia*) Yellowish or greenish flowers, either in broad umbels or growing in the axils. See pp. 408 and 432.

Climbing Fumitory, Mountain Fringe or **Allegheny Vine** (*Adlumia fungosa*) Vine with divided leaves. See p. 108.

WILDFLOWERS WITH BASAL LEAVES ONLY
(and 3 regular parts) / Leaves Entire

Yellow, Blue, or Purple-Brown Flowers

Yellow-eyed Grasses (*Xyris*) Yellow flowers, ¼″ wide, in a scaly head. Leaves grasslike. Bogs and wet shores. Summer. Yellow-eyed Grass Family.

> **Slender Yellow-eyed Grass** (*X. torta*) Base of plant enlarged, like a small bulb. Leaves very narrow, ⅛″ or less wide, often spirally twisted.

> **Carolina Yellow-eyed Grass** (*X. caroliniana*) Base of plant soft and flat. Leaves usually broader than those of Slender Yellow-eyed Grass, and not twisted.

Wild Ginger (*Asarum canadense*) Low plant with a curious purple-brown flower, about 1″ wide with 3 pointed lobes, that grows at the base of the 2 heart-shaped leaves. Root with the distinct taste and smell of ginger. Rich woods. Spring. Birthwort Family.

Irises (*Iris*) Yellow or blue flowers, 2–4″ wide; leaves narrow. See p. 120.

Yellow Pond Lilies (*Nuphar*) Yellow flowers; aquatic plants with heart-shaped leaves. See p. 176.

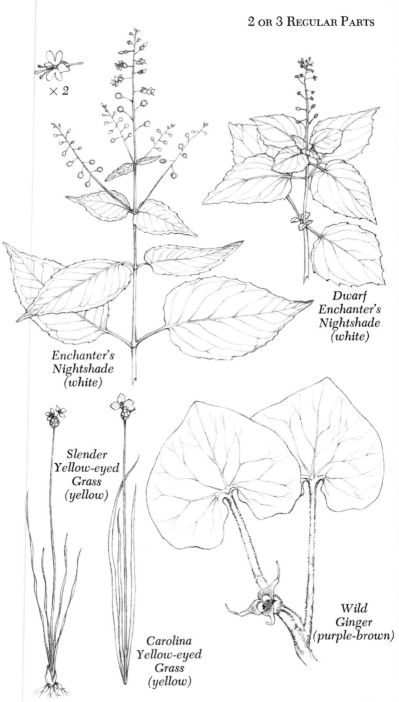

× 2

Enchanter's Nightshade (white)

Dwarf Enchanter's Nightshade (white)

Slender Yellow-eyed Grass (yellow)

Carolina Yellow-eyed Grass (yellow)

Wild Ginger (purple-brown)

× ½

White or Pink Flowers

Water Plantains (*Alisma*) White or pinkish flowers, ⅛–½″ wide, in a widely branched cluster. Leaves elliptical or egg-shaped, long-stalked. Muddy shores. Summer. Water Plantain Family.

Small Water Plantain (*A. subcordatum*) Flowers about ⅛″ wide; petals about as long as the sepals.

Large Water Plantain (*A. triviale*) † Flowers over ¼″ wide; petals much longer than the sepals. Less common.

Arrowheads (*Sagittaria*) White flowers, ½–1″ wide, growing in whorls of 3 (usually) from an unbranched stalk. Several other species, which are identified by their fruit, are found in this area. Shallow water and marshes. Summer. Water Plantain Family.

1. MOST OR ALL OF THE LEAVES ARROW-SHAPED

Common Arrowhead (*S. latifolia*) Flowers 1–1½″ wide; stamens 25–40. The leaves vary from broadly to very narrowly arrow-shaped. Common.

Engelmann's Arrowhead (*S. engelmanniana*) † Flowers ⅔–1″ wide; stamens 15–25. Leaves usually very narrowly arrow-shaped. Mass. south.

2. LEAVES ONLY OCCASIONALLY ARROW-SHAPED

Sessile-fruited Arrowhead (*S. rigida*) Leaves narrowly lance-shaped to oval (occasionally with lobes at the base); lowest flower (or fruit) stalkless. The flower cluster is shorter than the leaves, and the stalk of the cluster is usually bent over. Flowers ½–¾″ wide.

Grass-leaved Arrowhead (*S. graminea*) Leaves narrowly lance-shaped, with a flat blade; lowest flowers (or fruit) long-stalked. Flowers ½″ wide; flower cluster erect.

Slender Arrowhead (*S. teres*) Leaves without blades, round in cross section and tapering to the tip. Flowers ½″ wide. Sandy shores near the coast, Mass. to Md.

Flowering Rush (*Butomus umbellatus*) * Rose-colored flowers, ¾–1″ wide, in umbels. The leaves are sword-shaped, triangular in cross section. 1–4′ high. Muddy shores, St. Lawrence River system, Lake Champlain and Great Lakes. Summer. Flowering Rush Family.

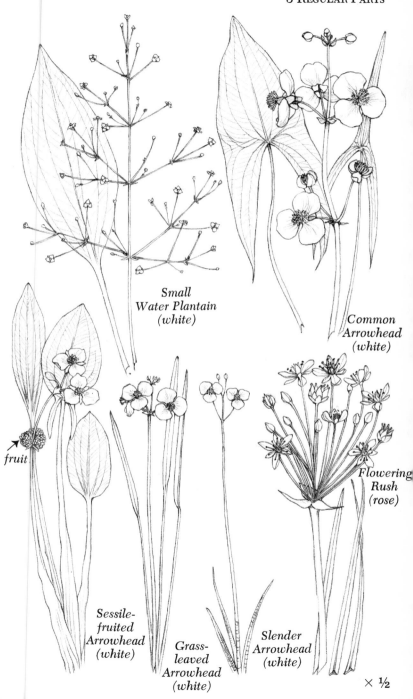

Small
Water Plantain
(white)

Common
Arrowhead
(white)

fruit

Sessile-
fruited
Arrowhead
(white)

Grass-
leaved
Arrowhead
(white)

Slender
Arrowhead
(white)

Flowering
Rush
(rose)

× ½

Flowers Large (¾″ or More Wide)

Spiderworts (*Tradescantia*) Blue or purple flowers, ¾–1½″ wide, with broad petals; flowers in umbel-like clusters with 2 long, leaf-like bracts below the flower cluster. Leaves long and narrow. 8–36″ high. Woods and meadows, s. N.Eng. to Minn. south; often cultivated. Spring and summer. Spiderwort Family.

Spiderwort (*T. virginiana*) Leaves green; sepals and flower stalks hairy.

Ohio Spiderwort (*T. ohiensis*) † Leaves whitened with a bloom; sepals hairy only at the tip, if at all, and flower stalks smooth.

Virginia Dayflower (*Commelina virginica*) Blue flowers, ¾–1″ wide, with broad petals; each flower growing from a heart-shaped spathe. Lower petal slightly smaller than the other 2. Leaves lance-shaped. 1–4′ high. Moist woods and clearings, s. N.J. to Kan. south. Summer and fall. Spiderwort Family.

Irises (*Iris*) Flowers 2–4″ wide, blue or violet with yellow markings or yellow. The 3 large outer divisions are the sepals; the 3 smaller, erect, inner parts are the petals. Leaves long and narrow, sheathing the stem. Iris Family.

1. PLANT 1–3′ HIGH

Larger Blue Flag (*I. versicolor*) Blue flowers with yellow veining; leaves ½–1″ wide. The flowers are about 4″ wide. Common in marshes and wet meadows, Can. south to Va., n. Ohio, Mich. and Wis. Late spring and early summer.

Slender Blue Flag (*I. prismatica*) Similar to the Larger Blue Flag, but leaves ⅛–¼″ wide and flowers 3″ wide. Marshes and meadows, near the coast. Early summer.

Yellow Iris (*I. pseudacorus*) * Yellow flowers, 4″ wide. Escaped from cultivation to marshes and banks of streams. Late spring and summer.

2. PLANT 2–8″ HIGH

Dwarf or **Vernal Iris** (*I. verna*) Sepals blue with a yellow band at the base, the band smooth or slightly downy; leaves very narrow. Dry woods and barrens, Pa. south. Spring.

Crested Iris (*I. cristata*) Sepals blue with conspicuous orange or whitish crest; leaves lance-shaped. Rich woods and slopes, s. Pa. to Ind. south. Spring.

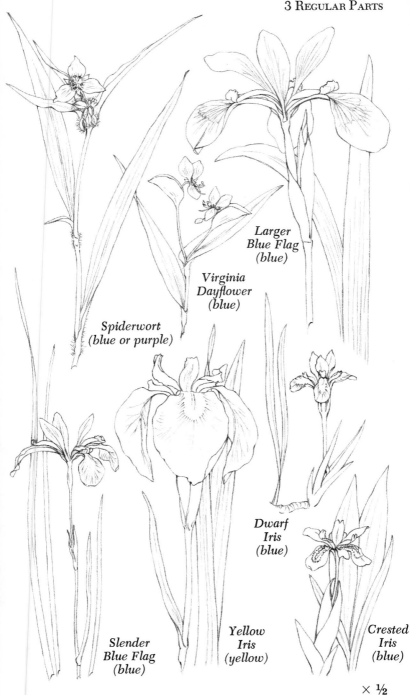

Larger
Blue Flag
(blue)

Virginia
Dayflower
(blue)

Spiderwort
(blue or purple)

Dwarf
Iris
(blue)

Slender
Blue Flag
(blue)

Yellow
Iris
(yellow)

Crested
Iris
(blue)

× ½

Flowers Small (under ½″ Wide)

Virginia Snakeroot (*Aristolochia serpentaria*) Brownish-purple flowers on 1–2″ stalks at the base of the plant. The flowers are about ½″ long, curved in the middle like an S, with 3 flaring lobes. Leaves heart-shaped at the base, long-pointed. 4–18″ high. Rich woods, sw. Conn., se. N.Y., Pa. to s. Ill. south. Early summer. Birthwort Family.

Redroot (*Lachnanthes tinctoria*) Dull yellow flowers, ⅓″ wide, in a dense branching cluster at the top of the stem. Leaves narrow, pointed. The plant is woolly at the top. Juice red. 8–30″ high. Sandy swamps and also a weed in cranberry bogs, N.S. and s. Mass. south. Summer and fall. Bloodwort Family.

Sweet Goldenrod (*Solidago odora*) Very small, yellow flowers in one-sided clusters. See p. 448.

Black Crowberry (*Empetrum nigrum*) Very small, purplish flowers in the axils. See p. 126.

Pinweeds (*Lechea*) Very small, greenish, reddish or brownish flowers in loose, branched clusters. See p. 408.

Lily Family (Liliaceae) Flowers composed of 6 parts, the outer 3 larger than the inner 3. See flowers with 6 regular parts, pp. 332–353.

WILDFLOWERS WITH ALTERNATE LEAVES /
Leaves Toothed, Lobed or Divided

False Mermaid (*Floerkea proserpinacoides*) Tiny, white flowers, long-stalked, growing in the axils. Leaves with 3–5 lance-shaped or oblong leaflets. Weak-stemmed annual, 4–15″ long. Wet woods and stream valleys, N.S., sw. Que. and Vt. to N.D. south. Spring. False Mermaid Family.

Mermaid Weed (*Proserpinaca palustris*) Tiny, green flowers, stalk-less, growing in the axils. Leaves vary from sharply toothed above the water to divided into narrow segments under water. Prostrate or sprawling plant of muddy places. Summer and fall. Water Milfoil Family.

Goldenrods (*Solidago*) Small, yellow flowers. See pp. 446–453.

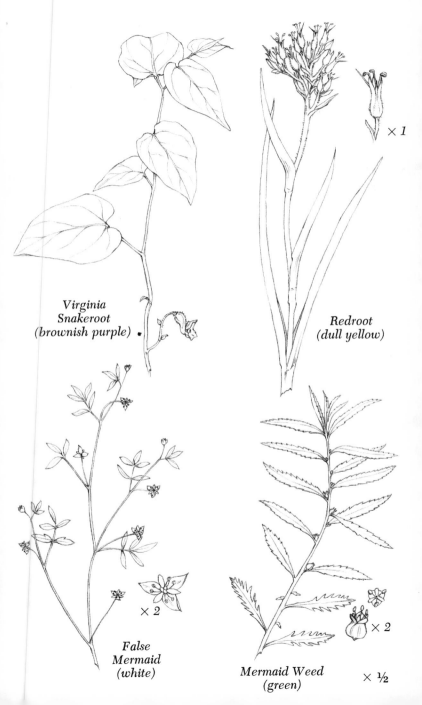

Virginia
Snakeroot
(brownish purple)

Redroot
(dull yellow)

× 1

False
Mermaid
(white)

× 2

Mermaid Weed
(green)

× 2

× ½

Trilliums (*Trillium*) Leaves in a single whorl of 3; flower large, solitary. A distinctive group of woodland plants. Spring. Lily Family.

1. LEAVES STALKLESS OR NEARLY SO

a. *Flower stalkless*

Toad Trillium or **Toadshade** (*T. sessile*) Maroon flower (or green in a variety), the petals erect and not spreading outward. Leaves generally mottled. 4–12″ high. Rich woods, w. N.Y. to Ill. south.

b. *Flower-stalk horizontal or bent downward*

Nodding Trillium (*T. cernuum*) Flower stalk ½–1½″ long, bent downward so flower nods beneath the leaves; petals recurved at the tip; anthers pink. Flower white or pale pink. 6–20″ high. Moist woods.

Drooping Trillium (*T. flexipes*) † Flower stalk 1½–3″ long, horizontal or drooping; petals not recurved at the tip; anthers creamy white. Flower white, rarely purple. Moist woods, c. N.Y. to s. Minn. south.

c. *Flower stalk erect or ascending*

Large-flowered Trillium (*T. grandiflorum*) Flower showy, funnel-shaped at base and flaring outward from the middle; petals 1½–2½″ long. Flower white, turning pink as it fades. 6–20″ high. Rich woods, w. Me. to Minn. south.

Wake-robin, Birthroot or **Purple** or **Red Trillium** (*T. erectum*) Flower normally maroon or dark purple, ill scented; petals ½–1½″ long, spreading outward from the base. A white, scentless variety is found; also rarely yellowish or green. 6–20″ high. Rich woods, south to Mich., Pa., Del. and in the mts. to Ga.

2. LEAVES DISTINCTLY STALKED

Painted Trillium (*T. undulatum*) White flower, with crimson veining at the base of each petal. Leaves taper-pointed. 8–20″ high. Cool moist woods, south to Wis., Mich., Pa., N.J., and in the mts. to Ga.

Snow Trillium or **Dwarf White Trillium** (*T. nivale*) Dwarf, early-blooming species with a white flower and small, oval, blunt leaves. 2–6″ high. Wooded hillsides and shady ledges, w. Pa. to Minn. south. Early spring.

Prairie Trillium (*T. recurvatum*) Maroon, stalkless flower with erect petals and drooping sepals. 6–18″ high. Rich woods, Ohio to Iowa south.

Continued

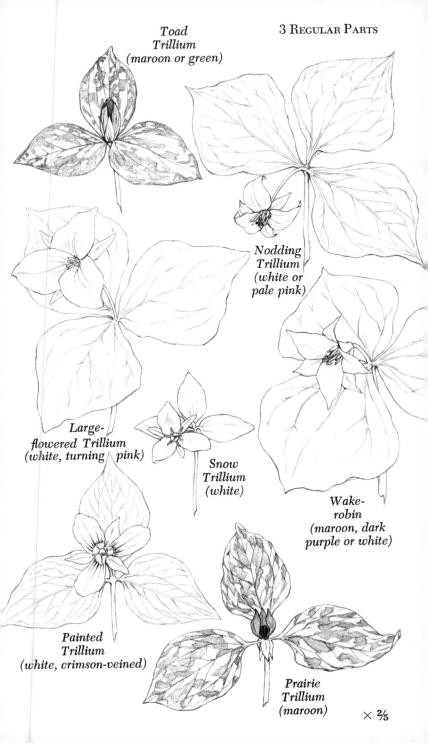

*Toad
Trillium
(maroon or green)*

*Nodding
Trillium
(white or
pale pink)*

*Large-
flowered Trillium
(white, turning pink)*

*Snow
Trillium
(white)*

*Wake-
robin
(maroon, dark
purple or white)*

*Painted
Trillium
(white, crimson-veined)*

*Prairie
Trillium
(maroon)*

× 2/5

Bedstraws (*Galium*) Leaves in whorls of 4–6; tiny, white flowers. A few flowers may be 4-lobed. Weak-stemmed. Swamps and low grounds. Summer and fall. Madder Family.

Clayton's Bedstraw (*G. tinctorium*) Leaves mostly in 5's or 6's, lance-shaped or oblong; flower stalks straight.

Small Bedstraw (*G. trifidum*) † Leaves narrow, in 4's; flower stalks long and arching.

SHRUBS

Black Crowberry (*Empetrum nigrum*) Low, straggling shrub of n. regions, south into mts. of n. N.Eng. and N.Y.; on Me. coast and e. Long I. Tiny, purplish flowers, solitary in the axils. Leaves narrow, thick, evergreen, ¼″ long. Fruit a black berry, ¼″ in diameter. **Purple Crowberry** (*E. atropurpureum*) of N.Eng. mts. and N.S. north has purple-black or red berries, and its branches are white-woolly when they are young. Rocky or peaty soil. Early summer. Crowberry Family.

VINES

Dutchman's Pipe (*Aristolochia durior*) Large, twining vine with heart-shaped leaves. The brown-purple flowers are shaped like a Dutch pipe, 1″ long, 3-lobed at the end, and grow from the axils. Rich woods and along streams, sw. Pa. and W.Va. south; culti-vated and sometimes escaped north to N.Eng. Early summer. Birthwort Family.

WILDFLOWERS WITH NO APPARENT LEAVES AT FLOWERING TIME (and 4 regular parts)

Yellow Bartonia (*Bartonia virginica*) Yellowish or straw-colored flowers, ⅛″ long, in a stiff raceme or branched cluster. Leaves scalelike, in pairs. Stem wiry. 2–12″ high. Dry woods or sandy bogs. Late summer. Gentian Family.

Indian Pipe or **Corpse Plant** (*Monotropa uniflora*) Waxy-white, solitary flower. See p. 172.

Pinesap or **False Beechdrops** (*Monotropa hypopithys*) Tan, yellow or red flowers, ½″ long. See p. 172.

Pennywort (*Obolaria virginica*) Dull-white or purplish flowers, ½″ long, surrounded by purplish bracts. See p. 158.

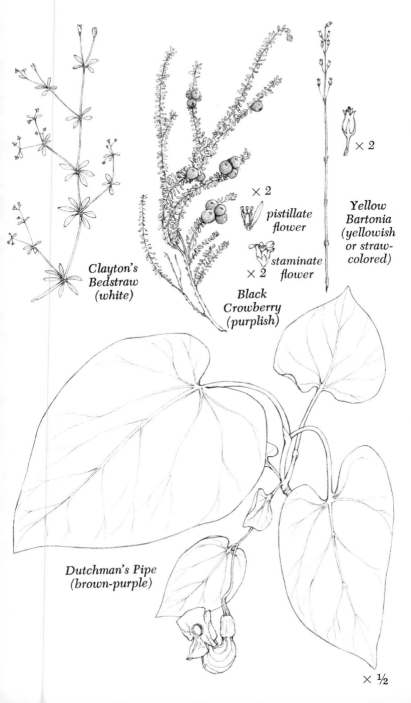

Clayton's
Bedstraw
(white)

× 2
pistillate
flower

staminate
× 2 flower

Black
Crowberry
(purplish)

Yellow
Bartonia
(yellowish
or straw-
colored)

× 2

Dutchman's Pipe
(brown-purple)

× ½

Whitlow Grass (*Draba verna*) * Very small, white flowers in racemes. Petals deeply cleft. Leaves ½–1″ long. Dry fields, Mass. to Ill. south. Spring. Mustard Family.

Yellow Pond Lilies (*Nuphar*) Yellow flowers; aquatic plants with heart-shaped leaves. See p. 176.

Golden Club (*Orontium aquaticum*) Yellow flowers in a dense spike. See p. 336.

Plantains (*Plantago*) Whitish or greenish flowers in dense heads or spikes. See p. 398.

WILDFLOWERS WITH ALTERNATE LEAVES / Leaves Entire

White or Pink Flowers; Leaves under 1″ Long, Evergreen

Creeping Snowberry (*Gaultheria hispidula*) Prostrate plant with very small, white, bell-shaped flowers hidden beneath the leaves. Leaves dark green, egg-shaped. The fruit is a white berry with wintergreen flavor. 3–12″ long. Mossy woods and bogs, mostly in the mts., south to Pa., Mich., Wis. and Ida., and in mts. to N.C. Spring and early summer. Heath Family.

Mountain Cranberry (*Vaccinium vitis-idaea*) Creeping plant with erect branches and pink, bell-shaped flowers in a small terminal cluster. Leaves oval, shining above, paler and black-dotted beneath. Fruit a dark-red, acid berry. 3–8″ high. Rocky and dry, peaty places south to Me. coast, mts. of N.Eng. and n. Minn. Summer. Heath Family.

Cranberries (*Vaccinium*) Trailing plants with ascending branches and pale-pink flowers having four recurved petal-like lobes. Flowers nodding, long-stalked. The stamens form a cone protruding from the center of the flower like a shooting star. Fruit a red, acid berry. Heath Family.

Large Cranberry (*V. macrocarpon*) Leaves blunt, only slightly paler beneath and with the edges slightly turned in. The flower stalk has 2 bracts which are above the middle of the stalk. The cranberry of commerce. Bogs. Summer.

Small Cranberry (*V. oxycoccos*) Smaller throughout; margins of leaves strongly rolled inward; leaves somewhat pointed, much paler beneath. Flower stalk has 2 bracts at or below the middle of the stalk. Berries spotted when young. Cold bogs, south to N.J., Pa., n. Ohio, Mich. and Wis., and in mts. to N.C. Late spring and summer.

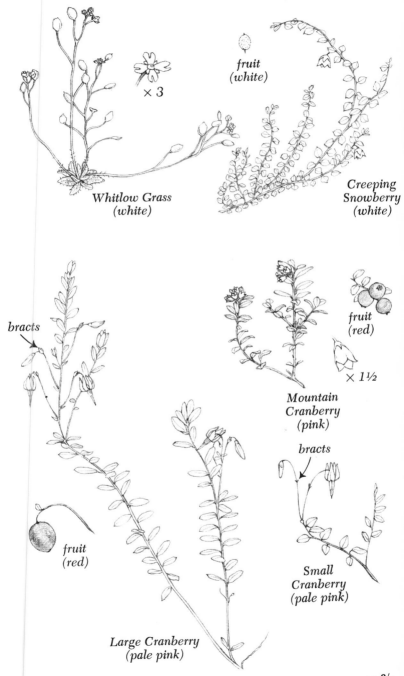

× 3

fruit
(white)

Whitlow Grass
(white)

Creeping
Snowberry
(white)

bracts

fruit
(red)

fruit
(red)

× 1½

Mountain
Cranberry
(pink)

bracts

Small
Cranberry
(pale pink)

Large Cranberry
(pale pink)

× ⅔

White, Pink, Magenta or Purple Flowers; Leaves Not Evergreen

PLANTS OF WOODS, FIELDS, ROCKS AND WASTE PLACES

Canada Mayflower or **Wild Lily-of-the-valley** (*Maianthemum canadense*) Small woodland plant with 2 or 3 leaves, which are heart-shaped at the base. White flowers in a small raceme. Fruit a speckled, red berry. 2–6″ high. Woods; very common. Spring. Lily Family.

Fireweed or **Great Willow Herb** (*Epilobium angustifolium*) Large (¾–1″ wide) magenta flowers in a long, spikelike raceme. Leaves lance-shaped, pale beneath, entire or minutely toothed. 2–8′ high. Roadsides, clearings and burned woodlands. Summer and early fall. Evening Primrose Family.

Jumpseed or **Virginia Knotweed** (*Tovara virginiana*) Very small, greenish-white flowers in slender, thinly flowered spikes 4–12″ long. Leaves egg-shaped or elliptical. Stem jointed, 1–4′ high. Woods and thickets, c. and s. N.Eng. to Minn. south. Summer and fall. Buckwheat Family.

Hoary Alyssum (*Berteroa incana*) * Tiny white flowers in racemes, the petals deeply cleft. The stem and leaves are covered with a grayish down. Leaves lance-shaped, ½–1½″ long. Pod oblong. 1–2′ high. Dry fields and waste places. Summer. Mustard Family.

Narrow-leaved White-topped Aster (*Sericocarpus linifolius*) White flowers in a flat-topped cluster. See p. 202.

Roseroot (*Sedum rosea*) Purplish flowers in a branched, terminal cluster; leaves fleshy, under 1½″ long. See p. 140.

PLANTS OF WET PLACES

Halberd-leaved Tearthumb (*Polygonum arifolium*) Prickly-stemmed plant with broadly arrow-shaped leaves. See p. 402.

Willow Herbs (*Epilobium*) Small pink or whitish flowers with petals notched at the tip. See p. 156.

Mountain Watercress (*Cardamine rotundifolia*) Plant of springy places with roundish or egg-shaped, entire or wavy-toothed leaves and white flowers in a short raceme. See p. 140.

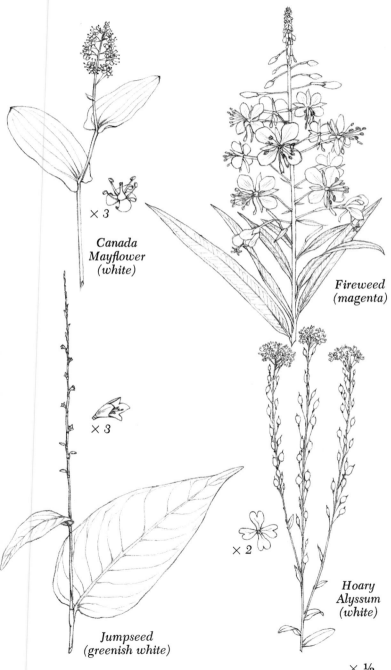

× 3

*Canada
Mayflower
(white)*

*Fireweed
(magenta)*

× 3

*Jumpseed
(greenish white)*

× 2

*Hoary
Alyssum
(white)*

× ½

Yellow or Green Flowers

FLOWERS ½″ OR MORE WIDE

Sundrops (*Oenothera*) Petals yellow, broad, notched at the tip. Species of Evening Primrose whose flowers open during the day. Summer. Evening Primrose Family.

Sundrops (*O. fruticosa*) Flowers 1–2″ wide. See p. 134.

Small Sundrops (*O. perennis*) Flowers ½–¾″ wide, in a leafy raceme. Leaves lance-shaped, blunt, 1–2″ long. 6–24″ high. Open woods and fields.

Seedbox (*Ludwigia alternifolia*) Petals yellow, not notched; flowers ½–¾″ wide and grow singly in the axils. Leaves lance-shaped, pointed. The seed capsule is square at the top. 2–3′ high. Swamps and shores, s. N.Eng. to s. Mich. south. Summer. Evening Primrose Family.

FLOWERS UNDER ½″ WIDE

Wormseed or **Treacle Mustard** (*Erysimum cheiranthoides*) * Yellow flowers, ⅓″ wide, with 4 petals; leaves 1–4″ long. Flowers in racemes or terminal clusters. Leaves sometimes slightly toothed. Pods narrow and erect. 6–36″ high. Waste places and fields. Summer. Mustard Family.

Common Smartweed or **Water Pepper** (*Polygonum hydropiper*) Green flowers in slender spikes, the spikes 1–3″ long and drooping at the tip. Leaves lance-shaped, wavy-margined. Stem jointed, often reddish, 8–24″ high. Common weed of moist soil. Summer and fall. Buckwheat Family.

Mossy Stonecrop or **Wallpepper** (*Sedum acre*) Bright yellow flowers, ⅓″ wide; leaves fleshy, ⅛–¼″ long. See p. 186.

Sweet Goldenrod (*Solidago odora*) Small, yellow flowers in one-sided, curving clusters. See p. 448.

Spurges (*Euphorbia*) Yellowish or greenish flowers, mostly in a broad, terminal umbel; juice milky. See p. 408.

Roseroot (*Sedum rosea*) Yellowish flowers, ¼″ wide, in a terminal cluster; leaves ½–1½″ long, fleshy, egg-shaped or oval, crowded. See p. 140.

Purslane or **Pusley** (*Portulaca oleracea*) Prostrate, fleshy weed of gardens and waste places; flowers ¼″ wide, growing singly in the leaf clusters. See p. 186.

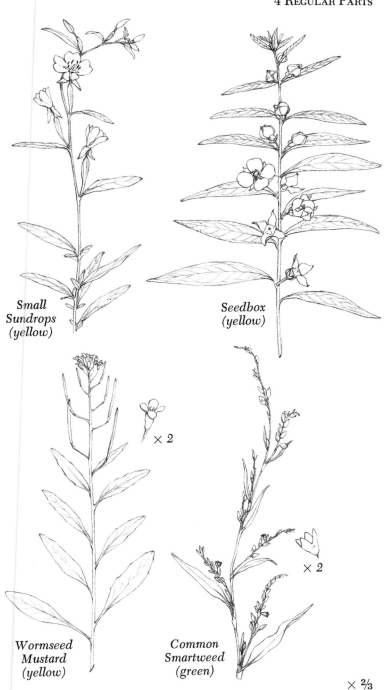

Small
Sundrops
(yellow)

Seedbox
(yellow)

Wormseed
Mustard
(yellow)

× 2

Common
Smartweed
(green)

× 2

× ⅔

Yellow Flowers

Evening Primroses and **Sundrops** (*Oenothera*) Flowers ½–2″ wide, with a prominent cross-shaped stigma in the center. Below the flower is a long, slender calyx tube, and the sepals are usually bent backward. Flowers in spikes or racemes. The Sundrops opens during the day, while Evening Primroses open at twilight. Small Sundrops (*O. perennis*) has entire leaves (p. 132). Dry open places. Summer and fall. Evening Primrose Family.

1. PETALS NARROW

Cross-shaped Evening Primrose (*O. cruciata*) Flowers relatively small, ½–1″ wide, with narrow petals. Leaves lance-shaped. 1–4′ high. N.Eng. to Mich.

2. PETALS BROAD, USUALLY INDENTED AT THE TIP

Sundrops (*O. fruticosa*) Flowers wide open during the day; pods about twice as long as wide. Flowers 1–2″ wide. 1–3′ high. Fields and meadows, s. N.Eng. to Mich. south.

Common Evening Primrose (*O. biennis*) Flowers wide open at twilight; pods 4 times longer than broad; leaves lance-shaped, wavy-edged and slightly toothed. Flowers 1–2″ wide. 1–6′ high. Common.

Cut-leaved Evening Primrose (*O. laciniata*) Flowers open at twilight; larger leaves deeply lobed. Flowers ½–1½″ wide. Weak-stemmed, 4–30″ high.

Seabeach Evening Primrose (*O. humifusa*)† Flowers open at night; plant silvery-downy throughout. Flowers about 1″ wide; leaves wavy-toothed. Sprawling plant of seabeaches, N.J. south.

Charlock (*Brassica kaber*) Flowers about ½″ wide; upper leaves egg-shaped or oblong. See p. 142.

Wormseed Mustard (*Erysimum cheiranthoides*) Flowers small (⅓″ wide), in racemes or small terminal clusters; leaves lance-shaped, nearly entire, 1–4″ long. See p. 132.

Goldenrods (*Solidago*) Flowers small and numerous, in one-sided clusters or in the axils. See pp. 446–453.

Roseroot (*Sedum rosea*) Yellowish flowers, ¼″ wide, in a terminal cluster; leaves ½–1½″ long, crowded. See p. 140.

Mustard Family (Cruciferae) Flowers in racemes; leaves irregularly toothed or lobed. See pp. 142–145.

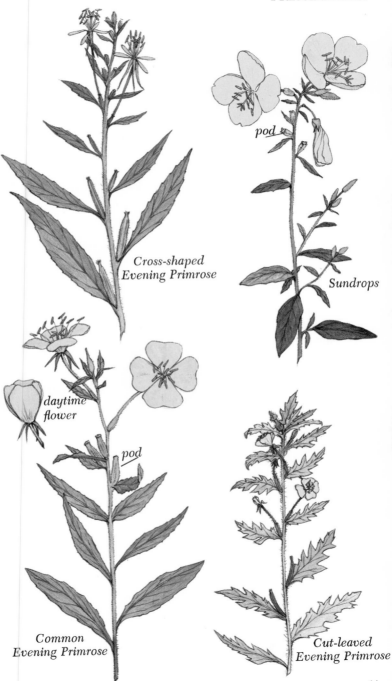

Cross-shaped
Evening Primrose

pod

Sundrops

daytime
flower

pod

Common
Evening Primrose

Cut-leaved
Evening Primrose

× ½

White Flowers; Leaves with an Arrow-shaped Base, Which Clasps the Stem

FLOWERS TINY (UNDER ⅛" WIDE); PODS BROAD

Field Peppergrass (*Lepidium campestre*) * Stem gray-green, fine-hairy; basal leaves mostly entire or slightly toothed; pods egg-shaped and slightly indented at the tip. 10–18" high. Fields and roadsides. Spring to fall. Mustard Family.

Field Pennycress (*Thlaspi arvense*) * Stem smooth; basal leaves (if present) unlobed; pods nearly round, broadly winged and deeply notched at the tip. 6–18" high. Fields and waste places. Spring and summer. Mustard Family.

Shepherd's Purse (*Capsella bursa-pastoris*) Basal leaves deeply lobed; pods triangular. See p. 150.

FLOWERS LARGER (⅛–¼" WIDE); PODS NARROW

Tower Mustard (*Arabis glabra*) Yellowish-white flowers; the upper stem has a whitish bloom; pods stiffly erect. The base of the stem has spreading hairs. 2–4' high. Fields and ledges. Spring and summer. Mustard Family.

Smooth Rock Cress (*Arabis laevigata*) Greenish-white or white flowers; stem smooth throughout, with a whitish bloom; pods spread horizontally. 1–3' high. Rocky woods and ledges. Spring and summer. Mustard Family.

Hairy Rock Cress (*Arabis hirsuta*) Stem hairy, without whitish bloom. White flowers. Leaves numerous, the lower ones over-lapping and hairy; basal leaves in a rosette. Pods erect. 6–24" high. Rocks and ledges. Spring and early summer. Mustard Family.

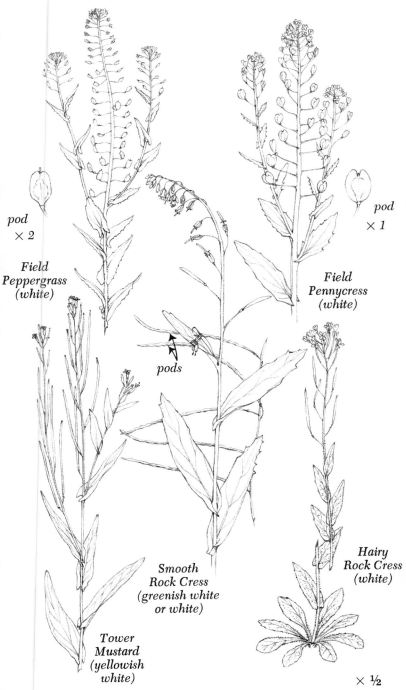

pod
× 2

*Field
Peppergrass
(white)*

pod
× 1

*Field
Pennycress
(white)*

pods

*Smooth
Rock Cress
(greenish white
or white)*

*Hairy
Rock Cress
(white)*

*Tower
Mustard
(yellowish
white)*

× ½

White, Pink or Purple Flowers in 1 or More Spikes or Racemes; Stem Leaves Not Arrow-shaped

BASAL LEAVES OR LOWEST STEM LEAF MORE THAN TWICE AS LONG AS WIDE

Dame's Violet or **Dame's Rocket** (*Hesperis matronalis*) * Large, showy (¾–1″ wide) purple flowers (sometimes pink or white); stamens and style mostly concealed in the flower tube. Flowers fragrant. 2–3′ high. Escaped from gardens to fields and roadsides. Spring and summer. Mustard Family.

Biennial Gaura (*Gaura biennis*) White flowers, turning pink as they fade, ⅓″ wide; stamens long and conspicuous, drooping beneath the flower. Sepals reflexed. Leaves lance-shaped, slightly toothed. 2–5′ high. Fields and meadows, Mass. and w. Que. to Minn. south. Summer. Evening Primrose Family.

Sea Rocket (*Cakile edentula*) Light-purple flowers, ¼″ wide; fleshy plant of béaches. Leaves wavy-toothed, narrowed at the base. Pods constricted in the middle. Bushy, branched plant, 6–12″ high. Summer and fall. Along the seashore and the Great Lakes. Mustard Family.

Horseradish (*Armoracia lapathifolia*) * White flowers, ¼″ wide; coarse plant of moist, open places with large, long-stalked basal leaves, 6–12″ long. 2–3′ high. Cultivated for its thick root. Escaped to roadsides and along streams. Spring and summer. Mustard Family.

Sicklepod (*Arabis canadensis*) Creamy-white flowers, ¼″ wide, slightly nodding; slender plant of woods and rocky places. Stem leaves narrowed at both ends, sparingly toothed. Pods long and bent downward. 1–3′ high. Me. to Minn. south. Spring and early summer. Mustard Family.

Fireweed (*Epilobium angustifolium*) Magenta flowers, ¾–1″ wide; stamens and style conspicuous. See p. 130.

Wild Peppergrass (*Lepidium virginicum*) Tiny, white flowers; pods nearly round. See p. 150.

LOWER LEAVES HEART-SHAPED OR TRIANGULAR; FOUND IN DRY PLACES

Garlic Mustard (*Alliaria officinalis*) * Leaves coarsely toothed, long-stalked. White flowers, ¼–⅓″ wide. Leaves smell of garlic when crushed. 1–3′ high. Roadsides and open woods. Spring and early summer. Mustard Family.

Continued

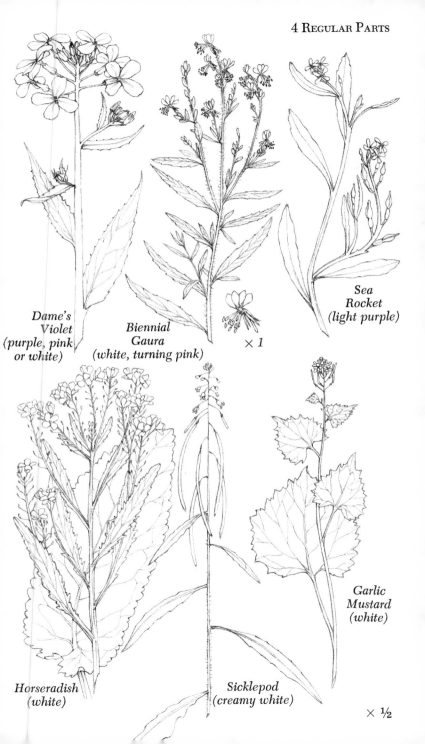

Dame's
Violet
(purple, pink
or white)

Biennial
Gaura
(white, turning pink)

× 1

Sea
Rocket
(light purple)

Horseradish
(white)

Sicklepod
(creamy white)

Garlic
Mustard
(white)

× ½

White, Pink or Purple Flowers in 1 or More Spikes or Racemes; Stem Leaves Not Arrow-shaped (cont.)

LOWEST LEAF ROUNDISH OR OBLONG, UNDER 1½" LONG; FOUND IN WET PLACES

Cresses (*Cardamine*) Slender plants of springy places with roundish, oblong or slightly heart-shaped, long-stalked, basal leaves. Spring and early summer. Mustard Family.

Purple Cress (*C. douglassii*) Rose-purple or pink flowers, ½–¾" wide. Stem usually hairy. 6–12" high. W. Mass. to Wis. south.

Spring Cress (*C. bulbosa*) White flowers, ½" wide; stem leaves oblong or lance-shaped, with a few teeth. Stem erect. 6–24" high. S. and w. N.Eng. to Minn. south.

Mountain Watercress (*C. rotundifolia*) Similar to Spring Cress, but stem leaves roundish or egg-shaped, wavy-toothed or entire. Creeping at base with erect branches. N.Y. and Ohio south.

White, Pink or Purple Flowers, Not in Spikes or Racemes

Willow Herbs (*Epilobium*) Petals notched or indented at the tip. Flowers in the upper axils; the base of the flower formed into a narrow, stalklike tube. For other species, see pp. 156 and 160. Summer and fall. Evening Primrose Family.

Purple-leaved Willow Herb (*E. coloratum*) Small white or pink flowers; leaves narrowly lance-shaped, with numerous, fine, sharp teeth, gray-green, sometimes purplish. Seed hairs brown. 1–3' high. Swamps and moist thickets.

Northern Willow Herb (*E. glandulosum*) Like the Purple-leaved Willow Herb, but leaves broader, not grayish, somewhat shining above, with fewer teeth. See p. 160.

Hairy Willow Herb (*E. hirsutum*) Rose-purple flowers, 1" wide; leaves usually opposite. See p. 160.

Roseroot (*Sedum rosea*) Purplish (pistillate) or yellowish (staminate) flowers, ¼" wide, in a branched, terminal cluster. Leaves fleshy, ½–1½" long, egg-shaped or oval, slightly toothed or entire. 4–12" high. Rocky coastal cliffs, Me. north, and very locally inland to Vt., N.Y., ne. Pa. and N.C. Spring and summer. Sedum Family.

Toothed White-topped Aster (*Sericocarpus asteroides*) White, asterlike flowers in a flat-topped cluster. See p. 210.

Tassel Rue or **False Bugbane** (*Trauvetteria carolinensis*) White flowers with conspicuous stamens; leaves lobed. See p. 420.

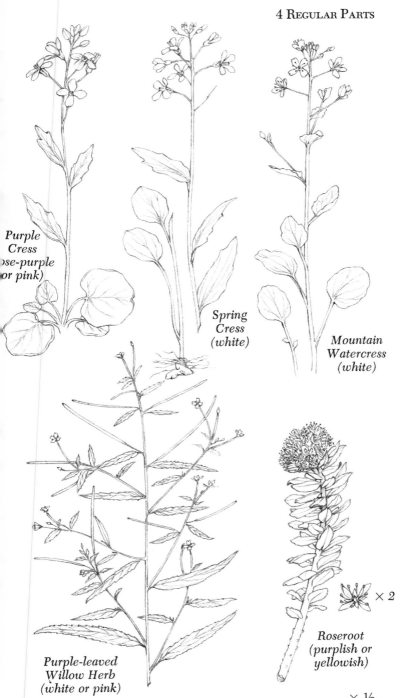

*Purple
Cress
(rose-purple
or pink)*

*Spring
Cress
(white)*

*Mountain
Watercress
(white)*

*Purple-leaved
Willow Herb
(white or pink)*

*Roseroot
(purplish or
yellowish)*

× 2

× ½

Yellow Flowers, ½″ or More Wide

STAMENS 10 OR MORE, CONSPICUOUS

Celandine (*Chelidonium majus*) * Flowers ½–¾″ wide, in small umbels. The leaves are divided into several irregularly lobed leaflets and are all alternate. Juice yellow. 1–2′ high. Damp soil or roadsides and waste places. Spring to fall. Poppy Family.

Horn Poppy or **Sea Poppy** (*Glaucium flavum*) * Flowers large (1–2″ wide); upper leaves wavy-toothed, clasping the stem. Lower leaves thick, deeply lobed, 3–8″ long. Juice yellow. Pods very long (6–10″) and slender, often curved. 2–3′ high. Gravelly beaches and waste places, local, s. N.Eng. to Mich. south. Summer. Poppy Family.

Celandine Poppy (*Stylophorum diphyllum*) Flowers large (1½–2″ wide); uppermost leaves opposite. See p. 162.

STAMENS 5 OR 6, NOT CONSPICUOUS

Wild Radish (*Raphanus raphanistrum*) * Stem more or less hairy; middle leaves deeply lobed; flowers ½–¾″ wide; petals pale yellow or white, with purple veins. The ripe pod is constricted between the seeds, somewhat like a pea pod. Fields and waste places. Spring to fall. Mustard Family.

Field Mustard or **Rape** (*Brassica rapa*) * Stem with whitish bloom; middle and upper leaves entire or toothed, and clasp the stem. Flowers about ½″ wide. 1–3′ high. Weed of cultivated ground. Spring to fall. Mustard Family.

Charlock (*Brassica kaber*) * Stem green, often hairy, at least near the base; middle and upper leaves toothed, neither lobed nor clasping; yellow flowers about ½″ wide. Lower leaves (when present) deeply lobed. 8–30″ high. Common weed of cultivated ground and waste places. Spring to fall. Mustard Family.

Indian Mustard (*Brassica juncea*) * Stem smooth, often with whitish bloom; uppermost leaves small, mostly entire, not clasping; yellow flowers about ½″ wide. Black Mustard (p. 144) has smaller flowers, a green stem with scattered hairs, and the pods are shorter and borne close to the stem. 1–4′ high. Fields and waste places. Summer and fall. Mustard Family.

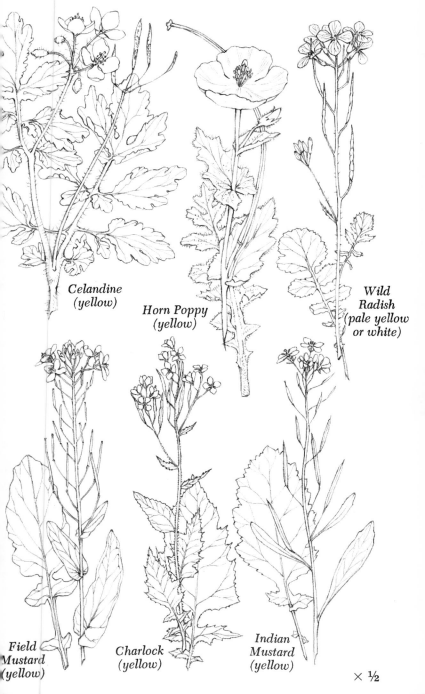

Celandine
(yellow)

Horn Poppy
(yellow)

Wild
Radish
(pale yellow
or white)

Field
Mustard
(yellow)

Charlock
(yellow)

Indian
Mustard
(yellow)

× ½

Yellow Flowers under ½" Wide

Mustard Family (Cruciferae) Flowers and pods forming racemes

1. TERMINAL LOBE OF BASAL LEAVES ROUNDED OR
   OVAL, NEARLY ENTIRE

Common Winter Cress or **Yellow Rocket** (*Barbarea vulgaris*) *
Basal leaves with 2–8 smaller lobes; upper leaves egg-shaped or
rounded, coarsely toothed, somewhat clasping. Pods narrow.
1–2′ high. Roadsides and meadows, common. Spring and
summer.

Early Winter Cress (*Barbarea verna*) * Like the Common
Winter Cress, but the basal leaves have 8–20 lobes and upper
leaves are pinnately lobed or divided. Spring.

2. TERMINAL LOBE OF BASAL OR LOWER LEAVES
   TOOTHED OR CUT

Black Mustard (*Brassica nigra*) * Upper leaves lance-shaped,
entire or toothed, not deeply lobed or divided; flowers about ⅓″
wide. Pods narrow and erect. Stem green, with scattered hairs.
Similar to Indian Mustard (p. 142). 1–7′ high. Common weed of
cultivated fields and waste places. Summer and fall.

Hedge Mustard (*Sisymbrium officinale*) * Most upper leaves
with 3 spreading lobes; flowers tiny (⅛″ wide); pods narrow and
stiffly erect. Stiffly branched, 1–3′ high. Waste places; common.
Spring to fall.

Marsh Yellow Cress (*Rorippa islandica*) Upper leaves toothed
or deeply cut; flowers very small (⅛–⅕″ wide); pods short and
plump, horizontally spreading. Petals no longer than the sepals.
1–4′ high. Wet shores and damp soil. Spring to fall.

Tumble Mustard (*Sisymbrium altissimum*) * Upper leaves divided into very narrow segments; pale-yellow flowers, ¼–⅓″
wide. Pods 2–4″ long, very narrow, stiff and spreading. The
lower leaves have numerous narrow divisions. Erect, branching plant, 2–4′ high. Fields and waste places. Late spring and
summer.

Creeping Yellow Cress (*Rorippa sylvestris*) * Upper leaves
deeply cut; bright-yellow flowers, ⅕–¼″ wide; pods narrow,
about ½″ long, spreading. Petals longer than sepals. Leaves
divided into lance-shaped or oblong, toothed segments. Plant
weakly erect or sprawling; creeps by underground stems. Wet
places, shores and roadsides. Late spring and summer.

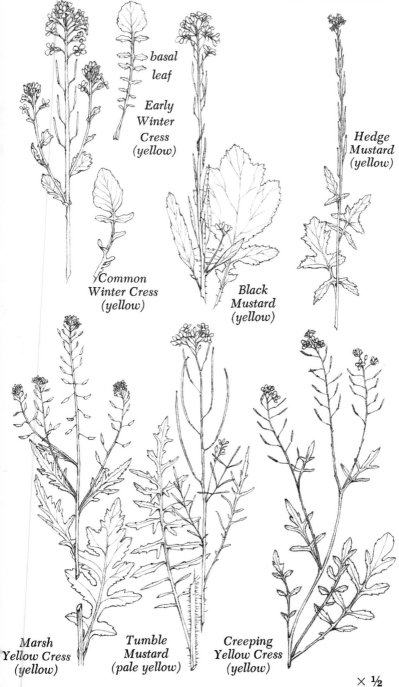

*basal
leaf*

**Early
Winter
Cress
*(yellow)***

**Hedge
Mustard
*(yellow)***

**Common
Winter Cress
*(yellow)***

**Black
Mustard
*(yellow)***

**Marsh
Yellow Cress
*(yellow)***

**Tumble
Mustard
*(pale yellow)***

**Creeping
Yellow Cress
*(yellow)***

$\times$ ½

White, Pink, Purplish or Greenish Flowers, with Numerous and Conspicuous Stamens

Canadian Burnet (*Sanguisorba canadensis*) Leaves pinnate, with 7–15 sharply toothed leaflets; white flowers in dense spikes. The flowers have a 4-lobed calyx, no petals, and long white stamens. 1–6′ high. Low meadows and bogs. Summer and fall. Rose Family.

Baneberries (*Actaea*) Leaves 2- to 3-times-pinnate, with many sharply toothed leaflets; white flowers in short racemes; woods. See p. 424.

Clammyweed (*Polanisia graveolens*) Leaves with 3 entire leaflets. Whitish flowers, ¼″ long, with purplish stamens; petals indented at the tip, narrowed at the base. The plant has a strong, unpleasant odor. 6–18″ high. Gravelly shores and banks, w. Que. to Man. south. Summer. Caper Family.

Meadow Rues (*Thalictrum*) Leaves 3-times-pinnate; leaflets short, with 2–9 blunt lobes. Flowers long-stalked, growing in large, branching clusters. Buttercup Family.

1. LEAFLETS WITH 5–9 LOBES

Early Meadow Rue (*T. dioicum*) Greenish flowers with drooping stamens and yellow anthers. Leaflets appear with the flowers in early spring. 6–24″ high. Rocky woods.

2. LEAFLETS WITH 2–3 LOBES; FLOWERS WHITE OR PURPLISH

Tall Meadow Rue (*T. polygamum*) Stamens club-shaped, white, not drooping. Leaves lighter green than the next two species. 3–8′ high. Common in sunny swamps and low meadows, Que. to Ont. south. Summer.

Waxy Meadow Rue (*T. revolutum*) Stamens slender and drooping; leaflets dark green, with waxy particles beneath, which give off a strong skunklike odor when touched. 2–6′ high. Rocky wooded slopes, or sometimes in meadows, Mass. to Ont. south. Late spring and early summer.

Purple Meadow Rue (*T. dasycarpum*) † Similar to the Waxy Meadow Rue, but leaves not waxy and without the odor. 3–6′ high. Low grounds and thickets, Ont. to Man. south. Early summer.

Queen-of-the-prairie (*Filipendula rubra*) Leaflets of lower leaves large, deeply lobed; flowers deep pink in branching clusters. See p. 234.

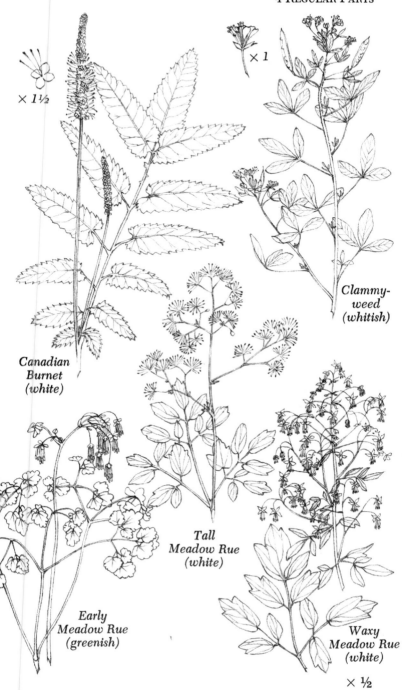

× 1½

× 1

Canadian
Burnet
(white)

Clammy-
weed
(whitish)

Early
Meadow Rue
(greenish)

Tall
Meadow Rue
(white)

Waxy
Meadow Rue
(white)

× ½

Flowers White, Pink or Purplish; Stamens 5 or 6, Inconspicuous

Yarrow or **Milfoil** (*Achillea millefolium*) Flowers in a flat-topped, branched cluster 1½–4″ wide; leaves finely dissected. See p. 220.

Mustard Family (Cruciferae) Flowers and pods forming racemes.

1. PLANTS OF WET PLACES

Cuckooflower or **Lady's Smock** (*Cardamine pratensis*) Erect plant with showy (½–¾″ wide) pink or white flowers. Leaves divided into 5–15 leaflets; the leaflets of the basal leaves are egg-shaped or roundish, the upper leaflets narrower. 6–20″ high. Wet meadows and swamps, occasionally on moist lawns. Spring.

Watercress (*Nasturtium officinale*) * Floating or creeping plant with small white flowers (about ¼″ wide); leaves divided into 3–9 nearly entire leaflets, the terminal leaflet largest and nearly round. The pungent leaves are used for salads. Springs and streams. Spring to fall.

Lake Cress (*Armoracia aquatica*) Aquatic, weak-stemmed plant with white flowers, ¼″ wide, and finely divided, underwater leaves. The upper leaves are toothed or entire. Lakes and slow streams, w. Que. and Vt. to Ont. south; rare and local in our area. Summer.

Pennsylvania Bitter Cress (*Cardamine pensylvanica*) Very small (⅛″ wide) white flowers; stem more or less erect, usually with a rosette of leaves at the base. Leaflets 3–15, the terminal leaflet wider than the others. Pods very narrow, mostly borne erect. 6–24″ high. Swamps and wet meadows; common. Spring and summer.

Continued

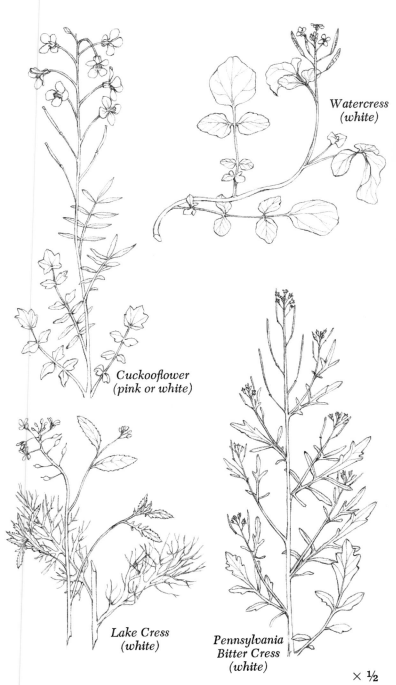

Watercress
(white)

Cuckooflower
(pink or white)

Lake Cress
(white)

Pennsylvania
Bitter Cress
(white)

$\times \frac{1}{2}$

Flowers White, Pink or Purplish; Stamens 5 or 6, Inconspicuous (cont.)

Mustard Family (Cruciferae) (cont.)

2. PLANTS OF WOODS, ROCKS AND WASTE PLACES

a. Stem leaves entire or toothed (not lobed or divided)

Shepherd's Purse (*Capsella bursa-pastoris*) * Stem leaves arrow-shaped, clasping the stem. Tiny white flowers. The distinctive pod is triangular, indented at the tip. Basal leaves deeply and irregularly lobed or divided. 6–20″ high. Very common weed of gardens and waste places. Early spring to late fall, sometimes in winter.

Wild Peppergrass (*Lepidium virginicum*) Stem leaves lance-shaped, toothed; tiny white flowers. Pods nearly round, slightly winged at the tip. The basal leaves (when present) have a broad terminal lobe with smaller lobes below. Common weed of roadsides and waste places. Spring to fall.

Lyre-leaved Rock Cress (*Arabis lyrata*) Upper leaves narrow, mostly entire; white flowers, ¼″ wide. The basal leaves are deeply lobed and grow in a rosette. Pods long and narrow. 4–12″ high. Rocky or sandy places, w. N.Eng. to Minn. south. Spring and summer.

b. Stem leaves deeply lobed or divided

Small-flowered Bitter Cress (*Cardamine parviflora*) Tiny white flowers. Small plant with leaves having 2–6 pairs of small leaflets and slender pods. 4–10″ high. Dry woods, ledges and sandy places. Spring and summer.

Large Toothwort (*Dentaria maxima*) White or pale-purple flowers, ½–¾″ wide; stem leaves 3 (rarely 2), each with 3 sharply toothed, egg-shaped leaflets. The rootstock is constricted into a series of joints. 4–12″ high. Moist or rich woods, local, s. Me. to Wis. south. Spring.

Toothwort or **Crinkleroot** (*Dentaria diphylla*) Similar to the Large Toothwort, but stem leaves normally 2, the leaflets with rounded teeth. Rootstock not constricted into joints. See p. 162.

Wild Radish (*Raphanus raphanistrum*) White or pale-yellow flowers, ½–¾″ wide, with purple veins; a weed of fields and waste places. See p. 142.

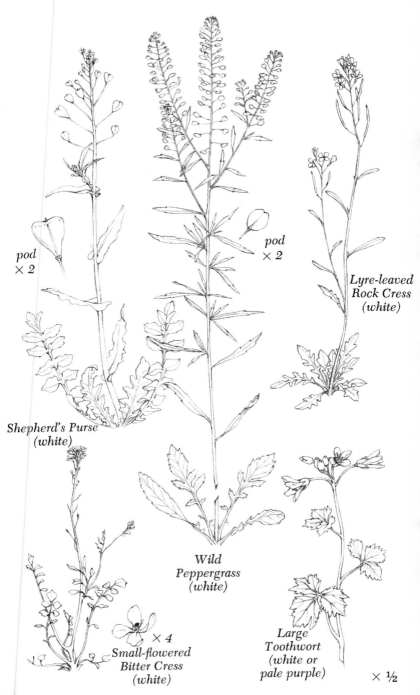

pod
× 2

pod
× 2

*Lyre-leaved
Rock Cress
(white)*

*Shepherd's Purse
(white)*

*Wild
Peppergrass
(white)*

× 4
*Small-flowered
Bitter Cress
(white)*

*Large
Toothwort
(white or
pale purple)*

× ½

Leaves in Whorls

Bunchberry or **Dwarf Cornel** (*Cornus canadensis*) Leaves usually 6, in a single whorl. "Flower" solitary, 1″ wide, consisting of 4 large, white, petal-like bracts surrounding a dense cluster of small greenish or yellowish flowers, each with 4 petals. Leaves broadly egg-shaped and pointed. Fruit a cluster of bright-red berries. 3–8″ high. Cool woods and bogs. Late spring and summer (mts.). Dogwood Family.

American Columbo or **Monument Plant** (*Swertia carolinensis*) Leaves in whorls of 4; flowers 1″ wide, greenish-yellow with purple dots, in a long cluster. Basal leaves large, up to 15″ long. 3–8′ high. Open woods and meadows, w. N.Y. to Wis. south. Spring and early summer. Gentian Family.

Bedstraws (*Galium*) Leaves in whorls of 4–8; flowers very small, in branching clusters. Stems square. A distinctive group of plants with over twenty species in our area. Two species have flowers with 3 parts (see p. 126). Madder Family.

1. WHITE FLOWERS (NOT GREENISH-WHITE)

a. Stems and leaves bearing hooked prickles

Cleavers (*G. aparine*) Leaves 1–3″ long; flowers 1–3 in a cluster, growing from the axils; fruit bristly. A sprawling, prickly plant of woods, thickets and shores. Late spring and early summer.

Rough Bedstraw (*G. asprellum*) Leaves ½–¾″ long; flowers numerous, in terminal clusters; fruit smooth. Weak-stemmed and reclining on other plants. Damp woods. Summer and fall.

b. Stems and leaves smooth or nearly so

Northern Bedstraw (*G. boreale*) Erect plant with leaves in whorls of 4. Leaves 1–2″ long. Flowers numerous, in dense terminal clusters. 1–3′ high. Rocky slopes and shores. Summer.

Marsh Bedstraw (*G. palustre*) Weak-stemmed plant of wet places, with leaves in whorls of 4–6. Leaves ½–¾″ long. Wet meadows and swamps, south to Pa., Mich. and Wis. Summer.

Shining Bedstraw (*G. concinnum*) † Similar to Marsh Bedstraw but grows in dry woods; leaves in whorls of 6. Leaves narrow, ½–¾″ long. N.J. to Minn. south. Summer.

Wild Madder (*G. mollugo*) * Plant of roadsides and fields; leaves on main stem in whorls of 7 or 8. Leaves ½–1½″ long. Erect or spreading. Flowers numerous in loose clusters. Late spring and summer.

Continued

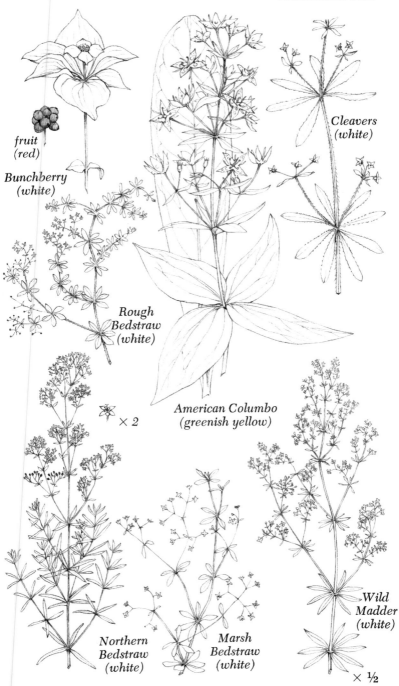

fruit
(red)

Bunchberry
(white)

Cleavers
(white)

Rough
Bedstraw
(white)

× 2

American Columbo
(greenish yellow)

Wild
Madder
(white)

Northern
Bedstraw
(white)

Marsh
Bedstraw
(white)

× ½

Leaves in Whorls (cont.)

Bedstraws (*Galium*) (cont.)

2. GREENISH-WHITE, GREEN OR PURPLE FLOWERS; FRUIT BRISTLY

a. Leaves in whorls of 6

Sweet-scented Bedstraw (*G. triflorum*) Greenish-white flowers.
Stems smooth and weak. Woods. Late spring and summer.

b. Leaves in whorls of 4

Wild Licorice (*G. circaezans*) Leaves broad with blunt tips,
3-veined. Green flowers. Woods. Summer.

Lance-leaved Wild Licorice (*G. lanceolatum*) Upper leaves tapering at the tip, 3-veined. Flowers usually purple. Dry woods.
Summer.

Hairy Bedstraw (*G. pilosum*) Leaves oval, usually hairy, ½–1″
long, with 1 main vein. Greenish-white to purple flowers, distinctly stalked. Dry woods and thickets, N.H. to Mich. south.
Summer.

3. YELLOW FLOWERS

Yellow Bedstraw (*G. verum*) * Leaves very narrow, in whorls of
6 or 8. Flowers in dense clusters. Stems stiff. 1–3′ high. Fields
and roadsides. Summer.

Wild Stonecrop (*Sedum ternatum*) Leaves mostly in whorls of 3;
white flowers, usually in a 3-branched cluster. See p. 272.

Leaves in Pairs; Yellow or Straw-colored Flowers

St. Peterswort and **St. Andrew's Cross** (*Ascyrum*) Yellow flowers,
½–1″ wide; dry sandy or rocky soil. Low, rather shrubby plants
with flattened stems. Two of the 4 sepals much larger than the
others. Summer. St. Johnswort Family.

St. Peterswort (*A. stans*) Leaves broadly oblong, partly clasping
the stem; petals egg-shaped. Styles 3 or 4. Erect; 1–2′ high.
Long Island, e. Pa. and Ky. south.

St. Andrew's Cross (*A. hypericoides*) Leaves narrowly oblong,
ʌnot clasping; petals narrowly oblong, forming an oblique cross.
Styles 2. Sprawling plant, 4–10″ high. Nantucket and N.J. to Ill.
south.

Golden Hedge Hyssop (*Gratiola aurea*) Yellow flowers, ½″ long;
grows in wet places. See p. 76.

Yellow Bartonia (*Bartonia virginica*) Yellowish or straw-colored
flowers, ⅛″ long, in a stiff cluster. See p. 126.

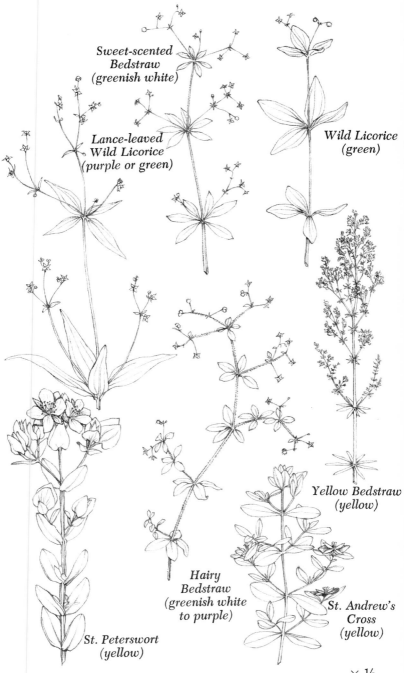

Sweet-scented
Bedstraw
(greenish white)

Lance-leaved
Wild Licorice
(purple or green)

Wild Licorice
(green)

Yellow Bedstraw
(yellow)

Hairy
Bedstraw
*(greenish white
to purple)*

St. Andrew's
Cross
(yellow)

St. Peterswort
(yellow)

× ½

Leaves in Pairs; Flowers Not Yellow or Straw-colored

PETALS OR FLOWER LOBES FRINGED OR INDENTED AT THE TIP

Fringed Gentians (*Gentiana*) Violet-blue flowers, 1–2½″ long, the flower lobes fringed or toothed. Gentian Family.

> **Fringed Gentian** (*G. crinita*) Upper leaves broadly lance-shaped or egg-shaped; tip of flower lobes fringed with long hairs. 1–3′ high. Moist meadows and low woods, c. Me. to Pa., south in mts. to Ga., west to Iowa and Man. Fall.

> **Smaller Fringed Gentian** (*G. procera*) Upper leaves narrow; flower lobes toothed at tip, fringed along sides. 6–20″ high. Wet places, w. N.Y. and O. to Ia. north. Late summer and fall.

Willow Herbs (*Epilobium*) Pink or whitish flowers, about ¼″ wide, the petals notched at the tip. Flowers in the upper axils. Leaves narrow or narrowly lance-shaped, with incurved edges, sometimes alternate. For other species, see pp. 140 and 160. 6–36″ high. Bogs and swamps. Summer and early fall. Evening Primrose Family.

> **Downy Willow Herb** (*E. strictum*) † Stem and leaves downy with whitish or grayish, spreading hairs. Leaves mostly wider than in the next species.

> **Narrow-leaved Willow Herb** (*E. leptophyllum*) Hairs of stem and leaves are short and turned inward.

PETALS OR FLOWER LOBES NOT FRINGED OR INDENTED

Partridgeberry (*Mitchella repens*) White or pinkish flowers, ½″ long, in pairs at the ends of the branches. A trailing plant with roundish, shining, evergreen leaves, ½–1″ long, often veined with white. Fruit a scarlet, edible berry. Woods. Late spring and early summer. Madder Family.

Bluets (*Houstonia*) Pale-blue or white flowers, with a yellow center, ⅓–½″ wide. Leaves ½″ or less long, mostly at the base of the plant, but with several pairs of very small stem leaves. Slender plants, 2–8″ high. Madder Family.

> **Bluets, Quaker Ladies** or **Innocence** (*H. caerulea*) Leaves elliptical; stem not creeping at the base. Grassy meadows, fields and open woods. Spring to fall.

> **Creeping Bluets** (*H. serpyllifolia*) Leaves nearly round; stem creeping at the base with erect flowering stems. Flowers usually deeper blue than those of the Bluets. Mts. of Pa. south. Spring and early summer.

Continued

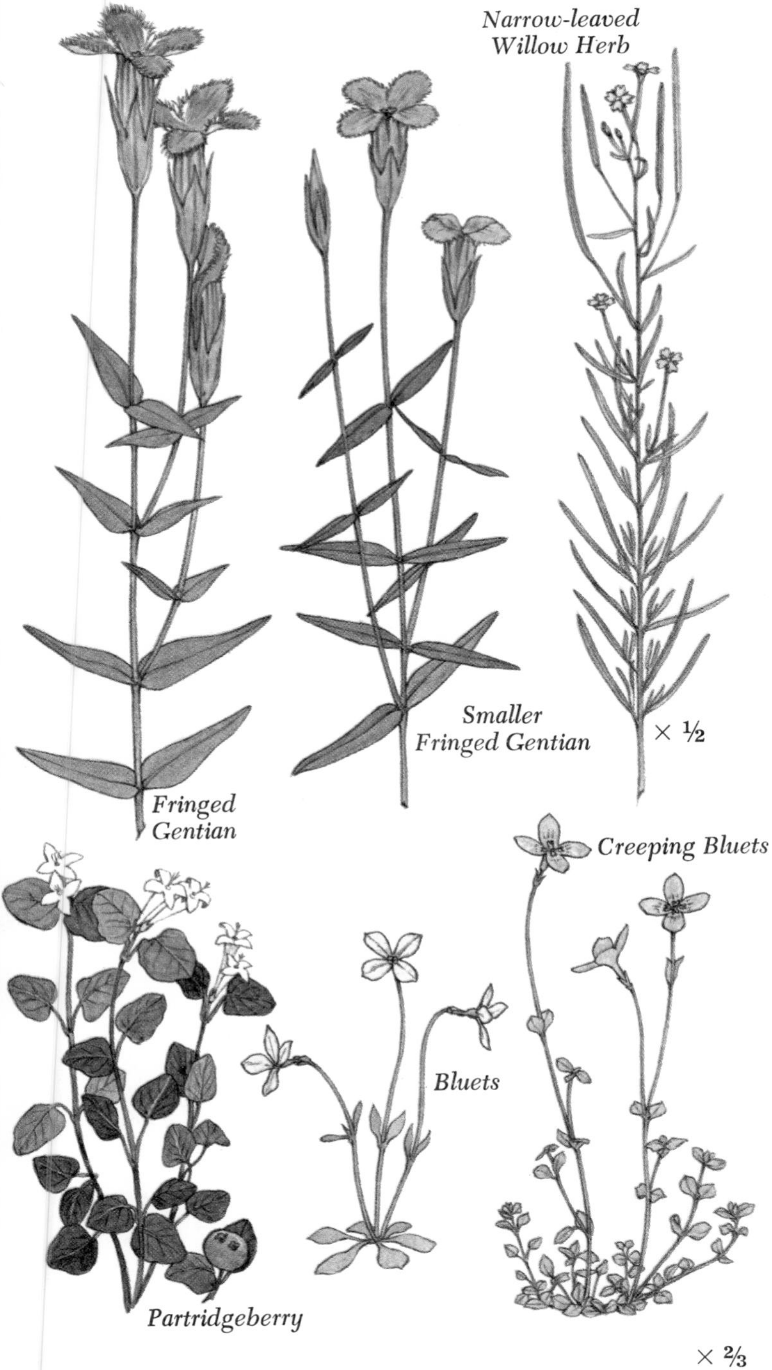

Narrow-leaved
Willow Herb

Smaller
Fringed Gentian

$\times$ 1/2

Fringed
Gentian

Creeping Bluets

Bluets

Partridgeberry

$\times$ 2/3

Leaves in Pairs; Flowers Not Yellow or Straw-colored (cont.)

PETALS OR FLOWER LOBES NOT FRINGED OR INDENTED
(CONT.)

Houstonias (*Houstonia*) White or pale-lilac flowers, ¼″ long, funnel-shaped with four flaring lobes, at the ends of the branches. Leaves ½–2″ long, some of them usually in a basal rosette. 4–18″ high. Dry woods or rocky banks. Spring to fall. Madder Family.

Narrow-leaved Houstonia (*H. tenuifolia*) Stem leaves very narrow. Plant widely branched. Dry woods and slopes, Pa. and W.Va. to Mo. south.

Large Houstonia (*H. purpurea*) Stem leaves egg-shaped or broadly lance-shaped, with 3–5 veins. Open woods and slopes. s. Pa. to Iowa south.

Long-leaved Houstonia (*H. longifolia*) Stem leaves lance-shaped or oblong, 1-veined; basal leaves smooth. Dry open woods and hillsides.

Fringed Houstonia (*H. canadensis*) † Similar to the Long-leaved Houstonia, but the edges of the basal leaves have small hairs. Rocky banks and shores, w. N.Y. to Minn. south.

Pennywort (*Obolaria virginica*) Dull-white or purplish flowers, ½″ long, usually in 3's in the axils of purplish, wedge-shaped bracts. A fleshy plant, 3–6″ high, with scalelike lower leaves. Rich woods, N.J. to Ill. south. Spring. Gentian Family.

Buttonweed (*Diodia teres*) Small (¼″ long), white or pale-purple, funnel-shaped flowers in the axils of the narrow leaves. Leaves stiff, with bristles at their base. 4–30″ long. Dry sandy soil, R.I. to Mich. and Wis. south. Summer and fall. Madder Family.

Water Purslane (*Ludwigia palustris*) Very small, green flowers stalkless in the axils. Leaves egg-shaped or oval, ½–1″ long. Plant of wet places, floating in water or rooted in the mud. Summer and fall. Evening Primrose Family.

Spurred Gentian (*Halenia deflexa*) Purplish or greenish flowers, ⅓–½″ long, with 4 downward-pointing spurs. Flowers in a terminal cluster or in the upper axils. Leaves egg- or lance-shaped, 1–2″ long, in widely spaced pairs. 6–30″ high. Moist woods, n. and w. N.Eng., N.Y., s. Ont., Ill., Minn. north. Summer. Gentian Family.

Speedwells (*Veronica*) White or blue, 4-lobed flowers, ¼″ wide, the lower lobe smaller than the others. See p. 74.

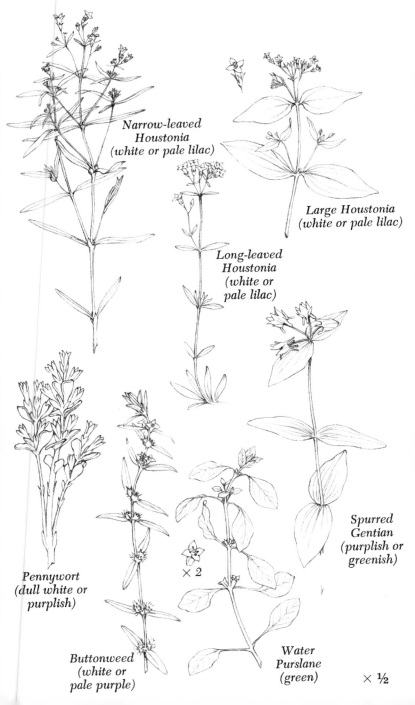

Narrow-leaved
Houstonia
(white or pale lilac)

Large Houstonia
(white or pale lilac)

Long-leaved
Houstonia
*(white or
pale lilac)*

Spurred
Gentian
*(purplish or
greenish)*

Pennywort
*(dull white or
purplish)*

× 2

Buttonweed
*(white or
pale purple)*

Water
Purslane
(green)

× ½

Flowers with 4 Separate Petals or Flower Rays

Meadow Beauties (*Rhexia*) Purple flowers, 1″ wide, with 8 conspicuous yellow stamens. Leaves 1–2″ long, toothed, with 3 main veins. 6–24″ high. Low meadows and sandy swamps. Summer. Meadow Beauty Family.

> **Meadow Beauty** or **Deergrass** (*R. virginica*) Leaves egg-shaped or oval, rounded at the base; stem square. Bright-purple flowers.

> **Maryland Meadow Beauty** (*R. mariana*) Leaves lance-shaped, narrowed to a short stalk; stem roundish. Pale-purple flowers. North to Cape Cod, e. Pa., Va., s. Ind., s. Ill.

Willow Herbs (*Epilobium*) Petals notched or indented in the center. Flowers in the upper axils. For other species, see pp. 140, 156. Summer and fall. Evening Primrose Family.

1. FLOWERS ¼″ OR LESS WIDE

> **Northern Willow Herb** (*E. glandulosum*) Leaves green, somewhat shining above, shallowly toothed and broadly lance-shaped. Lower leaves usually opposite. Pink to lilac flowers. Seed hairs whitish. 1–3′ high.

> **Purple-leaved Willow Herb** (*E. coloratum*) Leaves gray-green, sometimes purplish, narrowly lance-shaped, with numerous teeth. See p. 140.

2. ROSE-PURPLE FLOWERS, 1″ WIDE

> **Hairy Willow Herb** (*E. hirsutum*) * Leaves lance-shaped, sharply toothed, sometimes alternate. Stem stout, hairy, branched. 2–6′ high. Damp thickets, waste places.

Galinsoga or **Quickweed** (*Galinsoga ciliata*) Flowers with 3-toothed rays and a yellow central disk. See p. 284.

Enchanter's Nightshades (*Circaea*) Small, white flowers, in short racemes; leaves egg-shaped, long-stalked. See p. 116.

Flowers 4-lobed, the Parts Obviously Joined

Teasel (*Dipsacus sylvestris*) * Stem prickly. Lilac flowers, small and slightly irregular, in a large, thistlelike head. Leaves lance-shaped or oblong. 2–6′ high. Fields and roadsides. Summer and fall. Teasel Family.

Culver's Root (*Veronicastrum virginicum*) Leaves in whorls of 3–7. White, tubular flowers in spikes. Leaves lance-shaped, sharply toothed. 2–7′ high. Woods and meadows, c. N.Eng. to Man. south. Summer. Figwort Family.

Continued

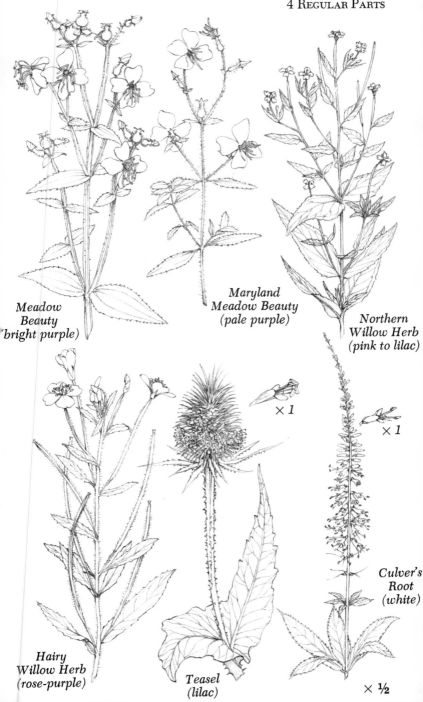

Meadow
Beauty
(bright purple)

Maryland
Meadow Beauty
(pale purple)

Northern
Willow Herb
(pink to lilac)

× 1

× 1

Culver's
Root
(white)

Hairy
Willow Herb
(rose-purple)

Teasel
(lilac)

× ½

Flowers 4-lobed, the Parts Obviously Joined (cont.)

Golden Saxifrage or **Water Carpet** (*Chrysosplenium americanum*)
Tiny, greenish or yellowish flowers; grows in wet places. Flowers
at the ends of the branches. Leaves roundish, under 1″ long, obscurely toothed. Creeping plant, forming a mat in springy places.
Spring. Saxifrage Family.

Mint Family (Labiatae) Flowers in dense whorls or spikes; stem
square. See p. 90.

Speedwells (*Veronica*) White or blue flowers; the lower flower
lobe smaller than the others. See p. 96.

Spotted Spurges (*Euphorbia*) Juice milky; green, reddish or whitish flowers. See p. 432.

WILDFLOWERS WITH OPPOSITE LEAVES /
Leaves Divided

Celandine Poppy (*Stylophorum diphyllum*) Deep-yellow flowers,
1½–2″ wide, solitary or in a small cluster at the top of the stem. The
leaves are deeply lobed and divided, usually with a pair of stem
leaves and 1 or more basal leaves. Juice yellow. 1–1½′ high. Open
woods, w. Pa. to Wis. south. Spring. Poppy Family.

Toothworts (*Dentaria*) White or pink flowers, ½–1″ wide, in a
small terminal cluster. Stem leaves 2 or 3, divided into 3 coarsely
toothed or lobed leaflets, attached near the center of the stem. The
roots have a peppery taste. Large Toothwort (*D. maxima*) (p. 150)
has alternate leaves, generally with 3 egg-shaped leaflets. 8–15″
high. Rich woods. Spring. Mustard Family.

> **Toothwort** or **Crinkleroot** (*D. diphylla*) Stem leaves normally 2,
> the leaflets egg-shaped. Basal leaves similar.

> **Cut-leaved Toothwort** or **Pepperroot** (*D. laciniata*) Stem leaves
> 3, the leaflets lance-shaped, deeply toothed or lobed; no basal
> leaves at flowering time; upper stem downy.

> **Slender Toothwort** (*D. heterophylla*) Stem leaves generally 2,
> the 3 leaflets narrow, entire or toothed, noticeably different from
> the egg-shaped leaflets of the basal leaves. N.J. to Ohio south.

> **Fine-leaved Toothwort** (*D. multifida*) † Stem leaves 2 or 3, di-
> vided into 3–7 very narrow segments; basal leaves (if present)
> similar; upper stem smooth. S. Ohio and s. Ind. south.

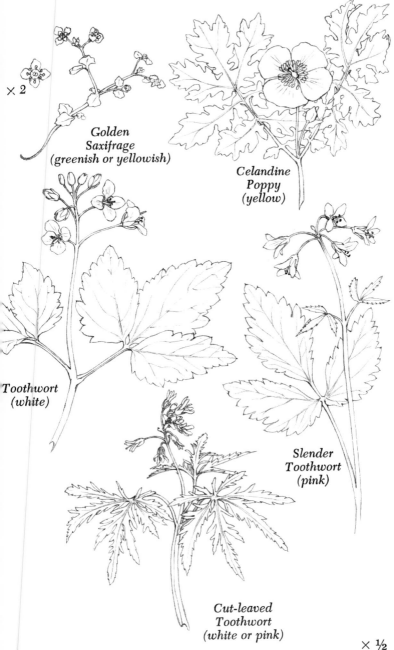

× 2

*Golden
Saxifrage
(greenish or yellowish)*

*Celandine
Poppy
(yellow)*

*Toothwort
(white)*

*Slender
Toothwort
(pink)*

*Cut-leaved
Toothwort
(white or pink)*

× ½

Shrubs under 2′ High

Bog or **Alpine Bilberry** (*Vaccinium uliginosum*) Low and branching, with thick, dull-green leaves, which are pale and finely veined beneath. The white or pinkish flowers are bell-shaped, and grow in the axils. Fruit blue or black, with a bloom, and edible. 6–24″ high. Can. south to barrens and shores of n. Mich. and n. Minn., and mt. summits of n. N.Eng. and N.Y. Summer. Heath Family.

Heather or **Ling** (*Calluna vulgaris*) * Tiny, needlelike leaves, ⅛″ long. Pink (sometimes white) flowers, ⅛″ long, in one-sided spikes. Low, evergreen shrub, 6–24″ high (rarely higher). Sandy or peaty soil; local. Summer to fall. Heath Family.

Mountain Cranberry (*Vaccinium vitis-idaea*) Low, creeping shrub with shining, oval, evergreen leaves; pink, bell-shaped flowers. See p. 128.

St. Peterswort and **St. Andrew's Cross** (*Ascyrum*) Yellow flowers, ½–1″ wide. See p. 154.

Shrubs over 2′ High; Flowers Bell-shaped or Tubular

Buttonbush (*Cephalanthus occidentalis*) Shrub of wet places with flowers in round, ball-like heads. The white, tubular flowers are about ⅓″ long and each has a long, protruding style. Leaves egg-shaped, 3–6″ long, opposite or whorled. 3–10′ high. Summer. Madder Family.

Privet (*Ligustrum vulgare*) * Small white flowers in dense panicles. Flowers tubular with flaring lobes, about ¼″ wide. Leaves lance-shaped or oblong and opposite, 1–2″ long. 6–20′ high. Escaped from cultivation to thickets and roadsides. Late spring and early summer. Olive Family.

Snowberry and **Indian Currant** (*Symphoricarpos*) Pink, greenish or purplish flowers in small terminal or axillary clusters, and broad, oval or roundish leaves. See p. 296.

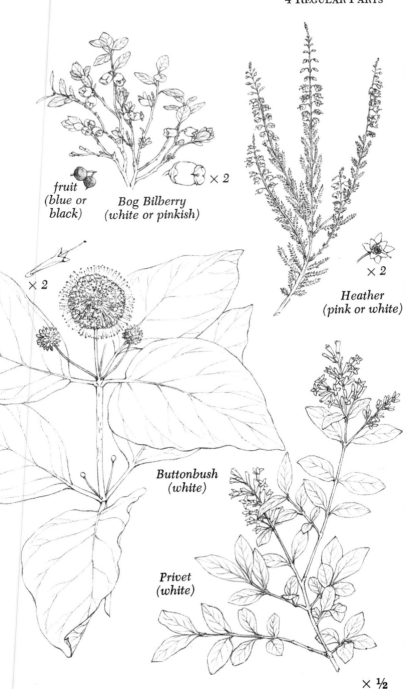

fruit
(blue or
black)

Bog Bilberry
(white or pinkish)

× 2

× 2

Heather
(pink or white)

Buttonbush
(white)

Privet
(white)

× ½

Shrubs over 2′ High; Flowers with 4 Petals

Flowering Dogwood (*Cornus florida*) Showy white flowers (actually bracts), 2–4″ wide. The true flowers are greenish-white and clustered in the center of the 4 petal-like bracts, which are notched at the tip. Leaves opposite and egg-shaped or oval. Large woodland shrub or tree, 7–40′ high. Woods, c. N.Eng. to Ill. south. Spring. Dogwood Family.

Dogwoods (*Cornus*) Small white flowers in broad, branching clusters. A group of large shrubs, best distinguished by the color of their fruit and young branches. Spring and early summer. Dogwood Family.

1. LEAVES OBVIOUSLY GROWING IN PAIRS

a. Flower cluster nearly as high as wide and not flat-topped

Panicled or **Gray Dogwood** (*C. racemosa*) Branches gray. Leaves pale beneath. The fruits are white with red stalks. Roadsides and thickets.

b. Flower cluster flat or slightly rounded

Round-leaved Dogwood (*C. rugosa*) Branches green, purple-spotted; largest leaves broadly egg-shaped or roundish, about 1½ times longer than wide, with 7–8 pairs of veins. Fruit light blue. Rich or rocky woodlands.

Silky Dogwood (*C. amomum*) Stalks of the flower cluster silky-hairy; leaves rounded at the base, with 3–6 pairs of veins, and abruptly short-pointed; pith of young stems brown. Fruit bluish. Wet or moist places.

Pale Dogwood (*C. obliqua*) † Same as the Silky Dogwood, except that the leaves taper at both ends and are pale beneath.

Red-osier Dogwood (*C. stolonifera*) Stalks of the flower cluster smooth or slightly hairy; leaves with 5–7 pairs of veins, pale beneath; pith of young stems white. Young branches usually bright red. Fruit white or lead-colored. Wet places and shores.

2. LEAVES ALTERNATE OR CLUSTERED AT THE ENDS OF THE BRANCHES

Alternate-leaved Dogwood (*C. alternifolia*) Branches greenish; fruit bluish-black. A shrub or small tree with nearly horizontal branches. Woods and borders.

Continued

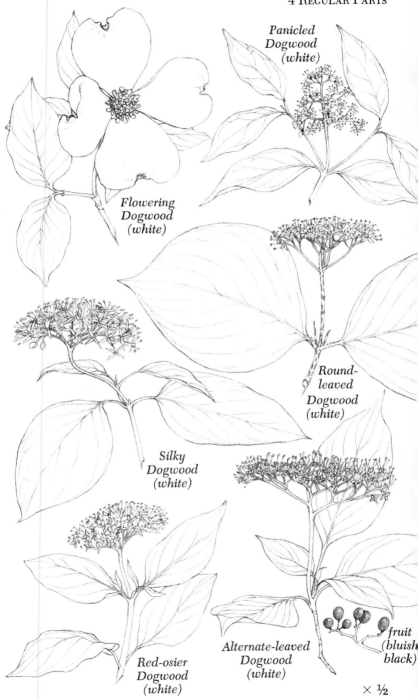

*Panicled
Dogwood
(white)*

*Flowering
Dogwood
(white)*

*Round-
leaved
Dogwood
(white)*

*Silky
Dogwood
(white)*

*Red-osier
Dogwood
(white)*

*Alternate-leaved
Dogwood
(white)*

*fruit
(bluish
black)*

× ½

Shrubs over 2' High; Flowers with 4 Petals (cont.)

Fringe Tree (*Chionanthus virginicus*) White flowers with long, narrow petals, in drooping clusters. Leaves oval or oblong. Fruit dark purple, oblong, ½″ long. Moist woods, N.J. to s. Ohio south. Spring. Olive Family.

Mountain Holly (*Nemopanthus mucronata*) Small, greenish-white or yellowish flowers in the axils. Flowers inconspicuous, long-stalked, with 4 or 5 narrow petals. Leaves elliptical. Fruit red, long-stalked. Cool swamps and bogs. Spring. Holly Family.

SHRUBS /
Leaves Toothed or Lobed

Witch Hazel (*Hamamelis virginiana*) Flowers with narrow, yellow petals; blooms in late fall. Leaves 2–5″ long, egg-shaped or oval, wavy-toothed. The flowers grow in small clusters in the axils. 5–15′ high. Woods. Witch Hazel Family.

Mountain Winterberry or **Large-leaved Holly** (*Ilex montana*) Small white flowers growing singly or in small clusters in the axils. Leaves egg-shaped or broadly lance-shaped, sharply toothed, rather long-pointed. Petals 4 or 5. The commoner Winterberry (*I. verticillata*) has 6–8 petals (p. 396). Fruit red. Upland woods, w. N.Eng. and N.Y. south. Late spring and early summer. Holly Family.

Common Buckthorn (*Rhamnus cathartica*) * Very small, greenish flowers in axillary clusters. Many of the branches are spiny-tipped. Leaves elliptical or egg-shaped, 1½–2½″ long, bluntly toothed. Fruit black. 6–20′ high. Originally cultivated as a hedge, the shrub has now spread to woods and borders. Spring. Buckthorn Family.

Burning Bush or **Wahoo** (*Euonymus atropurpureus*) Purple flowers in axillary clusters. Flowers ¼–⅓″ wide. Leaves oblong or elliptical, pointed, and finely toothed. Fruit a purplish-red, 4-lobed capsule with scarlet seeds. 6–25′ high. Rich woods and thickets, N.Y. and Ont. to Mont. south; escaped from cultivation elsewhere. Late spring and early summer. Staff Tree Family.

Wild Hydrangea (*Hydrangea arborescens*) White flowers in broad clusters at the ends of the branches. See p. 302.

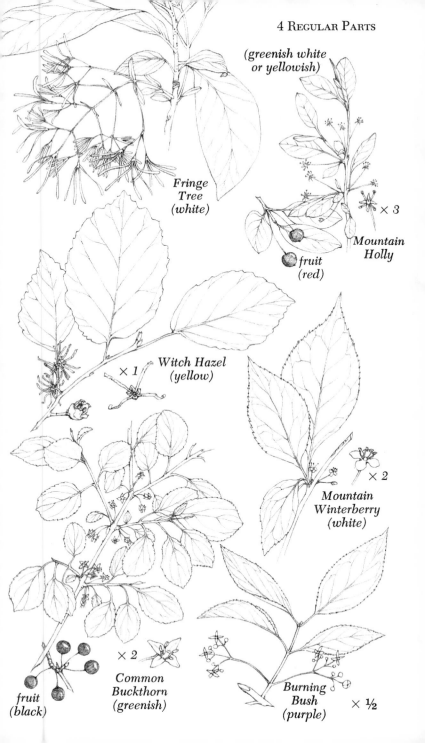

4 REGULAR PARTS

(greenish white
or yellowish)

Fringe
Tree
(white)

Mountain
Holly

fruit
(red)

× 3

Witch Hazel
(yellow)

× 1

Mountain
Winterberry
(white)

× 2

Common
Buckthorn
(greenish)

× 2

fruit
(black)

Burning
Bush
(purple)

× ½

SHRUBS /
Leaves Divided

Hop Tree or **Wafer Ash** (*Ptelea trifoliata*) Leaflets 3. Small, greenish-white flowers in branching clusters. The leaflets are egg-shaped, entire or obscurely toothed. The round, winged fruits are about ¾″ in diameter. 5–15′ high. Woods and thickets, sw. Que. and N.Y. to Neb. south; escaped from cultivation in N.Eng. Late spring and early summer. Rue Family.

Northern Prickly Ash or **Toothache Tree** (*Xanthoxylum americanum*) Leaflets 5–11, entire; stems prickly. Very small, greenish flowers in axillary clusters, appearing before the leaves are fully developed. Fruit brownish, containing a shining black seed. The bark and fruits are aromatic. 4–25′ high. Rocky woods and thickets, w. Que. and w. N.Eng. to N.D. south. Spring. Rue Family.

VINES /
Leaves Divided

Virgin's Bowers (*Clematis*) Vines with 3–7 leaflets and white, purple or blue flowers. Flowers with 4 colored sepals and small or no petals. The plants climb by twisting their leaf stalks around the supporting vegetation. The distinctive fruit is a cluster of feathery hairs called Old Man's Beard. Buttercup Family.

Virgin's Bower (*C. virginiana*) White flowers in a cluster. The 3 leaflets are coarsely toothed. Moist thickets. Summer and fall.

Leatherflower (*C. viorna*) Purple, bell-shaped flowers with very thick sepals recurved at the tip. Flowers grow singly. Leaflets 3–7, entire or occasionally lobed or divided. Rich woods, Pa. to Ill. south. Spring and summer.

Purple Virgin's Bower (*C. verticillaris*) Dull-purple or purplish-blue flowers, solitary in the axils, with the 4 colored sepals thin and nearly translucent. Leaflets 3, slightly toothed or entire. Rocky woods and slopes, south to Del., Ohio, Mich., and Wis., and in mts. to N.C. Spring.

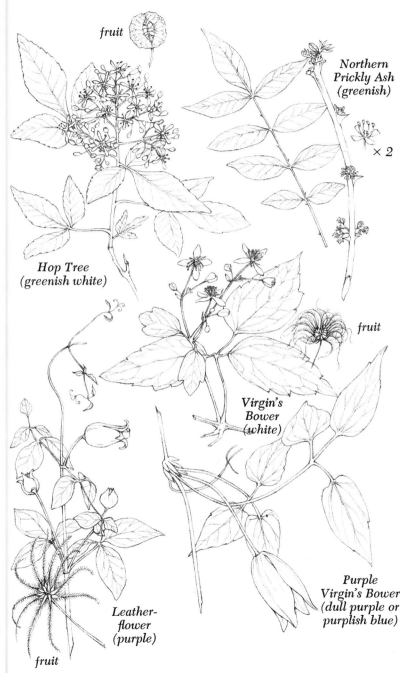

fruit

Northern Prickly Ash (greenish)

× 2

Hop Tree (greenish white)

fruit

Virgin's Bower (white)

Leather-flower (purple)

fruit

Purple Virgin's Bower (dull purple or purplish blue)

× ½

FLOWER SOLITARY

Indian Pipe or **Corpse Plant** (*Monotropa uniflora*) White, waxy plant of woodlands; stem scaly. Occasional plants are pinkish. The flower is at first nodding, but turns upright in fruit. Saprophyte. 4–10″ high. Summer. Pyrola Family.

One-flowered Cancerroot or **Ghost Pipe** (*Orobanche uniflora*) Pale-lavender or whitish flower, ¾–1″ long, shaped like a curved tube with a flaring end of 5 nearly regular lobes. A parasitic plant of woods and thickets. 3–10″ high. Spring. Broomrape Family.

FLOWERS SEVERAL TO MANY

Pinesap or **False Beechdrops** (*Monotropa hypopithys*) Tan, yellow or red, fleshy plant with ½″ nodding flowers. There are 3–10 flowers in the cluster. 4–12″ high. Saprophyte of pine or oak woods. Summer. Pyrola Family.

Orange Grass or **Pineweed** (*Hypericum gentianoides*) Very small, yellow flowers at the ends of the branches. The tiny, scalelike leaves grow in pairs. Stem wiry. 3–10″ high. Barren soil. Summer and fall. St. Johnswort Family.

Sand Jointweed (*Polygonella articulata*) Tiny pink or white flowers in racemes. The wiry stem is jointed and bears small threadlike leaves. Sandy soil, sw. Me. south to N.C., and inland along the Great Lakes to Minn. and Iowa. Late summer and fall. Buckwheat Family.

Giant Bird's Nest or **Pinedrops** (*Pterospora andromedea*) Small, white or reddish, bell-shaped flowers in a long raceme. Stem stout, purplish-brown, with scales at the base, and covered with sticky hairs. 1–4′ high. Dry, mostly pine, woods, Can. south to Vt., N.Y., Mich. west; very rare and local in our area. Summer. Pyrola Family.

Harbinger-of-spring (*Erigenia bulbosa*) Small white flowers in umbels; blooms in early spring. See p. 224.

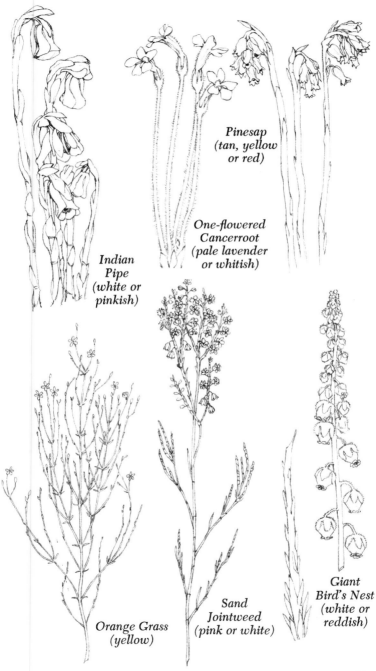

Indian Pipe
(white or pinkish)

Pinesap
(tan, yellow or red)

One-flowered Cancerroot
(pale lavender or whitish)

Orange Grass
(yellow)

Sand Jointweed
(pink or white)

Giant Bird's Nest
(white or reddish)

× ⅔

Flower Stalk Bearing More Than 1 Flower

Sundews (*Drosera*) Small, insectivorous plants of bogs and wet sand, with leaves covered with reddish hairs. The glandular hairs on the leaves exude dewlike drops of a sticky fluid that entraps insects. Flowers in one-sided racemes (raceme occasionally forked), opening only in sunshine. Summer. Sundew Family.

Round-leaved Sundew (*D. rotundifolia*) Leaves round, long-stalked. White (rarely pink or red) flowers.

Spatulate-leaved Sundew (*D. intermedia*) Leaves spoon-shaped, 2 or 3 times as long as wide. White flowers.

Thread-leaved Sundew (*D. filiformis*) Leaves very long (4–12″) and narrow. Purple flowers. Along the coast, from s. Mass. south.

Shooting Star (*Dodecatheon meadia*) Nodding pink, lilac or white flowers in an umbel, the flower lobes bent backwards like a "shooting star." Stamens form a cone in the center of the flower. Leaves lance-shaped. 6–20″ high. Open woods and meadows, D.C. and w. Pa. to Wis. south. The smaller *D. amethystinum* has deep red-purple flowers, and is found locally on shaded cliffs and streambanks in e. Pa., Ky., and the Miss. Valley. Spring. Primrose Family.

Sea Lavender or **Marsh Rosemary** (*Limonium nashii*) Plant of salt marshes with very small purple or lavender flowers in a much-branched cluster. The leaves are lance-shaped, tapering at the base, with a prominent midrib. Calyx somewhat hairy. *L. carolinianum* from s. N.Y. south has a smooth calyx. 6–24″ high. Summer and fall. Leadwort Family.

Fameflower (*Talinum teretifolium*) Small (½″ wide), deep-pink flowers in a branched cluster. The fleshy, slender, cylindrical leaves are 1–2″ long in a basal rosette. The flowers open around noon for a few hours. 4–12″ high. Dry rocks, se. Pa. to W.Va. south. Summer. Purslane Family.

Pyrolas (*Pyrola*) Nodding flowers in a raceme; flowers with a prominent style. See p. 178.

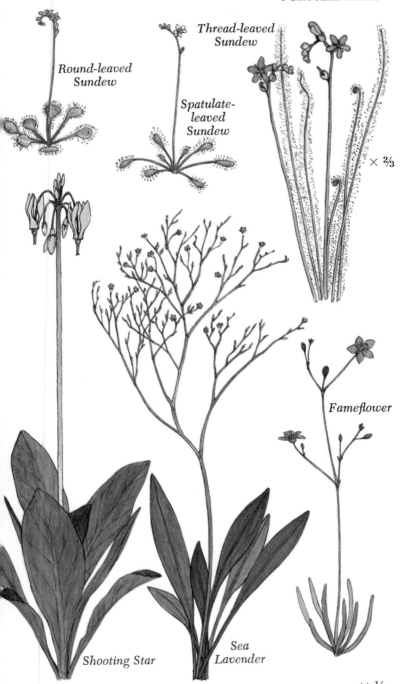

Round-leaved
Sundew

Thread-leaved
Sundew

Spatulate-
leaved
Sundew

× ⅔

Fameflower

Shooting Star

Sea
Lavender

× ½

Each Flower Stalk Bearing a Single Flower

Floating Heart (*Nymphoides cordata*) Aquatic plant with white flowers ¼–½" wide. Leaves heart-shaped and long-stalked, floating, and bear near the surface a small cluster of tubers from which the flowers grow. Ponds, Nfld. to Ont., south along the coastal plain. Summer and early fall. Gentian Family.

Yellow Pond Lilies (*Nuphar*) Aquatic plants with yellow flowers and heart-shaped leaves. The flowers have 5 or 6 large yellow sepals and numerous small petals, resembling stamens. Ponds and slow streams. Spring to fall. Water Lily Family.

> **Spatterdock, Yellow Pond Lily** or **Cow Lily** (*N. variegatum*) Flowers 1½–3" wide; leaves 4–12" long, most of them floating on the surface. The V-shaped notch between the lobes of the leaf is narrow and the leaf stalk is slightly flattened. South to Del., Ohio, n. Ill. and Mont.

> **Southern Pond Lily** (*N. advena*) † Flowers 1½–3" wide; most of the leaves held above the water. Leaves have a wide notch and a round leaf stalk. S. Me. to Wis. south; more common southward.

> **Small Yellow Pond Lily** (*N. microphyllum*) A species smaller than the two preceding, with flowers ½–1" wide and leaves 2–4" long. South to N.J., Pa., Mich. and Wis.

Diapensia (*Diapensia lapponica*) Low plant of alpine summits, forming dense cushions. White flower about ½" wide. The leaves are ¼–½" long and grow in a tight rosette. High mts. of N.Eng. and N.Y. north. Summer. Diapensia Family.

Creeping Spearwort (*Ranunculus reptans*) Low, creeping plant of wet shores with small yellow flowers (⅓" wide). Petals 4–7. Leaves usually very narrow, 1–2" long, sometimes lance-shaped. South to N.J., Pa., Mich. and Wis. Summer. Buttercup Family.

Mudwort (*Limosella subulata*) Small plant with tiny white flowers that grows in tidal mud. The leaves are very narrow and are longer than the flower stalks. Creeps and forms mats. Along the coast. Summer and fall. Figwort Family.

Grass-of-Parnassus (*Parnassia glauca*) White flowers, ¾–1½" wide, the petals veined with green; bogs and wet meadows. See p. 198.

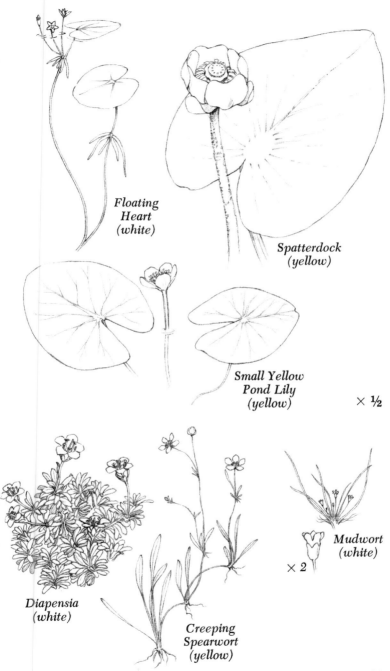

Floating
Heart
(white)

Spatterdock
(yellow)

Small Yellow
Pond Lily
(yellow)

× ½

Diapensia
(white)

Creeping
Spearwort
(yellow)

Mudwort
(white)

× 2

× ⅔

Flowers in a Raceme or Spike

Foamflower or **False Miterwort** (*Tiarella cordifolia*) Numerous white flowers with conspicuous stamens. The leaves are deeply heart-shaped at the base and have 5–7 shallow lobes. 6–12″ high. Rich woods. Spring. Saxifrage Family.

Naked Miterwort (*Mitella nuda*) Flowers few, greenish, with fringed petals. Leaves roundly heart-shaped, bluntly toothed. 3–8″ high. Cold northern woods. Spring and summer. Saxifrage Family.

Pyrolas or **Shinleafs** (*Pyrola*) Nodding flowers with a prominent style. Leaves obscurely toothed. Dry or moist woods. Summer. Pyrola Family.

1. FLOWERS IN A ONE-SIDED CLUSTER; STYLE PROTRUDING

One-sided Pyrola (*P. secunda*) White or greenish flowers on one side of the flowering stem. 3–8″ high.

2. FLOWER CLUSTER NOT ONE-SIDED; STYLE PROTRUDING

a. White or greenish flowers

Round-leaved Pyrola (*P. rotundifolia*) Leaves shining, leathery, nearly round, 1–3″ long, the stalk no longer than the blade. White flowers. 4–12″ high.

Greenish-flowered Pyrola (*P. virens*) Leaves thick and nearly round, not shining, ½–1½″ long, the stalk generally longer than the blade. Green or greenish-white flowers. 4–10″ high.

Shinleaf (*P. elliptica*) Leaves not shining, 1–3″ long, thinner than in the two preceding species, and longer than wide. Leaf blade usually longer than its stalk. White flowers. 4–12″ high.

b. Pink or purple flowers

Pink Pyrola or **Bog Wintergreen** (*P. asarifolia*) Leaves round and leathery, often shining and slightly heart-shaped at the base. Rich woods and swamps, south to n. and w. N.Eng., N.Y., n. Ind., Minn. west.

3. FLOWER CLUSTER NOT ONE-SIDED; STYLE NOT PROTRUDING

Lesser Pyrola (*P. minor*) Style short and straight, not protruding beyond petals. Northern species with white or pinkish flowers and dull, roundish leaves. 2–8″ high. Cool woods, south to n. N.Eng., n. Mich. west.

Galax or **Beetleweed** (*Galax aphylla*) Small white flowers in a dense spike; leaves evergreen, shining, roundly heart-shaped. 8–24″ high. Woods, Va. and W.Va. south. Late spring and early summer. Diapensia Family.

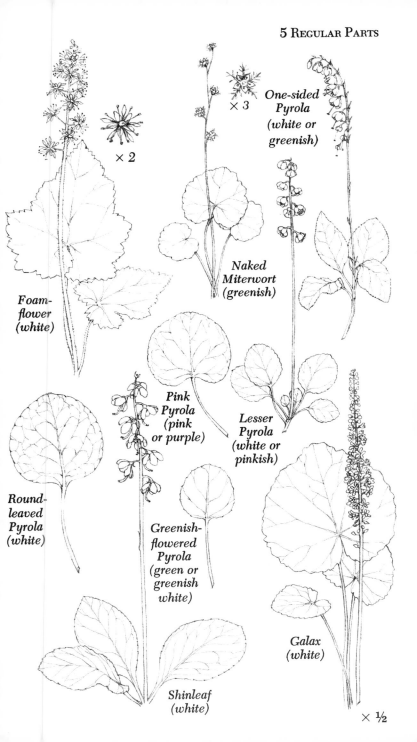

One-sided Pyrola (white or greenish)

× 3

Naked Miterwort (greenish)

Foam-flower (white)

× 2

Pink Pyrola (pink or purple)

Lesser Pyrola (white or pinkish)

Round-leaved Pyrola (white)

Greenish-flowered Pyrola (green or greenish white)

Galax (white)

Shinleaf (white)

× ½

Flowers in an Umbel or Branched Cluster

FLOWERS IN AN UMBEL

Primroses (*Primula*) Pink, light-purple or sometimes white flowers, usually with a yellow eye, the flower lobes notched at the tip. The lance-shaped, slightly toothed leaves grow in a rosette. Rocky banks and shores. Spring and summer. Primrose Family.

>   **Bird's-eye Primrose** (*P. laurentiana*) Plant stoutish, 4–18″ high; leaves usually mealy on the underside; calyx ¼–⅜″ long. C. Me. north.

>   **Dwarf Canadian Primrose** (*P. mistassinica*) † Similar to Bird's-eye Primrose but plant more slender, 1–8″ high, with leaves green on both sides; calyx ⅛–¼″ long. N. N.Eng., c. N.Y., n. Ill. to Iowa north.

Umbellate Water Pennywort (*Hydrocotyle umbellata*) Greenish-white flowers, very small and numerous. Leaves round, with scalloped edges, the leaf stalk attached to the center of the leaf. Wet places. Summer and fall. Parsley Family.

FLOWERS IN A BRANCHED CLUSTER

Alumroot (*Heuchera americana*) Leaves long-stalked, roundly heart-shaped with blunt teeth and 5–9 shallow lobes, often with dark veins. Flowers ¼″ long, green or purplish with protruding stamens. Occasionally there are 1 or 2 stem leaves. 1–3′ high. Woods and rocks, Conn. to s. Ont. and Mich. south. Late spring and summer. Saxifrage Family.

Saxifrages (*Saxifraga*) Leaves egg-shaped, oblong or lance-shaped. White, greenish or purple flowers in a terminal cluster. Spring or early summer. Saxifrage Family.

>   **Early Saxifrage** (*S. virginiensis*) Leaves egg-shaped, ½–3″ long; white flowers. 4–12″ high. Rocks and shaded banks. Spring.

>   **Swamp Saxifrage** (*S. pensylvanica*) Leaves lance-shaped, 4–8″ long, slightly toothed; green or greenish-white (rarely purple) flowers. Flowering stalk stout and somewhat hairy. 1–4′ high. Swamps. Spring.

>   **Lettuce Saxifrage** (*S. micranthidifolia*) Leaves lance-shaped, 4–12″ long, coarsely toothed; white flowers. 1–3′ high. Brooks and wet banks, Pa. south along the mts. Spring and early summer.

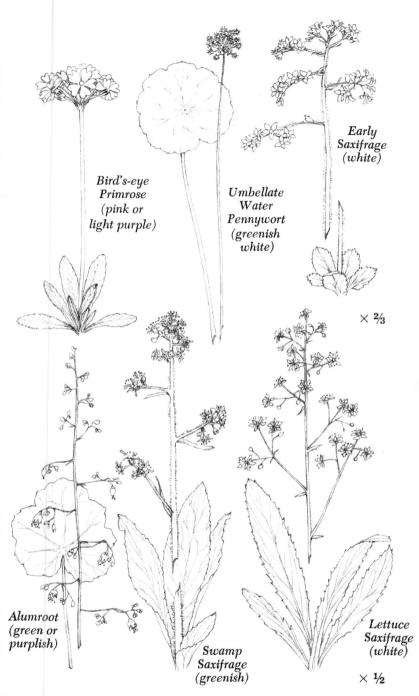

Bird's-eye Primrose (pink or light purple)

Umbellate Water Pennywort (greenish white)

Early Saxifrage (white)

× 2/3

Alumroot (green or purplish)

Swamp Saxifrage (greenish)

Lettuce Saxifrage (white)

× 1/2

Flowers Growing Singly or 2 or 3 in a Cluster

Dalibarda or **Dewdrop** (*Dalibarda repens*) White, erect flowers with numerous stamens. Leaves heart-shaped, dark green. Flowers ½″ wide, barely taller than the leaves. Stem creeping. Rich woods, south to N.C., Ohio and Mich. Summer. Rose Family.

One-flowered Pyrola (*Moneses uniflora*) White or light-rose, nodding flower, ½–¾″ wide, with a prominently protruding style. The leaves are roundish, 1″ long, finely toothed and evergreen, in a basal rosette. 2–6″ high. Cool woods. Summer. Pyrola Family.

Pitcher Plant (*Sarracenia purpurea*) A curious insectivorous plant with large (2″ wide), nodding, dark-red flowers and pitcher-shaped, hollow leaves which hold water and entrap insects. Leaves 4–10″ long, usually purple-veined, lined on the inside with downward-pointing hairs. 1–2′ high. Peat bogs. Late spring and summer. Pitcher Plant Family.

Violets (*Viola*) Lower petal with violet veins. See pp. 28–32.

Seaside Crowfoot (*Ranunculus cymbalaria*) Yellow flowers; sandy shores and salt marshes. See p. 364.

WILDFLOWERS WITH BASAL LEAVES ONLY /
Leaves Divided

Leaflets More Than 3

Silverweed (*Potentilla anserina*) Leaves with 7 or more sharply toothed, pinnate leaflets that are silvery beneath. Flowers yellow, ¾–1″ wide, with 5 (occasionally more) petals. Spreads by runners. Shores and salt marshes, Long I., Ind. to Iowa north. Summer. Rose Family.

Dwarf Cinquefoil (*Potentilla canadensis*) Low plant with 5 palmate leaflets. Yellow flowers ¼–¾″ wide. Distinguished from Common Cinquefoil (p. 240) by its leaflets, which are toothed only above the middle. Spreads by runners. Dry soil, w. N.S. to sw. Ont. south. Spring. Rose Family.

Wild Sarsaparilla (*Aralia nudicaulis*) Leaf umbrellalike over the flowers and divided into 3 groups of 5 leaflets. Flowers greenish-white, borne in 3 umbels (usually) at the top of a naked stalk. Berries purplish-black. 6–15″ high. Woods; very common. Late spring and early summer. Ginseng Family.

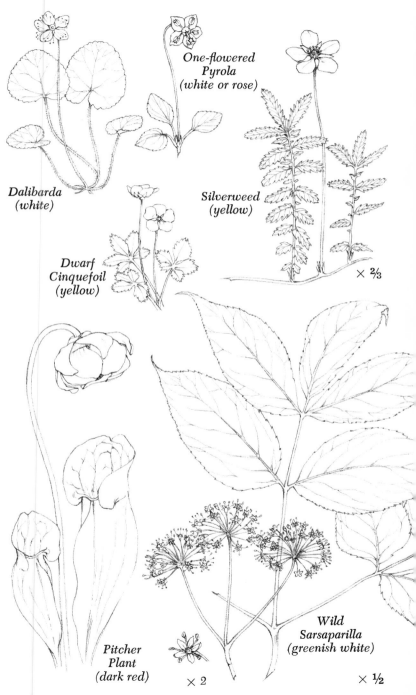

One-flowered
Pyrola
(white or rose)

Dalibarda
(white)

Silverweed
(yellow)

Dwarf
Cinquefoil
(yellow)

× ⅔

Pitcher
Plant
(dark red)

× 2

Wild
Sarsaparilla
(greenish white)

× ½

Leaflets 3

LEAFLETS TOOTHED

Goldthread (*Coptis groenlandica*) White flowers growing singly; evergreen, shining leaves. The flowers are ½″ wide, with 5–7 petal-like sepals. The common name is derived from the golden rootstocks. Moist woods and bogs. Spring. Buttercup Family.

Wild Strawberries (*Fragaria*) White flowers in a small cluster (occasionally 1-flowered); leaves not evergreen. The egg-shaped leaflets are coarsely toothed. Spreads by runners. Spring and early summer. Rose Family.

> **Wild Strawberry** (*F. virginiana*) Flowers ½–1″ wide; flower cluster (or fruit) usually no taller than the leaves; fruit red, roundish and juicy, with the seeds deeply imbedded in the surface. Fields.

> **Wood Strawberry** (*F. vesca*) Flowers about ½″ wide; flower cluster (or fruit) often overtopping the leaves and the flower stalks of unequal length; fruit cone-shaped, with the seeds on the surface. Open woods and rocky pastures.

Barren Strawberry (*Waldsteinia fragarioides*) Yellow flowers in a small cluster. The wedge-shaped leaflets resemble those of the Wild Strawberry. Fruit dry and inedible. Woods. Spring. Rose Family.

LEAFLETS ENTIRE OR NOTCHED AT THE TIP

Buckbean (*Menyanthes trifoliata* Bog plant with white flowers in a raceme. The inside of the flower is bearded with white hairs. Leaflets oval, entire. Spring and early summer. Gentian Family.

Wood Sorrels (*Oxalis*) Leaflets notched at the tip. Flowers solitary or in umbels. Wood Sorrel Family.

> **Common Wood Sorrel** (*O. montana*) White flowers veined with pink, solitary, ¾″ wide. 2–6″ high. Cool woods, south to c. N.Eng., Pa., Ohio, Mich. and Wis., and in the mts. to N.C.

> **Violet Wood Sorrel** (*O. violacea*) Purple flowers, ½″ wide, growing in an umbel. 4–8″ high. Open woods, Mass. to Minn. south. Spring and early summer.

> **Creeping Wood Sorrel** (*O. corniculata*) Yellow flowers. See p. 246.

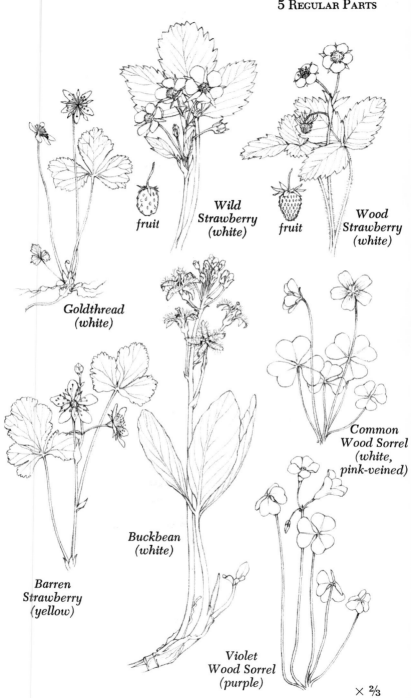

fruit

*Wild
Strawberry
(white)*

fruit

*Wood
Strawberry
(white)*

*Goldthread
(white)*

*Common
Wood Sorrel
(white,
pink-veined)*

*Barren
Strawberry
(yellow)*

*Buckbean
(white)*

*Violet
Wood Sorrel
(purple)*

× ⅔

Yellow or Orange Flowers; Largest Leaves under 2″ Long

Frostweed or **Rockrose** (*Helianthemum canadense*) Large flowers
(¾–1½″ wide) with wedge-shaped petals. The leaves are lance-shaped or oblong, ½–1½″ long. Flowers yellow, open only in sunlight and last one day. The plant later has numerous small flowers
without petals. 6–24″ high. Dry sandy soil. Late spring and early
summer. Rockrose Family.

Wild Yellow Flax (*Linum virginianum*) Slender, erect plant with
spreading branches and small (¼″ wide) yellow flowers. The leaves
are oblong or lance-shaped, ½–1″ long. 6–30″ high. Open woods
and clearings, s. N.Eng. to Ont. south. Summer. Flax Family.

Mossy Stonecrop or **Wallpepper** (*Sedum acre*) * Matted, fleshy-leaved plant with erect branches, 1–3″ high. Flowers yellow, ⅓″
wide, with 4 or 5 pointed petals. Leaves tiny, overlapping, thick
and fleshy. Escaped from cultivation to rocks and dry banks. Summer. Sedum Family.

Purslane or **Pusley** (*Portulaca oleracea*) * Prostrate, fleshy weed of
gardens and waste places, with leaves scattered along the stem and
clustered at the ends of the branches. The small (¼″ wide) yellow
flowers grow singly in the leaf clusters and open only a few hours
in the morning sun. Petals usually 5, but sometimes 4 or 6.
Leaves under 1″ long, blunt at the tip. Summer. Purslane Family.

Hoary Puccoon (*Lithospermum canescens*) Erect plant with or-ange-yellow, tubular flowers with 5 flaring lobes, about ½″ wide,
at the top of the stem. The fine-hairy stem and leaves are grayish.
6–18″ high. Dry open woods and prairies, s. Pa. and s. Ont. to Sask.
south. Spring. Borage Family.

Hudsonias (*Hudsonia*) Low, heathlike plants with crowded, scale-like or needlelike leaves. See p. 266.

Creeping Spearwort (*Ranunculus reptans*) Low, creeping plant of
wet shores. See p. 176.

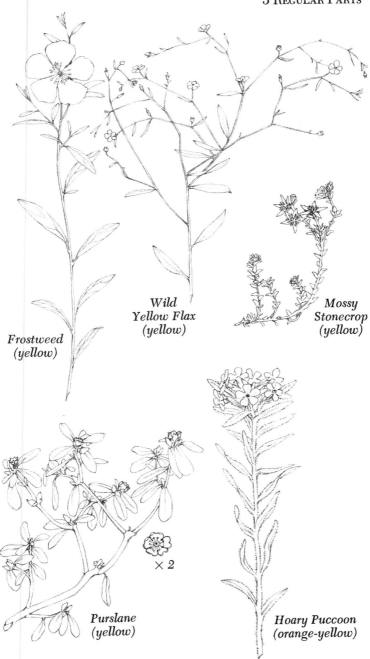

Frostweed
(yellow)

Wild
Yellow Flax
(yellow)

Mossy
Stonecrop
(yellow)

Purslane
(yellow)

× 2

Hoary Puccoon
(orange-yellow)

× ⅔

Yellow or Orange Flowers; Largest Leaves over 2" Long

Butterfly Weed or **Pleurisy Root** (*Asclepias tuberosa*) Showy, orange flowers in umbels. Leaves lance-shaped or narrow, 2–5" long. Stems hairy. 1–2' high. Our only milkweed with alternate leaves and colorless juice. Dry fields and banks, c. N.Eng. to Minn. south. Summer. Milkweed Family.

Common Mullein (*Verbascum thapsus*) * Coarse, woolly plant with a dense spike of yellow flowers. Flowers ¾–1" wide, slightly irregular. Noted for its large (4–12" long), soft-velvety, oblong leaves, the largest ones in a basal rosette. Leaves sometimes slightly toothed. 2–8' high. Fields and roadsides; very common. Summer and fall. Figwort Family.

Common Comfrey (*Symphytum officinale*) * Coarse, hairy plant with tubular flowers in one-sided racemes; flowers ½–¾" long, the flower lobes curving backward at the tip. The flowers vary in color and may be yellowish, whitish or purplish. Leaves lance-shaped or egg-shaped, 3–8" long. 2–3' high. Waste places. Summer. Borage Family.

False Gromwell (*Onosmodium virginianum*) Slender, hairy-stemmed plant with tubular flowers in a one-sided spike; flowers ⅓" long, the tips of the flower tube not recurved. Flowers yellow or orange. Leaves oblong or lance-shaped, 1–3½" long. 1–2½' high. Dry sandy soil, Mass. and N.Y. south. Summer. Borage Family.

Indian Mallow or **Velvetleaf** (*Abutilon theophrasti*) Heart-shaped, long-stalked velvety leaves. See p. 204.

Ground Cherries (*Physalis*) Nodding, greenish-yellow flowers with a dark center. See p. 204.

Goldenrods (*Solidago*) Numerous, small yellow flowers. See pp. 446–453.

Jointed-stemmed Plants with Arrow-shaped Leaves

Buckwheat (*Fagopyrum sagittatum*) * Erect plant with small, white flowers in branched clusters. The leaves are broadly arrow-shaped or triangular. 1–3' high. Commonly cultivated as a crop; escaped to fields and waste places. Summer and fall. Buckwheat Family.

Arrow-leaved Tearthumb (*Polygonum sagittatum*) Prickly, weak-stemmed plant with small clusters of white or pink flowers; leaves narrowly arrow-shaped. See p. 402.

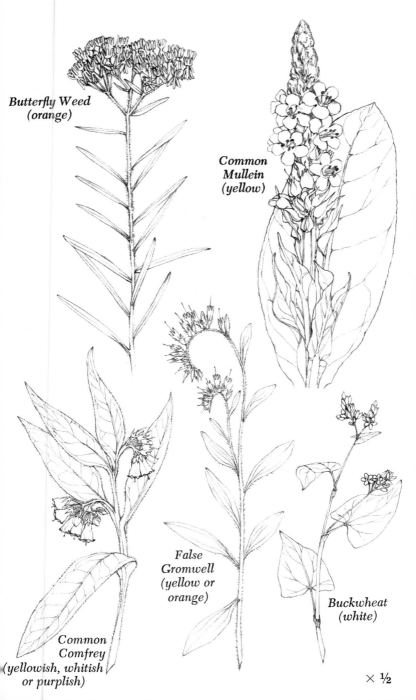

*Butterfly Weed
(orange)*

*Common
Mullein
(yellow)*

*False
Gromwell
(yellow or
orange)*

*Buckwheat
(white)*

*Common
Comfrey
(yellowish, whitish
or purplish)*

× ½

Jointed-stemmed Plants; Leaves Not Arrow-shaped
(Knotweeds and Smartweeds)

Sand Jointweed (*Polygonella articulata*) Plant with very narrow, threadlike leaves and wiry stems. See p. 172.

Knotweeds or **Smartweeds** (*Polygonum*) Leaves not threadlike. A large group of often weedy plants with very small flowers of 5 petal-like sepals, growing in spikes or spikelike racemes or in the axils. The stems are jointed and the stem immediately above each joint is surrounded by a membrane called a sheath. Of the 35 or so species in our area, the following are the most readily recognized. Summer and fall. Buckwheat Family.

1. FLOWERS IN NODDING SPIKES

a. Stem smooth

Nodding, Pale or **Dock-leaved Smartweed** (*P. lapathifolium*) Spikes dense, ¼–⅓" wide; flowers usually pink, but sometimes whitish or purplish. Sheaths mostly without fringe. 1–6' high. Damp soil.

Common Smartweed or **Water Pepper** (*P. hydropiper*) Spikes rather loose and often interrupted; greenish flowers; sheaths short-fringed. See p. 132.

b. Stem hairy

Carey's Knotweed (*P. careyi*) Leaves lance-shaped and short-stalked. Flowers purple, reddish or greenish, in rather loose-flowered spikes. Stem covered with bristly hairs. 1–3' high. Swamps or a weed in cleared ground.

Prince's Feather (*P. orientale*) * Leaves egg-shaped or heart-shaped at the base, long-stalked. Spikes rose-colored, dense. Stem soft-hairy. 1–8' high. Escaped from gardens.

2. FLOWERS IN ERECT SPIKES

a. Spikes loose and more or less interrupted

Mild Water Pepper (*P. hydropiperoides*) Plant weakly erect, 6–36" long. Pink or purplish, sometimes white or greenish, flowers. Shallow streams or wet places.

Japanese Knotweed (*P. cuspidatum*) * Large, bushy plant, 4–10' high, with broad, short-pointed leaves. The greenish-white flowers grow in branching spikes, mostly from the axils. Escaped from cultivation to waste places and roadsides.

Continued

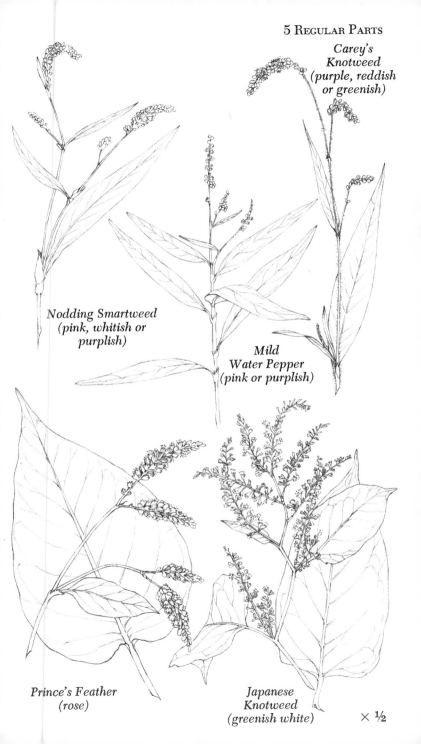

*Carey's
Knotweed
(purple, reddish
or greenish)*

*Nodding Smartweed
(pink, whitish or
purplish)*

*Mild
Water Pepper
(pink or purplish)*

*Prince's Feather
(rose)*

*Japanese
Knotweed
(greenish white)*

× ½

Jointed-stemmed Plants; Leaves Not Arrow-shaped (Knotweeds and Smartweeds) (cont.)

Knotweeds or **Smartweeds** (*Polygonum*) (cont.)

2. FLOWERS IN ERECT SPIKES (CONT.)

b. Spikes dense

Water Smartweed (*P. amphibium*) Plant of ponds and wet soil; spikes blunt, about 1″ long by ½″ wide. Flowers rose-colored. Leaves variable; those of aquatic forms are blunt or short-pointed; those of terrestrial forms, more slender and pointed.

Swamp Smartweed (*P. coccineum*) Plant of swamps and wet shores; spikes 1 or 2, slender, 1½–6″ long, 4 or more times longer than wide. Leaves like those of the Water Smartweed. Rose-colored flowers. 1–3′ high.

Lady's Thumb (*P. persicaria*) * Weed of gardens and waste places; leaves usually with a dark blotch in the center; tops of the sheaths fringed with hairs. Pink or purple flowers. 6–24″ high. Very common.

Pink Knotweed or **Pinkweed** (*P. pensylvanicum*) Weed of moist soil, damp shores and gardens; spikes thick, usually more than 2; sheaths without fringe; leaves lance-shaped, long-pointed, tapering at the base. Pink or rose-colored flowers. Upper part of stem bears numerous, short, glandular hairs. 8–36″ high.

Alpine Bistort (*P. viviparum*) Arctic plant found south to n. Mich. and Minn. and on alpine summits of n. N.Eng. Pale-pink or white flowers, the lower flowers replaced by red bulblets. Basal leaves long-stalked, lance-shaped or oblong. 2–10″ high.

3. FLOWERS GROWING SINGLY OR IN SMALL CLUSTERS
   IN THE AXILS

Doorweed or **Common Knotgrass** (*P. aviculare*) * Leaves blue-green. Flowers green with white or pink margins. Sheaths silvery; leaves narrow to broad, ½–1″ long. Usually prostrate, but may also grow half or fully erect. Common weed of dooryards and waste places.

Erect Knotweed (*P. erectum*) Leaves yellow-green. Flowers yellowish green. Leaves elliptical, ½–2½″ long. Erect or partly erect. 8–30″ high. Open ground and waste places.

Sea Knotweed (*P. glaucum*) Stem and leaves whitish. Leaves fleshy, narrowly oblong, ½–1″ long. Flowers pink. Prostrate plant of seashores, Mass. south.

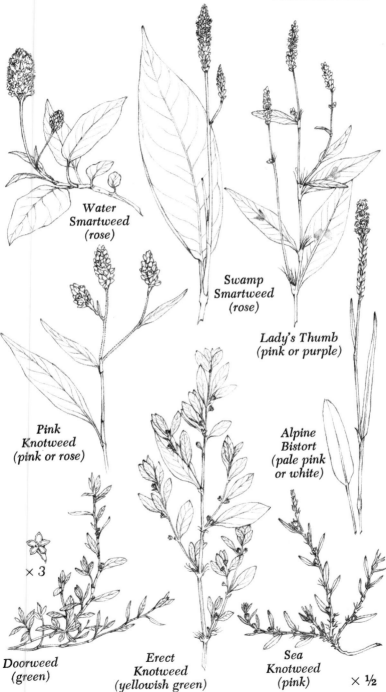

Water
Smartweed
(rose)

Swamp
Smartweed
(rose)

Lady's Thumb
(pink or purple)

Pink
Knotweed
(pink or rose)

Alpine
Bistort
(pale pink
or white)

× 3

Doorweed
(green)

Erect
Knotweed
(yellowish green)

Sea
Knotweed
(pink)

× ½

Blue, Violet or Purple Flowers; Stems Not Jointed

*STEM DOWNY OR HAIRY; FLOWERS IN MORE OR LESS
ONE-SIDED RACEMES OR SPIKES*

Forget-me-nots (*Myosotis*) Blue flowers with a yellow eye; found
in wet places. Leaves oblong or lance-shaped, 1–3″ long. Stems
downy, sprawling or weakly erect, 6–20″ long. Springs and muddy
shores. Late spring to fall. Borage Family.

    True Forget-me-not (*M. scorpioides*) * Flowers ¼–⅜″ wide. The
calyx lobes are only a quarter to a third the length of the calyx.

    Smaller Forget-me-not (*M. laxa*) Flowers ⅛–¼″ wide. Calyx
lobes one half the length of the calyx.

Hound's Tongues (*Cynoglossum*) Reddish-purple or blue flowers,
⅓″ wide; basal leaves large, stalked. Leaves oblong or broadly
lance-shaped. The fruit is composed of 4 bristly nutlets that cling
to clothing. 1½–3′ high. Borage Family.

    Hound's Tongue (*C. officinale*) * Reddish-purple (rarely white)
flowers. Leafy-stemmed, soft-hairy, mousy-smelling weed of
pastures and waste places. Spring and summer.

    Wild Comfrey (*C. virginianum*) Blue or pale-lilac flowers. The
upper stem leaves are few, and have a heart-shaped, clasping
base. Stem covered with bristly hairs. Open woods, s. Conn. to
Ill. south. Spring.

Small Bugloss (*Lycopsis arvensis*) * Stem and leaves covered with
bristly hairs; flowers small (¼″ wide), blue, in leafy-bracted clusters. The flower tube is bent at the base. Leaves lance-shaped,
entire or wavy-toothed, 1–3″ long. 1–2′ high. Dry fields and waste
places; local, except e. Can. Summer. Borage Family.

European Stickseed (*Lappula echinata*) * Tiny (⅛″ wide) blue
flowers in slender, leafy racemes; fruit a small, prickly bur, ⅛″ in
diameter. Leaves narrow, ½–2″ long. Stem hairy. 6–24″ high. Summer and fall. Borage Family.

Viper's Bugloss or **Blueweed** (*Echium vulgare*) Large, blue, funnel-shaped flowers with protruding stamens. See p. 50.

Common Comfrey (*Symphytum officinale*) Purplish, tubular
flowers, ½–¾″ long, with protruding style. See p. 188.

Continued

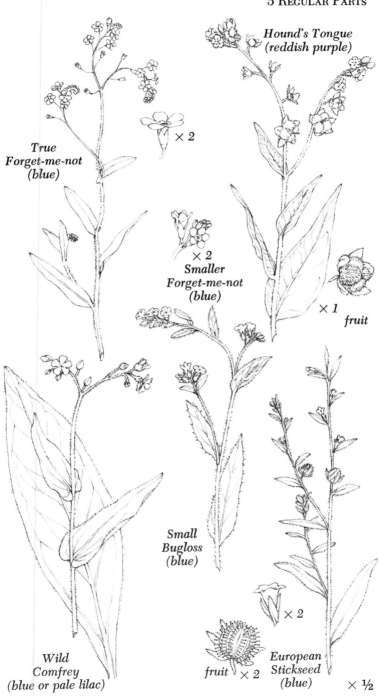

Hound's Tongue
(reddish purple)

True
Forget-me-not
(blue)

× 2

× 2
Smaller
Forget-me-not
(blue)

× 1   fruit

Wild
Comfrey
(blue or pale lilac)

Small
Bugloss
(blue)

fruit × 2

× 2

European
Stickseed
(blue)   × ½

Blue, Violet or Purple Flowers; Stems Not Jointed (cont.)

INDIVIDUAL FLOWERS IN HEADS

Blazing Stars (*Liatris*) Purple flowers in dense heads, arranged in a long, spikelike cluster (occasionally there is a solitary head). See p. 412.

Knapweeds (*Centaurea*) Rose-purple flowers in thistlelike heads, with fringed bracts covering the base of the flower head. See p. 210.

Large-flowered Marshallia (*Marshallia grandiflora*) Lavender, tubular flowers in a long-stalked head. See p. 202.

STEM SMOOTH OR ROUGH, BUT WITHOUT HAIRS; FLOWERS IN LOOSE CLUSTERS OR GROWING SINGLY

Harebell or **Bluebell** (*Campanula rotundifolia*) Plant with violet-blue flowers, ⅔–1″ long, and very narrow stem leaves. Flowers nodding, bell-shaped. The round, somewhat heart-shaped basal leaves usually disappear by flowering time. 6–20″ high. Rocky banks, shores and meadows. Summer and fall. Bluebell Family.

Virginia Bluebells or **Virginia Cowslip** (*Mertensia virginica*) Showy, nodding, trumpet-shaped flowers; blooms in spring. Flowers blue (pink when young) and about 1″ long. Leaves elliptical or egg-shaped, 2–5″ long. 1–2′ high. Rich woods and meadows, N.Y. to Minn. south. Spring. Borage Family.

Sea Lungwort or **Oysterleaf** (*Mertensia maritima*) Prostrate plant of seabeaches. Pale-blue (pink when young), bell-shaped flowers, ¼–⅓″ long. Leaves pale, fleshy, egg-shaped, 1–3″ long, tasting of oysters. 3–30″ long. Mass. north. Summer and fall. Borage Family.

Common Flax (*Linum usitatissimum*) * Blue flowers, ¾″ wide, with 5 broad petals. Leaves narrowly lance-shaped, ½–1½″ long. 1–2′ high. The flax of commerce; occasional in waste places. Summer. Flax Family.

Marsh Bellflowers (*Campanula*) Pale-blue, bell-shaped flowers, ¼–½″ long, found in wet meadows. See p. 212.

Loosestrifes (*Lythrum*) Marsh plants with purple flowers growing in the axils. See p. 348.

Harebell

Virginia Bluebells

Sea Lungwort

Common Flax

$\times$ ½

Low Plants with Evergreen or Floating Leaves

Trailing Arbutus or **Mayflower** (*Epigaea repens*) Early spring flower with leathery, oval leaves, 1–3″ long, and rounded or heart-shaped at the base. The spicy, pink or white flowers are about ½″ long and grow in small clusters at the ends of the branches. Stem trailing and hairy. Sandy or rocky woods. Heath Family.

Bearberry (*Arctostaphylos uva-ursi*) Trailing plant with compact clusters of nodding, bell-shaped, white or pale-pink flowers, slightly under ¼″ long. Leaves ½–1″ long, tapering to the base. Fruit a dry and mealy red berry. Open rocky and sandy places. Spring. Heath Family.

Pyxie or **Flowering Moss** (*Pyxidanthera barbulata*) Creeping plant of pine barrens with tiny, mosslike leaves. Numerous white or pinkish flowers, about ¼″ wide, dot the matlike surface. N.J. south. Early spring. Diapensia Family.

Moss Plant (*Cassiope hypnoides*) Alpine plant with needlelike foliage and small bell-shaped, nodding, white flowers. The flowers grow singly at the ends of the branches. Mosslike, matted plant, 1–5″ high. Alpine summits of N.H. and Me. north. Summer. Heath Family.

Wintergreen or **Checkerberry** (*Gaultheria procumbens*) Bell-shaped flowers nodding under the shining leaves. See p. 212.

Floating Heart (*Nymphoides cordata*) Aquatic plant with heart-shaped leaves and white flowers. See p. 176.

White Flowers, ¾″ or More Wide

Grass-of-Parnassus (*Parnassia glauca*) Showy (¾–1½″ wide) white flowers veined with green, on long stalks. The plant has a rosette of broad, long-stalked basal leaves, which are rounded or heart-shaped at the base, and one stalkless leaf clasping the flowering stalk. 6–24″ high. Swamps and wet meadows, in limy soil. Late summer and fall. Saxifrage Family.

Upright or **Low Bindweed** (*Convolvulus spithamaeus*) Large (1½–2″ wide) white, funnel-shaped flowers on long stalks, growing from the lower axils. Leaves oval, 1–3″ long, rounded or heart-shaped at the base. Weakly erect, 4–18″ high. Sandy or rocky fields or banks. Late spring and summer. Morning Glory Family.

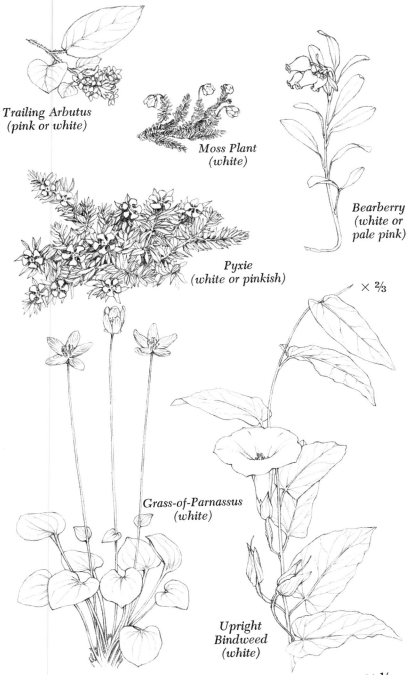

Trailing Arbutus
(pink or white)

Moss Plant
(white)

Bearberry
(white or
pale pink)

Pyxie
(white or pinkish)

× ⅔

Grass-of-Parnassus
(white)

Upright
Bindweed
(white)

× ½

Erect Plants, Not Evergreen, with White or Pink Flowers under ¾" Wide; Stems Not Jointed

FLOWERS IN SPIKES OR RACEMES

Pokeweed (*Phytolacca americana*) Stout, succulent, branching plant over 3' high, with racemes of white or pinkish flowers ¼" wide. Sepals 5, round and petal-like. Berries dark purple. Young shoots edible, but the root and possibly the berries are poisonous. 4–10' high. Moist soil. Summer and fall. Pokeweed Family.

Water Pimpernel or **Brookweed** (*Samolus parviflorus*) Plant of wet places with very small, long-stalked, white flowers, ⅛" wide. Leaves egg-shaped, 1–3" long. 4–18" high. Shallow water, often on tidal shores. Late spring to fall. Primrose Family.

Virginia Stickseed or **Beggar's Lice** (*Hackelia virginiana*) Plant of dry places with tiny (under ⅛" wide) whitish flowers in one-sided racemes; stem leaves elliptical or lance-shaped, 2–8" long. Basal leaves large, usually absent at flowering time. Fruit a prickly bur that clings to clothing. Stem fine-hairy, widely branched. 1–4' high. Dry woods. Summer and fall. Borage Family.

Spring Forget-me-not (*Myosotis verna*) Plant of dry places with tiny white flowers in racemes; leaves oblong, ½–1½" long. Stem hairy. 3–15" high. Dry woods and banks. Spring and early summer. Borage Family.

Common Comfrey (*Symphytum officinale*) Tubular, whitish flowers, ½–¾" long, in one-sided racemes. See p. 188.

Sand Jointweed (*Polygonella articulata*) Tiny pink or white flowers in racemes; leaves very narrow. See p. 172.

FLOWERS STALKLESS, GROWING SINGLY IN THE UPPER AXILS

Gromwells (*Lithospermum*) Small (¼" long or less), tubular, stalkless, whitish flowers in the axils of leafy bracts. Stem downy, usually branched. Fruit 1–4 seedlike nutlets. Fields and waste places. Spring and summer. Borage Family.

European Gromwell (*L. officinale*) * Leaves very numerous, lance-shaped, pointed, with obvious veins. Nutlets white or pale brown, shining. 1½–3' high.

Corn Gromwell (*L. arvense*) * Leaves narrowly lance-shaped, short-pointed, with only the middle vein obvious. Nutlets brown, wrinkled. 6–30" high.

Continued

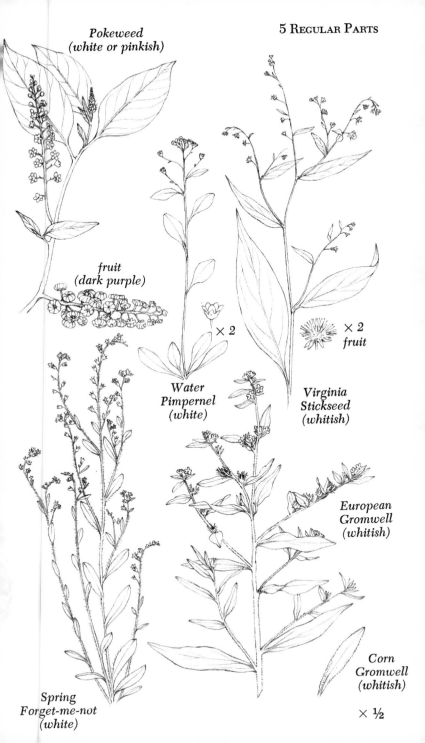

Pokeweed
(white or pinkish)

fruit
(dark purple)

Water
Pimpernel
(white)

× 2

Virginia
Stickseed
(whitish)

× 2
fruit

Spring
Forget-me-not
(white)

European
Gromwell
(whitish)

Corn
Gromwell
(whitish)

× ½

Erect Plants, Not Evergreen, with White or Pink Flowers under ¾" Wide; Stems Not Jointed (cont.)

FLOWERS IN UMBELS, BRANCHING CLUSTERS OR HEADS

Star or **Bastard Toadflax** (*Comandra umbellata*) Small (⅛" wide) greenish-white, 5-pointed flowers in a terminal cluster of small cymes. The flowers have a 5-lobed, bell-shaped calyx and no petals. Leaves oblong, ½–1½" long. Parasitic. 6–15" high. Dry fields and open woods, Me. to Mich. south. Late spring and early summer. Sandalwood Family.

Flowering Spurge (*Euphorbia corollata*) White flowers, ¼" wide, with 5 roundish petal-like parts (actually bracts surrounding the tiny flowers), in an open cluster. A whorl of leaves at the top of the stem; lower leaves alternate. Juice milky. 1–3' high. Dry fields, open woods, N.Y. to Minn. south; introduced in N.Eng. Summer and fall. Spurge Family.

Snow-on-the-mountain (*Euphorbia marginata*) * White flowers clustered in the center of conspicuous, white-margined bracts and leaves. Leaves oval or egg-shaped. Juice milky. 1–3' high. Escaped from cultivation to waste places; native to the Prairie States. Summer and fall. Spurge Family.

Black Nightshade (*Solanum nigrum*) * Drooping, white flowers in small umbels along the branches. Flowers star-shaped, ¼" wide, with a cone of stamens in the center. Leaves egg-shaped, entire or wavy-toothed. Fruit a black berry. Stem branched. 1–2½' high. Woods and waste places. Summer and fall. Nightshade Family.

Narrow-leaved White-topped Aster (*Sericocarpus linifolius*) Aster-like flowers, ½" wide, with 4 or 5 white rays, in a flat-topped cluster. Leaves very narrow, 1–3" long. 1–2½' high. Dry fields and woods, s. N.H. to Ohio south. Summer and early fall. Composite Family.

Large-flowered Marshallia (*Marshallia grandiflora*) Pink or laven der, tubular flowers in a long-stalked head. Larger leaves lance shaped, with 3 main veins. 10–36" high. Stream banks and clea ings, s. Pa. to Ky. south. Summer. Composite Family.

Marsh Bellflowers (*Campanula*) Slender plants of wet meadow and shores with bell-shaped flowers. See p. 212.

Tuberous Indian Plantain (*Cacalia tuberosa*) Whitish flowers, ¼" long, in a large, open, flattish, branching cluster. See p. 414.

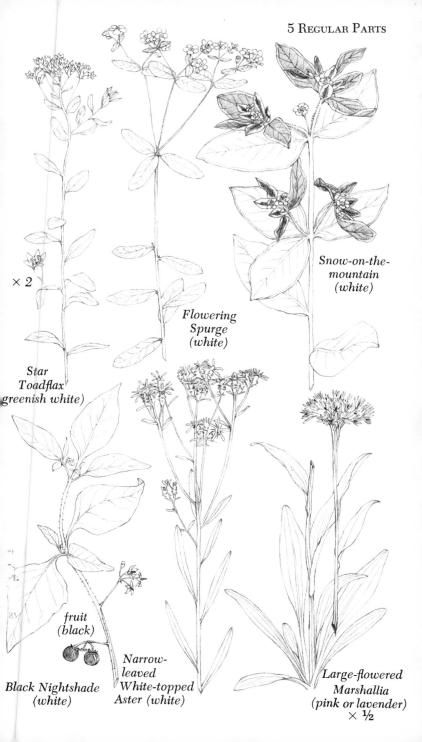

× 2

Star
Toadflax
greenish white)

Flowering
Spurge
(white)

Snow-on-the-
mountain
(white)

fruit
(black)

Black Nightshade
(white)

Narrow-
leaved
White-topped
Aster (white)

Large-flowered
Marshallia
(pink or lavender)
× ½

Yellow Flowers; the Largest Leaves About as Wide as Long

Marsh Marigold or **Cowslip** (*Caltha palustris*) Showy spring flower (1–1½″ wide) of wet places, with 5–9 bright-yellow sepals and no petals. Leaves heart-shaped, long-stalked and shallowly toothed. Stem hollow. 1–2′ long. Swamps and meadows. Buttercup Family.

Indian Mallow or **Velvetleaf** (*Abutilon theophrasti*) * The large, velvety, heart-shaped leaves taper at the point and are slightly toothed or entire. The yellow flowers are ½–1″ wide, borne singly or in small clusters in the axils. Stem branched, soft-hairy. 2–6′ high. Waste places. Summer and fall. Mallow Family.

Hooked Crowfoot (*Ranunculus recurvatus*) Both upper and lower stem leaves deeply cleft into 3 egg-shaped segments. Pale-yellow flowers, ⅓″ wide, with the petals no longer than the sepals. Stem hairy. 6–24″ high. Brooksides and damp woods. Spring and early summer. Buttercup Family.

Crowfoots (*Ranunculus*) Upper stem leaves divided into narrow segments; flowers about ¼″ wide. See p. 244.

Mountain Avens (*Geum peckii*) Alpine plant of the White Mts., N.H. See p. 238.

Yellow Violets (*Viola*) Woodland plants with the lower petal of the flowers veined with violet. See p. 54.

Yellow Flowers; the Largest Leaves Longer Than Wide

Ground Cherries (*Physalis*) Nodding, greenish-yellow flowers with a dark center, growing from the axils. The flowers are open-bell–shaped, with 5 shallow lobes. Branching plants, 1–3′ high, with hanging lanternlike pods. Fields, clearings and open woods. Summer. Nightshade Family.

Clammy Ground Cherry (*P. heterophylla*) Leaves broadly egg-shaped, rounded or heart-shaped at the base; stems covered with sticky hairs. Leaves often coarsely toothed. The commonest species.

Virginia Ground Cherry (*P. virginiana*) Leaves narrowly egg-shaped, tapering at the base, sparingly toothed; stems downy. S. N.Eng. to Man. south.

Smooth Ground Cherry (*P. subglabrata*) † Leaves similar to the Virginia Ground Cherry, but stem and leaves are smooth or nearly so. Vt. to Mich. south.

Continued

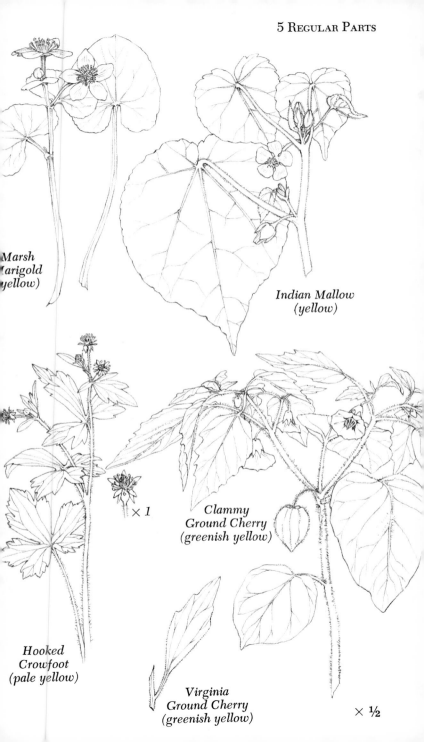

Marsh
Marigold
(yellow)

Indian Mallow
(yellow)

× 1

Clammy
Ground Cherry
(greenish yellow)

Hooked
Crowfoot
(pale yellow)

Virginia
Ground Cherry
(greenish yellow)

× ½

Yellow Flowers; the Largest Leaves Longer Than Wide (cont.)

Mulleins (*Verbascum*) Large (¾–1″ wide) yellow flowers in spikes or racemes. Flowers with 5 deep, slightly irregular lobes. Fields and roadsides. Summer and fall. Figwort Family.

    Common Mullein (*V. thapsus*) Plant with velvety leaves and flowers in a dense spike. See p. 188.

    Moth Mullein (*V. blattaria*) * Flowers yellow or white, tinged with purple on the back, in a loose raceme. Leaves smooth, toothed or lobed. 2–4′ high.

Prickly Mallow (*Sida spinosa*) * Yellow, 5-petaled flowers, ¼–½″ wide, on short stalks in the axils. Leaves egg-shaped or oblong, long-stalked, 1–2″ long. The stalks of the larger leaves have a small, blunt spur at the base. 8–24″ high. Waste places, Mass. to Mich. south. Summer and fall. Mallow Family.

Water-plantain Spearwort (*Ranunculus ambigens*) Flowers about ½–¾″ wide, with 5 yellow, oblong petals, in a small terminal cluster. Leaves lance-shaped, slightly toothed, 3–6″ long. Stem weakly erect. 1–3′ long. Ditches and swamps, Me. to Minn. south. Summer. Buttercup Family.

Wingstem (*Actinomeris alternifolia*) Tall plant with drooping flower rays; flower heads 1–2″ wide. See p. 376.

Goldenrods (*Solidago*) Flowers small and numerous; flowering from mid-summer to fall. See pp. 446–453.

Plants Prostrate or Creeping over the Ground; Leaves as Wide as Long

Common Mallow or **Cheeses** (*Malva neglecta*) * Prostrate plant with pale-lilac or white flowers, ½–¾″ wide, growing in the axils. The roundish, toothed leaves have 5–7 shallow lobes. 4–24″ long. Common weed of waste places and barnyards. Spring to fall. Mallow Family.

Water Pennywort (*Hydrocotyle americana*) Creeping plant of moist or wet places with tiny, whitish flowers growing in the axils. The leaves are roundly heart-shaped with scalloped edges. Summer and early fall. Parsley Family.

Geraniums or **Cranesbills** (*Geranium*) Pink or purple flowers, ¼–½″ wide; leaves deeply lobed. See p. 280.

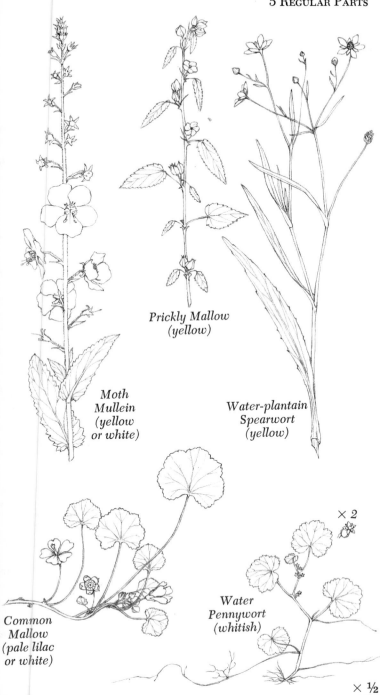

Prickly Mallow
(yellow)

Moth
Mullein
(yellow
or white)

Water-plantain
Spearwort
(yellow)

× 2

Common
Mallow
(pale lilac
or white)

Water
Pennywort
(whitish)

× ½

Erect Plants; the Largest Leaves as Wide as Long; Flowers Not Yellow

BLUE, VIOLET OR LARGE, ROSE-PURPLE FLOWERS

Venus's Looking-glass (*Specularia perfoliata*) Blue or violet flowers, ½–¾" wide, growing in the upper axils. The heart-shaped leaves clasp the stem and are ½–1" long. 6–30" high. Spring and summer. Lobelia Family.

High Mallow (*Malva sylvestris*) * Showy (1–2" wide) rose-purple flowers with petals that are red-veined and concave at the tip. Leaves with 5–7 shallow lobes. Musk Mallow (p. 234) has deeply cleft leaves and paler flowers. 10–30" high. Roadsides and waste places. Summer. Mallow Family.

Harebell or **Bluebell** (*Campanula rotundifolia*) Nodding, blue, bell-shaped flowers. See p. 196.

WHITE, GREENISH OR PURPLISH FLOWERS

Broad-leaved Waterleaf (*Hydrophyllum canadense*) White or purplish flowers in a loose cluster at the base of the maple-leaf-shaped upper leaf. Flowers open-bell–shaped, about ½" long, with protruding stamens. Appendaged Waterleaf (p. 228) has lavender flowers, borne above the leaves, and divided lower leaves. 8–24" high. Rich woods, w. N.Eng. to Mich. south. Early summer. Waterleaf Family.

Cloudberry or **Baked-apple Berry** (*Rubus chamaemorus*) Solitary white flower, ¾–1" wide, on erect branches from a creeping rootstock. Leaves usually with 5 shallow lobes. Fruit a reddish or yellowish, edible berry. 3–10" high. Peat bogs and heaths, Montauk Pt. on Long I., Me. and the mts. of N.H. north. Summer. Rose Family.

Tall White Lettuce (*Prenanthes altissima*) Nodding, greenish-white flowers, ½" long; basal leaves (if present) triangular or with 3–5 deep lobes. See p. 212.

Indian Plantains (*Cacalia*) Erect heads of white flowers, ¼–½" long, in a flattish cluster. See p. 420.

Alumroot (*Heuchera americana*) Small (¼" long) greenish or purplish flowers in a loose, branching cluster; leaves roundly heart-shaped, 2–4" wide. See p. 180.

Naked Miterwort (*Mitella nuda*) Low plant with green flowers in a short raceme; leaves roundly heart-shaped, 1–1½" wide. See p. 178.

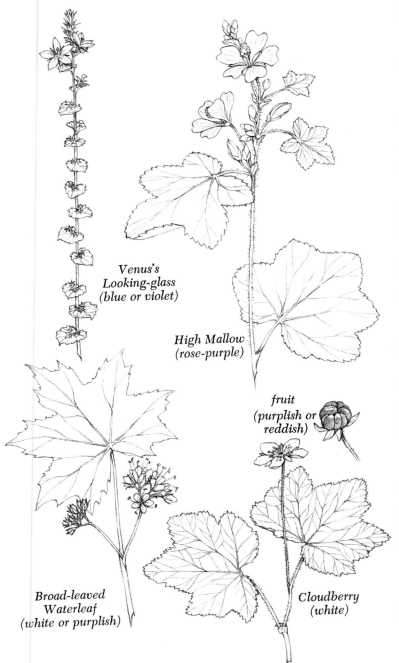

Venus's
Looking-glass
(blue or violet)

High Mallow
(rose-purple)

fruit
(purplish or
reddish)

Broad-leaved
Waterleaf
(white or purplish)

Cloudberry
(white)

× ½

Purple, White or Bluish Flowers in Heads; Leaves Longer Than Wide

Ironweeds (*Vernonia*) Tall plants (3–10′ high) with small purple flowers in heads ½–¾″ wide. The leaves are lance-shaped and finely toothed, 3–10″ long. Moist meadows. Late summer and fall. Composite Family.

> **New York Ironweed** (*V. noveboracensis*) Bracts with long, threadlike tips cover the base of the flower head; each head has 30–50 flowers. Mass. to s. Ohio south.

> **Tall Ironweed** (*V. altissima*) Bracts blunt or short-pointed; flower heads with 13–30 flowers. N.Y. to s. Mich. south.

Knapweeds (*Centaurea*) Rose-purple flowers with fringed bracts covering the base of the flower head. Heads ¾–1¾″ wide. Leaves oblong or lance-shaped, with a few teeth or lobes. Spotted Knapweed (p. 234) has divided leaves. 1–3′ high. Fields, roadsides. Summer and fall. Composite Family.

> **Black Knapweed** (*C. nigra*) * Floral bracts with blackish comb-like fringes. Usually without showy marginal flowers.

> **Brown Knapweed** (*C. jacea*) * Floral bracts brownish, with a finely fringed border. Showy marginal flowers present.

Wild Quinine or **American Feverfew** (*Parthenium integrifolium*) Small heads (¼″ wide) with 5 tiny, white rays widely spaced around the margin. Heads numerous, in a large, branched cluster. Basal leaves elliptical or egg-shaped, long-stalked, rough-surfaced, and up to 12″ long. 1–4′ high. Open woods and thickets, se. N.Y., Pa. to Mich. south. Summer and fall. Composite Family.

Toothed White-topped Aster (*Sericocarpus asteroides*) Asterlike flowers with 4–6 narrow, white rays, growing in a flat-topped cluster. Flowers about ½″ wide. There is usually a rosette of sparsely toothed, egg-shaped leaves at the base and a few stem leaves. Narrow-leaved White-topped Aster (p. 202) has narrow, entire leaves. 6–24″ high. Dry woods and clearings, s. Me. to Mich. south. Summer and fall. Composite Family.

Tall Thistle (*Cirsium altissimum*) Prickly-leaved plant with purple flowers. See p. 430.

Rattlesnake Master or **Button Snakeroot** (*Eryngium yuccifolium*) White, greenish-white or bluish flowers in buttonlike heads; leaves stiff, spiny-edged. See p. 418.

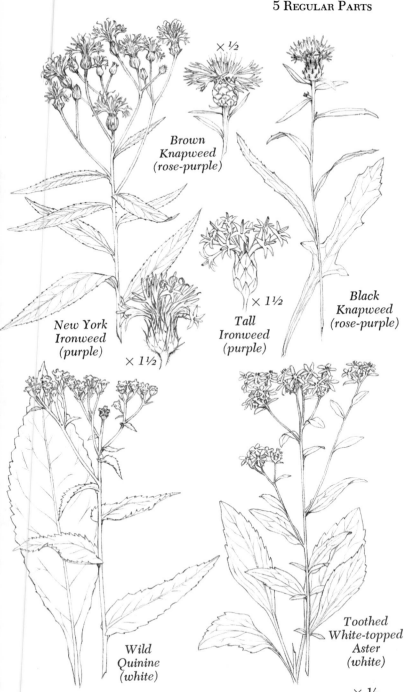

× ½

Brown
Knapweed
(rose-purple)

Black
Knapweed
(rose-purple)

New York
Ironweed
(purple)

× 1½

× 1½

Tall
Ironweed
(purple)

Wild
Quinine
(white)

Toothed
White-topped
Aster
(white)

× ½

White, Violet or Blue Flowers, Bell-shaped or Funnel-shaped; Leaves Longer Than Wide

Wintergreen or **Checkerberry** (*Gaultheria procumbens*) Low ever green with 1 or more small white flowers hanging beneath the leaves. Flowers ¼″ long, bell-shaped, constricted at the tip, with 5 small teeth. Leaves dark green and shining, oval, obscurely toothed, tasting strongly of wintergreen. Fruit an edible, bright red berry. 2–6″ high. Summer. Woods. Heath Family.

Tall White Lettuce (*Prenanthes altissima*) Greenish-white, nod ding flowers, ½″ long, with protruding style. Leaves very vari able, the stem leaves usually shallowly lobed or toothed; basal leaves, if present, broad and either triangular or palmately lobed or divided. Plant with milky juice. 2–7′ high. Rich, moist woods Late summer and fall. Composite Family.

Bellflowers (*Campanula*) Blue or white, bell-shaped flowers. Tall Bellflower (p. 216) has star-shaped flowers. Bluebell Family.

1. PLANTS OF WET MEADOWS AND SHORES WITH SMALL WHITE OR PALE-BLUE FLOWERS

Marsh or Bedstraw Bellflower (*C. aparinoides*) Flowers white or white tinged with blue, ¼–⅓″ long. Plant with spreading flower ing branches. Leaves narrow, slightly toothed or entire. Stem weak, slightly rough and clinging. Summer.

Blue Marsh Bellflower (*C. uliginosa*) Similar to the Marsh Bellflower, but the flowers are pale blue, almost ½″ long, and the branches less widely spreading.

2. PLANTS OF FIELDS, WOODS AND ROCKY PLACES WITH BLUE FLOWERS

Creeping Bellflower (*C. rapunculoides*) * Nodding, blue bells 1–1½″ long, in a long, one-sided raceme. Lower leaves egg shaped with a heart-shaped base, long-stalked; the upper, very short-stalked or stalkless. 1–3′ high. Fields and roadsides Summer.

Southern Harebell (*C. divaricata*) Blue flowers, about ¼″ long in a branching cluster. Leaves lance- or egg-shaped, sharply toothed. 1–3′ high. Woods and rocky slopes, Md., W.Va. and Ky south. Summer and fall.

Harebell or **Bluebell** (*C. rotundifolia*) Nodding, blue bells ⅔–1″ long; stem leaves narrow. See p. 196.

Continued

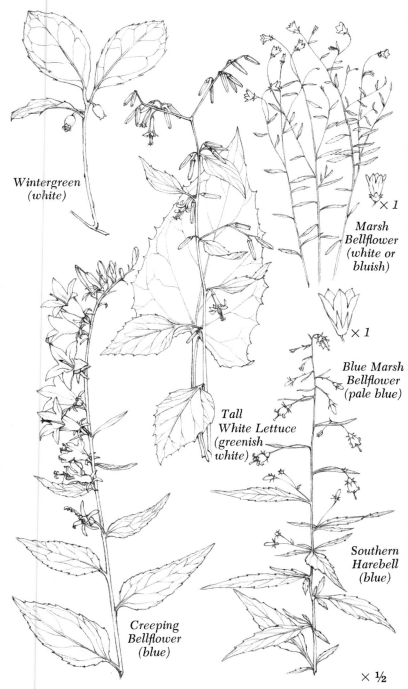

Wintergreen
(white)

Marsh
Bellflower
(white or
bluish)

× 1

× 1

Blue Marsh
Bellflower
(pale blue)

Tall
White Lettuce
(greenish
white)

Southern
Harebell
(blue)

Creeping
Bellflower
(blue)

× ½

White, Violet or Blue Flowers, Bell-shaped or Funnel-shaped; Leaves Longer Than Wide (cont.)

Jimsonweed or **Thorn Apple** (*Datura stramonium*)* A coarse weed with large (2½–4″ long) funnel-shaped flowers. The color of the flowers varies from white to violet or lavender. Leaves egg-shaped, pointed, coarsely toothed, 2–8″ long. Fruit a spiny pod, 2″ long. Ill-smelling and poisonous. Waste places. 1–5′ high. Summer and fall. Nightshade Family.

Small Bugloss (*Lycopsis arvensis*) Hairy plant with small (¼″ wide) blue flowers in close clusters. See p. 194.

Showy, Pink or White Flowers (Over 1″ Wide) with Large, Veiny Petals (Mallows)

Rose Mallows (*Hibiscus*) Very large flowers, 4–6″ wide; petals 2–3″ long. Pink or white flowers, some varieties with a purple or crimson center. As is characteristic of all mallows, the stamens are united into a column arising from the center of the flower. Leaves broad, long-stalked. 3–7′ high. Late summer and fall. Mallow Family.

> **Swamp Rose Mallow** (*H. palustris*) Stem and undersurface of leaves whitish-downy. Leaves egg-shaped or 3-lobed, with a rounded or heart-shaped base. Brackish or fresh marshes, Mass. south along the coast, and inland from w. N.Y. along the Great Lakes.

> **Halberd-leaved Rose Mallow** (*H. militaris*) Stem and undersurface of leaves smooth. At least the lower leaves are 3-lobed and spear-shaped. Riverbanks and swamps, s. Pa. to Minn. south.

Marshmallow (*Althaea officinalis*) * Velvety, gray-green plant with pale-rose flowers, 1–1½″ wide; petals ½–¾″ long. Leaves egg-shaped and either coarsely toothed or 3-lobed. The roots are the original source of marshmallow. 2–4′ high. Salt marshes, Conn. south and locally inland to Mich. Summer and fall. Mallow Family.

Seashore Mallow (*Kosteletzkya virginica*) Flowers intermediate in size between the Rose Mallows and the Marshmallow, with rose-colored flowers 1½–2½″ wide, and petals ¾–1¼″ long. Leaves egg-shaped, usually 3-lobed. The stem is minutely downy or rough. 2–4′ high. Brackish meadows, Long I. south. Summer. Mallow Family.

Jimson Weed

*Swamp
Rose Mallow*

*Halberd-
leaved
Rose Mallow*

Marshmallow

*Seashore
Mallow*

× 1/3

Flowers Star-shaped or Wheel-shaped, Not Yellow; Leaves Longer Than Wide

FLOWERS ¾–1″ WIDE

Tall Bellflower (*Campanula americana*) Light-blue, star-shaped flowers in a leafy spike. Leaves narrowly egg- or lance-shaped, tapering at the base. 2–6′ high. Moist thickets, N.Y. to Minn. south. Summer and fall. Bluebell Family.

Horse Nettle (*Solanum carolinense*) Prickly plant with violet or white, star-shaped flowers in a small cluster. The stamens form a cone in the center of the flower. Leaves coarsely toothed or lobed. Fruit a yellow berry. 1–4′ high. Sandy fields and waste places. Summer and fall. Nightshade Family.

Moth Mullein (*Verbascum blattaria*) White flowers in a loose raceme. See p. 206.

FLOWERS ⅛–½″ WIDE

Live-forevers (*Sedum*) Plants with fleshy, coarsely toothed leaves. The star-shaped flowers are purple, pink or white, about ¼″ wide, in cymes. Summer and fall. Sedum Family.

　　Live-forever (*S. purpureum*) * Pink-purple flowers; leaves green. 8–30″ high. Roadsides and fields, escaped from cultivation. Many plants do not flower, but propagate vegetatively.

　　Wild Live-forever (*S. telephioides*) Pale-pink or white flowers; leaves whitened. The leaves have fewer teeth than those of the Live-forever. 6–16″ high. Cliffs and rocks, Pa. to Ill. south.

Ditch Stonecrop (*Penthorum sedoides*) Small, yellowish-green flowers in a branching cluster of one-sided spikes; grows in wet places. Leaves broadly lance-shaped or elliptical, finely toothed, 2–4″ long. 6–30″ high. Ditches and swamps. Summer and fall. Saxifrage Family.

Black Nightshade (*Solanum nigrum*) White, star-shaped flowers in small umbels along the branches, ¼″ wide. See p. 202.

Phacelias or **Scorpionweeds** (*Phacelia*) Blue (rarely white) flowers in more or less one-sided racemes. See p. 234.

Striped or **Spotted Wintergreen** (*Chimaphila maculata*) Plant with variegated leaves and white, waxy flowers. See p. 284.

Toothed White-topped Aster (*Sericocarpus asteroides*) Asterlike flowers with 5 narrow, white rays. See p. 210.

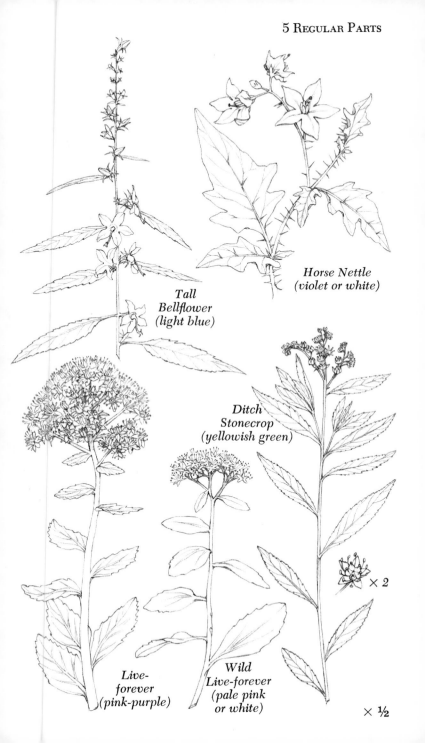

Tall
Bellflower
(light blue)

Horse Nettle
(violet or white)

Ditch
Stonecrop
(yellowish green)

× 2

Live-
forever
(pink-purple)

Wild
Live-forever
(pale pink
or white)

× ½

Very Small Flowers in Dense Spikes, Racemes or Heads

Goatsbeard (*Aruncus dioicus*) White flowers in a large branching cluster of dense spikes 2–3″ long. The leaves are 2- to 3-times pinnate, with large, egg-shaped leaflets. 3–7′ high. Rich woods and banks, Pa. to Iowa south. Late spring and early summer. Rose Family.

Baneberries (*Actaea*) White flowers in a single raceme 1–2″ long; stamens white and conspicuous. See p. 424.

Spotted Knapweed (*Centaurea maculosa*) Pink, purple or whitish flowers in thistlelike heads, the base of the heads covered with black-fringed bracts. See p. 234.

Thistles (*Cirsium*) Flowers in dense heads; leaves prickly. See p. 430.

Very Small, White or Greenish Flowers in Umbels; Leaves Palmate with 3–5 Leaflets

Cow Parsnip (*Heracleum maximum*) Very broad (4–8″ wide) cluster of white flowers. The petals are indented at the tip, and the outer petals are apt to be larger and deeply cleft. Base of leaves enlarged into a clasping sheath. Leaflets 3, broad and more or less heart-shaped at the base. Stem woolly. 4–10′ high. Moist rich ground. Summer. Parsley Family.

Honewort (*Cryptotaenia canadensis*) Tiny white flowers in small umbels with unequal rays; upper leaves alternate. The leaves have 3 sharply and irregularly toothed, often lobed, leaflets. 8–36″ high. Rich woods. Summer and fall. Parsley Family.

Sanicles or **Black Snakeroots** (*Sanicula*) Inconspicuous, greenish or whitish flowers in small umbels; upper leaves opposite. See p. 426.

× 3

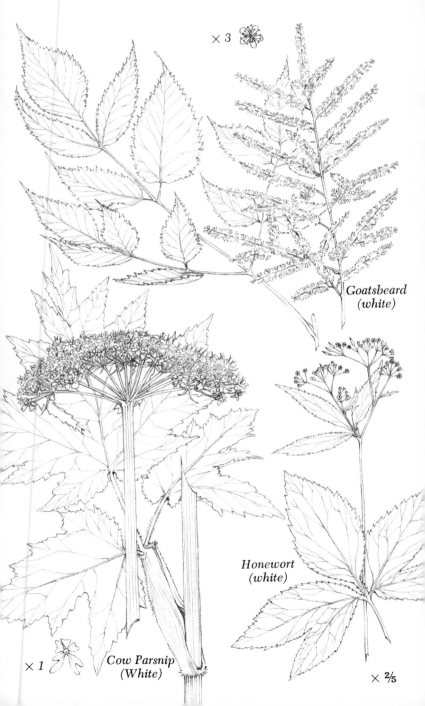

Goatsbeard
(white)

Honewort
(white)

× 1   *Cow Parsnip*
(White)

× 2/5

Very Small, White or Pink Flowers in Umbels or Flat Clusters; Leaves Finely Divided

WHITE OR PINK FLOWERS IN FLAT-TOPPED CORYMBS

Yarrow or **Milfoil** (*Achillea millefolium*) * Each flower has 4–6 rays that are 3-toothed. Leaves lance-shaped in outline and finely dissected. 1–3′ high. Fields and roadsides; common. Late spring to fall. Composite Family.

WHITE FLOWERS IN UMBELS; PLANTS OF FIELDS, WOODS AND WASTE PLACES

Wild Carrot, Queen Anne's Lace or **Bird's Nest** (*Daucus carota*) * Stem covered with bristly hairs; bracts beneath the umbel deeply and narrowly lobed. Umbels 2–4″ wide, with (usually) 1 purple floret in the center; they become concave in fruit to form a "bird's nest." 1–3′ high. Very common weed of dry fields and waste places. Summer and fall. Parsley Family.

Caraway (*Carum carvi*) * Smooth, slender plant, 1–2′ high, of dry, open places; bracts beneath the umbel entire and narrow, or absent. Umbels 1–2½″wide. Seeds aromatic. Commoner to the north. Late spring and summer. Parsley Family.

Poison Hemlock (*Conium maculatum*) * Coarse plant of waste places (occasionally riverbanks) with a smooth, spotted stem; bracts beneath umbel entire. Base of leaves enlarged and sheathing the stem. Deadly poisonous if eaten. 2–6′ high. Late spring and summer. Parsley Family.

Harbinger-of-spring or **Pepper-and-salt** (*Erigenia bulbosa*) Very early spring flower under 10″ high. See p. 224.

WHITE FLOWERS IN UMBELS; PLANTS OF SWAMPS AND MARSHES

Hemlock Parsley (*Conioselinum chinense*) Leaves divided into oblong, deeply lobed segments. Stem smooth, unspotted. Plant slender, 6–60″ high. Cold swamps, wet woods and riverbanks. Summer and fall. Parsley Family.

Mock Bishop's Weed (*Ptilimnium capillaceum*) Leaves divided into threadlike, untoothed segments. Stem slender. 1–3′ high. Fresh or brackish marshes, s. N.Eng. south along the coast, inland in the s. states north to s. Ill. Summer and fall. Parsley Family.

Bulb-bearing Water Hemlock (*Cicuta bulbifera*) Leaves divided into narrow, sparingly toothed leaflets; slender plant of swamps. See p. 222.

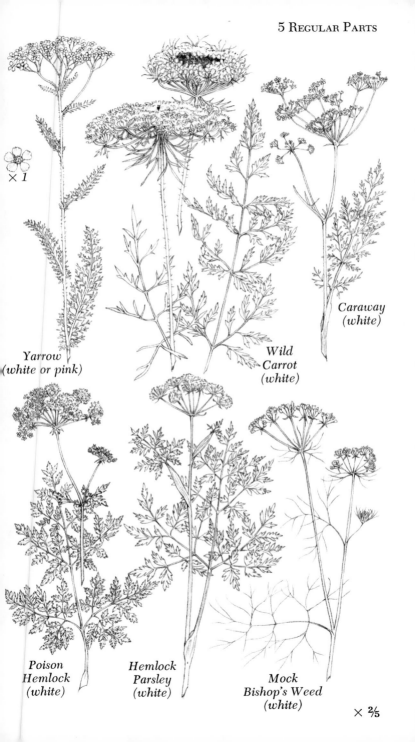

× 1

Yarrow
(white or pink)

Wild
Carrot
(white)

Caraway
(white)

Poison
Hemlock
(white)

Hemlock
Parsley
(white)

Mock
Bishop's Weed
(white)

× 2/5

Very Small, White Flowers in Umbels; Leaves Once-pinnate

Water Parsnip (*Sium suave*) Leaflets toothed along the entire margin. Leaves with 7–17 narrow or lance-shaped leaflets, the lowest leaves often finely divided. Stem angled. 2–6′ high. Swamps, muddy banks. Summer and fall. Parsley Family.

Cowbane (*Oxypolis rigidior*) Leaflets sparsely toothed, mostly above the middle, or entire. The 5–16 leaflets are lance-shaped or oblong. 2–6′ high. Poisonous. Swamps and wet woods, N.Y. to Minn. south. Late summer and fall. Parsley Family.

Very Small, White Flowers in Umbels; Leaves 2- to 3-times-divided into Leaflets, Not Finely Divided

PLANTS OF FRESHWATER SWAMPS AND DAMP MEADOWS

Water Hemlock or **Spotted Cowbane** (*Cicuta maculata*) Leaflets lance-shaped with numerous teeth; umbels flat, 2–4″ wide. Stem branching, usually mottled with purple. 3–6′ high. All parts are deadly poisonous to taste. Swamps and low meadows. Summer and fall. Parsley Family.

Bulb-bearing Water Hemlock (*Cicuta bulbifera*) Leaflets narrow, sparsely toothed; umbels 1–2″ wide. Little bulblets are clustered in the upper axils. 1–4′ high. Deadly poisonous. Swamps. Summer and fall. Parsley Family.

Great Angelica (*Angelica atropurpurea*) Leaflets egg-shaped; umbels roundish, 3–10″ wide. Flowers greenish white. Base of the leaves with veiny, enlarged sheaths. Stem purple or purple-blotched. 4–7′ high. Low meadows and stream banks. Late spring to fall. Parsley Family.

MARITIME PLANTS OF SALT MARSHES, BEACHES AND ROCKS

Seaside Angelica (*Coelopleurum lucidum*) Upper leaves with a broad, open sheath at the base; flowers greenish white. 2–4′ high. Beaches and rocks along the coast, N.Y. north. Summer. Parsley Family.

Scotch Lovage (*Ligusticum scothicum*) Upper leaves with narrow sheath at the base; flowers white; leaflets broad, wedge-shaped. 1½–2′ high. Salt marshes and rocks, N.Y. north. Summer and fall. Parsley Family.

Water Hemlock or **Spotted Cowbane** (*Cicuta maculata*) Upper leaves with narrow sheath; leaflets lance-shaped. See above.

Continued

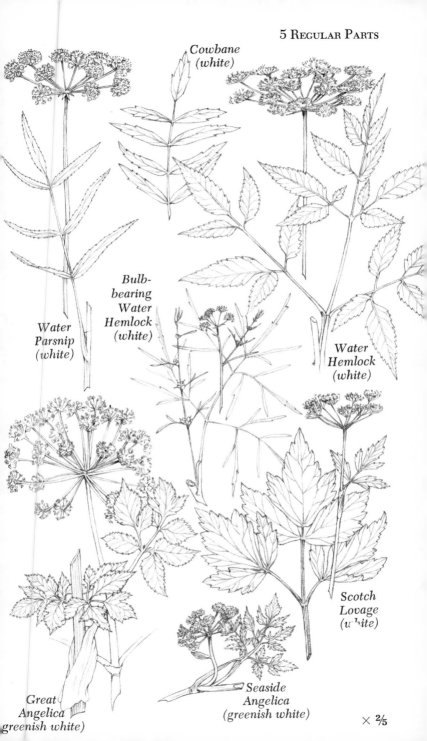

*Cowbane
(white)*

*Water
Parsnip
(white)*

*Bulb-
bearing
Water
Hemlock
(white)*

*Water
Hemlock
(white)*

*Scotch
Lovage
(white)*

*Great
Angelica
greenish white)*

*Seaside
Angelica
(greenish white)*

× **2/5**

Very Small, White Flowers in Umbels; Leaves 2- to 3-times-divided into Leaflets, Not Finely Divided (cont.)

PLANTS OF WOODLANDS AND DRY OPEN PLACES

Spikenard (*Aralia racemosa*) Greenish-white flowers in a long, branching cluster of umbels. Leaflets large and heart-shaped at the base. Fruit a dark-purple berry. Noted for its aromatic root. Stem widely branched. 3–6' high. Rich woods. Summer. Ginseng Family.

Bristly Sarsaparilla (*Aralia hispida*) Whitish flowers in round umbels; lower stem bristly. Leaflets egg-shaped and sharply toothed. The umbels are on long stalks that extend above the leaves. Fruit dark purple. 1–3' high. Open woods and clearings. Summer. Ginseng Family.

Sweet Cicelies (*Osmorhiza*) Woodland plants 1–3' high, with small umbels of white flowers in spring and early summer. The fernlike leaves have egg-shaped leaflets that are deeply lobed and toothed. Fruit club-shaped, blackish, clinging to clothing. Parsley Family.

Sweet Cicely (*O. claytoni*) Styles shorter than the petals, becoming (at the tip of the fruit) $\frac{1}{16}$" long. Stem hairy. Root aromatic.

Aniseroot (*O. longistylis*) Styles longer than the petals, becoming (at the tip of the fruit) $\frac{1}{8}$" long. Stem nearly smooth or occasionally hairy. Root carrotlike, with a pleasant anise odor.

Harbinger-of-spring or **Pepper-and-salt** (*Erigenia bulbosa*) Very early spring flower under 10" high. Flowers white with red-brown anthers. The stem leaves (1 or 2) and the several basal leaves are divided into narrow or oblong segments, and are often not fully developed at flowering time. Root a small, round tuber. Open woods, w. N.Y. and w. Pa. to Minn. south. Parsley Family.

Hairy Angelica (*Angelica venenosa*) Plant 2–6' high, with thick, oval, finely toothed leaflets; flowers from midsummer to fall. Umbels 2–4" wide. The upper leaves have tubular sheaths at their base. Dry woods and clearings, w. Mass. to Mich. south. Parsley Family.

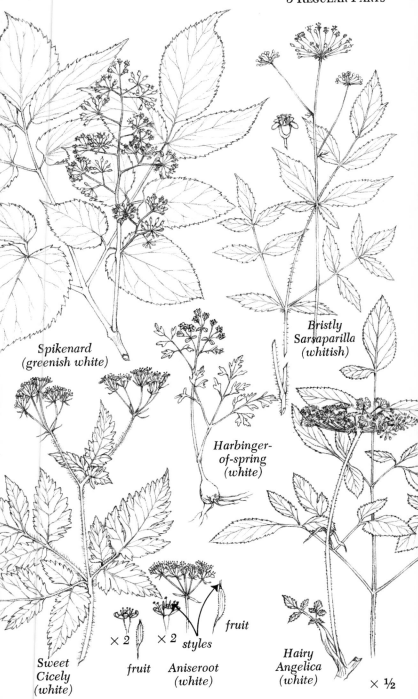

Spikenard
(greenish white)

Bristly
Sarsaparilla
(whitish)

Harbinger-
of-spring
(white)

Hairy
Angelica
(white)

Sweet
Cicely
(white)

× 2

fruit

× 2 *styles*

fruit

Aniseroot
(white)

× ½

Very Small, Yellow Flowers (Purple in 1 Species), in Umbels

LARGER LEAVES WITH MORE THAN 5 LEAFLETS

Wild Parsnip (*Pastinaca sativa*) * Leaves pinnate (the leaflets in pairs along 1 central stalk). The 5–15 leaflets are egg-shaped, sharply toothed or lobed. Umbels 2–6″ wide. Stem stout, grooved. 2–5′ high. The wild state of the cultivated parsnip. Roadsides and waste places. Summer and fall. Parsley Family.

Golden Alexanders (*Zizia aurea*) Leaves 2- to 3-times-divided; leaflets finely toothed. Leaflets lance-shaped or egg-shaped with numerous sharp teeth. Stem branching. 1–2½′ high. Meadows, shores and open woods. Spring and early summer. Parsley Family.

Yellow Pimpernel (*Taenidia integerrima*) Leaves 2- to 3-times-divided; leaflets entire. Leaflets egg-shaped or oval. The umbels have slender rays. 1–3′ high. Open woods and rocky slopes, Que. and w. N.Eng. to Minn. south. Spring and early summer. Parsley Family.

Hairy-jointed Meadow Parsnip (*Thaspium barbinode*) Leaves 2- to 3-times-divided, the leaflets coarsely toothed or cleft. Flowers pale yellow. Stem hairy at the leaf joints. 1–4′ high. Rich woods and open rocky slopes, N.Y. to Minn. south. Late spring and early summer. Parsley Family.

*LEAVES WITH 3 OR 5 LEAFLETS OR ELSE
HEART-SHAPED*

Heart-leaved Alexanders (*Zizia aptera*) Stem leaves with 3, sometimes 5, leaflets; basal leaves heart-shaped; central flower in each small flower cluster stalkless; ribs of fruit rounded. The basal leaves are long-stalked and sometimes divided into 3 leaflets. Woods and thickets, N.Y. to B.C. south. Spring and early summer. Parsley Family.

Meadow Parsnip (*Thaspium trifoliatum*) Flowers yellow or purple; very like Heart-leaved Alexanders, but the central flower in the clusters is stalked, the ribs of fruit have thin wings, and the basal leaves are more often divided into 3 leaflets. Woods and thickets, N.Y. to Minn. south. Spring and early summer. Parsley Family.

Clustered Snakeroot (*Sanicula gregaria*) Stem and basal leaves divided into 5 leaflets; flowers greenish-yellow, in small roundish clusters. See p. 426.

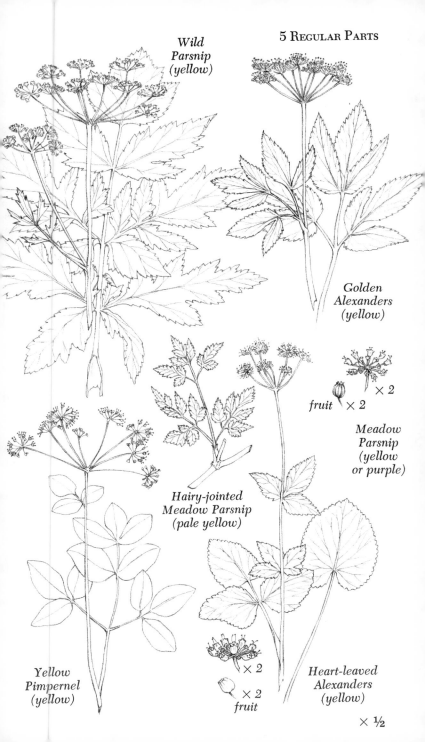

Wild
Parsnip
(yellow)

5 REGULAR PARTS

Golden
Alexanders
(yellow)

fruit × 2   × 2

Meadow
Parsnip
*(yellow
or purple)*

Hairy-jointed
Meadow Parsnip
(pale yellow)

Yellow
Pimpernel
(yellow)

× 2

× 2
fruit

Heart-leaved
Alexanders
(yellow)

× ½

Bell-shaped or Nodding Flowers

Columbines (*Aquilegia*) Large (1–2″ wide), showy, nodding flowers. Each petal has a long, narrow spur at the back. The leaflets grow in 3's and are usually deeply lobed. 1–3′ high. Spring and early summer. Buttercup Family.

> **Wild Columbine** (*A. canadensis*) Scarlet flowers with yellow center and long, protruding stamens. Rocky woods and ledges

> **Garden** or **European Columbine** (*A. vulgaris*) * Blue, purple or white flowers, about as wide as long. The stamens do not protrude from the flower. Roadsides and fields; more common northward.

Water or **Purple Avens** (*Geum rivale*) Nodding, purplish flowers, ½″ long; grows in wet places; leaflets toothed. Sepals purple; petals yellowish and about as long as the sepals. The basal leaves have a large, terminal segment; stem leaves mostly divided or cleft into 3 segments. 1–3′ high. Swamps and wet meadows. Spring and summer. Rose Family.

Waterleafs (*Hydrophyllum*) Small (⅓″ long), white, lavender, blue or violet flowers in close clusters; leaflets toothed; in rich woods; spring and early summer. The larger leaves are divided into 5–13 pinnate segments. Broad-leaved Waterleaf (p. 208) has broad leaves with 5–7 lobes. 1–2′ high. Waterleaf Family.

> **Virginia Waterleaf** (*H. virginianum*) Stem leaves pinnately 5–7-lobed; stamens long-protruding; stem smoothish. Leaves usually mottled as though water-stained. Flowers white to lavender. Stems rather weak. Que. and w. N.Eng. to Man. south.

> **Large-leaved Waterleaf** (*H. macrophyllum*) † Similar to the Virginia Waterleaf, but the stem is hairy. Leaves with 7–13 lobes. W. Va. to Ill. south.

> **Appendaged Waterleaf** (*H. appendiculatum*) Stem leaves palmately 5–7-lobed, like those of a maple leaf; stamens slightly protruding. Flowers lavender, borne above the leaves. Broad-leaved Waterleaf (p. 208) has similar stem leaves. Stem hairy. S. Ont. and w. Pa. to Minn. south.

Tall White Lettuce (*Prenanthes altissima*) Greenish-white, nodding flowers ½″ long, in a widely branched cluster; late summer and fall. See p. 212.

Continued

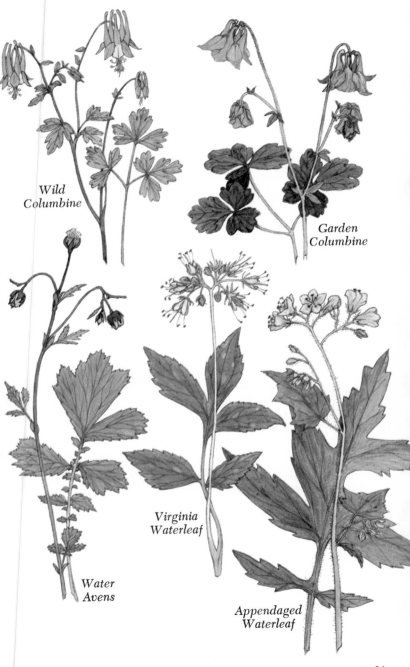

Wild
Columbine

Garden
Columbine

Virginia
Waterleaf

Water
Avens

Appendaged
Waterleaf

$\times \frac{1}{2}$

Bell-shaped or Nodding Flowers (cont.)

Jacob's Ladders (*Polemonium*) Blue or purple, bell-shaped flowers with entire leaflets. Leaves pinnate, with numerous leaflets. Flowers ½–¾" wide. Phlox Family.

Jacob's Ladder (*P. van-bruntiae*) Blue-purple flowers; stamens long-protruding. Lower leaves with 15–21 narrowly egg-shaped leaflets. Stem erect. 1½–2½' high. Swamps and mountain glades, Vt. and N.Y. south. Summer.

Greek Valerian (*P. reptans*) Deep-blue flowers; stamens not protruding. Lower leaves with 11–17 lance-shaped or oval leaflets. Stems weak and reclining. 6–18" high. Rich woods, N.Y. to Minn. south. Spring.

White, Pink or Purple Flowers, ¼" or More Wide, Not Bell-shaped or Nodding; Stem Leaves with 3 or More Entire, Toothed or Shallowly Lobed Leaflets

LEAFLETS ENTIRE OR WITH A FEW TEETH OR LOBES

Three-toothed Cinquefoil (*Potentilla tridentata*) Evergreen leaves with 3 leaflets, the leaflets 3-toothed at the tip. Flowers white, ¼–½" wide, and grow in a branched cluster. Spreads by underground stems. 1–12" high. Rocky or sandy soil, especially on mountaintops, Can. south to N.Y., Mich., Wis. and Iowa, and in mts. to Ga. Late spring and summer. Rose Family.

Buckbean (*Menyanthes trifoliata*) Bog plant with 3 entire leaflets. See p. 184.

Meadow Rues (*Thalictrum*) Leaflets with 2–9 blunt lobes, numerous. See p. 146.

LEAFLETS WITH NUMEROUS TEETH

Marsh or **Purple Cinquefoil** (*Potentilla palustris*) Bog plant with large (1" wide) purple flowers. Petals narrow and shorter than the broad, pointed, purple sepals. Leaflets 5–7, pinnate and blunt. Stem somewhat sprawling. 6–24" long. Swamps. Summer. Rose Family.

Tall Cinquefoil (*Potentilla arguta*) Basal leaves pinnate, with 7–11 egg-shaped leaflets. Flowers white, about ½" wide, and grow in a close cluster. Stem hairy. 1–3' high. Dry fields and rocky slopes. Late spring and summer. Rose Family.

Continued

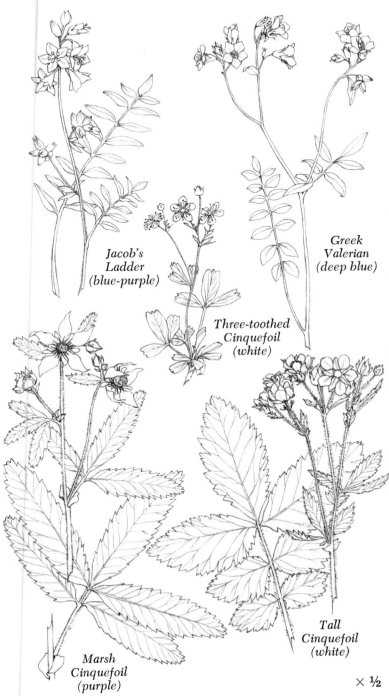

Jacob's
Ladder
(blue-purple)

Greek
Valerian
(deep blue)

Three-toothed
Cinquefoil
(white)

Marsh
Cinquefoil
(purple)

Tall
Cinquefoil
(white)

× ½

White, Pink or Purple Flowers, ¼″ or More Wide, Not Bell-shaped or Nodding; Stem Leaves with 3 or More Entire, Toothed or Shallowly Lobed Leaflets (cont.)

LEAFLETS WITH NUMEROUS TEETH (CONT.)

Bowman's Root and **American Ipecac** (*Gillenia*) White or pinkish flowers with long, narrow petals. The petals may be slightly unequal in length. Leaflets 3 or 5. 2–4′ high. Woods. Late spring and summer. Rose Family.

> **Bowman's Root** or **Indian Physic** (*G. trifoliata*) Leaflets 3. N.Y. to Mich. south.

> **American Ipecac** (*G. stipulata*) Leaflets apparently 5 (the bottom 2 are actually stipules). Sw. N.Y. to Ill. south.

Raspberries and **Blackberries** (*Rubus*) Stems prickly or else low and trailing over the ground. White flowers. Leaflets 3 or 5. Late spring and early summer. Rose Family.

1. STEMS TRAILING OVER THE GROUND (SEE P. 330)

2. STEMS ERECT OR ARCHED, PRICKLY

> **Common Blackberry** (*R. allegheniensis*) Flowers about 1″ wide, the petals longer than the sepals. Flowers in racemes. Fruit juicy, black. Divided by botanists into numerous species. 2–8′ high. Dry fields, clearings.

> **Thimbleberry** or **Black Raspberry** (*R. occidentalis*) Flowers ½″ wide, the petals no longer than the sepals; stem conspicuously whitened and bearing small, hooked prickles. The stems arch completely over and often root at the tip. Fruit purple-black. Dry or rocky soil.

> **Wild Red Raspberry** (*R. idaeus*) † Like the Thimbleberry, but the stem is only slightly whitened, and although usually arched, it does not root at the tip; the young stems are densely covered with bristles rather than prickly. Fruit red. 2–6′ high. Roadsides and thickets.

Avenses (*Geum*) Basal leaves with 1 or 3 large, terminal leaflets and several small leaflets along the stalk. White flowers. Stem leaves mostly of 3 toothed leaflets. 1–2½′ high. Rose Family.

> **White Avens** (*G. canadense*) Flowers ½″ wide, the petals as long as or longer than the sepals. Stem smooth to slightly hairy. Thickets and open woods. Summer, sometimes in fall.

> **Rough Avens** (*G. laciniatum*) Petals much shorter than the sepals. Stem hairy. Fruiting head a bristly ball, ¾″ in diameter. Damp meadows and roadsides. Late spring and summer.

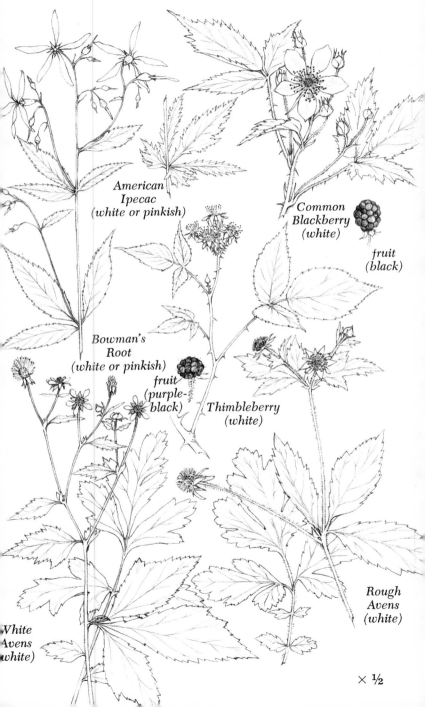

American
Ipecac
(white or pinkish)

Common
Blackberry
(white)

fruit
(black)

Bowman's
Root
(white or pinkish)

fruit
(purple-
black)

Thimbleberry
(white)

White
Avens
(white)

Rough
Avens
(white)

× ½

White, Pink, Purple or Blue Flowers, ¼″ or More Wide, Not Bell-shaped or Nodding; Stem Leaves or Leaflets Deeply Lobed or Divided

Musk Mallow (*Malva moschata*) * Large (1½–2″ wide), showy, white or pink flowers. Petals indented at the tip. Leaves deeply divided into narrow segments. 1–2½′ high. Waste places, roadsides. Summer. Mallow Family.

White Water Buttercup (*Ranunculus trichophyllus*) Aquatic plant with finely divided leaves. The flowers are white, ½–¾″ wide, and bloom just above the water surface. Ponds and streams. Summer and fall. Buttercup Family.

Queen-of-the-prairie (*Filipendula rubra*) Small (⅓″ wide), deep-pink flowers in large, branching clusters. Lower leaves very large, divided into 3–7 broad, deeply lobed leaflets. 2–8′ high. Meadows and prairies, Pa. to Mich. south, escaped from gardens east to N.Eng. Summer. Rose Family.

Spotted Knapweed (*Centaurea maculosa*) * Pink, purple or whitish flowers in thistlelike heads. Base of the heads covered with black-fringed bracts. Leaves divided into narrow segments. 1–3′ high. Roadsides and waste places. Summer. Composite Family.

Isopyrum or **False Rue Anemone** (*Isopyrum biternatum*) White flowers, ½–¾″ wide, in a small cluster; leaflets in 3′s and deeply lobed. 4–10″ high. Rich woods, s. Ont. to Minn. south. Spring. Buttercup Family.

Phacelias or **Scorpionweeds** (*Phacelia*) Blue (rarely white) flowers, about ½″ wide, in more or less one-sided racemes. Spring and early summer. Waterleaf Family.

Miami Mist (*P. purshii*) Petals fringed; stem leaves pinnately cleft and the upper stalkless. 6–18″ high. Rich woods and fields, Pa. to Wis. south.

Small-flowered Phacelia (*P. dubia*) † Similar to the Miami Mist, but the petals are not fringed. N.Y. and Ohio south.

Fern-leaved Phacelia (*P. bipinnatifida*) Petals not fringed; stem leaves long-stalked and pinnate. 10–24″ high. Rich woods, Va. to Ill. south.

Storksbill or **Alfilaria** (*Erodium cicutarium*) Pink or purple flowers (almost ½″ wide) in small umbels; leaves finely cut and *pinnately* divided. See p. 288.

Herb Robert (*Geranium robertianum*) Similar to the Storksbill, but the leaves are *palmately* divided. See p. 288.

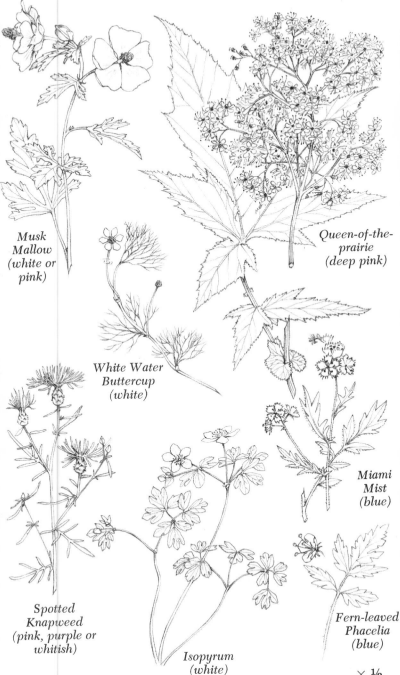

*Musk
Mallow
(white or
pink)*

*Queen-of-the-
prairie
(deep pink)*

*White Water
Buttercup
(white)*

*Miami
Mist
(blue)*

*Spotted
Knapweed
(pink, purple or
whitish)*

*Isopyrum
(white)*

*Fern-leaved
Phacelia
(blue)*

× ½

Yellow Flowers, ¼" or More Wide; Basal (or Lowest) Leaves Pinnately Divided or Lobed

Sennas (*Cassia*) Leaflets entire. Leaves pinnate, with numerous leaflets. Fruit a many-seeded pod. Pea Family.

Wild Senna (*C. hebecarpa*) Plant 3–5′ high with 5–9 pairs of leaflets. The yellow flowers are about ¾″ wide and grow in racemes. Stamens chocolate-brown. Stipules very narrow and pointed; joints of pods as long as wide. Roadsides and thickets, Mass. to Mich. south. Summer. The very similar *C. marilandica* (Pa. to Iowa south) has narrowly lance-shaped stipules, and the joints of the pods are much shorter than broad.

Partridge Pea (*C. fasciculata*) Plant 6–30″ high with 8–15 pairs of leaflets; showy yellow flowers 1–1½″ wide growing in the axils. Flowers long-stalked; stamens 10, 4 with yellow anthers, 6 with purple. Sandy fields, Mass. to Minn. south. Summer and fall.

Wild Sensitive Plant (*C. nictitans*) Like the Partridge Pea but smaller, with short-stalked flowers about ¼″ wide. Stamens 5. Leaves sensitive to touch. Sandy soil, Mass. and s. Vt. to Ill. south. Summer and fall.

Agrimonies (*Agrimonia*) Leaflets 5–15, toothed; flowers in slender spikes or racemes. The leaflets (including the terminal one) are of uniform shape, but diminish in size toward the base of the leaf, and there are usually very small leaf segments growing between them. Flowers ¼–½″ wide. Fruit bristly, clings to clothing. 1½–6′ high. Woods and thickets. Summer and early fall. Rose Family.

1. LARGER LEAFLETS 5–9

Agrimony (*A. gryposepala*) Leaflets smooth on the underside, except for a few hairs along the veins; raceme with scattered, spreading hairs. Fruit with spreading bristles. The commonest species.

Woodland Agrimony (*A. striata*) Leaflets downy beneath; raceme with hairs pressed to the stem. Fruit with erect bristles. Commoner in the n. parts of our area; begins to bloom later than the Agrimony.

Beaked Agrimony (*A. rostellata*) Raceme without hairs; leaflets broad, with a few, coarse, blunt teeth. Mass. to Ill. south.

2. LARGER LEAFLETS 11–15

Small-flowered Agrimony (*A. parviflora*) Recognized by its narrower, more numerous leaflets. Stem densely hairy. W. Conn. to Ill. south.

Continued

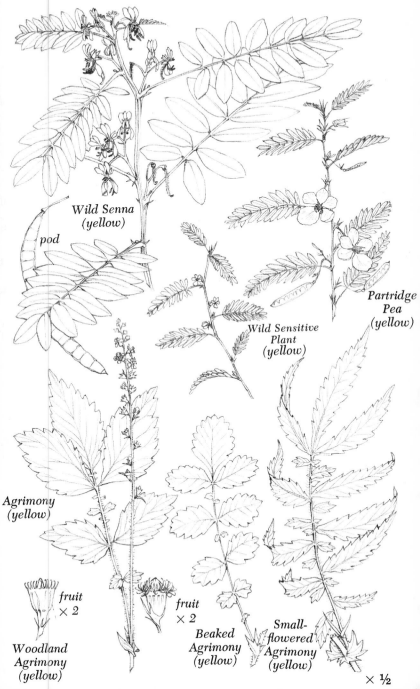

Wild Senna
(yellow)

pod

Partridge
Pea
(yellow)

Wild Sensitive
Plant
(yellow)

Agrimony
(yellow)

fruit
× 2

Woodland
Agrimony
(yellow)

fruit
× 2

Beaked
Agrimony
(yellow)

Small-
flowered
Agrimony
(yellow)

× ½

Yellow Flowers, ¼" or More Wide; Basal (or Lowest) Leaves Pinnately Divided or Lobed (cont.)

Avenses (*Geum*) Terminal leaflet of basal leaves noticeably larger than other leaflets and often cleft or lobed; flowers in a branched cluster or solitary. Basal leaves often have small leaflets interspaced with larger ones. Rose Family.

1. GOLDEN-YELLOW FLOWERS, ½–1″ WIDE; BLOOM IN SUMMER

Yellow Avens (*G. aleppicum*) Terminal leaflet of basal leaves wedge-shaped at base and usually deeply cleft; the next set of leaflets is not much smaller. Stem somewhat hairy. 1–4′ high. Meadows, thickets and woods.

Mountain Avens (*G. peckii*) Alpine plant; terminal leaflet large, rounded; stem smoothish. There are usually several sets of very small leaflets along the stalks of the basal leaves and the terminal leaflet is indistinctly lobed. 6–20″ high. White Mts., N.H.

Large-leaved Avens (*G. macrophyllum*) Terminal leaflet much larger than the other leaflets, roundish, usually 3-lobed; stem hairs bristly. The basal leaves have several small leaflets along the stalk with much smaller ones interspaced. 1–3′ high. Moist woods and thickets, n. N.Eng. and N.Y. to Minn. north.

2. FLOWERS ¼–½″ WIDE; FOUND IN WOODS

Cream-colored Avens (*G. virginianum*) Pale or greenish-yellow flowers, ¼–½″ wide; petals shorter than the sepals; blooms June to August. The basal leaves may be undivided, deeply lobed, or divided into 3–7 leaflets. Stem erect and hairy, at least below. 1½–3′ high. Dry woods, Mass. to Ind. south.

Spring Avens (*G. vernum*) † Yellow to cream-colored flowers, about ¼″ wide; petals as long as sepals; blooms April to early June. Basal leaves as in Cream-colored Avens. Stem only slightly hairy, arching. 6–24″ high. Rich woods and borders, N.Y. to Mich. south.

3. NODDING FLOWERS, ½″ LONG ; FOUND IN SWAMPS

Water or **Purple Avens** (*G. rivale*) See p. 228.

Buffalo Bur (*Solanum rostratum*) * Stem prickly with yellow spines. Flowers about 1″ wide, with 5 lobes. Leaves irregularly lobed and divided. Fruit prickly. 1–2′ high. Weed of waste places. Summer and fall. Nightshade Family.

Buttercups (*Ranunculus*) Spring flowers with shiny petals, over ½″ wide. See p. 242.

False Foxgloves (*Gerardia*) Flowers funnel-shaped. See p. 278.

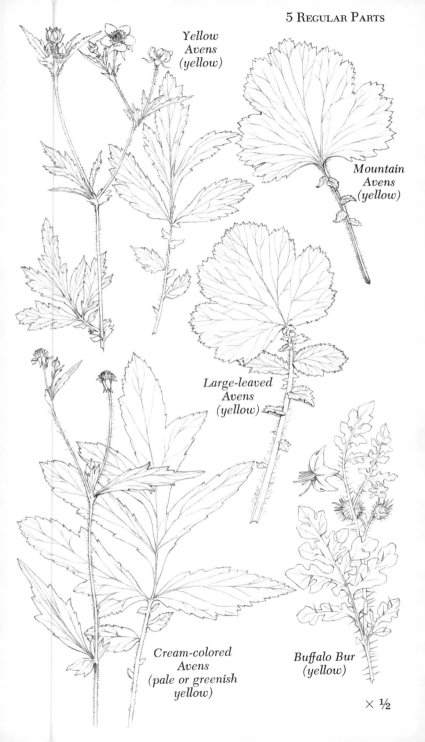

*Yellow
Avens
(yellow)*

*Mountain
Avens
(yellow)*

*Large-leaved
Avens
(yellow)*

*Cream-colored
Avens
(pale or greenish
yellow)*

*Buffalo Bur
(yellow)*

× ½

Yellow Flowers, ¼″ or More Wide; Leaves Palmate, the 3–7 Leaflets Regularly Toothed

Indian Strawberry (*Duchesnea indica*) * Leaflets 3; plant trailing. Flowers ½–¾″ wide, with a cluster of 3-toothed bracts below the calyx. Fruit red, resembling a strawberry but tasteless. Waste places, s. N.Y. to Iowa south. Spring and early summer. Rose Family.

Cinquefoils or **Five Fingers** (*Potentilla*) Leaflets 5–7, palmate, except for two nontrailing species that have 3 leaflets. Some species have white or purple flowers and one is a shrub (p. 316). Rose Family.

1. LEAFLETS 3

> **Rough Cinquefoil** (*P. norvegica*) Plant with stout, hairy stem; 4–36″ high. Flowers ¼–½″ wide, the calyx lobes slightly longer than the petals. Clearings, roadsides and waste places. Common. Late spring to fall.

> **Dwarf Mountain Cinquefoil** (*P. robbinsiana*) Alpine plant of the White Mts., N.H. Plant in a dense tuft, dwarf, ½–2″ high. Flower about ¼″ wide. Rare and local.

2. LEAFLETS 5, SILVERY-WHITE BENEATH

> **Silvery Cinquefoil** (*P. argentea*) * The silvery leaflets are deeply toothed, almost lobed. Flowers ¼–⅜″ wide, the petals not much longer than the sepals. 4–18″ long. Dry open places. Late spring to fall.

3. LEAFLETS 5–7, NOT SILVERY-WHITE BENEATH

> **Rough-fruited** or **Sulphur Cinquefoil** (*P. recta*) * Stout, erect plant, 10–24″ high, with pale-yellow flowers ½–¾″ wide. The 5–7 leaflets are lance-shaped, coarsely toothed. Dry fields and roadsides. Summer.

> **Common Cinquefoil** (*P. simplex*) Low, weak-stemmed plant, the 5 leaflets toothed for three-quarters of their length. Flowers ¼–½″ wide, growing on long stalks from the axils. 3–24″ long. Fields and open woods. Spring and early summer.

> **Dwarf Cinquefoil** (*P. canadensis*) Similar to the Common Cinquefoil, but the 5 leaflets are toothed only above the middle. See p. 182.

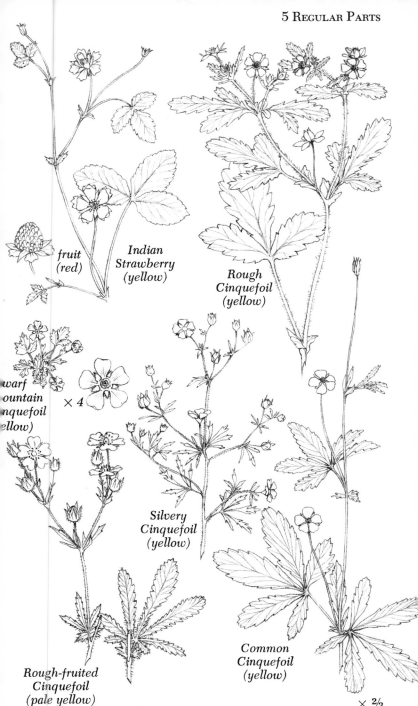

fruit
(red)

Indian
Strawberry
(yellow)

Rough
Cinquefoil
(yellow)

Dwarf
Mountain
Cinquefoil
(yellow)

× 4

Silvery
Cinquefoil
(yellow)

Rough-fruited
Cinquefoil
(pale yellow)

Common
Cinquefoil
(yellow)

× ⅔

Yellow Flowers, ¼" or More Wide; Leaves Palmate, the Segments Deeply Lobed or Divided

Buttercups (*Ranunculus*) Showy, golden-yellow flowers, ½–1½" wide. A well-known group of plants with shining petals and usually 3-divided leaves, the divisions variously cut and lobed. Buttercup Family.

1. AQUATIC; LEAVES FINELY DIVIDED

Yellow Water Buttercup (*R. flabellaris*) The submerged leaves are divided into threadlike segments; the leaves above water may be less cleft. Stem hollow. 6–24" long. Ponds and muddy shores. Spring and early summer.

2. NONAQUATIC; SEPALS BENT DOWN AGAINST THE FLOWER STALK

Bulbous Buttercup (*R. bulbosus*) * Flowers about 1" wide. The only species with a bulbous base. Stem usually hairy. 6–18" high. Fields and roadsides. Spring and early summer.

3. NONAQUATIC; SEPALS SPREADING

a. Plants of dry or rich woods and ledges; petals oblong, longer than wide

Hispid Buttercup (*R. hispidus*) Basal leaves, about as wide as long, cleft or divided into 3 segments which are either egg-shaped or oblong. Stem spreading. 6–24" long. S. N.Eng. to Wis. south. Spring.

Early Buttercup (*R. fascicularis*) Basal leaves pinnately divided, mostly longer than wide, the divisions lance-shaped or narrow. 6–12" high. S. N.H. to Ont. and Minn. south. Spring.

b. Plants of wet woods, swamps, moist open places and fields

Creeping Buttercup (*R. repens*) * Lower leaves with at least the terminal leaflet stalked, the largest leaflets normally 1–1½" long; leaves dark green, usually mottled; plant creeping at the base, often forming patches. Fruit short-beaked. 6–18" high. Ditches and low grounds. Spring and summer.

Swamp Buttercup (*R. septentrionalis*) Lower leaves with all leaflets stalked, the largest leaflets normally 1½–4" long and wedge-shaped; leaves not mottled; stem spreading, later rooting. Fruit long-beaked. 1–3' high. Wet woods, meadows. Spring and early summer.

Tall Buttercup (*R. acris*) * Larger leaves divided into 3–7, deeply cleft parts, all of them stalkless. Stem erect, usually hairy. 1–3' high. Fields and meadows. Common. Spring to fall.

Continued

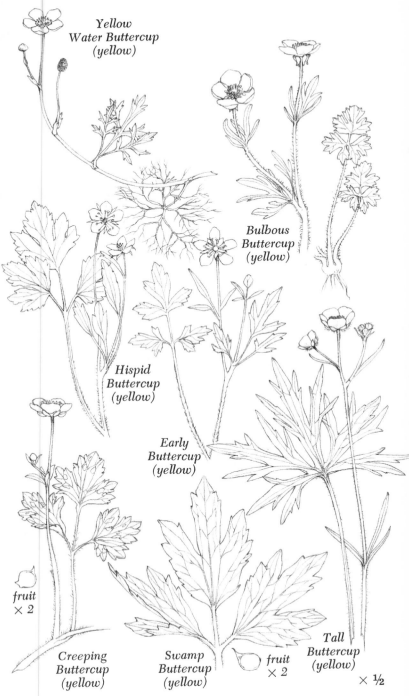

Yellow Water Buttercup (yellow)

Bulbous Buttercup (yellow)

Hispid Buttercup (yellow)

Early Buttercup (yellow)

fruit × 2

Creeping Buttercup (yellow)

Swamp Buttercup (yellow)

fruit × 2

Tall Buttercup (yellow)

× ½

Yellow Flowers, ¼″ or More Wide; Leaves Palmate, the Segments Deeply Lobed or Divided (cont.)

Crowfoots (*Ranunculus*) Small flowers (¼–⅜″ wide); sepals usually bent downward, as long as or longer than the petals. The stem leaves are deeply lobed and divided, but in several species at least some of the basal leaves are heart-shaped and toothed. The leaves of the Hooked Crowfoot (*R. recurvatus*) (p. 204) are deeply cleft into 3 lobes. Buttercup Family.

1. STEM HAIRY

Bristly Crowfoot (*R. pensylvanicus*) Hairy plant of wet meadows and ditches. The flowers are pale yellow. Leaves divided into 3 deeply cleft leaflets. 6–24″ high. Summer.

2. STEM SMOOTH

Small-flowered Crowfoot (*R. abortivus*) Some of the basal leaves roundish and toothed, heart-shaped at the base; seeds with a minute, usually straight beak at the tip. Stem leaves and usually a few basal leaves divided into oblong or narrow segments. 6–24″ high. Woods and moist slopes. Spring and early summer.

Mountain Crowfoot (*R. allegheniensis*) Similar to the preceding species, but the seeds have a noticeably curved hook. S. and w. N.Eng. to s. Ohio south.

Cursed Crowfoot (*R. sceleratus*) Basal leaves all deeply lobed; grows in wet places. Pale-yellow flowers, ¼–⅜″ wide. Leaves deeply cleft or divided into 3 segments. Stem hollow, fleshy. 6–24″ high. Pools and wet ditches. Spring and summer.

Spreading Globeflower (*Trollius laxus*) Large (1–1½″ wide) greenish-yellow, solitary flower; grows in wet places. The leaves are palmately divided into 5–7 segments. Petals minute, but with 5 or 6 large, spreading sepals. 1–2′ high. W. Conn. to Mich., south to Del. and Ohio; rare and local. Spring. Buttercup Family.

Flower-of-an-hour (*Hibiscus trionum*) * Pale-yellow flowers with a dark center, 1–2½″ wide; grows in waste places. Leaves divided into 3 segments, the middle one longest. The flowers last only a few hours. Low, spreading plant. Summer and fall. Mallow Family.

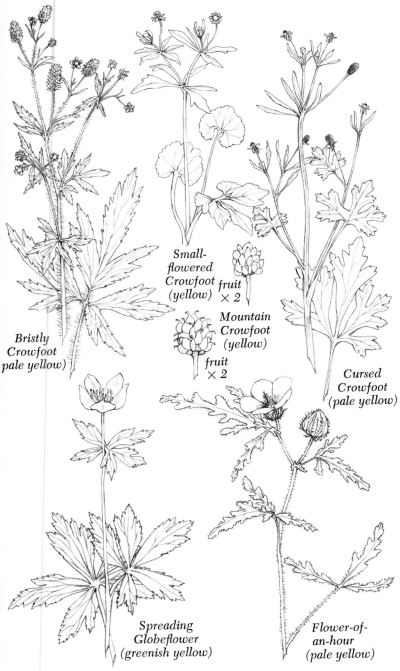

Small-
flowered
Crowfoot
(yellow)

fruit
× 2

Mountain
Crowfoot
(yellow)

fruit
× 2

Bristly
Crowfoot
pale yellow)

Cursed
Crowfoot
(pale yellow)

Spreading
Globeflower
(greenish yellow)

Flower-of-
an-hour
(pale yellow)

× ½

Yellow Flowers; Leaflets Entire or Notched at the Tip

Yellow Wood Sorrels (*Oxalis*) Leaflets in 3's, notched at the tip. Low plants with flowers in small long-stalked clusters. Leaves sour to the taste. Spring to fall. Wood Sorrel Family.

Yellow Wood Sorrel (*O. europaea*) Flowers ¼–½″ wide; stem more or less erect, not creeping. Stalks of pods erect or ascending. 3–15″ high. Common weed of gardens and roadsides. The very similar *O. stricta* has the stalks of the pods horizontal or bent abruptly downward.

Great Wood Sorrel (*O. grandis*) A large-flowered species with flowers ¾–1″ wide. The leaflets usually have a narrow purple border. Stalks of pods erect or spreading. 8–36″ high. Woods and shaded banks, Pa. to Ill. south.

Creeping Wood Sorrel (*O. corniculata*) * A creeping plant with smaller flowers and leaves than the preceding two species. Stalks of pods bent downward. Usually found as a weed around greenhouses.

WILDFLOWERS WITH OPPOSITE LEAVES /
Leaves Entire

Flowers Terminal, Flat-topped, the Lobes Very Narrow at the Base and United to Form a Slender Tube (Phloxes)

Phloxes (*Phlox*) Showy flowers, ½–1″ wide, with the rounded flower lobes joined to the flower tube with a very narrow base. The flowers of the Pink Family (pp. 258 and 259) are very similar, but the petals are completely separate. Phlox Family.

1. MATTED OR WIDELY BRANCHED; LEAVES STIFF AND NARROW

Moss Phlox, Moss Pink or **Ground Pink** (*P. subulata*) Flower lobes indented at the tip (not cleft). Rose-magenta to white flowers. Prostrate plant of dry, sandy or rocky places, N.Y. to Mich. south; escaped from cultivation in N.Eng. Spring.

Cleft Phlox or **Sand Phlox** (*P. bifida*) Flower lobes cleft about to the middle, forming a ten-pointed star. Flowers pale purple, with two dots at the base of each lobe. Dry ledges and sandhills, s. Mich. to Iowa south.

Continued

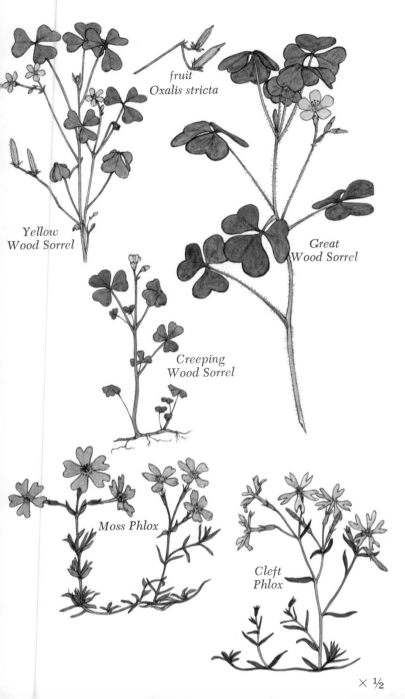

fruit
Oxalis stricta

*Yellow
Wood Sorrel*

*Great
Wood Sorrel*

*Creeping
Wood Sorrel*

Moss Phlox

*Cleft
Phlox*

× ½

Flowers Terminal, Flat-topped, the Lobes Very Narrow at the Base and United to Form a Slender Tube (Phloxes) (cont.)

Phloxes (*Phlox*) (cont.)

2. ERECT PLANTS OR, IF NOT ERECT, THE LEAVES NOT NARROW

a. Upper stem and calyx hairy; blooming in spring

Downy Phlox (*P. pilosa*) Leaves narrow or narrowly lance-shaped, sharp-pointed, 5 or more times longer than wide. Pink or purple flowers, the lobes entire. Stem usually soft-hairy, without prostrate, leafy shoots at base. 1–2' high. Open woods and grasslands, s. Conn. to Wis. south.

Wild Blue Phlox (*P. divaricata*) Leaves lance-shaped, egg-shaped or oblong; flower lobes about as long as the tube, often indented at tip. Blue to purple flowers; stamens not protruding. Stem with prostrate shoots at base. Woods, w. N.Eng. to Mich. south.

Creeping Phlox (*P. stolonifera*) Lower leaves egg-shaped; flower lobes about half as long as the tube, mostly entire. Violet or purple flowers; stamens slightly protruding. Stem creeping at the base. Moist woods, Pa. and Ohio south.

b. Upper stem and calyx smooth or nearly so

Wild Sweet William or **Meadow Phlox** (*P. maculata*) Middle leaves widest just above their base; stem erect, usually spotted with purple; flower cluster longer than wide. Purple or pink (rarely white) flowers. 1–3' high. Meadows and banks of streams, w. N.Eng. to Minn. south. Late spring and summer.

Garden Phlox or **Perennial Phlox** (*P. paniculata*) Middle leaves widest near the center, with prominent side veins, broadly lance-shaped, 3 or 4 times longer than wide; stem erect. Magenta-pink flowers (in the wild); cultivated in many color shades. 2–6' high. N.Y. to Iowa south; escaped from cultivation in N.Eng. Woods and borders. Summer and fall.

Smooth Phlox (*P. glaberrima*) Middle leaves narrowly lance-shaped, 5–7 times longer than wide, long-pointed; stem erect. Pink or purple flowers. 1–4' high. Low woods and moist open places, Va. and Ohio to Wis. south. Spring and early summer.

Mountain Phlox (*P. ovata*) † Stem sprawling, with erect flowering branches; middle leaves elliptical or egg-shaped. Deep-pink or purple flowers. 1–2' high. Woods, s. Pa. to Ind. south. Spring and early summer.

Downy Phlox
(pink or purple)

Wild Blue
Phlox
(blue to purple)

Creeping
Phlox
(violet or purple)

Smooth
Phlox
(pink or purple)

Wild
Sweet
William
(purple or pink)

Garden
Phlox
(magenta-pink)

× ½

Bell-shaped, Cup-shaped or Tubular Flowers under ½″ Long, Clustered at the Ends of the Branches

Dogbanes (*Apocynum*) Plants with milky juice. The flowers, ⅛–¼″ long, are bell-shaped or tubular, with 5 lobes. Leaves oblong or egg-shaped, 2–4″ long. Widely branched plants, 1–4′ high, with clusters of pink, white or greenish flowers. Pods long and narrow, in pairs. Summer. Dogbane Family.

1. FLOWERS PINK OR PINK-STRIPED (AT LEAST WITHIN)

Spreading Dogbane (*A. androsaemifolium*) Pink flowers with flaring, recurved lobes, more nodding than those of the other species. Common in dry fields and thickets.

Intermediate Dogbane (*A. medium*) Flowers pale pink, at least within, the lobes spreading but not recurved. Intermediate between the preceding and the following species, and treated by some botanists as a hybrid rather than a distinct species. Roadsides and thickets.

2. WHITE OR GREENISH FLOWERS WITH ERECT OR SPREADING LOBES

Indian Hemp (*A. cannabinum*) Greenish-white flowers, smaller than the preceding two species; lowest leaves rounded at the base, distinctly stalked. Stems usually more erect than those of the two preceding species. Shores and thickets. 1–3′ high.

Clasping-leaved Dogbane (*A. sibiricum*) Milk-white flowers; lowest leaves practically stalkless, sometimes with a heart-shaped, clasping base; the ends of the leaves rounded, with a short, bristlelike tip. The side veins of the leaves meet the midrib at a wider angle than those of Indian Hemp. 1–2′ high. Gravelly soil and stream banks.

Heart-leaved Umbrellawort or **Wild Four-o'clock** (*Mirabilis nyctaginea*) Pink or purple flowers in clusters of 2–5 above a star-shaped cup (involucre), which becomes greatly enlarged after flowering. The leaves are egg-shaped with a heart-shaped or rounded base, all with stalks except the upper ones. 1–3′ high. Prairies, roadsides and waste places. Late spring and summer. Four-o'clock Family.

Knawel (*Scleranthus annuus*) Sprawling plant with tiny, green flowers; leaves narrow, ¼–1″ long. See p. 432.

Corn Salad or **Lamb's Lettuce** (*Valerianella olitoria*) Tiny bluish or whitish flowers in close clusters. See p. 284.

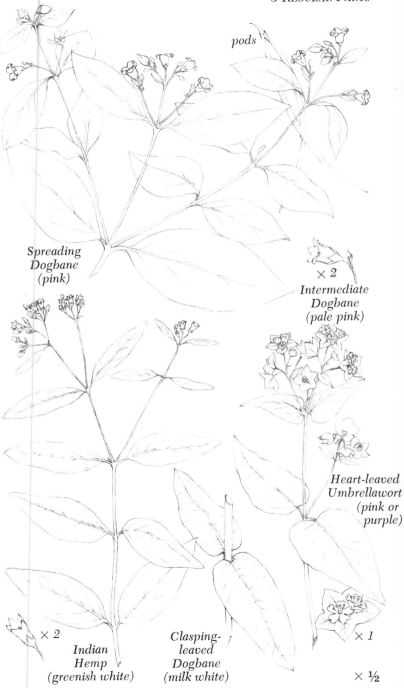

pods

Spreading
Dogbane
(pink)

× 2
Intermediate
Dogbane
(pale pink)

Heart-leaved
Umbrellawort
(pink or
purple)

× 2
Indian
Hemp
(greenish white)

Clasping-
leaved
Dogbane
(milk white)

× 1

× ½

Flowers ½″ or More Long, Funnel- or Club-shaped, or Tubular with Small Flaring Lobes; Some of the Flowers Terminal

BLUE, VIOLET OR GREENISH-WHITE FLOWERS

Ruellias (*Ruellia*) Lavender-blue or pale-violet, funnel-shaped flowers with round, flaring lobes. See p. 256.

Gentians (*Gentiana*) Showy flowers, either funnel-shaped with pointed lobes or club-shaped, blooming in late summer and fall. The Fringed Gentians (p. 156) have 4 flower lobes. Gentian Family.

1. FLOWERS CLUB-SHAPED OR NARROWLY TUBE-SHAPED, THE LOBES BLUNT AT THE TIP; BLUE OR VIOLET FLOWERS

a. Leaves narrow or narrowly lance-shaped

Narrow-leaved Gentian (*G. linearis*) Blue or violet flowers with the tips of the flower lobes erect or bent inward. 6–24″ high. Damp woods and meadows, Pa., W.Va., Md. and Minn. north. Late July to fall.

b. Leaves broad, egg-shaped or oblong

Closed or **Bottle Gentian** (*G. clausa*) Flowers closed at the tip, the fringes between the flower lobes seen only when flower is forced open; leaves slender-pointed. Blue-violet flowers, 1–1½″ long. Moist woods and meadows.

Fringe-tip Closed Gentian (*G. andrewsii*) Similar to the Closed Gentian, but the fringes between the flower lobes are slightly longer than the lobes and are visible at the tip of the closed flower. W. and s. N.Eng. (where rare) to Man. south.

Soapwort Gentian (*G. saponaria*) Flowers slightly open at the tip or closed, paler than the preceding two species; leaves with a broad point. Fringes between the flower lobes shorter than the lobes; calyx lobes narrower than in the other two species. Sandy swamps, shores, N.Y. to Minn. south.

2. FLOWERS FUNNEL-SHAPED, THE LOBES SPREADING AT THE TIP

Pine-barren Gentian (*G. autumnalis*) Large (2″ long), usually solitary flower with widely spreading lobes. Flowers deep blue, speckled on the inside. Leaves very narrow. 6–18″ high. Pine barrens, N.J. south.

Downy Gentian (*G. puberula*) Funnel-shaped, blue flowers with slightly spreading lobes, 1½–2″ long, clustered at the top of the stem. Leaves lance-shaped, 1–2″ long. 8–18″ high. Prairies and sandy open places, w. N.Y. to N.D. south.

Continued

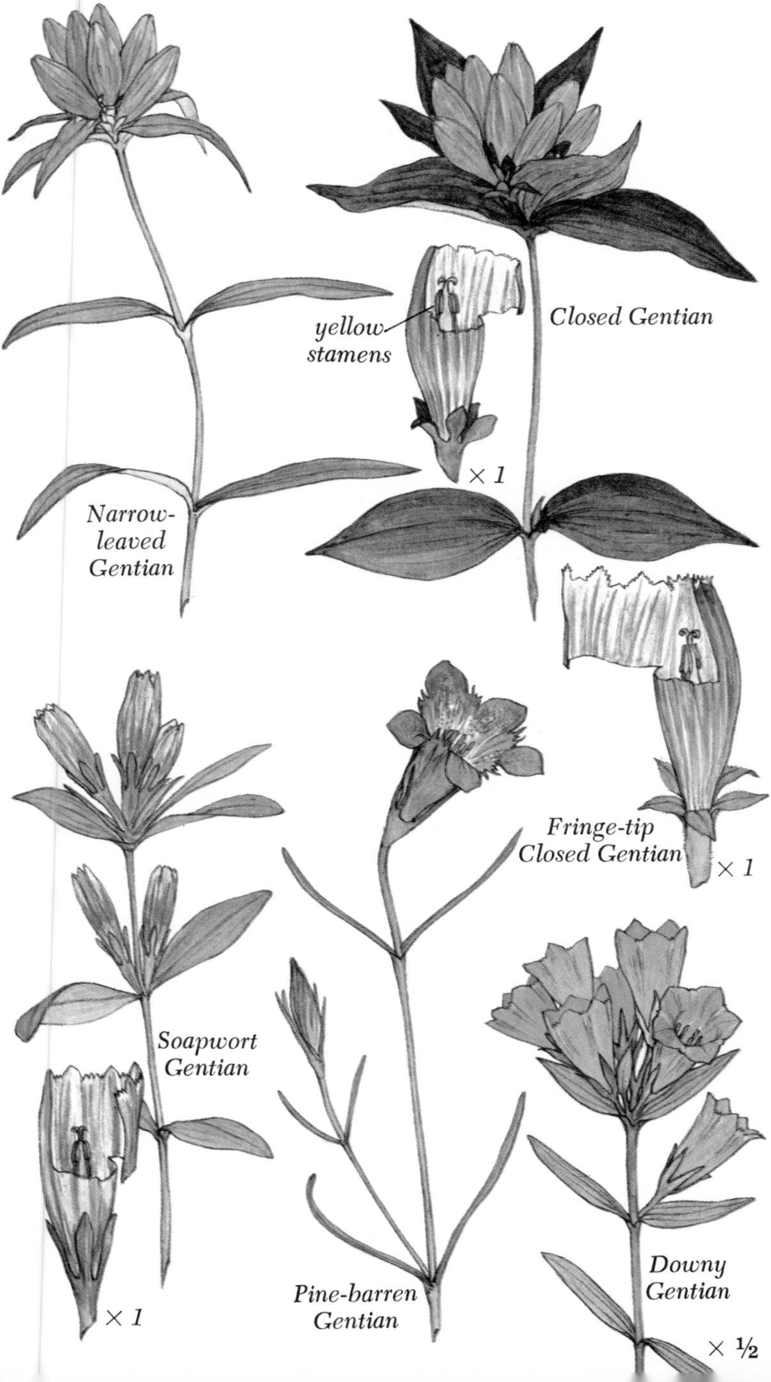

yellow-stamens

Closed Gentian

× 1

Narrow-leaved Gentian

Fringe-tip Closed Gentian × 1

Soapwort Gentian

× 1

Pine-barren Gentian

Downy Gentian

× ½

Flowers ½″ or More Long, Funnel- or Club-shaped, or Tubular with Small Flaring Lobes; Some Flowers Terminal (cont.)

BLUE, VIOLET OR GREENISH-WHITE FLOWERS (CONT.)

Gentians (*Gentiana*) (cont.)

3. FLOWER LOBES POINTED AT THE TIP, ERECT, NOT SPREADING

Stiff Gentian or **Agueweed** (*G. quinquefolia*) Flowers ½–1″ long, pale violet or whitish. Flowers narrow, funnel-shaped, with bristle-tipped lobes. Upper leaves with a rounded, clasping base. Stem 4-angled. 2–30″ high. Woods and damp meadows, sw. Me. to s. Ont. south.

Sampson's Snakeroot or **Striped Gentian** (*G. villosa*) Flowers about 1½″ long, greenish-white with purple stripes inside. Leaves blunt, narrowing toward the base. Open woods, N.J. to s. Ind. south.

PURPLE, PINK OR YELLOW FLOWERS

Gerardias (*Gerardia*) Purple or pink flowers, broadly funnel-shaped, with rounded lobes; leaves very narrow, under 2″ long. Flowers ½–1½″ long, the lobes regular or somewhat irregular. Twelve other local species are found in our area. Summer and fall. Figwort Family.

1. FLESHY PLANT OF SALT MARSHES; CALYX LOBES BLUNT

Seaside Gerardia (*G. maritima*) Leaves thick and blunt. Flowers ½–¾″ long. Along the coast.

2. PLANTS OF MOIST MEADOWS, BOGS AND DRY WOODS; CALYX LOBES POINTED

Purple Gerardia (*G. purpurea*) Flower stalks mostly under ¼″ long; flowers ¾–1½″ long. 10–30″ high. Moist meadows, shores, bogs, s. N.Eng. to Minn. south.

Small-flowered Gerardia (*G. paupercula*) Like the Purple Gerardia, but flowers ½–¾″ long. 6–18″ high.

Slender Gerardia (*G. tenuifolia*) Flower stalks mostly over ¼″ long. Flowers light purple, ½–¾″ long. 6–24″ high. Dry woods and fields, or sometimes in damper situations.

Centaury (*Centaurium umbellatum*) * Pink or rose flowers, ½″ long, the lobes longer than wide. Flower tube slender, a little longer than the lobes. Flower cluster somewhat flat-topped. Leaves oblong, some in a basal rosette. 6–15″ high. Meadows and fields. Summer and fall. Gentian Family.

Entire-leaved False Foxglove (*Gerardia laevigata*) Yellow flowers, 1–1½″ long, with flaring lobes. See p. 278.

Stiff
Gentian

Sampson's
Snakeroot

Seaside
Gerardia

Purple
Gerardia

Small-
flowered
Gerardia

Slender
Gerardia

Centaury

× ½

Flowers Tubular, Funnel- or Bell-shaped, All Growing in the Axils

BLUE OR VIOLET FLOWERS

Myrtle or **Periwinkle** (*Vinca minor*) * Trailing plant with shining leaves. Flowers blue-violet, about 1″ wide, funnel-shaped, with flaring lobes. Commonly cultivated and escaping to roadsides and woods. Spring. Dogbane Family.

Ruellias or **Wild Petunias** (*Ruellia*) Erect plants with large (1–2″ long), funnel-shaped, lavender-blue or pale-violet flowers with flaring lobes. Leaves egg-shaped. Flowers occasionally terminal. 1–3′ high. Woods, clearings, N.J. to Ill. south. Late spring and summer. Acanthus Family.

> **Hairy Ruellia** (*R. caroliniensis*) Stem hairy; flowers stalkless or nearly so.

> **Smooth Ruellia** (*R. strepens*) † Stem smooth or nearly so; flowers growing on short stalks from the middle axils.

False Pennyroyal (*Isanthus brachiatus*) Pale-blue flowers, ¼″ long, with 5 nearly equal lobes. Leaves lance-shaped, the larger ones 3-veined, sometimes with a few teeth. Plant somewhat sticky-hairy. 6–18″ high. Dry, sandy soil, w. N.Eng. to Minn. south. Late summer and fall. Mint Family.

FLOWERS NOT BLUE OR VIOLET

Sea Milkwort (*Glaux maritima*) Low plant of salt marshes and seabeaches with stalkless, white, pink or purple flowers. Flowers without petals. Leaves fleshy, oblong or narrow, about ½″ long. 4–12″ long. Summer. Primrose Family.

Horse Gentians or **Feverworts** (*Triosteum*) Broad-leaved plants with reddish, purplish or brown tubular flowers, ½–¾″ long, stalkless in the axils. Stem stout. 2–4′ high. Late spring and early summer. Honeysuckle Family.

> **Wild Coffee** or **Feverwort** (*T. perfoliatum*) Middle pairs of leaves broadly joined at base and obviously pierced by the stem; purplish-brown or greenish flowers. Fruit an orange-yellow berry. Woods and thickets, s. N.Eng. to Minn. south.

> **Orange-fruited Horse Gentian** (*T. aurantiacum*) Leaves stalkless, but not joined together; purplish-red, slightly irregular flowers. See p. 78.

Wintergreen or **Checkerberry** (*Gaultheria procumbens*) White flowers, ¼″ long, hanging beneath the leaves. See p. 212.

Gerardias (*Gerardia*) Purple or pink, funnel-shaped flowers and very narrow leaves. See p. 254.

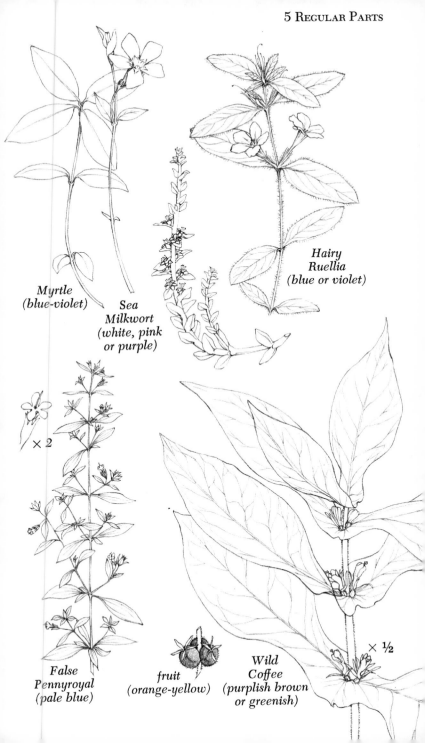

Myrtle
(blue-violet)

Sea
Milkwort
(white, pink
or purple)

Hairy
Ruellia
(blue or violet)

× 2

False
Pennyroyal
(pale blue)

fruit
(orange-yellow)

Wild
Coffee
(purplish brown
or greenish)

× ½

Petals Separate; Sepals United into a Tube, Cup or Bladder; Plants of Dry Habitats

Bouncing Bet or **Soapwort** (*Saponaria officinalis*) * Leaves oval, with 3–5 prominent ribs; pink or white flowers, 1″ wide, often double, in dense clusters. Petals indented at the tip. Stem smooth, stout. 1–2′ high. Roadsides and waste places; common. Summer and early fall. Pink Family.

Corn Cockle (*Agrostemma githago*) * Calyx teeth very long and pointed, projecting beyond the petals; purplish-red flowers, 1–1½″ wide. Leaves narrow, 2–4″ long. Stem covered with whitish hairs. 1–3′ high. Weed of grain fields and waste places. Summer. Pink Family.

Pinks (*Dianthus*) Petals pink, more or less toothed along the edge, and either with dark markings near the center or dotted with white; leaves narrow. Flowers ¼–¾″ wide. 6–15″ high. Pink Family.

> **Deptford Pink** (*D. armeria*) * Deep-pink flowers, dotted with white, ½″ wide. Leaves 1–2″ long. Fields and roadsides. Summer and fall.

> **Maiden Pink** (*D. deltoides*) * Pink flowers with a dark ring at the center, ½–¾″ wide. Petals toothed at tip. Leaves under 1″ long. Fields and roadsides. Summer.

Campions and **Catchflies** (*Silene* and *Lychnis*) Leaves with one main rib, calyx teeth short, and petals neither white-dotted nor with dark markings. Plants of both genera are called Campions — normally *Silene* has 3 styles and *Lychnis* has 5 styles. The Catchflies have sticky stems. Pink Family.

1. BRIGHT RED OR SCARLET FLOWERS

> **Fire Pink** (*S. virginica*) Flowers few, 1–1½″ wide, long-stalked, in a loose cluster; petals narrow, shallowly or deeply cleft. Weakly erect, 6–20″ high, with basal leaves that taper at the base. Rocky slopes and woods, N.J. to Minn. south. Late spring and early summer.

> **Royal Catchfly** (*S. regia*) Flowers 1″ wide, in a close cluster usually longer than wide; petals entire or slightly toothed. Leaves with a round base, stalkless. 2–4′ high. Dry woods and prairies, Ohio to s. Ill. south. Summer.

> **Scarlet Lychnis** (*L. chalcedonica*) * Flowers ¾–1″ wide, short-stalked, in a dense cluster; petals deeply cleft. Leaves egg-shaped or broadly lance-shaped. Stem hairy and leafy. 1–3′ high. Escaped from gardens to roadsides and thickets. Summer.

Continued

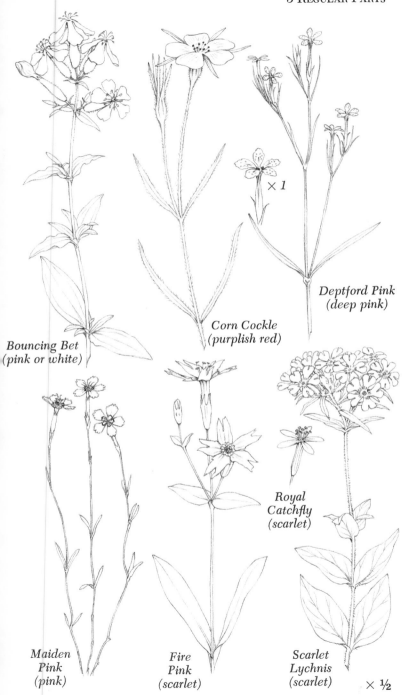

Bouncing Bet
(pink or white)

Corn Cockle
(purplish red)

Deptford Pink
(deep pink)

× 1

Maiden
Pink
(pink)

Fire
Pink
(scarlet)

Royal
Catchfly
(scarlet)

Scarlet
Lychnis
(scarlet)

× ½

Petals Separate; Sepals United into a Tube, Cup or Bladder; Plants of Dry Habitats (cont.)

Campions and **Catchflies** (*Silene* and *Lychnis*) (cont.)

2. ROSE, PINK, WHITE OR LILAC FLOWERS

a. Petals fringed ¼ of their length or deeply 4-lobed

Starry Campion (*S. stellata*) Petals deeply fringed; middle leaves mostly in whorls of 4. White flowers, ¾" wide. 1–3′ high. Open woods, Mass. to Minn. south. Summer.

Ragged Robin or **Cuckooflower** (*L. flos-cuculi*) * Petals divided into 4 narrow lobes, appearing tattered. Deep-pink (sometimes white) flowers, ¾–1" wide. 1–2′ high. Fields and meadows, Pa. north. Summer.

b. Petals deeply cleft for at least ¼ of their length

Bladder Campion (*S. cucubalus*) * Upper stem and leaves smooth. Calyx swollen-bladder–shaped, prominently veined. White flowers, ½–¾" wide; styles 3. Fields and roadsides. Spring and summer.

White Campion (*L. alba*) * Upper stem and leaves downy; white or pinkish flowers, about 1" wide, opening in the evening; styles 5. Calyx more or less inflated, finely veined. Fields and waste places. Late spring to fall.

Night-flowering Catchfly (*S. noctiflora*) * Similar to White Campion, but flowers smaller (about ¾" wide) and styles 3. Sticky-hairy weed of gardens and waste places. Late spring to fall.

Red Campion (*L. dioica*) *† Similar to White Campion, but flowers rose-colored, opening in the morning. Found infrequently.

c. Petals notched, shallowly fringed, or nearly entire

Wild Pink (*S. caroliniana*) Pink flowers, 1" wide; petals broadest at the tip, indented, slightly toothed or nearly entire. Low plant of sandy and rocky places with a rosette of lance-shaped basal leaves. 4–10" high. N.H. to Ohio south. Spring.

Sleepy Catchfly (*S. antirrhina*) Pink or white flowers, about ⅛" wide; petals notched at the tip. The flowers open only for a short time in the sun. Stem with dark, sticky sections. 8–30" high. Dry woods and waste places. Summer.

Moss Campion (*S. acaulis*) Dwarf alpine plant with pink or lilac flowers, ½" wide. Leaves narrow, ½" long. Summits of White Mts., N.H. Summer.

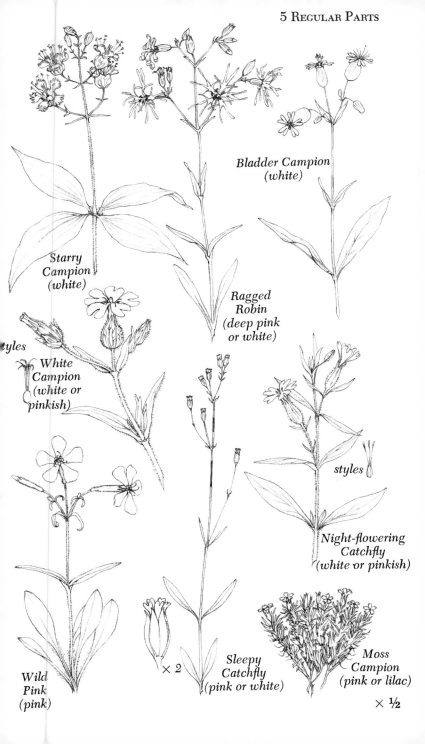

Bladder Campion
(white)

Starry
Campion
(white)

Ragged
Robin
(deep pink
or white)

styles

White
Campion
(white or
pinkish)

styles

Night-flowering
Catchfly
(white or pinkish)

Wild
Pink
(pink)

× 2

Sleepy
Catchfly
(pink or white)

Moss
Campion
(pink or lilac)

× ½

Petals Separate; Sepals United into a Tube, Cup or Bladder; Plants of Swamps and Wet Meadows

Swamp Loosestrife or **Water Willow** (*Decodon verticillatus*) Flowers all clustered in the upper axils; leaves mostly in whorls of 3 or 4. Stem rather woody, with 4–6 angles and usually arching. Flowers magenta, ½–¾″ wide. Leaves lance-shaped. Swamps and pond margins. Summer. Loosestrife Family.

Purple Loosestrife (*Lythrum salicaria*) Flowers in dense spikes; leaves mostly in pairs. See p. 351.

Ragged Robin (*Lychnis flos-cuculi*) Flowers in a loose, terminal cluster; petals deeply 4-lobed. See p. 260.

Plants with Milky Juice; Flowers Not Bell-shaped

Flowering Spurge (*Euphorbia corollata*) or **Snow-on-the-mountain** (*Euphorbia marginata*) White flowers, ¼″ wide; lower leaves alternate. See p. 202.

Milkweeds (*Asclepias*) Flowers in umbels and with their petal-like parts bent downward. The distinctive flowers have five erect hoods (the corona) comprising the upper part of the flower, with a curved horn projecting from each hood. Butterfly Weed (p. 188) has orange flowers and alternate leaves. Summer. Milkweed Family.

1. ROSE-PURPLE, DEEP-PURPLE OR PURPLISH-RED FLOWERS

Swamp Milkweed (*A. incarnata*) Plant of swamps and shores; leaf veins form an acute angle with the midrib. Flowers vary from pink to rose-purple. Hoods about ⅛″ long, the horns longer than the hoods. Leaves lance-shaped, usually tapering to the tip. 2–6′ high. Common.

Purple Milkweed (*A. purpurascens*) Plant of dry fields and thickets; veins form nearly a right angle with the midrib. Purplish-red flowers. Hoods about ¼″ long; horns short and horizontal (see Common Milkweed, p. 264). Leaves egg-shaped or oblong, downy beneath. Pods downy, but not warty. S. N.H. to Minn. south.

Red Milkweed (*A. rubra*) Plant of wet pinelands and bogs; veins form nearly a right angle with the midrib. Purplish-red flowers. Hoods about ⅓″ long; horns nearly erect and almost as long as the hoods. Leaves broadly lance-shaped or egg-shaped, tapering to the tip. 1–4′ high. Long I. south along the coast.

Continued

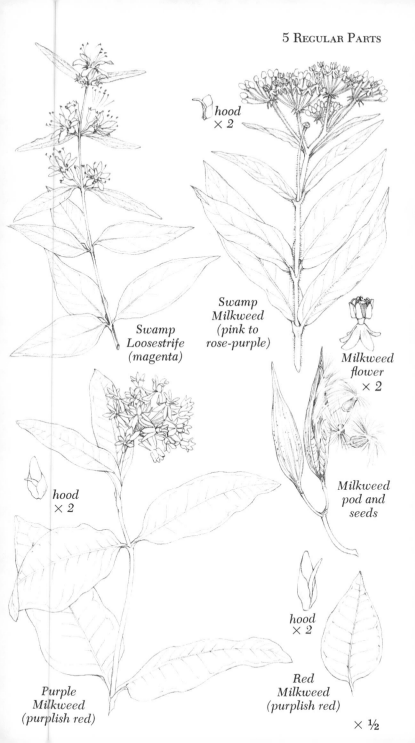

hood
× 2

Swamp
Milkweed
*(pink to
rose-purple)*

Swamp
Loosestrife
(magenta)

Milkweed
flower
× 2

Milkweed
*pod and
seeds*

hood
× 2

Purple
Milkweed
(purplish red)

hood
× 2

Red
Milkweed
(purplish red)

× ½

Plants with Milky Juice; Flowers Not Bell-shaped (cont.)

Milkweeds (*Asclepias*) (cont.)

2. BROWNISH-PINK, DULL-PURPLISH OR GREENISH-PURPLE
FLOWERS

Common Milkweed (*A. syriaca*) Leaves short-stalked, oblong or oval, grayish-downy beneath. Flowers fragrant. Hoods ⅛–⅙″ long; horns curved, easily seen. Pods with a warty surface. Coarse plant of fields and roadsides; common.

Blunt-leaved Milkweed (*A. amplexicaulis*) Leaves stalkless, clasping the stem at the base, wavy-margined and blunt at both ends. Pods smooth. Dry, usually sandy soil, s. N.Eng. to Minn. south.

Sullivant's Milkweed (*A. sullivantii*) † Leaves nearly stalkless, smooth, not wavy-margined. Moist soil, s. Ont. to Minn. south.

3. PALE-PINK, WHITE, GREENISH-WHITE OR GREEN FLOWERS

a. *Leaves very narrow*

Whorled Milkweed (*A. verticillata*) Greenish-white flowers. Leaves in whorls of 3–6. Dry fields, s. N.Eng. to Sask. south.

b. *Leaves lance-shaped, oval or oblong*

Four-leaved Milkweed (*A. quadrifolia*) Pale-pink or white flowers in 1–3 loose umbels; plant 1–2′ high; middle leaves usually in a whorl of 4. Leaves broadly lance-shaped, taper-pointed. Dry wooded slopes. Late spring and early summer.

Poke Milkweed (*A. exaltata*) Cream-white flowers, tinged with lavender or green, in loose, drooping umbels; plant 2–6′ high. Leaves oval, tapering to both ends, in pairs. Rich woods and borders, s. Me. to Minn. south.

White Milkweed (*A. variegata*) White flowers with a purple center, in dense umbels. Leaves oblong, not tapering at the tip, in pairs, the middle ones rarely in a whorl of 4. 1–3′ high. Dry woods, s. Conn. to s. Ill. south.

Green Milkweed (*A. viridiflora*) Green flowers in dense, nearly stalkless umbels. Leaves very thick, oval to lance-shaped, in pairs or some alternate, usually wavy-edged. Stem leaning or weakly erect. 1–3′ high. Dry, sandy woods and clearings, s. N.Eng. to s. Ont. and Man. south.

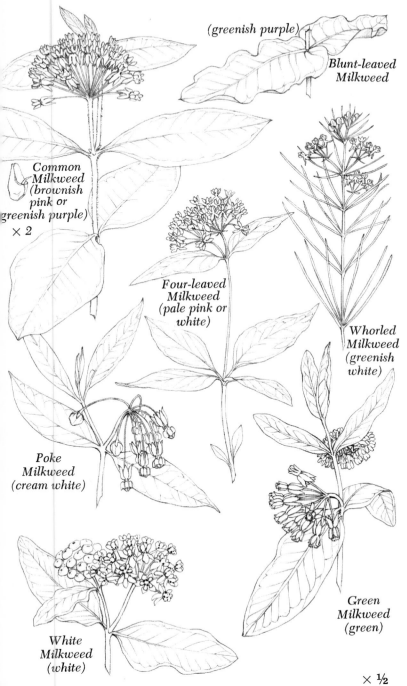

(greenish purple)

Blunt-leaved
Milkweed

Common
Milkweed
(brownish
pink or
greenish purple)
× 2

Four-leaved
Milkweed
(pale pink or
white)

Whorled
Milkweed
(greenish
white)

Poke
Milkweed
(cream white)

Green
Milkweed
(green)

White
Milkweed
(white)

× ½

Yellow Flowers; Petals Separate or Appearing So

Hudsonias (*Hudsonia*) Low, bushy plants with tiny, crowded, scalelike or needlelike leaves. The numerous flowers are about ⅓″ wide. 3–8″ high. Dry sandy places. Late spring and summer. Rockrose Family.

> **Golden Heather** (*H. ericoides*) Leaves needlelike and spreading outward. Plant greenish. Along the coast.

> **False Heather, Beach Heath** or **Poverty Grass** (*H. tomentosa*) Leaves scalelike, bluntish, pressed to the stem. Plant covered with grayish-white hairs. Along the coast and inland along the Great Lakes.

Moneywort (*Lysimachia nummularia*) * Creeping plant with roundish leaves. Flowers about 1″ wide, long-stalked, in the axils. 6–24″ long. Damp ground. Summer. Primrose Family.

Fringed Loosestrifes (*Lysimachia*) Petals nearly round and either toothed or abruptly pointed at the tip, slightly joined together at the base. Yellow, unspotted flowers, ½–1″ wide, usually nodding on long stalks. 1–3′ high. Moist thickets and shores. Summer. Primrose Family.

> **Fringed Loosestrife** (*L. ciliata*) Leaves egg-shaped, on long stalks fringed with hairs.

> **Lance-leaved Loosestrife** (*L. hybrida*) Leaves lance-shaped, tapering to the base.

Loosestrifes (*Lysimachia*) Flowers ¼–½″ wide, either in racemes or spikes, *or* all of the flowers grow singly on long stalks from the axils; petals longer than wide, slightly joined together at the base. Yellow flowers with dark streaks or dots. 1–2½′ high. Summer. Primrose Family.

> **Swamp Candles** or **Yellow Loosestrife** (*L. terrestris*) Flowers in a terminal raceme. Leaves lance-shaped, 1–3″ long. Wet places.

> **Whorled Loosestrife** or **Four-leaved Loosestrife** (*L. quadrifolia*) Flowers growing on long stalks in the axils. Leaves whorled, usually in 4's or 5's. Woods, thickets and shores, Me. to Wis. south.

> **Tufted Loosestrife** (*L. thrysiflora*) Flowers in short, spikelike racemes in the axils of the middle leaves. Petals 5 or 6. Leaves lance-shaped, in pairs, 2–4″ long. Cold swamps. Late spring and early summer.

Continued

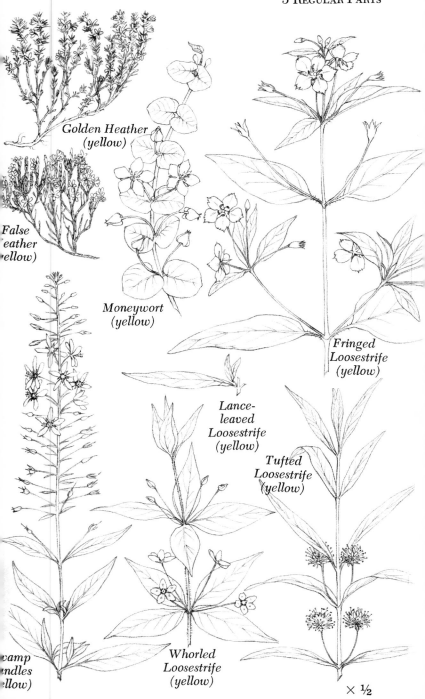

Golden Heather
(yellow)

False
Heather
(yellow)

Moneywort
(yellow)

Fringed
Loosestrife
(yellow)

Lance-
leaved
Loosestrife
(yellow)

Tufted
Loosestrife
(yellow)

Swamp
Candles
(yellow)

Whorled
Loosestrife
(yellow)

× ½

Yellow Flowers; Petals Separate or Appearing So (cont.)

St. Johnsworts (*Hypericum*) Flowers terminal, mostly in branching clusters; petals entirely separate. Yellow flowers with or without dark lines. Marsh St. Johnswort (p. 270) has pink flowers. Summer and fall. St. Johnswort Family.

1. STAMENS NUMEROUS (20 OR MORE); FLOWERS ⅓–1" WIDE

a. *Petals (usually) and leaves spotted with black or translucent dots*

Common St. Johnswort (*H. perforatum*) * Leaves 1½" or less long, narrowly oblong. Flowers ¾–1" wide, golden yellow, petals dotted on the margins. Common weed of fields and waste places.

Spotted St. Johnswort (*H. punctatum*) Leaves 1½–3" long, oblong, with rounded tip. Flowers ⅓–⅔" wide, dotted on the back. Damp places.

b. *Petals and leaves without dark markings*

Great St. Johnswort (*H. pyramidatum*) Flowers 1–2" wide; leaves 1½–5" long, partly clasping the stem. Petals curl lengthwise as the flower fades. 2–6' high. Meadows and banks of streams. Summer.

Pale St. Johnswort (*H. ellipticum*) Flowers ½–¾" wide; leaves growing upward, under 1½" long; stem obscurely 4-angled. 8–20" high. Shores and wet places.

Coppery St. Johnswort (*H. denticulatum*) Like Pale St. Johnswort, but flowers copper-yellow, leaves more nearly erect, and stem sharply 4-angled. Slender plant, 10–30" high. Wet sandy soil, N.J. to s. Ind. south. Summer.

2. STAMENS FEW (5–12); FLOWERS ⅛–⅓" WIDE

a. *Leaves narrow, lance-shaped or scalelike*

Orange Grass or **Pineweed** (*H. gentianoides*) Leaves tiny, scalelike. See p. 172.

Canada St. Johnswort (*H. canadense*) Leaves narrow, the larger upper leaves with 1–3 veins, 5–10 times longer than wide. Flowers about ¼" wide; pods red. 4–20" high. Wet or moist soil.

Larger Canada St. Johnswort (*H. majus*) Leaves lance-shaped, the larger upper leaves 3–4 times longer than wide, with 5 veins. Flowers ¼–⅓" wide. 6–30" high. Moist soil.

b. *Leaves elliptical or oval*

Dwarf St. Johnswort (*H. mutilum*) Leaves ½–1" long; flowers ⅙" wide. 6–30" high. Wet or moist open soil.

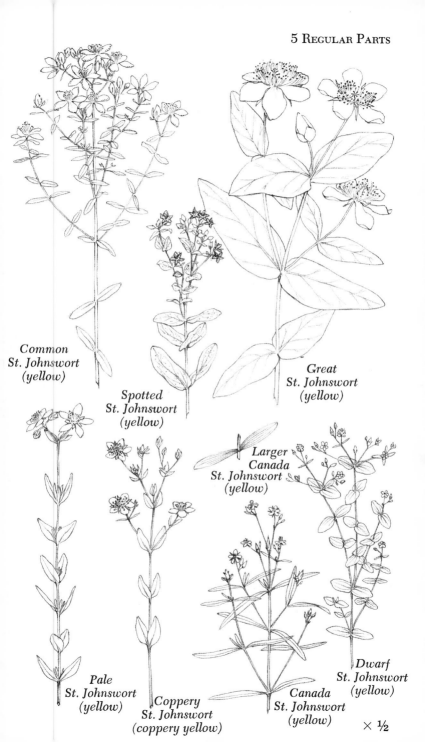

Common
St. Johnswort
(yellow)

Spotted
St. Johnswort
(yellow)

Great
St. Johnswort
(yellow)

Larger
Canada
St. Johnswort
(yellow)

Pale
St. Johnswort
(yellow)

Coppery
St. Johnswort
(coppery yellow)

Canada
St. Johnswort
(yellow)

Dwarf
St. Johnswort
(yellow)

× ½

Pink, Red, Blue or Purple Flowers; Petals and Sepals Separate, or Appearing So; Juice Not Milky

FLOWERS ½″ OR MORE WIDE

Marsh Pinks or **Sabatias** (*Sabatia*) Pink flowers, ¾–1½″ wide, with a yellow eye (sometimes white). Petals slightly joined together at the base; calyx very deeply lobed with very narrow segments. Large Marsh Pink (*S. dodecandra*) has 8–12 petals (see p. 386). Summer and early fall. Gentian Family.

> **Rose Pink** or **Bitterbloom** (*S. angularis*) Leaves egg-shaped, clasping at the base; stem sharply 4-square. 1–3′ high. Roadsides and meadows, s. N.Y. to Mich. and Wis. south.

> **Sea Pink** (*S. stellaris*) Leaves elliptical, narrowed at the base; calyx lobes shorter than the petals. Salt marshes along the coast, Mass. south.

> **Slender Marsh Pink** (*S. campanulata*) Similar to the Sea Pink, but leaves broadest near the base or very narrow, and calyx lobes about as long as the petals. Wet sands, Mass. south; inland north to Ind.

Spring Beauties (*Claytonia*) Pink or white flowers, veined with darker pink, ½–¾″ wide; stem bearing only a single pair of leaves. Flowers in a loose raceme. Low plants of moist woods. Spring. Purslane Family.

> **Spring Beauty** (*C. virginica*) Leaves narrow, 3–7″ long. S. and w. N.Eng. and sw. Que. to Minn. south.

> **Carolina Spring Beauty** (*C. caroliniana*) Leaves oval, 1–3″ long. South to N.Eng., mts. to Ga., n. Ill. and Minn.

Marsh St. Johnswort (*Hypericum virginicum*) Pink flowers, ½–¾″ wide, in small clusters, either terminal or in the upper axils; grows in bogs and swamps. Leaves oblong or egg-shaped, very blunt, 1–3″ long. 1–2′ high. Summer. St. Johnswort Family.

FLOWERS ⅛–¼″ WIDE

Pimpernel or **Poor Man's Weatherglass** (*Anagallis arvensis*) * Scarlet flowers (rarely blue or white), ¼″ wide, all growing on long stalks from the axils of the egg-shaped leaves. Petals slightly joined together at the base; calyx deeply cleft into 5 parts. The flowers open only in sunshine. Leaves under 1″ long. Low, sprawling plant of waste places and gardens. Summer. Primrose Family.

Continued

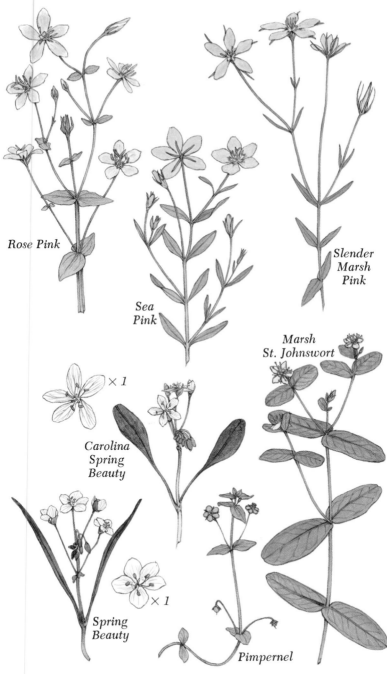

Rose Pink

Sea Pink

Slender Marsh Pink

Marsh St. Johnswort

× 1

Carolina Spring Beauty

Spring Beauty

× 1

Pimpernel

× ½

Pink, Red, Blue or Purple Flowers; Petals and Sepals Separate, or Appearing So; Juice Not Milky (cont.)

FLOWERS ⅛–¼" WIDE (CONT.)

Sand Spurreys (*Spergularia*) Matted or weak-stemmed plants with small (⅛" wide) pink or white flowers and very narrow leaves. Leaves ¼–1½" long. Late spring to fall. Pink Family.

Sand Spurrey (*S. rubra*) * Leaves growing in tufts; grows in dry, sandy places. The leaves are flat and not fleshy. Pink flowers.

Salt-marsh Sand Spurrey (*S. marina*) Leaves in pairs; grows in salt marshes and on seabeaches. The leaves are cylindrical and very fleshy. Pink or white flowers. Along the coast and in saline soil inland.

White Flowers with Whorled Leaves; Petals (if Present) and Sepals Separate; Juice not Milky

Carpetweed (*Mollugo verticillata*) * Prostrate plant with long-stalked flowers growing from the axils. Leaves ½–1" long, in whorls of 5 or 6, the blades widest toward the tip. Petals absent. Weed of gardens and waste places. Summer and fall. Carpetweed Family.

Corn Spurrey (*Spergula arvensis*) * Leaves 1–2" long, very narrow, in whorls of 10 or more. Flowers ¼" wide, growing in loosely branching clusters. 6–18" high. Weed of fields and waste places. Summer. Pink Family.

Wild Stonecrop (*Sedum ternatum*) Low, fleshy plant with creeping stems; the lower leaves mostly in whorls of 3. Flowers ½" wide, with 4 or 5 white petals, and usually grow in a 3-branched terminal cluster. 3–8" high. Rocks and banks, N.Y. to Mich. south. Spring. Stonecrop Family.

Rock Sandwort (*Arenaria stricta*) Plant of rocky places with stiff, very narrow leaves, ¼–¾" long, in dense clusters. Flowers ⅓" wide, the petals entire. Stem usually from a matted base with widely branched flower clusters. 6–15" long. Rocky ledges. Summer. Pink Family.

Pyxie or **Flowering Moss** (*Pyxidanthera barbulata*) Creeping plant of pine barrens with tiny, mosslike leaves. See p. 198.

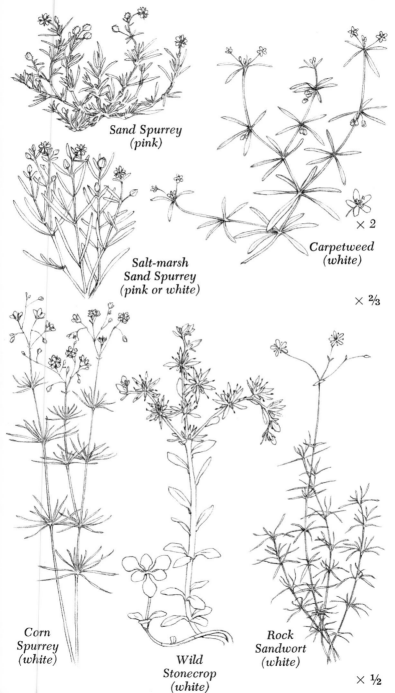

Sand Spurrey
(pink)

Salt-marsh
Sand Spurrey
(pink or white)

Carpetweed
(white)

× 2

× ⅔

Corn
Spurrey
(white)

Wild
Stonecrop
(white)

Rock
Sandwort
(white)

× ½

White or Green Flowers with Leaves in Pairs; Petals (If Present) and Sepals Separate; Juice Not Milky

PETALS WHITE, DEEPLY NOTCHED OR CLEFT

Chickweeds (*Stellaria* and *Cerastium*) Low, often weedy and insignificant plants of various habitats. The flowers usually grow in small terminal clusters. *Stellaria* has 3 styles; *Cerastium* has 5 styles. Pink Family.

1. PETALS 5 (CLEFT SO DEEPLY THEY APPEAR TO BE 10) OR NONE

a. Leaves egg-shaped, oblong or elliptical, less than 4 times as long as broad

Common Chickweed (*S. media*) * Weed of gardens and waste places; lower leaves long-stalked. Petals inconspicuous or sometimes absent. Very common. Spring to fall and occasionally winter.

Bog Chickweed (*S. alsine*) Plant of wet, springy places. Petals very inconspicuous or absent. Leaves ½–1″ long. Del. and Md. north. Spring and summer.

Great or **Star Chickweed** (*S. pubera*) Plant of woods and rocky slopes; flowers conspicuous, about ½″ wide. Plant spreading or erect, up to 1′ high. N.Y. to Ill. south. Spring.

b. Leaves lance-shaped or narrower, at least 5 times as long as broad; plants of grassy places

Lesser Stitchwort (*S. graminea*) * Leaves lance-shaped, broadest near the base, about 1″ long. Flower cluster terminal; petals slightly longer than the sepals. Fields and meadows. Spring to fall.

Long-leaved Stitchwort (*S. longifolia*) Leaves narrow, broadest near the middle, the longest 1½–2½″ long. Flower clusters mostly axillary; petals about equaling sepals. Damp to wet grassy places. Spring and summer.

2. PETALS 5, CLEFT HALF THEIR LENGTH OR LESS

Mouse-ear Chickweed (*C. vulgatum*) * Petals about as long as the sepals; flowers about ¼″ wide. Stem hairy. Leaves oblong, ½–1″ long. Common weed of gardens, lawns and roadsides. Spring to fall.

Field Chickweed (*C. arvense*) Petals 2 or 3 times as long as the sepals. Flowers ½″ wide; leaves narrow. Plant 4–12″ high, with tufts of leaves at the base. Rocky slopes. Spring and summer.

Great or **Star Chickweed** (*S. pubera*) Petals not much longer than sepals; flowers ½″ wide. See above.

Continued

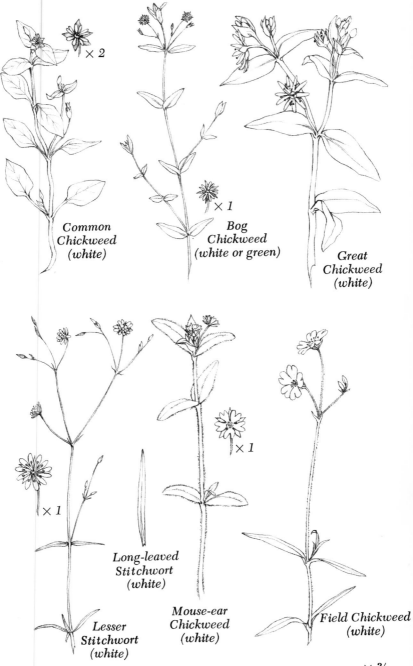

Common
Chickweed
(white)

× 2

Bog
Chickweed
(white or green)

× 1

Great
Chickweed
(white)

Lesser
Stitchwort
(white)

× 1

Long-leaved
Stitchwort
(white)

Mouse-ear
Chickweed
(white)

× 1

Field Chickweed
(white)

× ⅔

White or Green Flowers with Leaves in Pairs; Petals (If Present) and Sepals Separate; Juice Not Milky (cont.)

WHITE PETALS, ENTIRE OR SLIGHTLY INDENTED AT THE TIP

Seabeach Sandwort (*Arenaria peploides*) Fleshy, oval leaves; matted, spreading plant of seabeaches. Flowers ¼″ wide, terminal or growing in the axils. Summer. Pink Family.

Sandworts (*Arenaria*) Leaves short (¼–1″ long), not fleshy; small (¼–1″ wide) white flowers in terminal clusters. Low plants, often growing in tufts. Pink Family.

1. LEAVES EGG-SHAPED OR OVAL

Blunt-leaved or **Grove Sandwort** (*A. lateriflora*) Leaves ½–1″ long; flowers ¼–½″ wide. Flowers 1 to several in a cluster. Stems weakly erect. 2–10″ high. Open woods and gravelly shores. Spring and summer.

Thyme-leaved Sandwort (*A. serpyllifolia*) * Leaves about ¼″ long; flowers ⅛″ wide. A little plant (2–8″ high), usually widely branched, found in dry fields and stony places. Spring and summer.

2. LEAVES VERY NARROW

Mountain Sandwort (*A. groenlandica*) Grows on mountain summits and rocky ledges; leaves blunt, not stiff. Flowers about ½″ wide, the petals usually notched at the tip. 2–5″ high. Summer and fall.

Rock Sandwort (*A. stricta*) Grows on dry ledges; leaves stiff and pointed, smaller leaves growing in axils. See p. 272.

Pine-barren Sandwort (*A. caroliniana*) Grows in dry sands; leaves stiff and pointed. Petals white, green at base. Forms dense mats. R.I. south. Spring and summer.

Salt-marsh Sand Spurrey (*Spergularia marina*) Low plant with fleshy, very narrow leaves; salt marshes. See p. 272.

Marsh Pinks (*Sabatia*), **Spring Beauties** (*Claytonia*), **Pimpernel** (*Anagallis*) White forms of these plants. See p. 270.

GREEN FLOWERS WITH NO PETALS

Forked Chickweed (*Paronychia canadensis*) Widely branched, erect plant with tiny green flowers in the axils. Leaves elliptical, ¼–1″ long. 3–12″ high. Dry rocky or sandy places, s. N.H. to Minn. south. Summer and fall. Pink Family.

Common Chickweed (*Stellaria media*) or **Bog Chickweed** (*Stellaria alsine*) Plant prostrate on the ground. See p. 274.

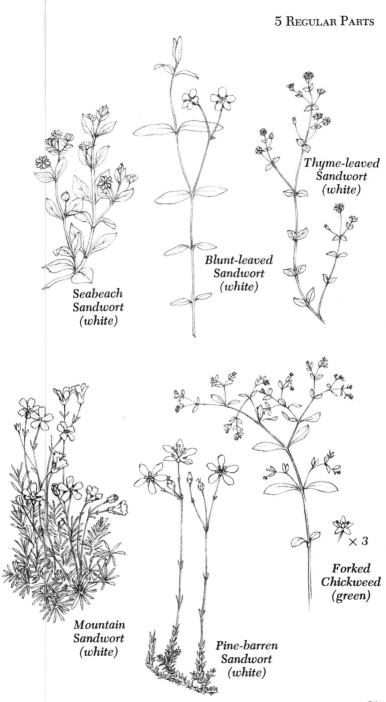

Seabeach
Sandwort
(white)

Blunt-leaved
Sandwort
(white)

Thyme-leaved
Sandwort
(white)

Mountain
Sandwort
(white)

Pine-barren
Sandwort
(white)

Forked
Chickweed
(green)

× 3

× 2/3

Yellow Flowers

False Foxgloves (*Gerardia*) Funnel-shaped flowers, 1–2″ long, 5-lobed at the tip. The flowers grow in leafy racemes. Parasitic on the roots of oak trees. Dry woods and clearings. Figwort Family.

1. STEM SMOOTH

Smooth False Foxglove (*G. flava*) Stem smooth and covered with a bloom, often purplish; most of the lower leaves deeply lobed or cleft, with pointed segments, but not finely divided. 3–6′ high. S. Me..to s. Minn. south. Summer and early fall.

Entire-leaved False Foxglove (*G. laevigata*) † Similar to Smooth False Foxglove but stem smooth, green; most of the leaves entire, although the lower leaves may be toothed or lobed. 2–6′ high. Pa. and Ohio south. Late summer and fall.

2. STEM DOWNY OR HAIRY

Downy False Foxglove (*G. virginica*) Stem and leaves downy; lower leaves more or less bluntly lobed, upper leaves usually entire. 2–4′ high. S. N.H. to Mich. south. Summer.

Fern-leaved False Foxglove (*G. pedicularia*) Stem sticky-hairy; leaves finely divided, fernlike. See p. 286.

Golden Star (*Chrysogonum virginianum*) Low plant with daisy-like flower heads 1–1½″ wide. The flower rays are broad and toothed at the tip. Leaves long-stalked, egg-shaped or oblong, 1–3″ long. 3–15″ high. Rich woods, s. Pa. and W.Va. south. Spring and early summer. Composite Family.

Small-flowered Leafcup (*Polymnia canadensis*) Plant with large, angularly lobed leaves and small heads of yellowish or whitish flowers, usually with 5 minute rays. The rays are sometimes absent or sometimes ½″ long and 3-lobed. Larger leaves with 3–5 lobes. Stem sticky-hairy. 2–5′ high. Moist shaded places, w. Vt. to Ont. south. Summer and fall. Composite Family.

Bur Marigolds (*Bidens*) Plants of wet places with flowers in small heads and lance-shaped leaves. See p. 392.

Yellow Violets (*Viola*) Flowers with 5 petals, the lower petal veined with violet. See p. 54.

Small Wood Sunflower (*Helianthus microcephalus*) Daisylike flower heads 1–1½″ wide. See p. 390.

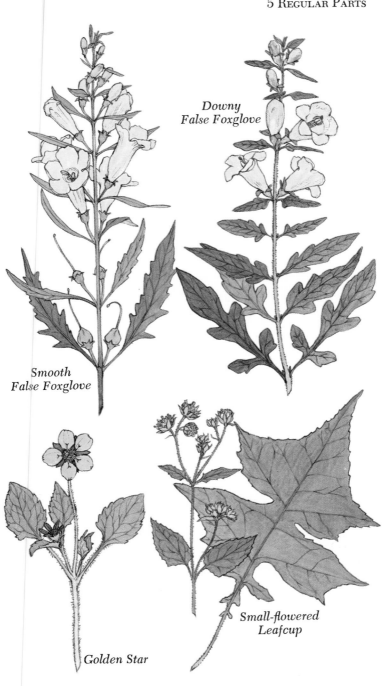

Downy
False Foxglove

Smooth
False Foxglove

Golden Star

Small-flowered
Leafcup

× 1/2

White, Pink, Purple or Blue Flowers with Leaves
Deeply Cleft or Lobed

Geraniums or **Cranesbills** (*Geranium*) Pink or purple flowers, ¼"
or more wide. Flowers solitary or in small clusters. Leaves deeply
and palmately lobed. Fruits shaped like a crane's bill. Herb Robert (p. 288) has 3 or 5 leaflets. Geranium Family.

1. FLOWERS 1" OR MORE WIDE

Wild Geranium or **Spotted Cranesbill** (*G. maculatum*) Rose-
purple flowers, 1–1½" wide. Leaves deeply and irregularly cleft
into 3–5 lobes, the lower leaves long-stalked. **Meadow Cranesbill** (*G. pratense*) * of n. N.Eng. and Maritime Provs. has deeper-
colored flowers and leaves more deeply cleft. 1–2' high. Common in woods and meadows. Spring and early summer.

2. FLOWERS ¼–½" WIDE

Carolina Cranesbill (*G. carolinianum*) Erect plant; flowers in
close clusters; beak of fruit short. Flowers pale pink or pale
purple, the flower stalk usually shorter than the calyx. 6–20"
high. Rocky woods and fields. Late spring and summer.

Bicknell's Cranesbill (*G. bicknellii*) Erect; flowers in loose clusters; beak of fruit long. Flowers pale purple, the flower stalk
longer than the calyx. 6–24" high. Open woods and clearings.
Summer.

Small-flowered Cranesbill (*G. pusillum*) * Prostrate or weak-
stemmed plant, with nearly round, very deeply lobed leaves;
stamens 5. Flowers pale purple. Beak of fruit short. 4–20" long.
Roadsides and waste places. Summer and fall.

Dove's-foot Cranesbill (*G. molle*) * Like the Small-flowered
Cranesbill, but with less deeply lobed leaves (about halfway)
and 10 stamens. Beak of fruit long. Weed of lawns and waste
places. Summer.

Canada Anemone (*Anemone canadensis*) Showy, white flowers,
1–1½" wide, on long stalks. Lower stem leaves in a whorl of 3,
deeply lobed, wedge-shaped and stalkless; upper leaves paired;
basal leaves long-stalked, with 5–7 lobes. 1–2' high. Damp
meadows and shores. Late spring and early summer. Buttercup
Family.

Blue Vervain (*Verbena hastata*) Violet-blue (rarely pink) flowers,
⅙" wide, in spikes. See p. 282.

Small-flowered Leafcup (*Polymnia canadensis*) Yellowish-white
flowers in a small, terminal cluster. See p. 278.

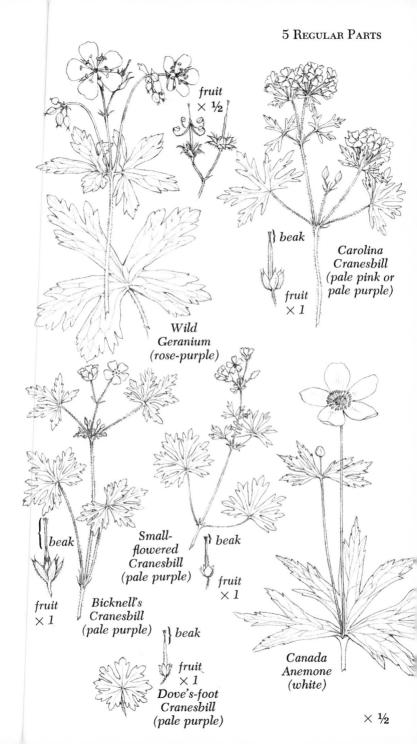

fruit
× ½

*Carolina
Cranesbill
(pale pink or
pale purple)*

} beak

*fruit
× 1*

*Wild
Geranium
(rose-purple)*

} beak

*Small-
flowered
Cranesbill
(pale purple)*

} beak

*fruit
× 1*

*fruit
× 1*

*Bicknell's
Cranesbill
(pale purple)*

} beak

*fruit
× 1*

*Dove's-foot
Cranesbill
(pale purple)*

*Canada
Anemone
(white)*

× ½

White, Purple or Blue Flowers in Slender Spikes or Racemes

Miterwort or **Bishop's Cap** (*Mitella diphylla*) Stem bearing a single pair of leaves in the middle. White flowers in a long raceme. Petals delicately fringed so that each flower resembles a snowflake. Stem leaves with 3–5 lobes and nearly stalkless; basal leaves heart-shaped at the base, long-stalked. 6–16″ high. Rich woods. Spring. Saxifrage Family.

Vervains (*Verbena*) Stem leaves more than 2. The spiked flowers are small, (⅛–⅓″ wide), tubular and 5-lobed at the end, a few opening at a time. Stem somewhat 4-sided. Summer and fall. Vervain Family.

1. WHITE FLOWERS

White Vervain (*V. urticifolia*) Spikes very slender and more or less interrupted. The leaves are egg-shaped and coarsely toothed. Stem usually hairy. 2–5′ high. Thickets and waste places.

2. BLUE OR PURPLE (SOMETIMES PINK) FLOWERS

Blue Vervain (*V. hastata*) Violet-blue (rarely pink) flowers; plant of moist thickets, shores and meadows. The leaves are lance-shaped, coarsely toothed and short-stalked. Lower leaves sometimes lobed. Spikes usually numerous. 2–6′ high.

Narrow-leaved Vervain (*V. simplex*) Purple flowers; leaves narrowly lance-shaped, tapering to the base and with fewer teeth than the Blue Vervain. Spikes solitary or few. 1–2′ high. Dry fields. w. N.Eng. to Minn. south.

Hoary Vervain (*V. stricta*) Purple (occasionally pink) flowers; leaves egg-shaped, coarsely toothed. Stem hairy with whitish hairs. Dry soil, s. Ont. to Mont. south; locally naturalized east to N.Eng.

White or Blue Flowers Growing in the Axils; Leaves Not Lobed

False Pennyroyal (*Isanthus brachiatus*) Pale-blue flowers, in small clusters in the axils. See p. 256.

Wintergreen or **Checkerberry** (*Gaultheria procumbens*) White, bell-shaped flowers, hanging beneath the leaves. See p. 212.

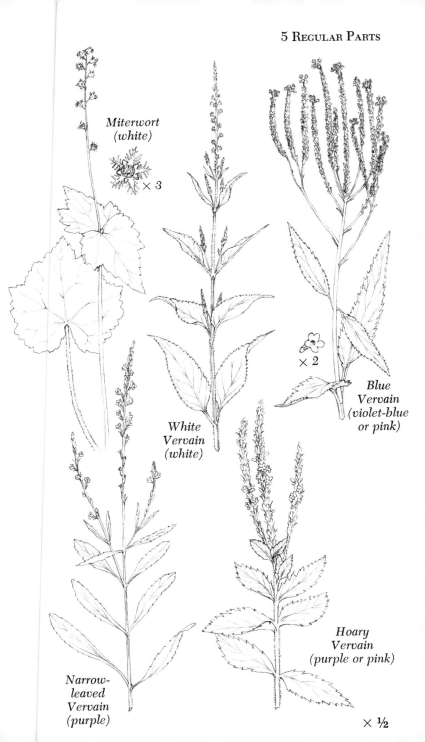

Miterwort (white)

× 3

White Vervain (white)

× 2

Blue Vervain (violet-blue or pink)

Narrow-leaved Vervain (purple)

Hoary Vervain (purple or pink)

× ½

White, Pink, Purple or Blue Flowers in Heads, or in Clusters of 1 to Several Flowers; Leaves Toothed or Shallowly Lobed

LOW PLANTS OF WOODLANDS OR BOGS

Twinflower (*Linnaea borealis*) Trailing plant with a pair of nodding, pink flowers on each flower stalk. The flowers are funnel-shaped and fragrant, about ½″ long. Leaves nearly round, obscurely toothed, under 1″ long. Cold woods and bogs, south to Long I., n. Ohio and n. Ind. and in mts. to W.Va. Summer and occasionally fall. Honeysuckle Family.

Pipsissewa or **Prince's Pine** (*Chimaphila umbellata*) Erect plant with dark-green and shining evergreen leaves. Flowers white or pinkish, waxy, ½″ wide, in a small cluster. Leaves finely toothed, wider toward the tip and mostly in whorls. 4–10″ high. Dry woods. Summer. Pyrola Family.

Striped or **Spotted Wintergreen** (*Chimaphila maculata*) Leaves variegated with white along the veins. The flowers and growth habit are very similar to the Pipsissewa, but the leaves are more pointed and either whorled or scattered along the stem. Dry woods, s. N.H. to Mich. south. Summer. Pyrola Family.

LOW WEEDS OF GARDENS AND WASTE PLACES

Galinsoga or **Quickweed** (*Galinsoga ciliata*) * Small (¼″ wide) flower heads with white, 3-toothed rays and a yellow central disk. Flower rays 4 or 5 . The leaves are egg-shaped, coarsely toothed, with 3 main veins. Stem hairy. 6–18″ high. Common weed of gardens. Summer and fall. Composite Family.

Corn Salad or **Lamb's Lettuce** (*Valerianella olitoria*) * Very small, bluish or whitish flowers in close clusters ¼–½″ wide. There is a circle of bracts beneath each cluster. Flowers tubular, 5-lobed at the tip, sometimes slightly irregular. Leaves blunt, the stem leaves with a few teeth, the basal leaves mostly entire. Stem forking. 6–15″ high. Fields and waste places. Spring. Valerian Family.

TALL PLANTS WITH FLOWERS IN BROAD CLUSTERS

Bonesets (*Eupatorium*) White flowers in heads. See p. 434.

Joe-Pye Weeds (*Eupatorium*) Purple or pink flowers in small heads. See p. 436.

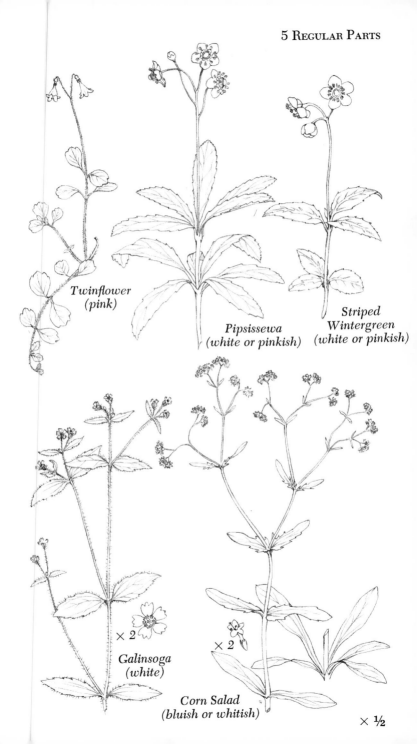

Twinflower
(pink)

Pipsissewa
(white or pinkish)

Striped
Wintergreen
(white or pinkish)

× 2

Galinsoga
(white)

× 2

Corn Salad
(bluish or whitish)

× ½

Yellow Flowers

False Foxgloves (*Gerardia*) Funnel-shaped flowers, 1–2″ long, 5-lobed at the tip. The flowers grow in leafy racemes. Dry woods. Figwort Family.

1. LEAVES DEEPLY LOBED, BUT NOT FINELY DIVIDED (SEE P. 278)

2. LEAVES FINELY DIVIDED, FERNLIKE

> **Fern-leaved False Foxglove** (*G. pedicularia*) Stem sticky-hairy; bushy plant, 1–4′ high. Flowers downy on the outside. S. Me. to Minn. south. Late summer and fall.

Yellow Wood Sorrels (*Oxalis*) Flowers with 5 separate petals; leaflets 3, notched at the tip. See p. 246.

Bur Marigolds (*Bidens*) Flowers in small heads; leaflets 3–5, toothed. See p. 440.

Individual Flowers under ¼″ Wide, Not Yellow

Ginsengs (*Panax*) Very small flowers in an umbel; leaves 3, whorled, palmate, each with 3–5 leaflets. Flowers with 5 petals and 5 stamens. Ginseng Family.

> **Ginseng** (*P. quinquefolius*) Green flowers; blooming in early summer. Leaflets 5, egg-shaped, short-pointed, stalked. Fruit bright red. Root long and tapering, often forked, prized by the Chinese for medicinal purposes. 6–16″ high. Rich woods, becoming rare.

> **Dwarf Ginseng** (*P. trifolium*) White flowers, blooming in spring. Leaflets 3–5, rather blunt, stalkless. Root a round tuber. 3–8″ high. Moist woods.

Valerians (*Valeriana*) Stem leaves pinnately divided into 5–25 lance-shaped or oblong leaflets or segments. Pale-pink or white, funnel-shaped flowers, ⅛–¼″ long, in branched clusters. Valerian Family.

> **Garden Valerian** or **Garden Heliotrope** (*V. officinalis*) * Basal leaves all divided; occasionally escapes from cultivation to roadsides and meadows. 2–5′ high. Summer.

> **Swamp Valerian** (*V. uliginosa*) Basal leaves entire or with a few lobes; plant of limy bogs. 1–3′ high. N. and w. N.Eng., N.Y. and Mich. north; rare in e. U.S. Late spring and early summer.

Spikenard (*Aralia racemosa*) Greenish-white flowers in a large branched cluster; leaflets heart-shaped at base. See p. 224.

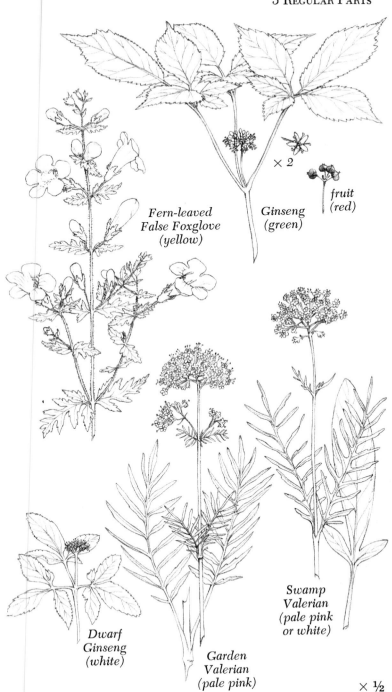

Fern-leaved
False Foxglove
(yellow)

Ginseng
(green)

× 2

*fruit
(red)*

Swamp
Valerian
*(pale pink
or white)*

Garden
Valerian
(pale pink)

Dwarf
Ginseng
(white)

× ½

Flowers ½" or More Wide, Not Yellow

Anemones (*Anemone*) Large white or greenish flowers on long stalks. The flowers are solitary or few, with 4–7 petal-like sepals and numerous stamens. Buttercup Family.

1. HEIGHT UNDER 1'; BLOOM IN SPRING

Wood Anemone or **Windflower** (*A. quinquefolia*) Leaves 3, in a whorl, each divided into 3–5 leaflets, some of the leaflets deeply cleft. Flower solitary, 1" wide, with usually 5 white or pinkish sepals. Moist woods.

Mountain Anemone (*A. lancifolia*) Similar to the Wood Anemone, but leaflets evenly toothed, usually not cleft. Sometimes over 1' high. Uplands, s. Pa. south.

2. HEIGHT 1–3'; STEM LEAVES LONG-STALKED; BLOOM IN SUMMER

Long-fruited Anemone (*A. cylindrica*) Lower stem leaves in a whorl of 5–9, with 3 leaves larger than the others. Greenish-white flowers, ¾" wide. Fruit a cylindrical head, ¾–1½" long. Fields and banks, w. Me. to Alta. south.

Large White-flowered Anemone (*A. riparia*) Lower stem leaves 2–3; center leaflet wedge-shaped at the base, with straight sides. Flowers usually white, 1–1½" wide. N. and w. N.Eng. and N.Y. to B.C. north. Rocky or gravelly places.

Thimbleweed or **Tall Anemone** (*A. virginiana*) Lower stem leaves 2–3; center leaflet wedge-shaped, with curved sides. Greenish flowers, ¾–1" wide, or sometimes white, 1–1½" wide. Fruiting "thimble" ¾–1" long. Rocky woods and banks, c. Me. to Minn. south; common.

3. HEIGHT 1–2'; STEM LEAVES STALKLESS

Canada Anemone (*A. canadensis*) Showy, white flower, 1–1½" wide. See p. 280.

Herb Robert (*Geranium robertianum*) Rose-purple (rarely white) flowers, ½" wide, with leaves *palmately* divided into 3 or 5 leaflets, the leaflets pinnately lobed. 6–18" high. Rocky woods. Spring to fall. Geranium Family.

Geraniums or **Cranesbills** (*Geranium*) Leaves deeply and palmately lobed, but not divided into leaflets. See p. 280.

Storksbill or **Alfilaria** (*Erodium cicutarium*) * Leaves *pinnately* divided into fine segments. Flowers pink or purple, almost ½" wide, in small, long-stalked umbels from the axils. Weak-stemmed plant of sandy fields and waste places. Spring to fall and occasionally in winter. Geranium Family.

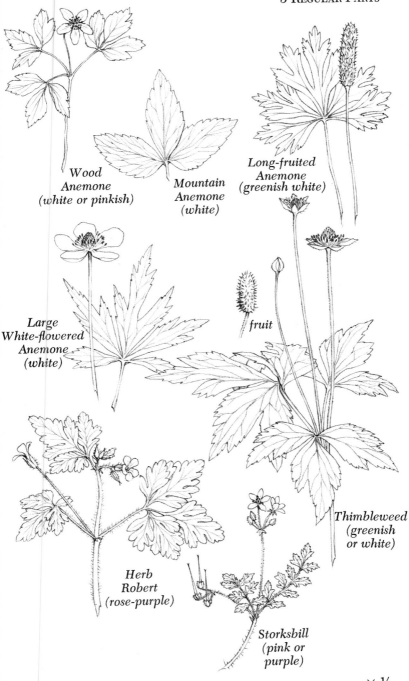

Wood
Anemone
(white or pinkish)

Mountain
Anemone
(white)

Long-fruited
Anemone
(greenish white)

Large
White-flowered
Anemone
(white)

fruit

Thimbleweed
*(greenish
or white)*

Herb
Robert
(rose-purple)

Storksbill
*(pink or
purple)*

× ½

SHRUBS /
With No Apparent Leaves at Flowering Time

Fragrant Sumac (*Rhus aromatica*) Tiny, yellowish flowers in short, dense spikes; flowering in early spring. See p. 318.

Shrub Yellowroot (*Xanthorrhiza simplicissima*) Small, purple flowers in drooping racemes. See p. 320.

SHRUBS /
Leaves Entire

Leaves Evergreen, Stiff and Leathery, under 1″ Long

Sand Myrtle (*Leiophyllum buxifolium*) Shrub of sandy pine barrens. The small (¼″ wide) white flowers grow in umbel-like clusters, and have 5 spreading petals and 10 protruding stamens. Leaves oval or oblong, ½″ long, dark green and shining. 4–18″ high. N.J. south. Spring. Heath Family.

Lapland Rosebay (*Rhododendron lapponicum*) Alpine plant with purple, open-bell–shaped, deeply 5-lobed flowers, ½–¾″ wide. The leaves are elliptical or oval, ½–¾″ long, and densely covered with brownish scales, especially beneath. Low, forming mats. Alpine summits of N.Eng. and N.Y. north. Early summer. Heath Family.

Mountain Heath (*Phyllodoce caerulea*) Alpine plant with purplish or lavender, nodding, bell-shaped flowers that are constricted at the tip. Flowers ⅓″ long, at the ends of the branches. Leaves needlelike, crowded, ¼–½″ long. 4–6″ high. Alpine summits of Me. and N.H. north. Early summer. Heath Family.

Alpine Azalea (*Loiseleuria procumbens*) Dwarf, spreading alpine plant with small pink or white flowers in small clusters. The flowers are bell-shaped, about ⅕″ long. Leaves dark green, narrowly oblong, ¼″ long, rather crowded, the margins turned under. Mts. of Me. and N.H. north. Late spring and early summer. Heath Family.

Moss Plant (*Cassiope hypnoides*) Dwarf alpine plant with nodding white flowers solitary at the ends of the branches. See p. 198.

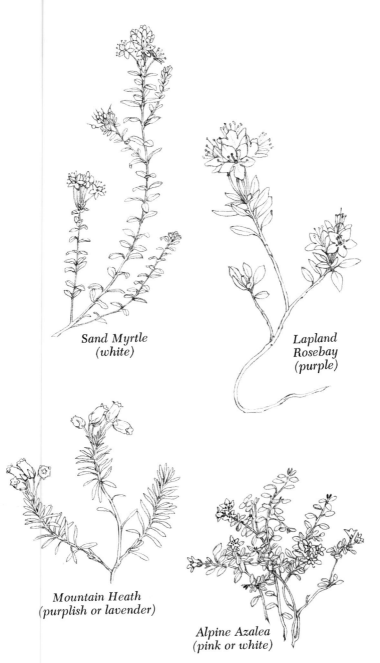

Sand Myrtle
(white)

Lapland
Rosebay
(purple)

Mountain Heath
(purplish or lavender)

Alpine Azalea
(pink or white)

× **2**/3

Leaves Evergreen, Stiff and Leathery, 1″ or More Long

Leatherleaf (*Chamaedaphne calyculata*) Bell-shaped, white flowers in one-sided, leafy racemes. The flowers are ¼″ long, narrowed at the tip. Leaves elliptical, dull green, the underside dotted with rusty scales; larger leaves 1–1½″ long. 1–4′ high. Bogs and swamps. Spring. Heath Family.

Bog Rosemary (*Andromeda glaucophylla*) Bell-shaped, nodding flowers in umbels; leaves white beneath, the margins rolled inward. The flowers are pink or white, ¼″ long. Leaves narrow, dark green above, 1–2″ long. 4–30″ high. Cold bogs. Spring and early summer. Heath Family.

Labrador Tea (*Ledum groenlandicum*) Small (⅓″ wide) white flowers with 5 petals; leaves brown-woolly beneath. Clusters many-flowered. Leaves with rolled-in edges, fragrant when crushed. 1–3′ high. Cold bogs, n. N.J. to Mich. and Wis. north. Spring and summer (mts.). Heath Family.

Rhododendrons (*Rhododendron*) Large (1½–2½″ wide), open-funnel–shaped flowers in showy clusters. Leaves dark green, 4–7″ long. 5–40′ high. Heath Family.

Great Laurel or **Rosebay** (*R. maximum*) Pink or white flowers, 1½–2″ wide; leaves usually fine-woolly beneath. Damp woods and swamps. Early summer.

Mountain Rosebay (*R. catawbiense*) † Rose- or lilac-purple flowers, 2–2½″ wide; leaves smooth beneath. Mountain woods, Va. and W.Va. south. Late spring and early summer.

Laurels (*Kalmia*) Saucer-shaped flowers, ¼–1″ wide, with 5 short lobes. Flowers showy, in branching clusters. Late spring and early summer. Heath Family.

Mountain Laurel (*K. latifolia*) Large shrub (3–20′ tall); pink or white flowers, ¾″ wide, in showy terminal clusters. Leaves dark green, shining, pointed at both ends. Rocky woods, N.Eng. to Ind. south.

Sheep Laurel or **Lambkill** (*K. angustifolia*) Shrub ½–3′ high; flowers clustered around the stem (not terminal). Crimson-pink flowers, ¼–½″ wide. Leaves not shining, paler beneath, the lower leaves usually drooping; foliage poisonous to livestock. Pastures, woods and swamps; south to Mich., Va., and in the mts. to Ga.; common.

Pale Laurel (*K. polifolia*) Crimson-pink flowers, ½–¾″ wide, growing in few-flowered, terminal clusters. Leaves whitened beneath, opposite. 6–24″ high. Cold bogs and mountaintops, south to n. N.J., Pa., Mich. and Minn.

Leatherleaf

Bog Rosemary

Labrador
Tea

Great
Laurel

Pale Laurel

Mountain
Laurel

Sheep Laurel

× ½

Leaves Growing in Pairs or 3's, Not Evergreen

Fly Honeysuckles (*Lonicera*) Long-stalked pairs of flowers growing from the axils. The flowers are tubular, 5-lobed, ½–¾″ long.
Leaves oblong or egg-shaped, 1–4″ long. For other species, see p.
104. Honeysuckle Family.

1. IN SWAMPS AND BOGS OR ON ALPINE SLOPES

Mountain Fly Honeysuckle (*L. villosa*) Flowers yellowish or
straw-colored, with 5 almost regular lobes. The leaves are blunt
and have a conspicuous fine veining. Berries blue. 1–3′ high.
Spring and early summer.

Swamp Fly Honeysuckle (*L. oblongifolia*) Flowers deeply 2-
lipped. See p. 104.

2. IN COOL WOODLANDS; NATIVE

American Fly Honeysuckle (*L. canadensis*) Greenish-yellow
flowers with short lobes. Leaves egg-shaped, rounded or
slightly heart-shaped at the base, with fine hairs along the
edges. Berries light red. 3–6′ high. Spring.

3. IN THICKETS AND ON ROADSIDES; INTRODUCED

Tartarian Honeysuckle (*L. tatarica*) * Leaves smooth beneath.
Pink (sometimes white), deeply lobed flowers, somewhat irregular. Leaves egg-shaped, slightly heart-shaped at the base. Berries red. 4–10′ high. Spring.

Morrow's Honeysuckle (*L. morrowi*) *† Like *L. tatarica*, but
leaves gray-downy beneath and flowers white, turning yellow. A
hybrid between the two, *L. bella*, has pink flowers, turning
yellow, and smoother leaves.

Shrubby St. Johnsworts (*Hypericum*) Golden-yellow flowers,
½–1″ wide, with numerous conspicuous stamens. Leaves oblong
or narrow, with tufts of smaller leaves growing in the axils. Summer. St. Johnswort Family.

Shrubby St. Johnswort (*H. spathulatum*) 2–7′ high; flowers at
the ends of the branches, and usually also in the upper axils,
forming an elongated cluster. Flowers about ¾″ wide; styles 3.
Leaves up to 3″ long. Pastures and rocky slopes, s. N.Y. to Minn.
south. **Dense-flowered St. Johnswort** (*H. densiflorum*) has
smaller flowers (about ½″ wide) and leaves (1–2″ long), and a
very dense flower cluster. Swamps and pine barrens, Long I. to
W.Va. south.

Kalm's St. Johnswort (*H. kalmianum*) † A small shrub (1–2′ high)
of the Great Lakes region; all the flowers in open branching
clusters wider than long; styles 5. Sandy soil.

Continued

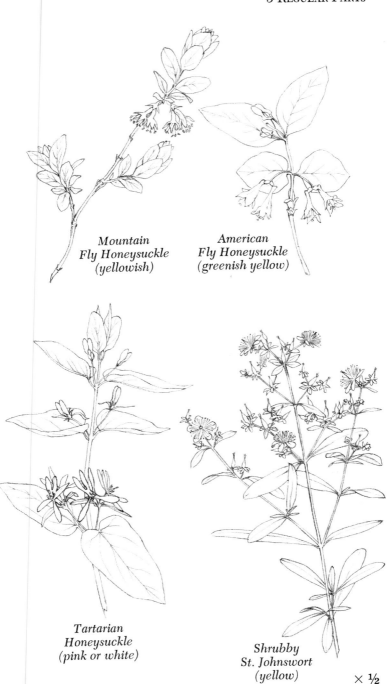

*Mountain
Fly Honeysuckle
(yellowish)*

*American
Fly Honeysuckle
(greenish yellow)*

*Tartarian
Honeysuckle
(pink or white)*

*Shrubby
St. Johnswort
(yellow)*

× ½

Leaves Growing in Pairs or 3's, Not Evergreen (cont.)

Snowberry (*Symphoricarpos albus*) Small (¼" long), pink, bell-shaped flowers in small axillary or terminal clusters. Flowers short-stalked, with 5 lobes. Leaves oval to nearly round; on young shoots, sometimes toothed. Fruit a waxy, white berry. 1–6' high. Native to limy ledges, but a cultivated variety has spread to roadsides and borders. Late spring to fall. Honeysuckle Family.

Indian Currant or **Coralberry** (*Symphoricarpos orbiculatus*) Greenish or purplish, bell-shaped flowers, ⅛" long, in axillary or terminal clusters. Leaves oval to nearly round. Berries coral-pink or purple. 1–5' high. Woods and thickets, Pa. to Minn. south; spread from cultivation north to N.Eng. and N.Y. Summer. Honeysuckle Family.

Naked Witherod or **Possum Haw** (*Viburnum nudum*) Small white flowers in broad, branching clusters. The leaves are shiny, somewhat leathery, but not evergreen, with the margins turned inward, entire or obscurely toothed. Witherod (*V. cassinoides*) (p. 302) is similar, but the leaves are not shiny and are usually toothed. 5–20' high. Thickets and swamps, s. Conn. south along the coastal plain; inland from Ky. south. Late spring and early summer. Honeysuckle Family.

Swamp Loosestrife (*Decodon verticillatus*) Plant of wet places with magenta flowers clustered in the upper axils. See p. 262.

Leaves Alternate or Clustered, Not Evergreen; Flowers Bell-shaped or Globe-shaped, ⅛–½" Long

Staggerbush (*Lyonia mariana*) Bell-shaped, nodding flowers, about ½" long; calyx lobes long and pointed, about ¼" long. The white or pinkish flowers are borne in clusters on leafless branches. Leaves oval or oblong. 1–6' high. Sandy or peaty soil, R.I. south along the coast, west to Tenn. and Ark. Spring and early summer. Heath Family.

Maleberry (*Lyonia ligustrina*) Globe-shaped (roundish and narrowly constricted at the tip), white flowers, ⅛" in diameter, in leafless clusters. Leaves oblong or egg-shaped. 2–10' high. Thickets, in wet or dry soil, N.Eng. to W.Va. and Ky. south. Spring and early summer. Heath Family.

Continued

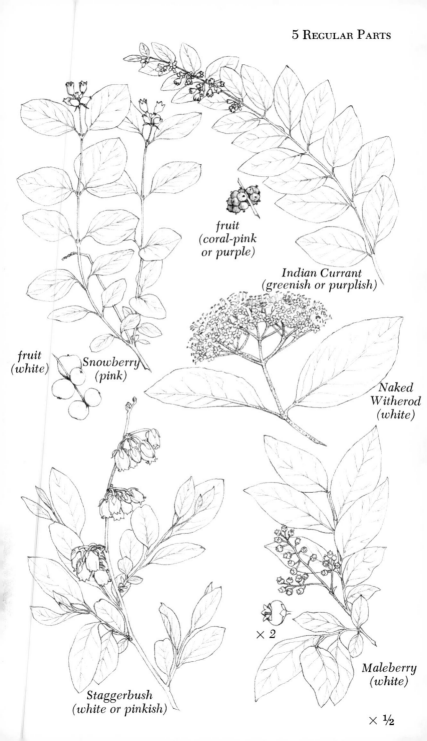

fruit
(coral-pink
or purple)

Indian Currant
(greenish or purplish)

fruit
(white)

Snowberry
(pink)

Naked
Witherod
(white)

× 2

Staggerbush
(white or pinkish)

Maleberry
(white)

× ½

Leaves Alternate or Clustered, Not Evergreen; Flowers Bell-shaped or Globe-shaped, ⅛–½" Long (cont.)

Blueberries and **Huckleberries** (*Vaccinium* and *Gaylussacia*) Bell-shaped flowers with short calyx lobes. Flowers in small racemes or clusters. For species with finely toothed leaves, see p. 308. Bog Bilberry (*V. uliginosum*) (p. 164) has 4 parts. Spring and early summer. Heath Family.

1. FLOWERS ABOUT AS WIDE AS LONG

Deerberry (*V. stamineum*) Stamens protruding. Greenish-white or purplish flowers, in leafy-bracted racemes. Leaves pale beneath. Berries green or purplish, not edible. 1–5' high. Dry woods, Mass. to Ont. south.

Dangleberry (*G. frondosa*) Stamens not protruding; flower stalks longer than the greenish or pinkish flowers. Leaves pale beneath. Berries blue, with a bloom, sweet. 2–5' high. Dry woods, s. N.Eng. to Ohio south.

Dwarf Huckleberry (*G. dumosa*) White or pink flowers on stalks no longer than the flowers. Leaves thick and shining, with a bristle tip. Fruit black, covered with short hairs. 6–24" high. Peaty bogs and dry barrens, along the coastal plain.

2. FLOWERS LONGER THAN WIDE, ¼–½" LONG, USUALLY CONSTRICTED SLIGHTLY NEAR THE TIP; PLANT OVER 3' HIGH

Highbush or **Swamp Blueberry** (*V. corymbosum*) White or pinkish flowers. 3–15' high. Swamps, pastures, woods. Berries blue. **Black Highbush Blueberry** (*V. atrococcum*) has shiny black berries; blooms earlier.

3. FLOWERS LONGER THAN WIDE, ABOUT ¼" LONG, USUALLY CONSTRICTED SLIGHTLY NEAR THE TIP; PLANT UNDER 3' HIGH

a. *Leaves much paler beneath*

Late Low Blueberry (*V. vacillans*) Greenish-pink or purplish flowers. See p. 308.

b. *Leaves green on both sides*

Black Huckleberry (*G. baccata*) Reddish flowers in short, one-sided clusters; leaves (under a lens) covered with shiny, resinous dots. Fruit black or bluish, sweet but seedy. 1–3' high. Woods, thickets.

Velvetleaf or **Sourtop Blueberry** (*V. myrtilloides*) Greenish flowers; leaves and young branches with spreading hairs. Fruit blue, with a heavy bloom, sour. 6–24" high. Moist or wet woods.

Early Low Blueberry (*V. angustifolium*) Flowers white or white tinged with pink; leaves minutely toothed. See p. 308.

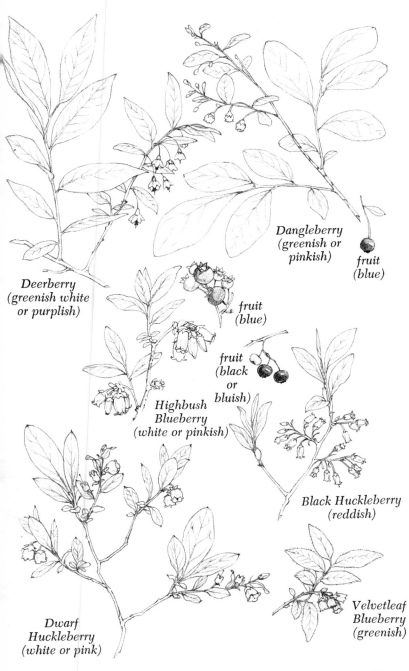

Dangleberry
*(greenish or
pinkish)*

*fruit
(blue)*

Deerberry
*(greenish white
or purplish)*

*fruit
(blue)*

*fruit
(black
or
bluish)*

**Highbush
Blueberry**
(white or pinkish)

Black Huckleberry
(reddish)

**Dwarf
Huckleberry**
(white or pink)

**Velvetleaf
Blueberry**
(greenish)

× ½

Leaves Alternate or Clustered, Not Evergreen; Flowers Not Bell-shaped or Globe-shaped

Azaleas (*Rhododendron*) Showy, funnel-shaped flowers, ½–2 wide. Stamens and style conspicuous. Heath Family.

1. BLOOMING IN EARLY SUMMER AFTER THE LEAVES ARE FULLY GROWN; FLOWERS USUALLY WHITE (SOMETIMES PINK)

Clammy Azalea or **Swamp Honeysuckle** (*R. viscosum*) Leaves hairy along the midrib beneath. Flowers sticky-hairy and very fragrant. 2–8′ high. Swamps, s. Me. to Ohio south.

Smooth Azalea (*R. arborescens*) Similar to the Clammy Azalea but leaves smooth beneath; Pa. to Ky. south. Stamens red. 4–20′ high. Moist woods and stream banks.

2. BLOOMING IN SPRING; PINK, PURPLE OR WHITE FLOWERS

a. Height 2′ or more; pink flowers

Pink Azalea or **Pinxter Flower** (*R. nudiflorum*) Flowers only faintly fragrant, if at all; underside of leaves hairy on the midrib only. Woods and swamps, Mass. to Ohio south.

Hoary or **Mountain Azalea** (*R. roseum*) † Like the Pink Azalea but the flowers very fragrant; underside of leaves soft-hairy all over; flower tube short, about as long as flower lobes. Rocky woods, s. Me. to sw. Que. south.

Woolly Azalea (*R. canescens*) † Similar to the Hoary Azalea, but flower tube slender, twice as long as the flower lobes. Woods and swamps, Del. to Ill. south.

b. Low shrub, 8–24″ high

Dwarf Azalea (*R. atlanticum*) † White, purple or pink flowers. A coastal species that spreads into colonies by underground stems. Sandy woods, s. N.J. and se. Pa. south.

3. BLOOMING IN SPRING; YELLOW, ORANGE OR SCARLET FLOWERS

Flame Azalea (*R. calendulaceum*) Flowers very variable in color, slightly fragrant. Commonly cultivated. 2–15′ high. Dry open woods, sw. Pa. and s. Ohio south.

Hudsonias (*Hudsonia*) Low, bushy plants with yellow flowers and tiny leaves. See p. 266.

Japanese Knotweed (*Polygonum cuspidatum*) Stem jointed; flowers small, greenish-white, in spikes. See p. 190.

Mountain Holly (*Nemopanthus mucronata*) Small, greenish or yellowish flowers in the axils; grows in swamps. See p. 168.

Clammy
Azalea

Smooth
Azalea

Pink
Azalea

Flame
Azalea

× ½

Leaves Opposite, Obviously Growing in Pairs; White Flowers in Broad, Branching Clusters

Wild Hydrangea (*Hydrangea arborescens*) Shrub of s. N.Y. to Ohio south; stamens 8 or 10; leaves with long (1–3″) stalks. Leaves egg-shaped, pointed, sharply toothed and 3–6″ long. 4–10′ high. Rocky banks and ravines. Early summer. Saxifrage Family.

Viburnums (*Viburnum*) Stamens 5. Leaf stalks usually less than 1″ long. Large shrubs of woodlands and borders. Spring and early summer. Honeysuckle Family.

1. LEAVES NOT LOBED

a. Leaves coarsely toothed

Arrowwood (*V. recognitum*) Twigs and flower cluster smooth. Leaves egg-shaped, prominently veined beneath. Fruit purplish-black. Woods and borders. **Downy Arrowwood** (*V. rafinesquianum*) has less prominent veins, shorter (under ¼″) leaf stalks, and pairs of narrow stipules (usually absent in Arrowwood).

Southern Arrowwood (*V. dentatum*) † Similar to the Arrowwood, but twigs and flower cluster downy. North to s. N.Eng. and Pa.

b. Leaves finely and sharply toothed

Hobblebush (*V. alnifolium*) Outer flowers large and showy, about 1″ wide, neutral (without stamens or pistils). Leaves broadly egg-shaped or roundish. Fruit changing from red to purple. Low woods, south to n. N.J. and Ohio and in uplands to Ga.

Sweet Viburnum or **Nannyberry** (*V. lentago*) Flowers of uniform size; leaves 2–4″ long, usually long-pointed. Leaf stalks normally winged, and often rusty in color. Fruit bluish-black, edible. Rich, moist soil.

Black Haw (*V. prunifolium*) Leaves mostly 1–2″ long, not long-pointed; flowers of uniform size. Fruit bluish-black, sweet and edible. Thickets and borders, sw. Conn. to Mich. south.

c. Leaves bluntly or obscurely toothed

Witherod or **Wild Raisin** (*V. cassinoides*) Leaves dull, thickish, with rounded, low teeth, or nearly entire; northern and upland species. Fruit bluish-black, sweet. Moist woods and swamps.

Naked Witherod or **Possum Haw** (*V. nudum*) Leaves shiny, nearly entire; southern species. See p. 296.

Continued

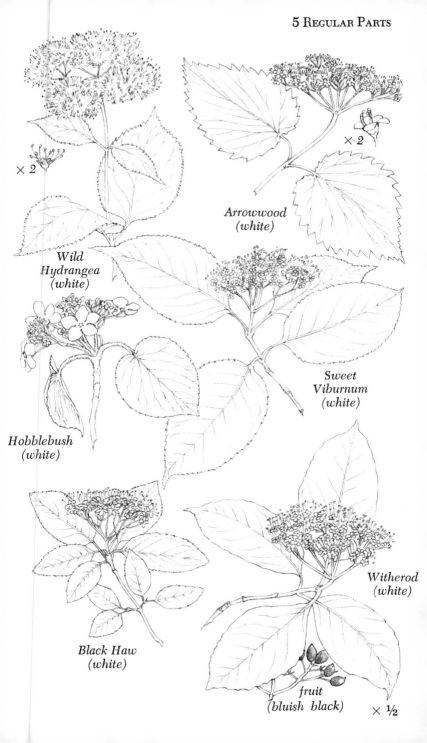

× 2

*Wild
Hydrangea
(white)*

*Arrowwood
(white)*

× 2

*Hobblebush
(white)*

*Sweet
Viburnum
(white)*

*Black Haw
(white)*

*Witherod
(white)*

*fruit
(bluish black)*

× ½

Leaves Opposite, Obviously Growing in Pairs; White Flowers in Broad, Branching Clusters (cont.)

Viburnums (*Viburnum*) (cont.)

2. LEAVES 3-LOBED

Highbush Cranberry (*V. trilobum*) Outer flowers in each cluster large and showy, ½–1″ wide, and neutral (no stamens or pistils). Leaves with 3 rather deep lobes and coarsely toothed. The acid, red fruit is used for preserves. Large, erect shrub, 3–10′ high. Cool moist woods and rocky slopes.

Maple-leaved Viburnum or **Dockmackie** (*V. acerifolium*) Flowers small and of uniform size; flower clusters 1½–2″ wide; common shrub of dry or rocky woods. The maplelike leaves are rounded or slightly heart-shaped at the base. Fruit purple-black. 3–6′ high.

Squashberry or **Mooseberry** (*V. edule*) Flowers all small; flower clusters ½–1¼″ wide; northern shrub of cool slopes and ravines. Leaves rather shallowly lobed, some unlobed. Fruit red, juicy. Straggling, 2–6′ high. N. N.Eng., n. N.Y., w. Pa., n. Mich. and Wis. north.

Leaves Opposite, Obviously Growing in Pairs; Yellow, Greenish or Purplish Flowers

Bush Honeysuckle (*Diervilla lonicera*) Yellow, funnel-shaped flowers, usually growing in 3's. The flowers, which may be slightly irregular, are about ¾″ long, and grow from the axils or at the ends of the spreading branches. Leaves egg-shaped, 2–5″ long. 1–3′ high. Dry rocky places. Late spring and summer. Honeysuckle Family.

Strawberry Bushes (*Euonymus*) Greenish or purplish, 5-petaled flowers growing in the axils. Flowers single or in small clusters. Leaves finely toothed; branches 4-sided. Fruit a rough-warty pod that splits open exposing scarlet seeds. Rich woods. Late spring and early summer. Staff Tree Family.

Strawberry Bush or **Bursting Heart** (*E. americanus*) Leaves practically stalkless, sharply pointed, widest in the middle, thickish; erect or semi-erect, with spreading branches, 2–6′ high. Se. N.Y. to s. Ill. south.

Running Strawberry Bush (*E. obovatus*) Leaves short-stalked, bluntly pointed, widest toward the tip, thin; trailing shrub, 1–2′ high. W. N.Y. to Mich. south.

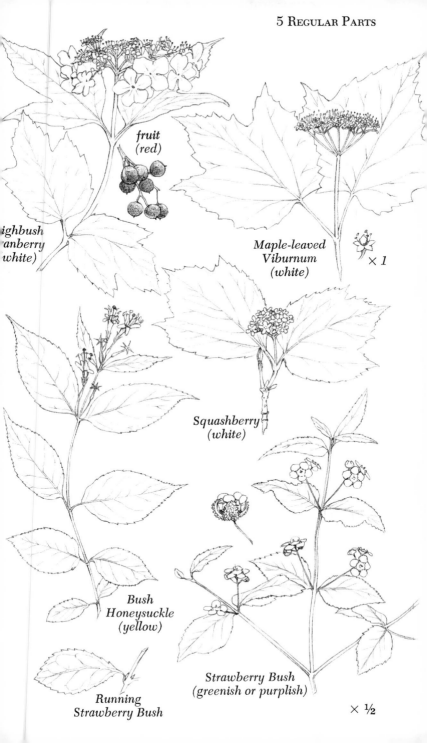

fruit (red)

*ighbush
anberry
white)*

*Maple-leaved
Viburnum
(white)*

× 1

*Squashberry
(white)*

*Bush
Honeysuckle
(yellow)*

*Strawberry Bush
(greenish or purplish)*

*Running
Strawberry Bush*

× ½

Leaves Alternate or Clustered, with 3–7 Lobes; Flowers Small and Inconspicuous, in the Axils

Currants and **Gooseberries** (*Ribes*) Spreading or straggling shrubs that are the alternate hosts of the destructive white pine blister rust. 1–5′ high. Spring and summer (mts.). Saxifrage Family.

1. BASE OF FLOWERS PRICKLY OR BRISTLY; FRUIT BRISTLY

Bristly Black Currant (*R. lacustre*) Flowering branches densely covered with bristles. Green or purplish flowers in racemes. Fruit purplish-black. Swamps and cold woods, n. and w. N.Eng. to Wis. north and west, and south in mts. to Tenn.

Prickly Gooseberry or **Dogberry** (*R. cynosbati*) Flowering branches with scattered prickles (sometimes absent); tubular, green flowers, 1–3 in a cluster. Fruit red-purple. Our commonest species. Rocky woods.

Skunk Currant (*R. glandulosum*) Branches smooth; whitish or pinkish flowers in racemes. A straggling shrub with a disagreeable skunklike odor when bruised. Fruit red. Cold damp woods and slopes, Canada and n. U.S., south in mts. to N.C.

2. BASE OF FLOWERS NOT PRICKLY OR BRISTLY; FRUIT SMOOTH

a. Flowers solitary or 2–3 in a cluster; branches usually bearing a few thorns

Smooth Gooseberry (*R. hirtellum*) Greenish-purple flowers; stamens slightly longer than the sepals. Fruit purplish or blackish. Woods and swamps.

Round-leaved Gooseberry (*R. rotundifolia*) Similar to the Smooth Gooseberry, but the stamens are much longer than the sepals. Rocky woods, w. N.Eng. and N.Y. south.

b. Flowers 5 or more, in racemes; branches without thorns

Wild Black Currant (*R. americanum*) Whitish or yellowish flowers, longer than wide; rich woods, moist thickets and stream banks. Fruit black.

Garden Currant (*R. sativum*) * Greenish flowers, wider than long; escaped to open woods and thickets. Fruit red.

Swamp Red Currant (*R. triste*) Pink or purplish flowers, wider than long; cold woods and swamps. Stems straggling. Fruit red. South to n. N.J., W.Va., s. Ont., Mich., Wis. and west to Ore.

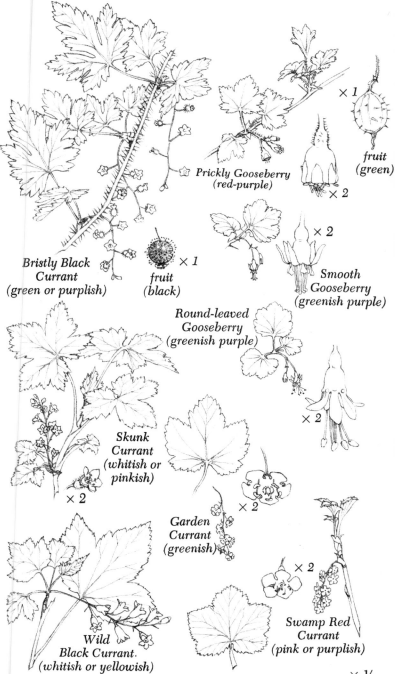

Prickly Gooseberry
(red-purple)

× 1

fruit
(green)

× 2

Bristly Black
Currant
(green or purplish)

fruit
(black)

× 1

× 2

Smooth
Gooseberry
(greenish purple)

Round-leaved
Gooseberry
(greenish purple)

× 2

Skunk
Currant
(whitish or
pinkish)

× 2

Garden
Currant
(greenish)

× 2

× 2

Wild
Black Currant.
(whitish or yellowish)

Swamp Red
Currant
(pink or purplish)

× ½

Leaves Alternate, with 3–7 Lobes; Showy, White or Rose-purple Flowers

Purple-flowering Raspberry (*Rubus odoratus*) Showy, rose-purple flowers, 1–2″ wide. The large leaves have 3–5 lobes and are heart-shaped at the base. Branches covered with bristly hairs. 3–6′ high. Rocky woods and borders, N.S. to Mich., south to Ga. and Tenn. Summer. Rose Family.

Ninebark (*Physocarpus opulifolius*) Numerous, white flowers in rounded clusters; stems without spines. The leaves are heart-shaped or wedge-shaped at the base, the larger 3-lobed. 3–10′ high, with long, curving branches on which the old bark peels off in layers. Rocky banks and shores. Late spring and early summer. Rose Family.

Hawthorns (*Crataegus*) White-flowered shrubs or small trees with branches bearing a few or many spines. A large, complex group with over 50 species in our area, most of them identifiable only by their fruit. For identification of species, refer to the technical manuals. Spring. Open woods and hillsides. Rose Family.

Leaves Alternate or Clustered, Not Lobed; Flowers Bell- or Funnel-shaped

Fetterbush (*Leucothoe racemosa*) White, bell-shaped flowers in one-sided racemes, the racemes 1–2″ long. Flowers ⅓″ long. Leaves lance-shaped or oblong, pointed. 5–10′ high. Moist thickets, Mass. south. Late spring and early summer. Heath Family.

Blueberries (*Vaccinium*) Small, bell-shaped flowers, solitary or in small clusters, the clusters not one-sided. Leaves finely toothed. For other species, see p. 298. Spring and early summer. Heath Family.

 Early Low Blueberry (*V. angustifolium*) Flowers several in a cluster, white or white tinged with pink. Leaves green on both sides, under ½″ wide. Dry, open soil.

 Dwarf Bilberry (*V. cespitosum*) Deep-pink flowers, solitary in the axils. Leaves shining, finely toothed. Gravelly soil, often alpine, n. N.Eng. and n. N.Y. to n. Wis. north.

 Late Low Blueberry (*V. vacillans*) Greenish-pink or purplish flowers; leaves much paler beneath. 6–36″ high. Dry open woods and clearings.

Azaleas (*Rhododendron*) Showy, funnel-shaped flowers, ½–2″ wide. See p. 300.

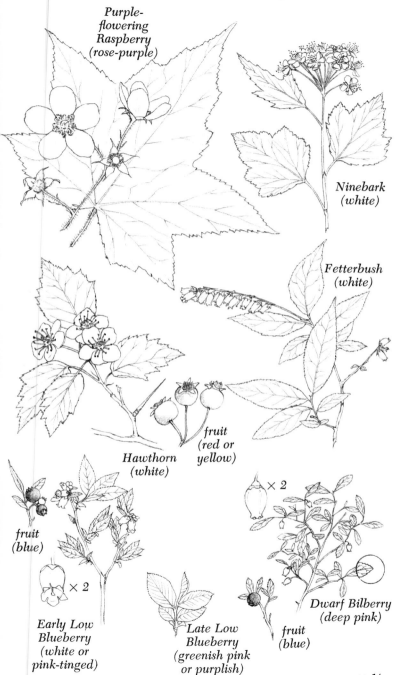

Purple-flowering Raspberry (rose-purple)

Ninebark (white)

Fetterbush (white)

fruit (red or yellow)

Hawthorn (white)

fruit (blue)

× 2

Early Low Blueberry (white or pink-tinged)

Late Low Blueberry (greenish pink or purplish)

fruit (blue)

× 2

Dwarf Bilberry (deep pink)

× ½

Leaves Alternate, Not Lobed; Greenish-white or Greenish Flowers Growing in the Axils

Alder-leaved Buckthorn (*Rhamnus alnifolia*) Low, sprawling shrub of cold bogs and swamps, 1½–3′ high. The greenish flowers have no petals, and grow 1–3 in a cluster at the base of the oval leaves. Berry black, inedible. Spring and early summer. Buckthorn Family.

Mountain Winterberry (*Ilex montana*) Erect shrub or small tree of mountain forests, 5–20′ high. See p. 168.

Leaves Alternate, Not Lobed; White or Pink Flowers with 5 Separate Petals; Blooming Mid-June to Fall

Sweet Pepperbush (*Clethra alnifolia*) Sweet-scented, white flowers in long racemes. The flowers are ⅓″ wide and have a protruding style. Leaves egg-shaped, sharply toothed above the middle. Swamps and moist, sandy woods, near the coast, s. Me. south. Summer. White Alder Family.

New Jersey Tea (*Ceanothus americanus*) Small, white flowers in short, dense clusters; leaves with 3 main veins. Flower clusters long-stalked. Leaves egg-shaped, rounded at the base and finely toothed. 1½–4′ high. Dry open woods and rocky banks. Summer. Buckthorn Family.

Meadowsweets (*Spiraea*) White or pale-pink flowers in branching clusters; leaves with 1 main vein. Flowers ⅙–¼″ wide. Summer and fall. Rose Family.

> **Meadowsweet** (*S. latifolia*) Flower cluster longer than wide; leaves egg-shaped or broadly lance-shaped, coarsely toothed. Twigs reddish- or purplish-brown, smooth. 2–6′ high. Moist or rocky soil; common in e. sections.

> **Narrow-leaved Meadowsweet** (*S. alba*) Flower cluster longer than wide; leaves lance-shaped, finely toothed. Twigs yellowish-brown, usually downy. 2–6′ high. Moist or wet places, sw. Que. and w. Vt. to Sask. south.

> **Corymbed Spiraea** (*S. corymbosa*) Flower cluster wider than long. Leaves egg-shaped or roundish, coarsely toothed above the middle. 1–3′ high. Rocky woods and banks, N.J. and Pa. south.

Steeplebush or **Hardhack** (*Spiraea tomentosa*) Rose-pink flowers in a steeplelike cluster. The stems and underside of the leaves are white-woolly. Flowers ⅛″ wide; leaves egg-shaped or oblong. 1–4′ high. Low grounds, fields and pastures. Summer and fall. Rose Family.

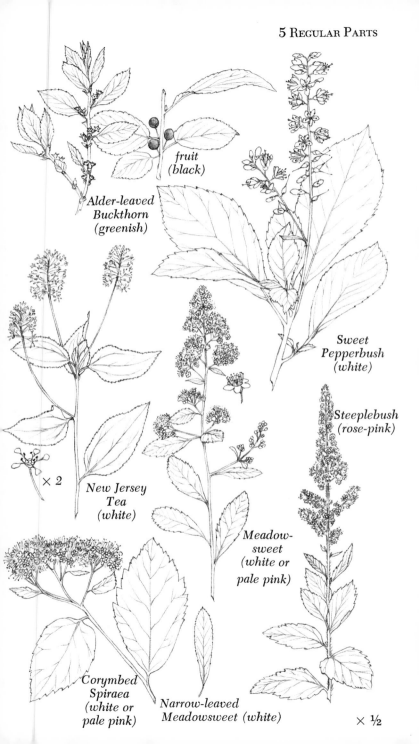

fruit
(black)

Alder-leaved
Buckthorn
(greenish)

Sweet
Pepperbush
(white)

× 2

Steeplebush
(rose-pink)

New Jersey
Tea
(white)

Meadow-
sweet
(white or
pale pink)

Corymbed
Spiraea
(white or
pale pink)

Narrow-leaved
Meadowsweet (white)

× ½

Leaves Alternate or Clustered, Not Lobed; White or Pink Flowers with 5 Separate Petals; Blooming in Spring

Plums and **Cherries** (*Prunus*) Flowers in small umbels along the stems (leaves or leaf buds growing at the ends of flowering branches). Flowers white, with roundish petals. Spring. Rose Family.

1. BUSHY SHRUBS, SELDOM OVER 6′ HIGH; FLOWERS ABOUT ½″ WIDE

Beach Plum (*P. maritima*) Leaves toothed to the base. Leaves egg-shaped, finely toothed. Fruit purple. 1–8′ high. Much-branched shrub of sandy soil near the coast, Me. to Del.

Sand Cherry (*P. susquehanae*) Leaves not toothed below the middle. Leaves narrowed toward the base. Fruit purple-black. 1–4′ high. Sandy or rocky soil. A similar, prostrate species, **Dwarf Cherry** (*P. depressa*), grows on gravelly beaches.

2. TALL SHRUBS OR SMALL TREES NORMALLY OVER 6′ HIGH

Bird, Pin or **Fire Cherry** (*P. pensylvanica*) Petals about ¼″ long; bark on flowering branches reddish brown. Leaves egg- or lance-shaped. Fruit red. Burned areas, woods and clearings.

Wild Plum (*P. americana*) Petals ⅜–½″ long; bark on flowering branches gray. Leaves egg-shaped, long-pointed. Branches often thorny. Fruit red to yellow. Woods and thickets, w. N.Eng. to Man. south.

Chokeberries (*Pyrus*) Petals roundish; flowers in branching, terminal clusters (no leaves or leaf buds at the ends of flowering branches); stems thornless. Flowers white or pink-tinged, ⅓–½″ wide. Leaves either egg-shaped (widest toward the tip) or elliptical, short-pointed and finely toothed. 3–12′ high. Spring. Rose Family.

Red Chokeberry (*P. arbutifolia*) Flower stalks woolly; calyx lobes longer than wide, bearing dark glands on the margin. Fruit red. Low woods and swamps.

Purple Chokeberry (*P. floribunda*) Flower stalks woolly; calyx lobes longer than wide, with few or no glands. Fruit purple-black. Low woods and swamps.

Black Chokeberry (*P. melanocarpa*) Flower stalks smooth; calyx lobes about as wide as long. Fruit black. Low woods, thickets and roadsides.

Continued

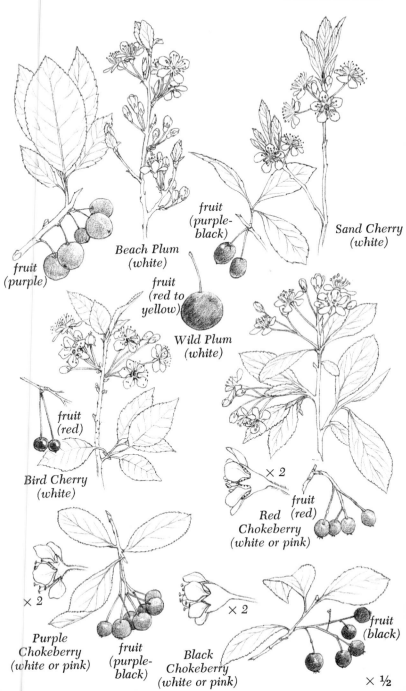

fruit (purple)

Beach Plum *(white)*

fruit (purple-black)

Sand Cherry *(white)*

fruit (red to yellow)

Wild Plum *(white)*

fruit (red)

Bird Cherry *(white)*

× 2

fruit (red)

Red Chokeberry *(white or pink)*

× 2

Purple Chokeberry *(white or pink)*

fruit (purple-black)

× 2

Black Chokeberry *(white or pink)*

fruit (black)

× ½

Leaves Alternate or Clustered, Not Lobed; White or Pink Flowers with 5 Separate Petals; Blooming in Spring (cont.)

Shadbushes, Juneberries or **Serviceberries** (*Amelanchier*) Petals longer than wide; white flowers, usually in short, loose racemes at the ends of the branches. A complex genus of shrubs or small trees, the species described below being the most distinctive. Leaves egg-shaped or oval, finely toothed. Fruit black or purplish, in most species sweet and edible. Spring. Rose Family.

1. PETALS ⅜–¾″ LONG; HEIGHT 6–40′

Smooth Shadbush (*A. laevis*) Leaves smooth or nearly so at flowering time. Fruit sweet and juicy. Woods and thickets.

Common Shadbush (*A. arborea*) † Similar to Smooth Shadbush but leaves white-woolly beneath at flowering time. Fruit dry and tasteless. Rich woods and thickets.

2. PETALS ¼–⅜″ LONG

Running Shadbush (*A. stolonifera*) In dry rocky places; 1–4′ high; leaves white-woolly at flowering time; spreads by underground stems, forming thickets. Fruit sweet and juicy. South to Va., Mich. and Minn.

Swamp Shadbush (*A. canadensis*) In swamps and moist soil, sometimes in drier situations; 4–20′ high; leaves white-woolly at flowering time; does not spread by underground stems. Flowers usually 5 or more in a cluster. Fruit juicy. Me. and sw. Que. south.

Mountain Shadbush (*A. bartramiana*) In bogs and on mountain slopes; 2–9′ high; leaves smooth at flowering time. Petals wider than those of the other species. Flowers in racemes, each with 1–4 flowers. N. N.Eng. to Minn. north; south in mts. to Mass. and Pa. Spring and early summer (high altitudes).

Chokecherry (*Prunus virginiana*) Petals roundish; white flowers in dense racemes, the racemes 1½–4″ long. Leaves egg-shaped, short-pointed, finely and sharply toothed. The flowers resemble those of the **Black Cherry** (*P. serotina*), a tree with bluntly toothed leaves. Fruit dark red to purplish, acid. 2–20′ high. Thickets and borders. Spring. Rose Family.

Hawthorns (*Crataegus*) Petals roundish; flowers in branching, *terminal* clusters; branches armed with scattered thorns. See p. 308.

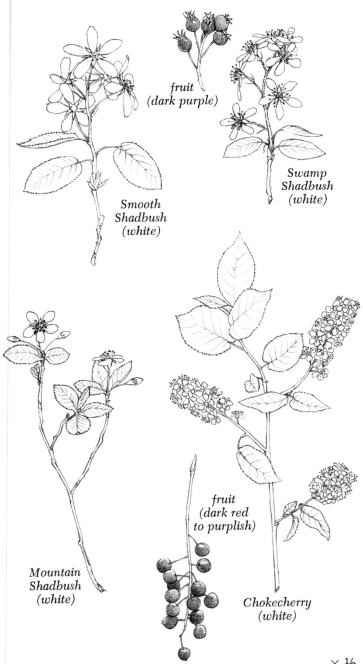

fruit
(dark purple)

Swamp
Shadbush
(white)

Smooth
Shadbush
(white)

Mountain
Shadbush
(white)

fruit
(dark red
to purplish)

Chokecherry
(white)

× ½

Flowers ½″ or More Wide

Shrubby Cinquefoil (*Potentilla fruticosa*) Yellow flowers, about
¾″ wide. The leaves have 5, sometimes 7, entire, narrowly oblong
or lance-shaped leaflets, ½–1″ long, which are silky-hairy on both
sides. 1–4′ high. Bogs, pastures and rocky places. Summer and fall.
Rose Family.

Roses (*Rosa*) Showy, white, pink or purple flowers, ¾–4″ wide, the
petals broadest at the tip and usually slightly indented. Leaves
with 3–9 pinnate leaflets and with stipules attached to the base of
the leaf stalks. About 20 species in our area, many of them escaped
from cultivation. Late spring and summer. Rose Family.

1. BUSHY SHRUBS (WITHOUT LONG, <u>ARCHING</u> FLOWERING STEMS)

a. Upper branches smooth except for scattered thorns

Swamp Rose (*R. palustris*) In wet soil; leaflets with very fine
teeth, dull green; prickles stout and usually hooked. Stipules
very narrow. 2–8′ high.

Pasture Rose (*R. carolina*) In dry, rocky or sandy soil; leaflets
dull green or slightly shining; stipules narrow; upper stems with
straight, slender thorns. Flowers usually solitary. 1–3′ high.

Virginia Rose (*R. virginiana*) In moist to dry thickets and meadows; leaflets dark green and shining, more coarsely toothed
than those of the Swamp Rose; stipules broadly winged, leaflike; thorns stout, flattened at the base, usually somewhat
curved. Flowers usually in small clusters. 2–8′ high.

Smooth Rose (*R. blanda*) On rocky slopes and shores; upper
stems without prickles or with a few scattered weak prickles;
leaflets dull green. Stipules broadened at the tip. 2–5′ high.

b. Upper branches covered with dense bristles

Rugosa Rose (*R. rugosa*) * Large (3–4″ wide) rose-purple flowers.
Leaflets dark green and shining, deeply veined. 2–8′ high. Seashore thickets, sand dunes and roadsides.

Shining Rose (*R. nitida*) Pink flowers, 1½–2½″ wide. Bristles
dark purple. Leaflets dark green and shining, finely toothed.
1–3′ high. Bogs and wet thickets, s. N.Eng. north.

Continued

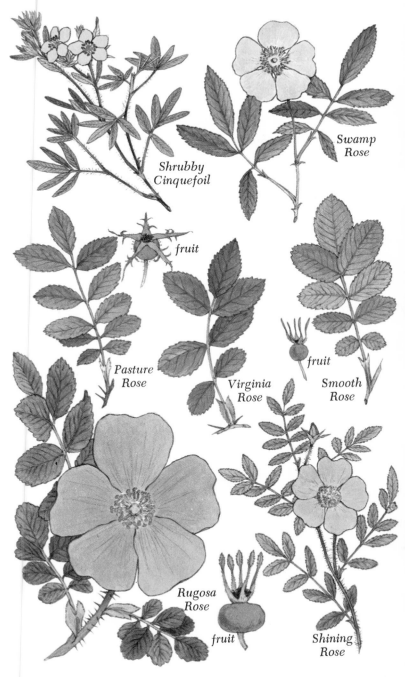

Shrubby
Cinquefoil

Swamp
Rose

fruit

Pasture
Rose

Virginia
Rose

Smooth
Rose

fruit

Rugosa
Rose

fruit

Shining
Rose

× ½

Flowers ½″ or More Wide (cont.)

Roses (*Rosa*) (cont.)

2. SHRUBS WITH SLENDER, ARCHING OR TRAILING,
FLOWERING STEMS

a. Leaflets on flowering stems usually 3

Prairie or **Climbing Rose** (*R. setigera*) Pink or whitish flowers, about 2½″ wide, in a small cluster. Leaflets sharply toothed and shining above. Stems either arching, trailing or climbing. 4–12′ long. Thickets and clearings, N.Y. to Ill. south; escaped from cultivation in N.Eng.

b. Leaflets on flowering stems usually 7–9

Multiflora Rose (*R. multiflora*) * Numerous, white flowers, ¾–1½″ wide. Stipules deeply fringed. 4–12′ long. Much cultivated, and now escaped to roadsides and moist thickets, s. N.Eng. south.

Sweetbrier or **Eglantine** (*R. eglanteria*) * Pink flowers, 1¼–2″ wide; leaflets very fragrant. Leaflets roundish to elliptical, double-toothed, hairy beneath. 4–8′ high. Roadsides and pastures.

Raspberries and **Blackberries** (*Rubus*) White flowers with petals longer than wide and widest in the middle. See p. 232.

Flowers under ½″ Wide; Leaflets 3

American Bladdernut (*Staphylea trifolia*) Drooping racemes of white flowers; leaflets finely toothed. Petals erect. Fruit an inflated, 3-pointed pod, 2–3″ long. Bark striped. 4–15′ high. Moist thickets and banks, Mass. and sw. Que. to Minn. south. Spring. Bladdernut Family.

Fragrant Sumac (*Rhus aromatica*) Yellowish flowers in short, dense spikes; blooms in early spring as the leaves unfold. Leaflets with blunt, coarse teeth, the terminal leaflet short-stalked or stalkless. 2–6′ high. Rocky woods, w. N.Eng. to Kan. south. Cashew Family.

Poison Ivy (*Rhus radicans*) Green flowers; terminal leaflet stalked; leaflets entire or slightly toothed. See p. 330.

Hop Tree or **Wafer Ash** (*Ptelea trifoliata*) Greenish-white flowers; terminal leaflet stalkless or nearly so, entire or obscurely toothed. See p. 170.

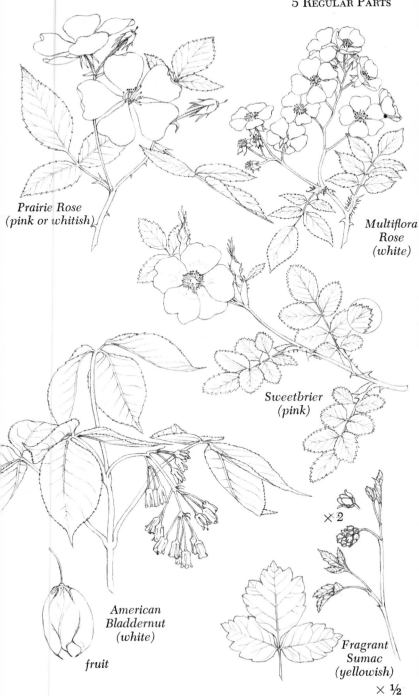

*Prairie Rose
(pink or whitish)*

*Multiflora
Rose
(white)*

*Sweetbrier
(pink)*

$\times 2$

*American
Bladdernut
(white)*

fruit

*Fragrant
Sumac
(yellowish)*

$\times \frac{1}{2}$

Flowers under ½" Wide; Leaflets 5 or More; Stems Not Prickly

LEAVES (AS WELL AS LEAFLETS) GROWING IN PAIRS

Elders (*Sambucus*) White or yellowish flowers in large terminal clusters. Flowers about ⅛" wide. Fruits berrylike and juicy. 3–10' high. Honeysuckle Family.

Common Elder (*S. canadensis*) White flowers in a cluster wider than long. Leaflets 5–11, usually 7, egg-shaped, sharply toothed. Fruit purplish-black, used for jelly and wine. Moist places. Late spring and summer.

Red-berried Elder (*S. pubens*) Creamy-white or yellowish flowers in a cluster longer than wide. Leaflets 5–7, lance- or egg-shaped, toothed. Fruit red, acid. Rocky woods. Spring and early summer.

LEAVES ALTERNATE OR CLUSTERED

Shrub Yellowroot (*Xanthorrhiza simplicissima*) Purple flowers in drooping racemes 2–3" long. Flowers ¼" wide. Leaflets usually 5, toothed or lobed, clustered at the top of the stem. 8–24" high. Damp woods and banks, N.Y. to W.Va. south; escaped in N.Eng. Spring. Buttercup Family.

American Mountain Ash (*Pyrus americana*) White flowers in broad, rounded or flattish clusters; bark smooth. Flowers ¼" wide, numerous. Leaves pinnate, with 11–17 sharply toothed leaflets. Fruit bright red. 5–30' high. Woods, mountain slopes. Late spring and early summer. Rose Family.

Sumacs (*Rhus*) Very small, greenish or yellowish flowers in clusters. Summer. Cashew Family.

1. IN SWAMPS; FRUIT SMOOTH

Poison Sumac or **Poison Dogwood** (*R. vernix*) *Very poisonous at all seasons.* Small, green flowers in a loose cluster. Leaflets entire. Fruit whitish or gray. 6–20' high. Late spring and early summer.

2. IN DRY SOIL; FRUIT COVERED WITH RED HAIRS

Staghorn Sumac (*R. typhina*) Branches densely covered with velvety hairs; leaflets with numerous, sharp teeth. 5–20' high.

Dwarf or **Shining Sumac** (*R. copallina*) Branches fine-hairy; leaflets entire or with a few, blunt teeth. Leaves shining, with winglike projections between the leaflets. 2–10' high. S. Me. to Ill. south.

Smooth Sumac (*R. glabra*)† Branches very smooth; leaflets sharply toothed. 3–10' high.

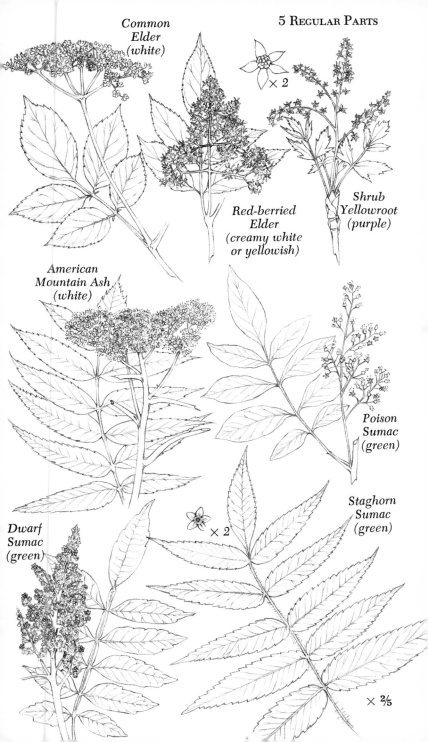

Common
Elder
(white)

5 REGULAR PARTS

× 2

Shrub
Yellowroot
(purple)

Red-berried
Elder
*(creamy white
or yellowish)*

American
Mountain Ash
(white)

Poison
Sumac
(green)

Staghorn
Sumac
(green)

Dwarf
Sumac
(green)

× 2

× 2/5

SHRUBS /
Leaves Divided

Flowers under ½" Wide; Leaflets 5 or More; Stems Prickly

Hercules' Club (*Aralia spinosa*) Large, spiny-trunked shrub; leaflets toothed. Small, white flowers in a large, branching cluster of umbels. Leaves up to 3' long, with egg-shaped leaflets and prickly stalks. Fruit black. Rich woods and clearings, w. N.Y. to Iowa south; escaped from cultivation in s. N.Eng., c. N.Y. and Mich. Summer. Ginseng Family.

Northern Prickly Ash or **Toothache Tree** (*Xanthoxylum americanum*) Stems prickly at leaf joints; leaflets entire. See p. 170.

VINES /
With No Apparent Leaves at Flowering Time

Common Dodder or **Love Vine** (*Cuscuta gronovii*) Parasitic plant with yellow or orange stems and dense clusters of small, white flowers. Flowers bell-shaped, ⅛" long, with 5 flaring lobes. Tightly twines around the stems of other plants and absorbs their sap through tiny suckers. There are 10 other species occasionally found in our area. Low grounds. Summer and fall. Morning Glory Family.

VINES /
Leaves Entire

Leaves Heart- or Arrow-shaped at the Base

False Buckwheats or **Bindweeds** (*Polygonum*) Very small, white or greenish flowers in racemes or in axillary clusters or solitary in the axils. Leaves heart- or arrow-shaped at the base. The twining or trailing stems are jointed. Buckwheat Family.

Fringed Bindweed (*P. cilinode*) White flowers in racemes; the sheaths surrounding the stem at the leaf joints are fringed with hairs. Fruit not winged. Rocky woods and slopes. Summer.

Climbing False Buckwheat (*P. scandens*) Yellow-green or greenish-yellow flowers in racemes; sheaths not fringed; flowering calyx winged on the back. Conspicuous in fall by its winged fruit. Moist woods and thickets. Late summer and fall.

Black Bindweed (*P. convolvulus*) * Inconspicuous green flowers mostly in few-flowered axillary racemes or clusters; calyx and fruit not winged. Common weed of gardens and waste places. Summer and fall.

Continued

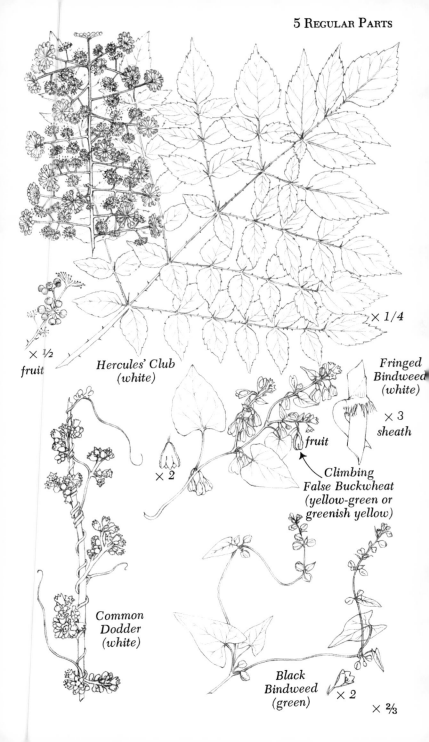

× 1/4

× ½
fruit

Hercules' Club
(white)

Fringed
Bindweed
(white)

× 3
sheath

× 2

fruit

Climbing
False Buckwheat
(yellow-green or
greenish yellow)

Common
Dodder
(white)

Black
Bindweed
(green)

× 2

× ⅔

Leaves Heart- or Arrow-shaped at the Base (cont.)

Bindweeds (*Convolvulus*) Showy, white or pink, funnel-shaped flowers; leaves triangular in outline (not heart-shaped). Upright Bindweed (*C. spithamaeus*) (p. 198) is a semi-erect species. Summer and fall. Morning Glory Family.

Hedge Bindweed (*C. sepium*) Flowers 1½–3″ long. Leaves usually with square lobes at the base. Moist thickets.

Field Bindweed (*C. arvensis*) * Flowers about ¾″ long. Leaves usually arrow-shaped at the base. Weed of fields and waste places.

Morning Glories (*Ipomoea*) Funnel-shaped flowers; leaves heart-shaped. Ivy-leaved Morning Glory (*I. hederacea*) (p. 326) and occasionally some of the following species have 3-lobed leaves. Summer and fall. Morning Glory Family.

1. FLOWERS 1¾–3″ LONG

Common Morning Glory (*I. purpurea*) * Calyx, and usually the stem, hairy, the sepals narrow and more or less pointed. The flowers are of various colors — blue, purple, red, white or variegated. Escaped from cultivation to fields and waste places.

Wild Potato Vine (*I. pandurata*) Calyx and stem smooth or nearly so, the sepals broad and blunt. White flowers with pink or purple stripes in the throat. Leaves heart-shaped or sometimes narrowed in the middle. The root is huge for the size of the plant — 1–3′ long and growing straight down. Dry hills or slopes, Conn. to Mich. south.

2. FLOWERS ½–1¼″ LONG

Small Red Morning Glory (*I. coccinea*) * Scarlet flowers, ¾–1¼″ long. Sepals with bristlelike tips. Leaves heart-shaped or sometimes lobed. Thickets and waste places, Mass. to Mich. south.

Small White Morning Glory (*I. lacunosa*) White flowers, ½–¾″ long (sometimes purple). The leaves are heart-shaped or 3-lobed, slender-pointed. Moist thickets, Pa. to Ill. south.

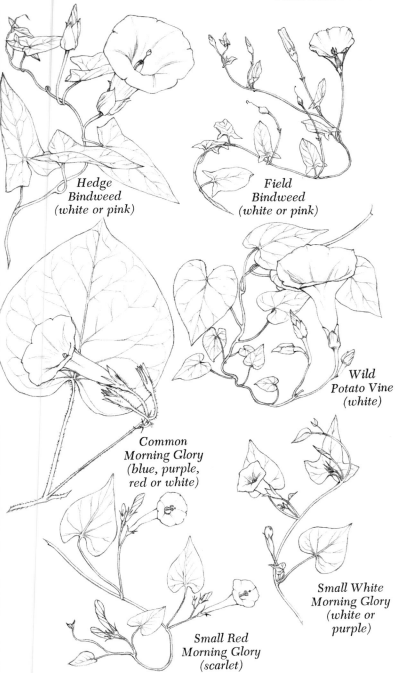

Hedge
Bindweed
(white or pink)

Field
Bindweed
(white or pink)

Wild
Potato Vine
(white)

Common
Morning Glory
(blue, purple,
red or white)

Small White
Morning Glory
(white or
purple)

Small Red
Morning Glory
(scarlet)

× ½

Leaves Not Heart- or Arrow-shaped

Trumpet or **Coral Honeysuckle** (*Lonicera sempervirens*) Scarlet (rarely yellow), trumpet-shaped flowers with a narrow tube, 1–2″ long. The flowers, which may be slightly irregular, grow in whorls at the ends of the branches. Leaves oblong, in pairs, the upper pairs joined together. Stem woody and high-climbing. Woods and thickets, s. Me. to Iowa south. Spring to fall. Honeysuckle Family.

Black Swallowwort (*Cynanchum nigrum*) * Dark-purple, fragrant flowers, about ¼″ wide, in small clusters in the axils. Leaves egg-shaped, in pairs or sometimes whorled. Fruit pods similar to those of the Milkweeds. 2–6′ long. Roadsides and fields. Late spring and summer. Milkweed Family.

VINES /
Leaves Toothed or Lobed

Vines without Tendrils

Climbing Bittersweets (*Celastrus*) Small greenish flowers; leaves unlobed. Fruit orange, conspicuous in fall, splitting open to reveal the showy, scarlet seeds. Stem woody, twining. Rich thickets and fencerows. Late spring and early summer. Staff Tree Family.

> **Climbing Bittersweet** (*C. scandens*) Flowers in terminal clusters; leaves finely toothed, pointed.

> **Asiatic Bittersweet** (*C. orbiculatus*) * Flowers in axillary clusters; leaves bluntly toothed, nearly round.

Common Hop (*Humulus lupulus*) * Small greenish flowers in loose, axillary clusters; leaves with 3–5 deep lobes. Staminate and pistillate flowers separate. Fruit a drooping cluster of overlapping bracts, 1–2½″ long. Stem rough, twining. Rich thickets. Summer. Hemp Family.

Morning Glories (*Ipomoea*) White, blue, purple or scarlet, funnel-shaped flowers. Leaves heart-shaped at the base. Summer and fall. Morning Glory Family.

1. CALYX LOBES WITH LONG, VERY NARROW TIPS AND HAIRY BASE

> **Ivy-leaved Morning Glory** (*I. hederacea*) * Blue or purple (sometimes white) flowers with a white tube, 1–1½″ long. Leaves with 3 deep lobes. Stem with backward-pointing hairs. Fields, waste places. Summer and fall.

2. CALYX LOBES OTHERWISE (SEE P. 324)

Continued

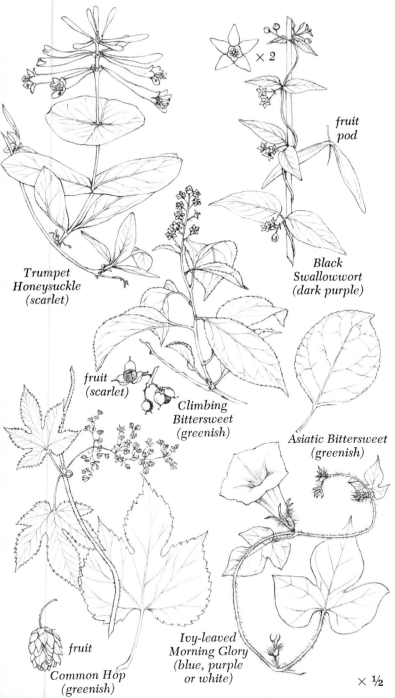

× 2

fruit pod

Trumpet Honeysuckle (scarlet)

Black Swallowwort (dark purple)

fruit (scarlet)

Climbing Bittersweet (greenish)

Asiatic Bittersweet (greenish)

fruit

Common Hop (greenish)

Ivy-leaved Morning Glory (blue, purple or white)

× ½

Vines without Tendrils (cont.)

Bittersweet Nightshade (*Solanum dulcamara*) Violet or purple flowers with backward-pointing lobes. See below.

Climbing Hempweed or **Climbing Boneset** (*Mikania scandens*) White or pink flowers in heads; leaves heart-shaped. See p. 444.

Vines Clinging by Tendrils

One-seeded Bur Cucumber (*Sicyos angulatus*) Stem covered with sticky hairs; small clusters of greenish-white flowers in the axils. Staminate flowers in long-stalked clusters; pistillate flowers in short-stalked clusters. Leaves broad, 5-lobed, heart-shaped at the base. Fruits prickly, ½" long, stalkless, in a small cluster. River-banks and moist thickets. Summer and fall. Gourd Family.

Grapes (*Vitis*) Vines with woody stems and many-branched clusters of small greenish flowers. See p. 444.

Passionflowers (*Passiflora*) Flowers ½–2" wide, growing singly or in pairs from the axils. See p. 396.

VINES   /
Leaves Divided

Flowers Not White or Green

Bittersweet Nightshade (*Solanum dulcamara*) * Violet or purple, shooting star–shaped flowers, ½" wide, the flower lobes pointed backward. Flowers in small clusters along the stem. Leaves divided into 3 leaflets, or deeply lobed with a large terminal segment, or entire. Fruit a red berry, somewhat poisonous. Moist thickets. Spring to fall. Nightshade Family.

Trumpet Creeper (*Campsis radicans*) Red or orange, trumpet-shaped flowers, 2½" long; leaflets 7–11, sharply toothed. Stem woody. Moist woods and thickets, N.J. to Iowa south; escaped north to N.Eng. Summer and fall. Bignonia Family.

Cross Vine (*Bignonia capreolata*) Orange or red, somewhat bell-shaped flowers, paler within, 2" long; leaflets 2, entire, oblong or egg-shaped. A cross section of the stem shows a cross. Woody vine with tendrils. Rich, moist woods, Md. to Ill. south. Spring. Bignonia Family.

Prairie or **Climbing Rose** (*Rosa setigera*) Large, pink flowers, 2½" wide; stem prickly. See p. 318.

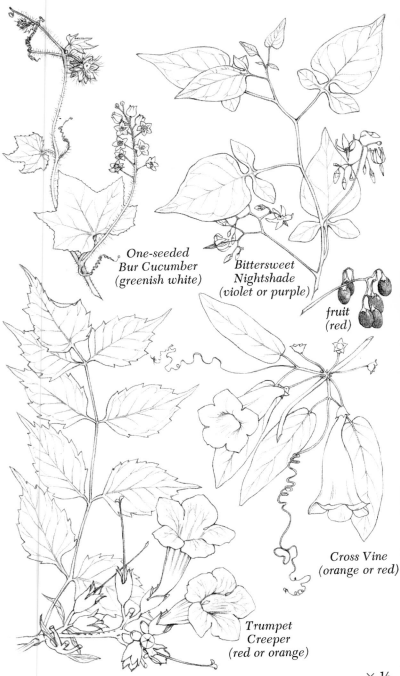

One-seeded
Bur Cucumber
(greenish white)

Bittersweet
Nightshade
(violet or purple)

fruit
(red)

Cross Vine
(orange or red)

Trumpet
Creeper
(red or orange)

× ½

White or Green Flowers

Blackberries or **Dewberries** (*Rubus*) Trailing plants with white flowers ¼–1″ wide, and leaves divided into 3 or 5 toothed leaflets. Flowers solitary or in small clusters. Rose Family.

Dewberry (*R. flagellaris*) Flowers about 1″ wide; leaves not shining; trailing stem prickly. Fruit black, large and sweet. Dry open places. Spring and early summer.

Swamp Dewberry (*R. hispidus*) Flowers ½–¾″ wide; leaves dark green and shining; stem bristly. Leaflets usually 3. Fruit reddish, black when fully ripe, about ½″ in diameter, acid. Swamps, open woods and clearings. Summer.

Dwarf Raspberry (*R. pubescens*) Flowers ¼–½″ wide, the petals erect at the base; stem without prickles. Sepals bent downward. Fruit dark red, about ½″ in diameter, juicy. Stem trailing, with erect, leafy branches. Wet woods, shores and banks. Spring and summer (mts.).

Poison Ivy (*Rhus radicans*) Very small (⅛″ wide), green flowers; leaflets 3, entire or with a few, coarse teeth. The flowers grow in small, branching clusters in the axils. Fruit gray or whitish. Sometimes bushy and erect. *Very poisonous to the touch at all seasons.* Open woods, thickets and fencerows. Late spring and early summer. Sumac Family.

Virginia Creeper or **Woodbine** (*Parthenocissus quinquefolia*) Very small, greenish or whitish flowers; leaflets 5, coarsely toothed. See p. 444.

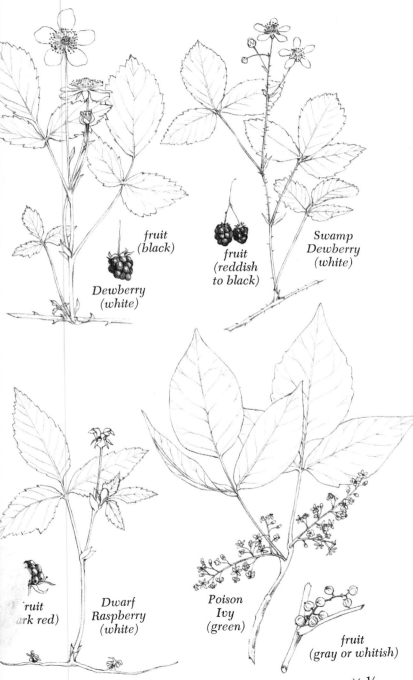

fruit (black)

Dewberry (white)

fruit (reddish to black)

Swamp Dewberry (white)

fruit (dark red)

Dwarf Raspberry (white)

Poison Ivy (green)

fruit (gray or whitish)

× ½

Wild Leek or **Ramps** (*Allium tricoccum*) White flowers in an umbel at the end of a long, naked stalk. Leaves elliptical, 8–10″ long, appearing in spring but disappearing before the plant blooms. Bulbs used as food in the s. Appalachians. 6–18″ high. Rich woods. Summer. Lily Family.

WILDFLOWERS WITH BASAL LEAVES ONLY / Leaves Entire

Blue or Violet Flowers with Narrow Leaves

Blue-eyed Grasses (*Sisyrinchium*) Flowers yellow-eyed, ½–¾″ wide, in a small umbel or solitary, each petal-like part with a bristle-tip. Stems wiry, 2-edged. 6–18″ long. Fields and meadows. Late spring and early summer. Iris Family.

1. STEM BEARING A LEAFLIKE BRACT IN THE MIDDLE, FROM WHICH THE LONG FLOWERING STEMS BRANCH

   Stout Blue-eyed Grass (*S. angustifolium*) Lower stem distinctly winged (with flat edges), over ⅛″ wide. Flowers often pale blue.

   Eastern Blue-eyed Grass (*S. atlanticum*) Lower stem barely winged, pale green, under ⅛″ wide.

2. STEM WITHOUT A BRACT IN THE MIDDLE AND UNBRANCHED; FLOWER CLUSTER OVERTOPPED BY A POINTED BRACT

   Common Blue-eyed Grass (*S. montanum*) Deep violet-blue flowers; stem distinctly winged (with flat edges), ⅛″ wide; leaves about as long as the flowering stems.

   Slender Blue-eyed Grass (*S. mucronatum*) † Violet-blue flowers; stem very slender, barely winged, 1⁄16″ wide; leaves much shorter than the flowering stems. N. Me. to Wis., south to N.C.

   White Blue-eyed Grass (*S. albidum*) † Pale-blue or white flowers. S. Ont. and Ohio to s. Wis. south.

Wild Hyacinth or **Eastern Camass** (*Camassia scilloides*) Pale-blue flowers, ½–¾″ wide, in a loose-flowered raceme. 1–2′ high. Meadows and open woods, w. Pa. to Mich. south. Late spring. Lily Family.

Grape Hyacinth (*Muscari botryoides*) * Deep-blue, globular flowers, ⅛″ wide, in a dense raceme. Leaves fleshy, grooved. 6–8″ high. Commonly cultivated, escaping to fields and roadsides. Spring. Lily Family.

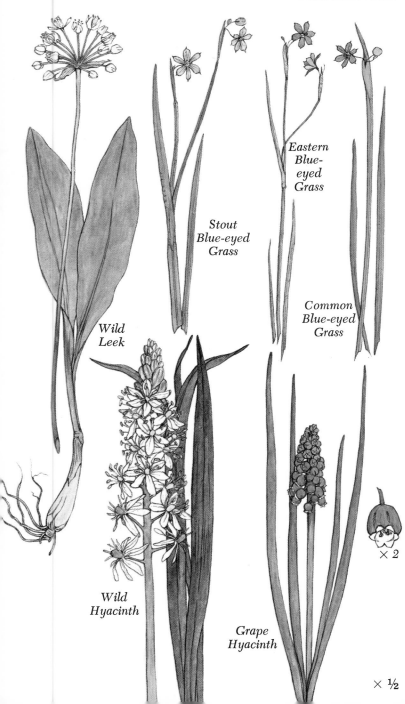

Eastern
Blue-
eyed
Grass

Stout
Blue-eyed
Grass

Common
Blue-eyed
Grass

Wild
Leek

Wild
Hyacinth

Grape
Hyacinth

× 2

× ½

White, Pink or Greenish Flowers with Narrow Leaves

FLOWERS OVER ¾″ WIDE

Star-of-Bethlehem (*Ornithogalum umbellatum*) * Slender plant of fields and meadows. Backs of the white petals green with white margins. Flower cluster rather flat-topped. The flowers open only in sunshine. Leaves grasslike with a pale midrib. 4–12″ high. Spring. Lily Family.

Yucca or **Spanish Bayonet** (*Yucca filamentosa*) Large plant (5–10′ high) of sandy places. The nodding, whitish flowers grow in a large panicle several feet long. Leaves thick and rigid, 1–2½′ long, with twisting threads. S. N.J. south; escaped northward. Summer. Lily Family.

Flowering Rush (*Butomus umbellatus*) Plant of muddy shores; roseate flowers in umbels. See p. 118.

FLOWERS UNDER ¾″ WIDE

Fly Poison (*Amianthium muscaetoxicum*) Flowers in a raceme; flowering stem smooth. White flowers, turning greenish with age. The grasslike leaves are somewhat blunt at the tip. 1½–4′ high. Open sandy woods, Long I. to Pa. south. Late spring and early summer. Lily Family.

False Asphodels (*Tofieldia*) Flowers in a raceme; flowering stem bears short, sticky hairs. See p. 344.

Wild Onions (*Allium*) Flowers in an umbel or solitary; leaves strongly onion-scented. Flower cluster either quite dense, or most or all of the flowers replaced by small bulbets. For other species, see pp. 332 and 348. 8–24″ high. Lily Family.

Wild Garlic (*A. canadense*) Flower cluster erect, containing numerous small bulbs and few, if any, flowers. Whitish or pink flowers. Leaves very narrow, 6–18″ long. Moist meadows and open woods. Late spring and early summer.

Nodding Wild Onion (*A. cernuum*) Flower cluster nodding, without bulbs. Pink or white flowers. Leaves very narrow. Rocky and gravelly places, N.Y. to B.C. south. Summer.

White Blue-eyed Grass (*Sisyrinchium albidum*) Flowers in an umbel or solitary; flower parts bristle-tipped. See p. 332.

Sweetflag or **Calamus** (*Acorus calamus*) Minute, yellow-green flowers in a dense spike. See p. 398.

*Yucca
(whitish)*

*Star-of-
Bethlehem
(white)*

× 2

*Fly Poison
(white or green)*

*Wild
Garlic
(whitish or pink)*

*Nodding
Wild Onion
(pink or white)*

× ⅖

Orange, Yellow or Greenish-yellow Flowers with Narrow Leaves

Yellow Stargrass (*Hypoxis hirsuta*) Yellow flowers, ½–¾″ wide, in a small cluster. Leaves grasslike, 4–12″ long. 3–6″ high at flowering time. Meadows and open woods, s. Me. to Man. south. Spring to fall. Amaryllis Family.

Day Lily (*Hemerocallis fulva*) * Tawny-orange, funnel-shaped flowers, 3–4″ wide. Flowers open for a day. Leaves 2′ long. 2–6′ high. Escaped from gardens to roadsides and meadows. Summer. Lily Family.

Blackberry Lily (*Belamcanda chinensis*) Purple-spotted, orange flowers, 1½–2″ wide. See p. 348.

Sweetflag or **Calamus** (*Acorus calamus*) Minute, greenish-yellow flowers in a dense spike. See p. 398.

Creeping Spearwort (*Ranunculus reptans*) Low, creeping plant of wet shores. See p. 176.

Leaves Lance-shaped or Wider; Flowers in a Spike or Raceme

Lily-of-the-valley (*Convallaria majalis*) * White, bell-shaped, nodding flowers, in a one-sided raceme. Leaves 2 or 3, oval, 6″ long. A familiar garden plant which is now established in woods and thickets. 4–10″ high. Late spring. Lily Family.

Colicroot (*Aletris farinosa*) Whitish flowers in a stiff, spikelike raceme 4–12″ long. Flowers tubular, ¼–⅓″ long, and rough on the outside. Leaves lance-shaped, in a basal rosette. Flowering stem usually bears a few small bracts. 1–3′ high. Sandy soil, s. Me. to Wis. south. Summer. Lily Family.

Swamp Pink (*Helonias bullata*) Pink or purplish flowers in a dense raceme. Flower stalk hollow, 1–2′ high. The leaves are evergreen and grow in a basal rosette. Bogs, s. N.Y. and Pa. south. Spring. Lily Family.

Golden Club (*Orontium aquaticum*) Yellow flowers in a compact spadix. The oblong, long-stalked leaves are often floating. 1–2′ high. Shallow water of ponds and streams, Mass. and c. N.Y. south. Spring. Arum Family.

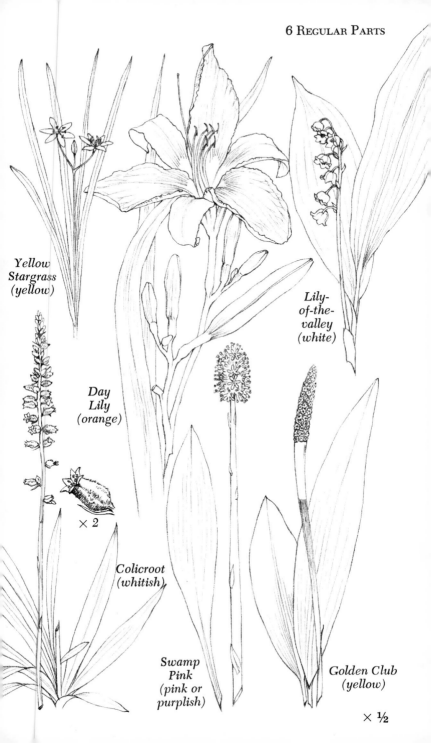

Yellow Stargrass (yellow)

Lily-of-the-valley (white)

Day Lily (orange)

× 2

Colicroot (whitish)

Swamp Pink (pink or purplish)

Golden Club (yellow)

× ½

Leaves Lance-shaped or Wider; Flowers Single or in a Small Cluster

Clintonias (*Clintonia*) Leaves oval; flowers in an umbel. Leaves usually 3 (sometimes 2 or 4), large and shining. 6–12″ high. Spring and early summer. Lily Family.

> **Yellow Clintonia** or **Bluebead** (*C. borealis*) Nodding, greenish-yellow flowers, ¾″ long. Fruit a dark-blue, beadlike berry. Moist woods, very common in mountainous areas.

> **White Clintonia** (*C. umbellulata*) Erect, white flowers, usually purple-dotted, ½″ long. Fruit black. Rich woods, w. N.Y. to e. Ohio south.

Trout Lilies or **Dogtooth Violets** (*Erythronium*) Leaves oval; flower solitary, nodding, ¾–1½″ long. The 2 leaves are 3–8″ long. Moist woods. Early spring. Lily Family.

> **Trout Lily** or **Yellow Adder's Tongue** (*E. americanum*) Yellow flowers. Leaves usually mottled with brown.

> **White Trout Lily** or **White Adder's Tongue** (*E. albidum*) Flower white or tinged with blue. Leaves usually slightly mottled or not mottled. S. Ont. to Minn. south.

Mud Plantain (*Heteranthera reniformis*) Pale-blue or white flowers, ¼–⅜″ wide, in a small cluster. Leaves roundish. Stems creeping in the mud of pond-margins. North to Conn., s. N.Y. and s. Ill. Summer and fall. Pickerelweed Family.

Yellow Pond Lilies (*Nuphar*) Aquatic plants with yellow flowers. See p. 176.

WILDFLOWERS WITH BASAL LEAVES ONLY /
Leaves Toothed, Lobed or Divided

Hepaticas (*Hepatica*) Leaves with 3 deep lobes and thickish. Blue, pink or white flowers, ½–1″ wide, with 6–12 petal-like sepals. Beneath the sepals are 3 green bracts resembling sepals. Hybrids occur with leaves intermediate between the two species. Woods. Early spring. Buttercup Family.

> **Round-lobed Hepatica** or **Liverleaf** (*H. americana*) Lobes of leaves rounded at the tip. The bracts beneath the flower are also rounded at the tip.

> **Sharp-lobed Hepatica** (*H. acutiloba*) Lobes of leaves and bracts sharply or bluntly pointed, not rounded.

Goldthread (*Coptis groenlandica*) Leaves divided into 3, toothed leaflets. See p. 184.

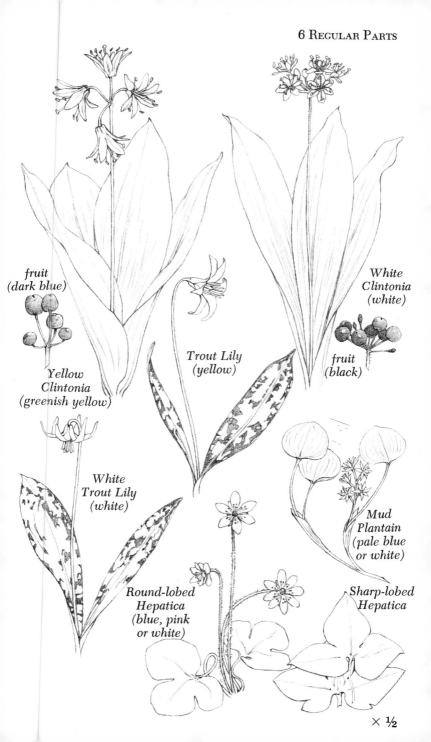

fruit
(dark blue)

White
Clintonia
(white)

Yellow
Clintonia
(greenish yellow)

Trout Lily
(yellow)

fruit
(black)

White
Trout Lily
(white)

Mud
Plantain
(pale blue
or white)

Round-lobed
Hepatica
(blue, pink
or white)

Sharp-lobed
Hepatica

× ½

Nodding, Bell-shaped Flowers

*YELLOW, YELLOWISH OR RED-ORANGE FLOWERS, ¾″ OR
MORE LONG*

Bellworts (*Uvularia*) Low, woodland plants with yellowish flowers. The flowers are usually solitary at the ends of the branches. Leaves oval or oblong. Stem forked above the middle. 6–24″ high. Spring. Lily Family.

1. LEAVES PIERCED BY THE STEM, NOT MERELY CLASPING

Bellwort (*U. perfoliata*) Pale-yellow flowers, ¾–1¼″ long; inside of flowers covered with orange granules. Leaves smooth beneath. Open woods and clearings, s. N.Eng. to s. Ont. south.

Large-flowered Bellwort (*U. grandiflora*) Orange-yellow flowers, 1–2″ long; inside of flowers bear few, if any, granules. Leaves usually whitish-downy beneath. Rich woods, chiefly in limestone regions, sw. Que. and w. N.Eng. to N.D. south.

2. LEAVES CLASPING, BUT NOT PIERCED BY THE STEM

Sessile-leaved Bellwort or **Wild Oats** (*U. sessilifolia*) Leaves pale beneath. Pale-yellow or straw-colored flowers, more slender than the preceding two species. Fruit a triangular pod. Common in woods and thickets.

Mountain Bellwort (*U. pudica*) † Similar to Sessile-leaved Bellwort but leaves green and shining on both sides. Flowers light-yellow, about 1″ long. Pine barrens, Long I., N.J. and Va., and in mountain woods, W.Va. and Va. south.

Tiger Lily (*Lilium tigrinum*) * Large, spotted, red-orange, nodding flowers, 3–4″ wide. The upper part of the stem is whitish-downy, and small black bulblets grow in the upper axils. Stem purple. 2–5′ high. Escaped from gardens to roadsides and persisting around old dwellings. Summer. Lily Family.

GREENISH FLOWERS, AT THE ENDS OF THE BRANCHES

Fairy Bells or **Yellow Mandarin** (*Disporum lanuginosum*) Flowers ½–¾″ long, composed of 6 pointed segments, and growing singly or a few in a cluster. The stem and leaves are downy; the last 2 leaves on each branch appearing opposite. Fruit a red berry. 1–2½′ high. Rich woods, w. N.Y. and s. Ont. south. Spring. Lily Family.

Continued

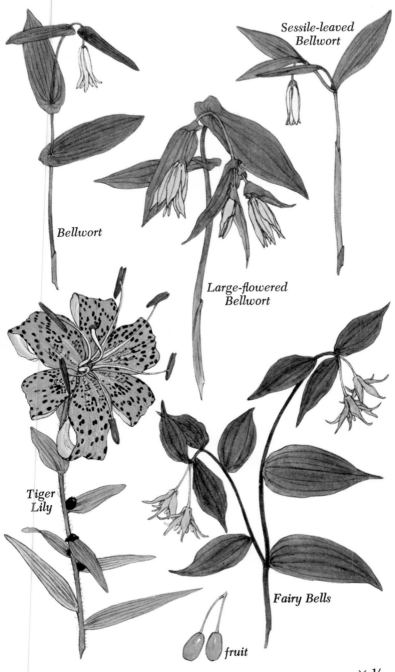

Sessile-leaved
Bellwort

Bellwort

Large-flowered
Bellwort

Tiger
Lily

Fairy Bells

fruit

× ½

Nodding, Bell-shaped Flowers (cont.)

*GREENISH, PURPLE OR PINK FLOWERS GROWING IN THE
AXILS OR ALONG THE BRANCHES*

Solomon's Seals (*Polygonatum*) Plants with an unbranched, arching stem, beneath which hangs a row of elongated greenish
bells with 6 short lobes. Leaves broadly lance-shaped or egg-
shaped. Fruit a dark-blue or blackish berry. The common name is
derived from the round scars found on the rootstock. Late spring
and early summer. Lily Family.

> **Great Solomon's Seal** (*P. canaliculatum*) Flowers ⅔–¾″ long;
> leaves smooth; flowers 2–10 in a cluster. Stem stout. 2–6′ high.
> Rich woods and river-banks, w. N.H. to Man. south.

> **Hairy Solomon's Seal** (*P. pubescens*) Flowers ⅜–½″ long; leaves
> (under magnification) hairy on the veins beneath. Flowers grow-
> ing singly or in pairs. Stem slender, 1–3′ high. Common in
> woods.

> **Smooth Solomon's Seal** (*P. biflorum*) † Similar to Hairy Solo-
> mon's Seal but flowers ½–⅔″ long; leaves smooth on both sides;
> flowers 1–4 in a cluster. Stem slender. 1–3′ high. Woods, Conn.
> to s. Mich. south.

Twisted Stalks (*Streptopus*) Broad-leaved, usually branching
plants with bell-shaped flowers having 6 recurved segments.
Flowers about ½″ long, with their stalks bent (or twisted) in the
middle. Leaves egg-shaped. Fruit a red berry. Cool moist woods,
mostly in the mts. Spring and early summer (mts.). Lily Family.

> **Twisted Stalk** or **White Mandarin** (*S. amplexifolius*) Greenish
> flowers. The leaves clasp the stem and have a whitish bloom
> beneath. 1–3′ high. N.Eng. to Wis. north and in mts. to N.C.

> **Rosybells, Rose Twisted Stalk** or **Rose Mandarin** (*S. roseus*)
> Rose-purple or pink flowers. The leaves are stalkless, but not
> clasping, and are green beneath. 1–2′ high. N.J., Pa., Mich. and
> Wis. north, and in mts. to Ga.

Asparagus (*Asparagus officinalis*) * Leaves (actually clusters of
short branches) very short and narrow, giving the plant a feathery
appearance. The flowers are small (¼″ long), yellow-green bells
hanging here and there along the branches. The true leaves are
tiny scales. Fruit a scarlet berry. 3–5′ high. Escaped from gardens
to fields and waste places. Late spring and early summer. Lily
Family.

Great
Solomon's
Seal
(greenish)

fruit
(dark
blue)

Hairy
Solomon's
Seal
(greenish)

fruit
(red)

Twisted
Stalk
(greenish)

× 1

Rosybells
(rose-purple
or pink)

Asparagus
(yellow-green)

× ½

Flowers in Racemes or Widely Branched Clusters; Leaves Long and Narrow

FLOWERS IN A BRANCHING CLUSTER

Featherfleece (*Stenanthium gramineum*) Petals and sepals narrow, four or more times longer than wide, pointed. White or greenish flowers in a large cluster. Stem smooth. 2–5′ high. Open woods, Pa. to Ill. south. Summer and fall. Lily Family.

Bunchflower (*Melanthium virginicum*) Petals and sepals abruptly narrowed to a short stalk. Greenish-white flowers, turning brownish as they age. Petals flat. Upper part of stem downy. Leaves grasslike, but rather broadly so. Broad-leaved Bunchflower (*M. hybridum*) (p. 346) has lance-shaped leaves and crinkled petals. 2–5′ high. Meadows and damp woods, s. N.Y. to Iowa south. Summer. Lily Family.

Golden Crest (*Lophiola americana*) White-woolly plant of bogs in the N.J. pine barrens. Flowers ¼″ wide, with a conspicuous yellow, woolly center. The similar *L. septentrionalis* is found locally in w. N.S. 1–2′ high. Early summer. Amaryllis Family.

FLOWERS IN A RACEME

Turkey Beard (*Xerophyllum asphodeloides*) White flowers; leaves stiff and needlelike, the basal ones forming a thick, bristly clump. Flowers in a dense raceme 3–10″ long. 2–5′ high. Pine barrens and mountain woods, N.J., Del. and Va. south. Late spring and early summer. Lily Family.

Bog Asphodel (*Narthecium americanum*) Yellow flowers. Leaves very narrow, mostly basal. 10–16″ high. Pine-barren bogs, N.J. and Del. Early summer. Lily Family.

False Asphodels (*Tofieldia*) White flowers; basal leaves irislike; stem covered with sticky hairs. 6–24″ high. Bogs and shores. Summer. Lily Family.

> **Sticky Tofieldia** (*T. glutinosa*) Stem sticky with short, black hairs. Canada south to n. N.Eng., w. N.Y. to Ill., and in mts. to Ga.

> **False Asphodel** (*T. racemosa*) † Hairs of stem not black. Along coast, N.J. south.

Fly Poison (*Amianthium muscaetoxicum*) White or greenish flowers; basal leaves somewhat blunt at the tip; stem smooth. See p. 334.

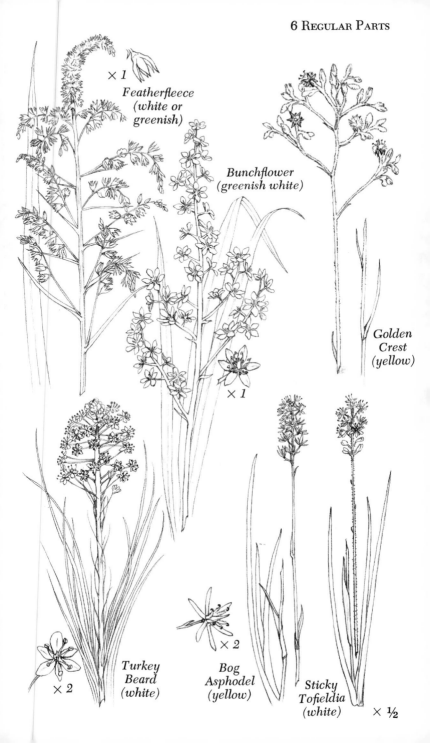

× 1
Featherfleece
(white or
greenish)

Bunchflower
(greenish white)

Golden
Crest
(yellow)

× 1

Turkey
Beard
(white)

× 2

Bog
Asphodel
(yellow)

× 2

Sticky
Tofieldia
(white)

× ½

Flowers in Racemes, Spikes or Widely Branched Clusters; Leaves Lance-shaped or Wider

Devil's Bit, Blazing Star or **Fairy Wand** (*Chamaelirium luteum*) Very small, white flowers in a slender spikelike raceme; basal leaves in a rosette. Male and female flowers on different plants, the female plant more leafy. Basal leaves blunt, widest toward the end; stem leaves narrower. 1–3' high. Moist meadows and woods, w. Mass. to Mich. south. Late spring and early summer. Lily Family.

False Solomon's Seals (*Smilacina*) Small, white flowers in branching clusters or racemes; no basal leaves. Fruit a speckled or striped, greenish berry, turning dull red. Late spring and early summer. Lily Family.

False Solomon's Seal or **Wild Spikenard** (*S. racemosa*) Flowers in a branched, pyramidal cluster. Leaves oblong, 3–6" long. Stem arching, zigzag. 1–3' high. Wooded banks and roadsides; common.

Star-flowered Solomon's Seal (*S. stellata*) Flower cluster unbranched; leaves more than 4. Flowers larger and fewer than the False Solomon's Seal, and leaves narrower. Fruit striped with black. 1–2' high. In several habitats — sandy banks and dunes, moist meadows and open shores.

Three-leaved Solomon's Seal (*S. trifolia*) Flower cluster unbranched; leaves usually 3 , sometimes 2 or 4. Its lance-shaped or elliptical, ascending leaves and slender flower cluster distinguish it from the common Canada Mayflower (p. 130). 2–8" high. Bogs and wet woods.

False or **White Hellebore**, or **Indian Poke** (*Veratrum viride*) Coarse, swampland plant with leafy stem and large, branching cluster of yellow-green flowers. Leaves large, oval, clasping the stem and strongly ribbed lengthwise. Root very poisonous. 2–6' high. Wet woods, south to Ga., west to Ont. and Minn. Late spring and summer. Lily Family.

Broad-leaved Bunchflower (*Melanthium hybridum*) Plant of open woods with greenish-white or greenish flowers in a large, branching cluster; basal leaves present. Petals narrowed to a stalk, crinkled. Leaves lance-shaped. Bunchflower (p. 344) has narrow leaves and flat petals. 2–4' high. S. Conn. and s. N.Y. south. Summer. Lily Family.

Field Sorrel or **Sheep Sorrel** (*Rumex acetosella*) Weed with very small, reddish or greenish flowers in racemes; stem jointed. See p. 402.

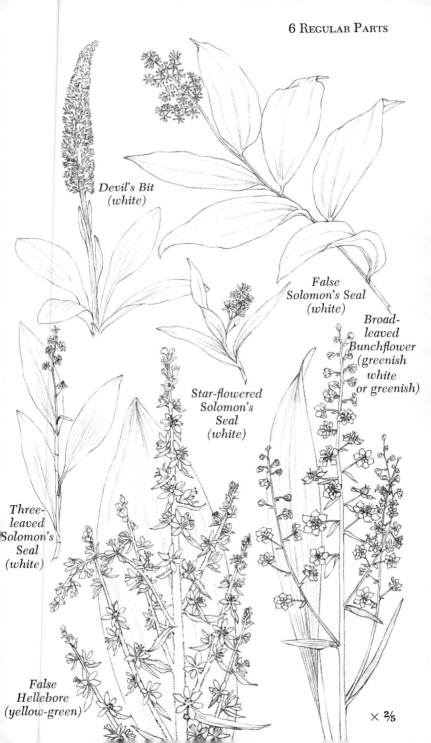

Devil's Bit
(white)

False
Solomon's Seal
(white)

Broad-
leaved
Bunchflower
(greenish
white
or greenish)

Star-flowered
Solomon's
Seal
(white)

Three-
leaved
Solomon's
Seal
(white)

False
Hellebore
(yellow-green)

× **2/5**

Flowers Solitary, or in Umbels or Small Clusters; Not Bell-shaped

YELLOW, ORANGE OR ORANGE-RED FLOWERS

Blackberry Lily (*Belamcanda chinensis*) * Orange, purple-spotted flowers, 1½–2″ wide, in a branching cluster. Leaves sword-shaped, irislike, 6–10″ long. The fruit resembles a blackberry. 1–3′ high. Escaped from cultivation to roadsides and open woods, Conn. to Neb. south. Summer. Iris Family.

Water Stargrass (*Heteranthera dubia*) Aquatic plant with pale-yellow flowers and grasslike leaves. Flowers ½–¾″ wide, with a slender tube, solitary. Ponds, streams or muddy shores. 1–3′ long. Summer and fall. Pickerelweed Family.

Wood Lily (*Lilium philadelphicum*) Large, orange-red or orange flowers, erect, not nodding. See p. 352.

BLUE FLOWERS

Blue-eyed Grasses (*Sisyrinchium*) Blue flowers with grasslike leaves. See p. 332.

PURPLE OR GREENISH FLOWERS

Carrion Flower (*Smilax herbacea*) Greenish, ill-smelling flowers in rounded umbels; tendril-bearing plant with a stem that arches or clambers over bushes. Leaves broad. Fruit a cluster of blue-black berries. 3–6′ long. Woods and thickets. Late spring and early summer. Lily Family.

Water Shield (*Brasenia schreberi*) Aquatic plant with oval, floating leaves. Flowers dull purple, ½–¾″ wide. Stalk attached to the center of the leaf, both leaf and stalk covered with a gelatinous film. Ponds and streams. Summer. Water Lily Family.

Field Garlic (*Allium vineale*) * Purplish or greenish flowers in an umbel; leaves very narrow, hollow. Flowers often replaced by bulblets. 1–3′ high. Serious pest of lawns, pastures and meadows, Mass. to Mich. south. Summer. Lily Family.

Loosestrifes (*Lythrum*) Purple flowers growing singly in the axils. Petals 5 or 6, somewhat erect. Stem 4-angled. Summer. Loosestrife Family.

    Hyssop Loosestrife (*L. hyssopifolia*) Leaves pale green, blunt; flowers tiny. 6–24″ high. Borders of marshes, Me. to N.J. and Pa.; s. Ohio.

    Winged Loosestrife (*L. alatum*) Leaves dark green, pointed; flowers ¼–½″ wide. 1–4′ high. Swamps and meadows; mostly inland.

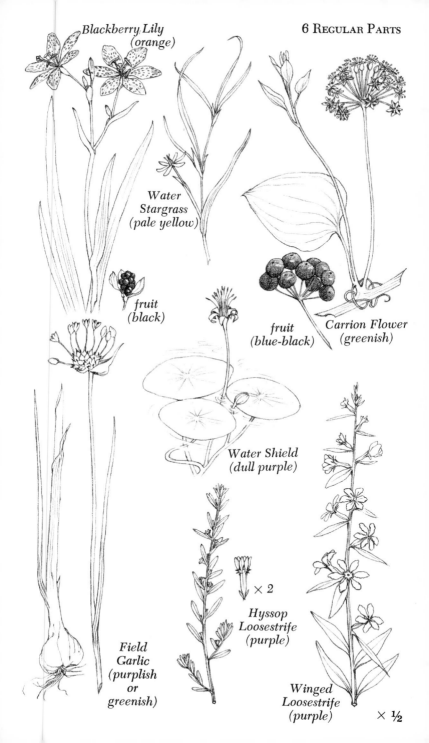

Blackberry Lily
(orange)

Water
Stargrass
(pale yellow)

fruit
(black)

fruit
(blue-black)

Carrion Flower
(greenish)

Water Shield
(dull purple)

× 2

Hyssop
Loosestrife
(purple)

Field
Garlic
(purplish
or
greenish)

Winged
Loosestrife
(purple)

× ½

WILDFLOWERS WITH ALTERNATE LEAVES /
Leaves Toothed or Lobed

YELLOW FLOWERS

Marsh Marigold or **Cowslip** (*Caltha palustris*) Showy spring flower; leaves heart-shaped; grows in wet places. See p. 204.

Water-plantain Spearwort (*Ranunculus ambigens*) Flowers ½–¾″ wide; leaves lance-shaped; grows in wet places. See p. 206.

Goldenrods (*Solidago*) Small and numerous yellow flowers in a large, branching cluster. See pp. 446–453.

Wingstem (*Actinomeris alternifolia*) Tall plant with drooping flower-rays; flowers 1–2″ wide. See p. 376.

WHITE OR GREENISH-WHITE FLOWERS

Tall White Lettuce (*Prenanthes altissima*) Nodding, greenish-white flowers, ½″ long. See p. 212.

White Wood Aster (*Aster divaricatus*) White flowers in a terminal cluster; lower leaves heart-shaped. See p. 454.

Toothed White-topped Aster (*Sericocarpus asteroides*) White flowers in a flat-topped cluster; lower leaves egg-shaped. See p. 210.

WILDFLOWERS WITH ALTERNATE LEAVES /
Leaves Divided

YELLOW FLOWERS

Buttercups (*Ranunculus*) Flowers golden-yellow. See p. 242.

Spreading Globeflower (*Trollius laxus*) Flowers greenish-yellow, 1–1½″ wide; grows in wet places. See p. 244.

WHITE, GREENISH OR PINK FLOWERS

Yarrow or **Milfoil** (*Achillea millefolium*) White or pink flowers in a flat-topped cluster; leaves finely divided. See p. 220.

Baneberries (*Actaea*) White flowers with conspicuous stamens in a dense raceme 1–2″ long. See p. 424.

Blue Cohosh (*Caulophyllum thalictroides*) Small (⅓–½″ wide) greenish flowers in a small cluster; leaflets with 2–5 lobes. See p. 354.

Tall White Lettuce (*Prenanthes altissima*) Nodding, greenish-white flowers, ½″ long; style protruding. See p. 212.

Asparagus (*Asparagus officinalis*) Yellow-green, bell-shaped flowers, ¼″ long; leaves very narrow. See p. 342.

White or Purple Flowers
The illustrations for this page are on p. 353.

Purple Loosestrife (*Lythrum salicaria*) * Purple flowers in a dense spike. Flowers showy, ½–¾″ wide, with 5 or 6 petals. The leaves are lance-shaped, somewhat clasping the stem, and grow in pairs or sometimes in whorls of 3. Swamps and wet meadows, often growing in large colonies to the exclusion of our native wild flowers. Summer. Loosestrife Family.

Narrow-leaved Loosestrife (*Lythrum lineare*) Light-purple or nearly white flowers growing in the axils; leaves narrow; stem smooth. A slender plant of salt marshes, 1–4′ high. For related species with mostly alternate leaves, see p. 348. Long I. south. Summer and fall. Loosestrife Family.

Clammy Cuphea or **Blue Waxweed** (*Cuphea petiolata*) Purple flowers growing in the axils; leaves broadly lance-shaped; plant sticky-hairy. See p. 76.

Starflower (*Trientalis borealis*) White flowers on long stalks above a single whorl of 5–10 leaves. See p. 386.

White Trout Lily or **White Adder's Tongue** (*Erythronium albidum*) Solitary, nodding, white flower; leaves 2, near the base of the plant. See p. 338.

Flowers neither White nor Purple

Lilies (*Lilium*) Large (2–4″ wide) and showy, yellow, orange or red flowers, solitary or in terminal clusters. Leaves lance-shaped, mostly in whorls. Tiger Lily (*L. tigrinum*) (p. 340) has alternate leaves. Summer. Lily Family.

Turk's-cap Lily (*L. superbum*) Nodding, orange-red flowers; the petals and sepals curl back so the tips nearly touch, completely disclosing the stamens; s. N.H. to N.Y. south. Green star at center of flower clearly defined. Leaves smooth to the touch. 3–8′ high. Damp meadows and borders of bogs.

Michigan Lily (*L. michiganense*) † Similar to Turk's-cap Lily, but occurring from s. Ont. and Ohio to Man. south. Green star at center of flower not clearly defined.

Canada Lily, Meadow Lily or **Wild Yellow Lily** (*L. canadense*) Flowers nodding; petals and sepals spreading or partly curled backward. Flowers variable in color and shape, the most common form being an open, spotted, yellow bell. A red-flowered form occurs from Pa. to Ind. south. Veins on the underside of the leaves rough to the touch. 2–5′ high. Meadows and swamps.

Wood Lily (*L. philadelphicum*) Flowers erect, the base of the petals and sepals narrowed to a stalk. Orange-red or orange flowers, purple-spotted within. The western form (var. *andinum*) has mostly scattered leaves. 1–3′ high. Dry thickets and open woods.

Indian Cucumber Root (*Medeola virginiana*) Leaves lance-shaped, in two whorls, one of 5–9 leaves near the middle of the stem and the other of 3–5 at the top. Greenish-yellow flowers, usually hanging down beneath the upper whorl of leaves. Styles · long and spreading, giving the flowers a spiderlike appearance. Berries dark purple, held above the leaves. 1–2′ high. Rich moist woods. Late spring and early summer. Lily Family.

Tufted Loosestrife (*Lysimachia thrysiflora*) Yellow flowers growing in short racemes from the axils. See p. 266.

Trout Lily or **Yellow Adder's Tongue** (*Erythronium americanum*) Solitary, nodding, yellow flower, ¾–1½″ long; leaves 2, near the base of the plant. See p. 338.

Asparagus (*Asparagus officinalis*) Yellow-green, bell-shaped flowers, ¼″ long; leaves very narrow. See p. 342.

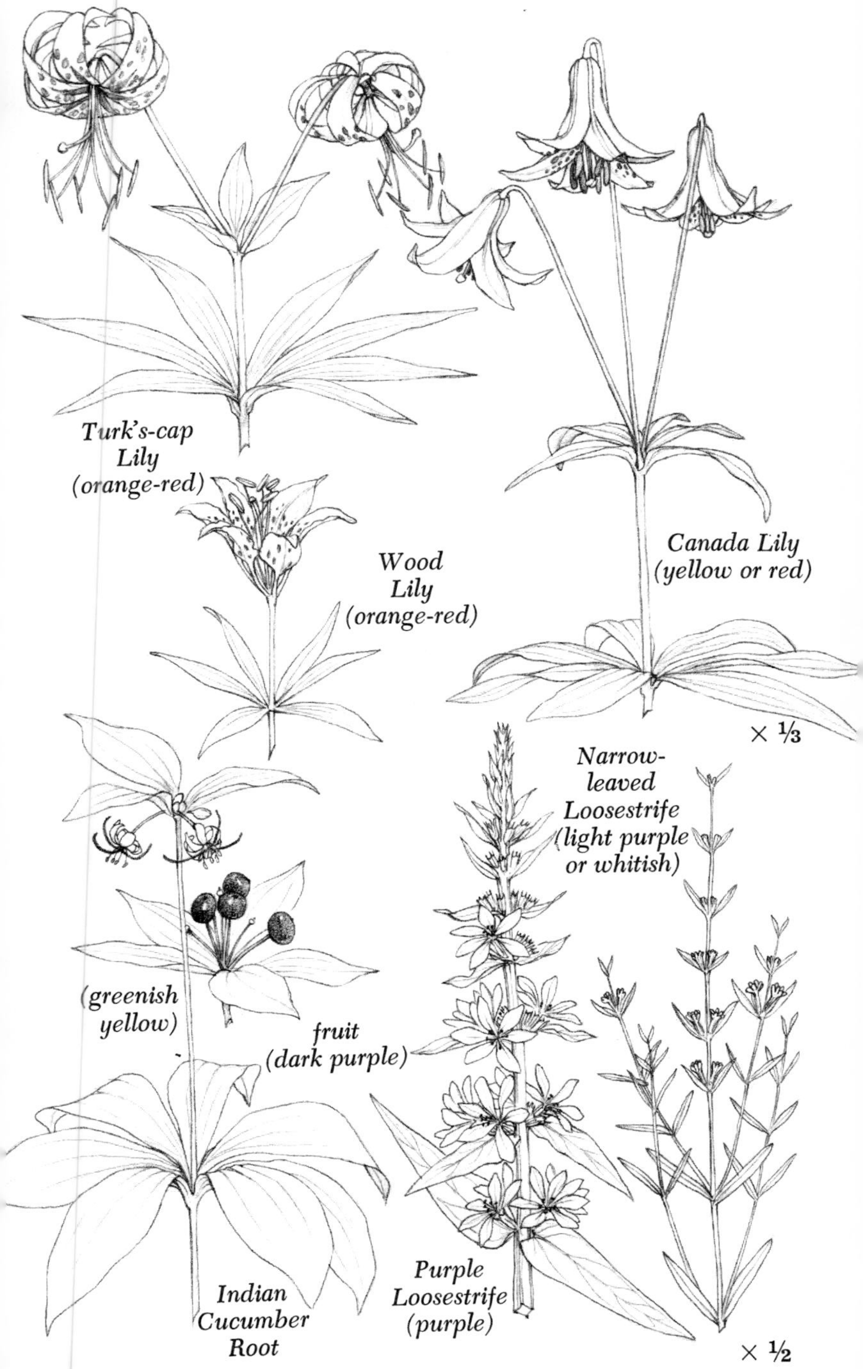

Turk's-cap Lily (orange-red)

Wood Lily (orange-red)

Canada Lily (yellow or red)

× ⅓

Narrow-leaved Loosestrife (light purple or whitish)

(greenish yellow)

fruit (dark purple)

Indian Cucumber Root

Purple Loosestrife (purple)

× ½

Mayapple or **Mandrake** (*Podophyllum peltatum*) Solitary, white flower growing beneath 2 large, deeply cleft leaves. The flower is 1½–2″ wide, with 6–9 waxy petals. Plants without flowers have a single, umbrellalike leaf. Fruit yellowish, lemon-shaped, 2″ long, edible. 1–1½′ high. Rich woods and pastures, w. Que. and w. N.Eng. to Minn. south. Spring. Barberry Family.

Blue Cohosh (*Caulophyllum thalictroides*) Yellow-green or purplish flowers in a branching, terminal cluster. The flowers are about ½″ wide, with a tiny petal at the inside base of each sepal. The leaves (which are actually alternate and stalkless) are divided into egg-shaped leaflets with 2–5 lobes. Seeds blue, berrylike. 1–3′ high. Rich woods. Spring. Barberry Family.

Rue Anemone (*Anemonella thalictroides*) White or pinkish flowers in a small umbel; leaves roundish, bluntly lobed. See p. 392.

Anemones (*Anemone*) Large, white or greenish flowers on long stalks; leaves sharply toothed or cleft. See p. 288.

Bur Marigolds or **Beggar Ticks** (*Bidens*) Yellowish, orange or greenish flowers in small heads. See pp. 392 and 440.

SHRUBS

Barberries (*Berberis*) Yellow flowers, ¼″ wide, growing from the axils; stems armed with spines. Leaves entire or toothed. Thickets and pastures. Spring. Barberry Family.

Common Barberry (*B. vulgaris*) * Flowers in drooping, many-flowered racemes; leaves bristly-toothed. 3–10′ high.

Japanese Barberry (*B. thunbergii*) * Flowers solitary or in a small umbel; leaves entire. 2–6′ high.

Spicebush (*Lindera benzoin*) Yellow flowers, ⅛″ wide, blooming in early spring before the leaves appear; grows in wet places. See p. 442.

Sweet Bay (*Magnolia virginiana*) White flowers, 2–3″ wide; leaves entire. See p. 396.

Hollies (*Ilex*) Small, white flowers in the axils; leaves toothed or nearly entire. See p. 396.

Black Crowberry (*Empetrum nigrum*) Low evergreen shrub with narrow leaves. See p. 126.

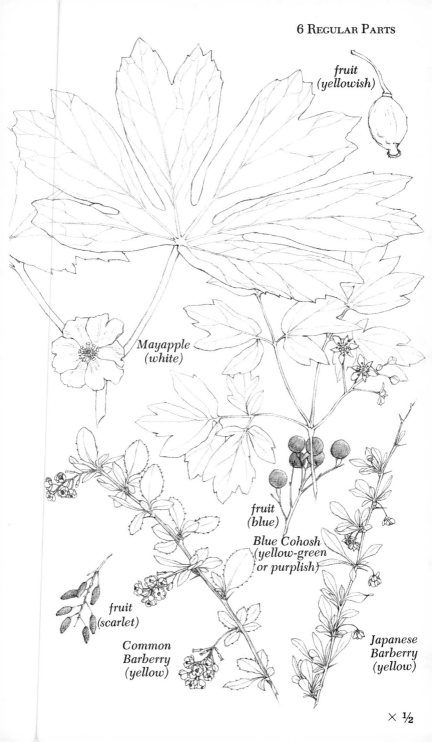

fruit
(yellowish)

Mayapple
(white)

fruit
(blue)

Blue Cohosh
(yellow-green
or purplish)

fruit
(scarlet)

Common
Barberry
(yellow)

Japanese
Barberry
(yellow)

× ½

WHITE OR WHITISH FLOWERS

Wild Balsam Apple or **Wild Cucumber** (*Echinocystis lobata*)
Leaves with mostly 5 deep lobes; plant with forked tendrils. The
greenish-white flowers are of two types: the staminate, which are
numerous in an erect, branched cluster; and the pistillate, which
are solitary or in small clusters from the same axils as the staminate. Fruit a spiny, green bladder about 2″ long. The similar One-
seeded Bur Cucumber (*Sicyos angulatus*) (p. 328) has 5 petals and
smaller fruits. Extensively climbing. Moist ground and thickets;
often cultivated. Summer and fall. Gourd Family.

Moonseed (*Menispermum canadense*) Leaves entire or shallowly
lobed; plant without tendrils. The whitish flowers are ⅛″ wide,
and grow in loose, axillary clusters, staminate and pistillate on
separate plants. Leaves very broad. Fruit black, resembling a cluster of grapes. 6–12′ long. Rich woods and thickets, w. Que. and w.
N.Eng. to Man. south. Early summer. Moonseed Family.

YELLOW OR GREEN FLOWERS

Wild Yamroot (*Dioscorea villosa*) Flowers in drooping racemes or
spikes; leaves long-pointed, heart-shaped at the base. Flowers
small, greenish-yellow, the staminate and pistillate in separate
clusters. Leaves entire and alternate, or the lower ones in whorls
of 3. Stem twining. 5–15′ long. Moist thickets, s. N.Eng. to Minn.
south. Summer. *D. quaternata* of Pa. to Ill. south blooms in
spring, has a more erect stem, and its lower leaves in whorls of
4–7. Yam Family.

Greenbriers (*Smilax*) Green flowers in umbels; stems woody,
prickly. Leaves entire, broadly egg-shaped or roundish, and heart-
shaped or rounded at the base. Berries blue-black or black. Carrion Flower (*S. herbacea*) (p. 348) is a more or less erect, non-
woody species. Woods and thickets. Spring and early summer.
Lily Family.

> **Common Greenbrier** or **Catbrier** (*S. rotundifolia*) Leaves green
> on both sides, shining above; thorns stout, rigid and green.
> Common.

> **Sawbrier** (*S. glauca*) † Leaves strongly whitened beneath. Dry
> sandy soil, s. N.Eng. to Ill. south.

> **Bristly Greenbrier** (*S. tamnoides*) Leaves green on both sides;
> thorns often blackish, bristly, very numerous near the base
> of the plant. N.Y. to Minn. south.

Carrion Flower (*Smilax herbacea*) Flowers in rounded umbels, ill-
scented; stems not prickly. See p. 348.

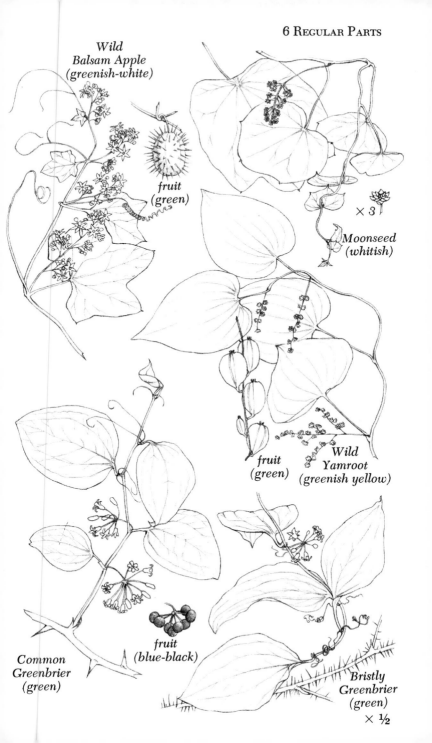

Wild Balsam Apple (greenish-white)

fruit (green)

Moonseed (whitish)

× 3

fruit (green)

Wild Yamroot (greenish yellow)

fruit (blue-black)

Common Greenbrier (green)

Bristly Greenbrier (green)

× ½

WILDFLOWERS WITH NO APPARENT LEAVES AT FLOWERING TIME

Coltsfoot (*Tussilago farfara*) * Yellow, dandelionlike flower heads, about 1″ wide, appearing in early spring before the leaves. The roundly heart-shaped leaves that develop later are toothed and shallowly lobed, 3–7″ wide. Stalk scaly. 3–18″ high. Damp soil of streamsides, banks and waste places. Composite Family.

Prickly Pear (*Opuntia humifusa*) A native cactus with yellow flowers 2–3″ wide. The large, swollen joints are armed with barbed bristles. Sprawling plant of sandy or rocky places, Mass. to Minn. south. Early summer. Cactus Family.

Sweet Coltsfoot (*Petasites palmatus*) Plant of swamps and wet woods, with scaly stalk and heads of cream-colored flowers ⅓–½″ wide. Blooms in spring before the leaves appear. Leaves long-stalked, deeply cleft into 5–7 segments. 6–24″ high. Mass., w. Conn. and N.Y. to Minn. north. Composite Family.

WILDFLOWERS WITH BASAL LEAVES ONLY /
Leaves Entire

Aquatic Plants

Water Lilies (*Nymphaea*) Aquatic plants with showy, white or pinkish flowers, 3–8″ wide. Petals numerous, in many rows. Leaves long-stalked, nearly round, cleft at the base, 3–10″ in diameter. Ponds. Summer and fall. Water Lily Family.

Sweet-scented Water Lily (*N. odorata*) Flowers very fragrant, 3–5″ wide; leaves usually purplish beneath. Petals slightly tapering toward the tip.

Tuberous Water Lily (*N. tuberosa*) † Flowers slightly, if at all, fragrant, 4–8″ wide; leaves usually green beneath. Petals broad at the tip. Sw. Que. and w. N.Eng. to Minn. south.

American Lotus (*Nelumbo lutea*) Very large, pale-yellow flower, 5–10″ wide, on a long stalk. Leaves round, 1′ or more wide, with the stalk attached in the center of the leaf. The flower and usually the leaves are held high above the water. Ponds and slow streams, s. N.Eng. to Minn. south; rare and local in the east. Summer. Water Lily Family.

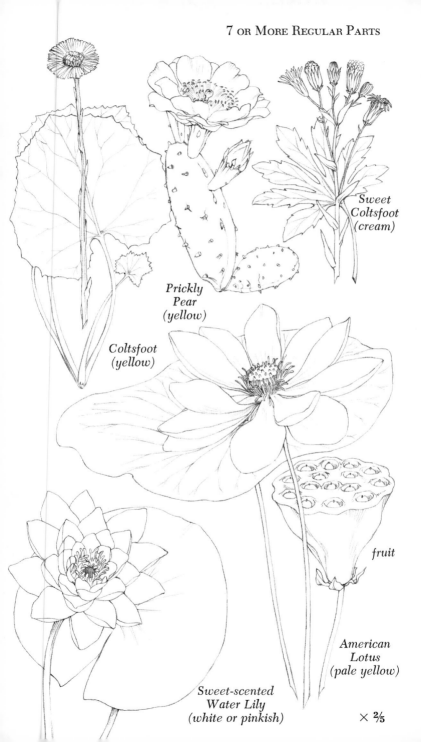

Sweet Coltsfoot (cream)

Prickly Pear (yellow)

Coltsfoot (yellow)

fruit

American Lotus (pale yellow)

Sweet-scented Water Lily (white or pinkish)

× 2/5

Plants of Dry Places

Hawkweeds (*Hieracium*) Yellow or orange, dandelionlike flowers in heads ½" or more wide. Heads in a branching cluster or solitary. The species described below have entire leaves or leaves with a few minute teeth; some occasionally have 1–3 stem leaves. For species with alternate leaves (3 or more), see pp. 368 and 372. 4–36" high. Mostly weedy plants of fields and roadsides, often spreading by runners and forming mats. Spring to fall. Composite Family.

1. RED-ORANGE FLOWERS

Orange Hawkweed or **Devil's Paintbrush** (*H. aurantiacum*) * Heads ¾–1" wide, in a small cluster. The stem and leaves are very hairy. Troublesome weed of fields and pastures.

2. YELLOW FLOWERS; LEAVES VEINED WITH PURPLE

Rattlesnake Weed (*H. venosum*) Heads usually numerous, ½–¾" wide. Stem smooth, sometimes bearing a few leaves. Dry woods and clearings, s. Me. to s. Ont. south.

3. YELLOW FLOWERS; LEAVES NOT PURPLE-VEINED

a. Flower heads 1–4, about 1" wide

Mouse Ear (*H. pilosella*) * Head usually solitary (sometimes 2); leaves white-woolly beneath. Stem slender.

Large Mouse Ear (*H. flagellare*) * Heads usually 2 to 4 (sometimes 1); leaves green beneath. Stem stout.

b. Flower heads 4 or more, ½–¾" wide

Field Hawkweed or **King Devil** (*H. pratense*) * Stem and upper and lower surfaces of leaves very hairy; stem green. Common.

Pale Hawkweed or **King Devil** (*H. floribundum*) *† Similar to Field Hawkweed, but upper surface of leaves nearly smooth and stem and leaves have whitish bloom. Produces prostrate runners from base of the plant.

Smooth Hawkweed or **King Devil** (*H. florentinum*) *† Similar to Field Hawkweed but stem and leaves nearly smooth. Does not form runners from the base of the plant. Leaves pale green or with a whitish bloom.

Dwarf Dandelion (*Krigia virginica*) Yellow, usually solitary, flower heads ¼–½" wide. See p. 362.

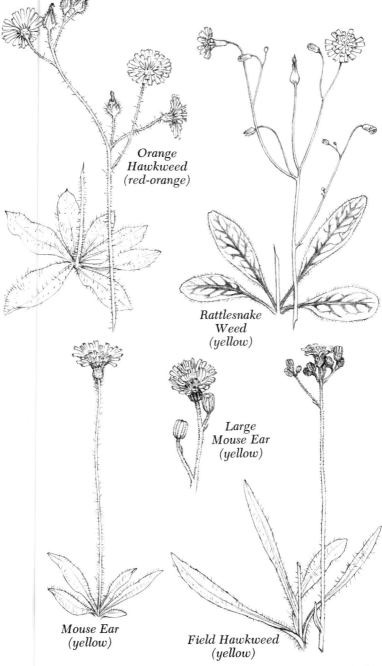

*Orange
Hawkweed
(red-orange)*

*Rattlesnake
Weed
(yellow)*

*Large
Mouse Ear
(yellow)*

*Mouse Ear
(yellow)*

*Field Hawkweed
(yellow)*

× ½

Yellow Flowers; Leaves Two or More Times Longer Than Wide

FLOWER HEADS (WHEN FULLY EXPANDED)
¾" OR MORE WIDE

Dandelions (*Taraxacum*) Stalk unbranched, naked, hollow. The flower heads are 1–2" wide. Leaves variously cleft and lobed. 2–18" high. Lawns, waste places. Composite Family.

Common Dandelion (*T. officinale*) * Heads 1–2" wide; seeds brown. Outer bracts at base of flower head turned downward. Leaves less deeply cleft than in the next species. Abundant weed. Spring to fall and occasionally in winter.

Red-seeded Dandelion (*T. erythrospermum*) * Heads about 1" wide; seeds red. Bracts of flower head spreading. Lobes of leaves cleft nearly to the midrib and more widely separated than in the Common Dandelion; and flowers somewhat paler. Spring and early summer.

Fall Dandelion (*Leontodon autumnalis*) * Stalk slender, bearing a few, very small scales and usually forked; leaves not noticeably hairy. Flower heads about 1" wide. 6–24" high. Fields and lawns. Summer and fall. Composite Family.

Cat's Ear (*Hypochoeris radicata*) * Leaves very hairy on both sides; stalk 8–18" high, usually bearing a few scales and branched. Flower heads 1–1½" wide. Fields, roadsides and lawns. Late spring to fall. Composite Family.

Prairie Dock (*Silphium terebinthinaceum*) Tall plant (4–10′ high) with very large, egg-shaped leaves. Heads numerous, 1½–3" wide. Leaves toothed or cleft. Prairies and open woods, Ohio and s. Ont. south. Summer and fall. Composite Family.

FLOWER HEADS ¼–¾" WIDE

Dwarf Dandelion (*Krigia virginica*) Flower heads ¼–½" wide, usually solitary; stalk very slender. The leaves are in a basal rosette and are variously lobed and toothed. Later in the year the plant may become branched and have stem leaves. Low plant of dry sandy soil, c. N.Eng. to Wis. south. Spring and summer. Composite Family.

Lamb Succory (*Arnoseris minima*) * Stalk swollen beneath the flower heads and usually branched. Flower heads ½–¾" wide. Leaves coarsely toothed. 3–12" high. Fields and waste places; local. Summer. Composite Family.

Hawkweeds (*Hieracium*) Flower heads in a branched cluster; leaves entire or with a few minute teeth. See p. 360.

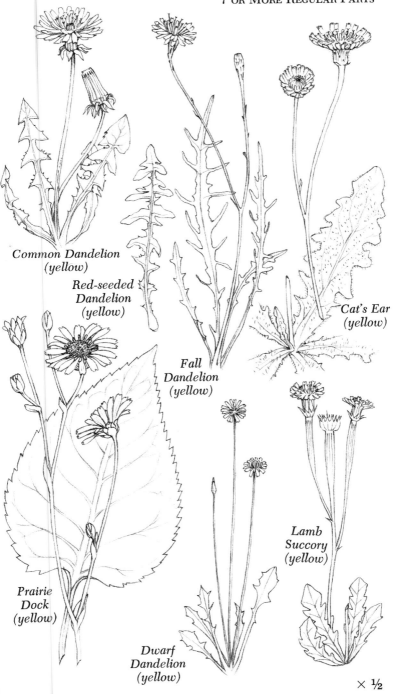

Common Dandelion
(yellow)

Red-seeded
Dandelion
(yellow)

Cat's Ear
(yellow)

Fall
Dandelion
(yellow)

Prairie
Dock
(yellow)

Lamb
Succory
(yellow)

Dwarf
Dandelion
(yellow)

× ½

Yellow Flowers; Leaves About as Wide as Long

Lesser Celandine (*Ranunculus ficaria*) * Buttercuplike flowers with 8–12 shining petals, 1″ wide. The leaves are heart-shaped, 1–2″ long, and bluntly toothed. Low plant of damp places; escaped from gardens. Spring. Buttercup Family.

Seaside Crowfoot (*Ranunculus cymbalaria*) Flowers about ¼″ wide, growing singly or in a small cluster; leaves roundish, bluntly toothed, under 1″ long. Low plant of salt marshes and sandy shores along the coast, and inland in saline soil and along the Great Lakes and St. Lawrence River. Summer. Buttercup Family.

Coltsfoot (*Tussilago farfara*) Dandelionlike flowers in heads about 1″ wide; stalk scaly. See p. 358.

White, Blue or Pink Flowers

LEAVES DIVIDED INTO 2 OR 3 LEAFLETS

Twinleaf (*Jeffersonia diphylla*) Leaves divided lengthwise into 2 leaflets. The white flowers are 1″ wide with 8 petals, and grow singly, 1 to a stalk. Fruit pear-shaped, about 1″ long, opening with a hinged lid. 6–8″ high when in bloom, taller in fruit. Rich woods, N.Y. and s. Ont. to Wis. south. Spring. Barberry Family.

Goldthread (*Coptis groenlandica*) Leaves divided into 3, shining, toothed leaflets. See p. 184.

LEAVES TOOTHED OR LOBED, NOT DIVIDED

Bloodroot (*Sanguinaria canadensis*) White flowers growing singly, 1–1½″ wide; the single leaf with 5–9 deep lobes. Petals 8 to 12, rarely pinkish. The juice is orange-red, whence the common name. 3–6″ high when in bloom, taller later. Rich woods. Early spring. Poppy Family.

Hepaticas (*Hepatica*) Flowers growing singly; leaves with 3 deep lobes. See p. 338.

Foamflower or **False Miterwort** (*Tiarella cordifolia*) White flowers in a raceme; leaves with 5–7 shallow lobes. See p. 178.

Sweet Coltsfoot (*Petasites palmatus*) Cream-colored flowers in a terminal cluster; grows in wet places. See p. 358.

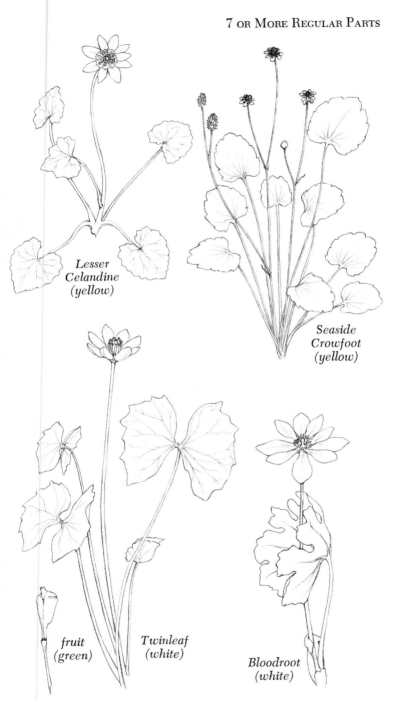

*Lesser
Celandine
(yellow)*

*Seaside
Crowfoot
(yellow)*

*fruit
(green)*

*Twinleaf
(white)*

*Bloodroot
(white)*

× ½

Yellow or Orange, Daisylike or Asterlike Flowers

Sneezeweeds (*Helenium*) Flower rays wedge-shaped, widest at the tip, with 3–4 teeth. In the center of the flower head is a prominent knobby disk. Sneezeweed (*H. autumnale*) has toothed leaves (p. 376). Summer and fall. Composite Family.

> **Purple-headed Sneezeweed** (*H. nudiflorum*) Disk brown or purple. See p. 374.

> **Fine-leaved** or **Bitter Sneezeweed** (*H. tenuifolium*) Disk yellow. Leaves very narrow, numerous. 8–24″ high. Fields and roadsides, s. U.S., locally north to Mass. and Mich.

Camphorweed (*Heterotheca subaxillaris*) Flower heads ½–¾″ wide; upper leaves broad, clasping stem. 1–3′ high. Dry soil, N.J. to Ill. south. Summer and fall. Composite Family.

Golden Asters (*Chrysopsis*) Flower rays widest in the middle; flower heads ½–1″ wide, with a yellow center; leaves not clasping. Dry sandy soil. Summer and fall. Composite Family.

> **Sickle-leaved Golden Aster** (*C. falcata*) Leaves very narrow, rather stiff, often curved. 4–12″ high, with white-woolly stem. Se. Mass. to N.J.

> **Maryland** or **Broad-leaved Golden Aster** (*C. mariana*) Leaves oblong or lance-shaped. Stem silky when young. 1–2½′ high. Se. N.Y. to s. Ohio south.

Narrow-leaved Sunflower (*Helianthus angustifolius*) Yellow flowers with purplish-black disk; heads 2–3″ wide; leaves narrow, stiff. Lower leaves usually opposite. 2–6′ high. Wet or damp places, Long I. to s. Ind. south.

Black-eyed Susan (*Rudbeckia serotina*) Orange flowers with a blackish-brown disk; rays narrowed at the tip. See p. 374.

Goldenrods (*Solidago*) Flower heads small (under ½″ wide) and numerous. See pp. 446–453.

Yellow, Dandelionlike Flowers

Yellow Goatsbeard (*Tragopogon pratensis*) * Flower heads 1–2½″ wide, on long stalks; leaves grasslike, clasping the stem. The flowers close at noon. 1½–3′ high. Fields and roadsides. Summer and fall. Composite Family.

Wild Lettuce (*Lactuca canadensis*) Pale-yellow or reddish-yellow flowers, the heads about ¼″ wide. See p. 372.

Coltsfoot (*Tussilago farfara*) Blooms in early spring; heads about 1″ wide; flower stalk scaly. See p. 358.

Continued

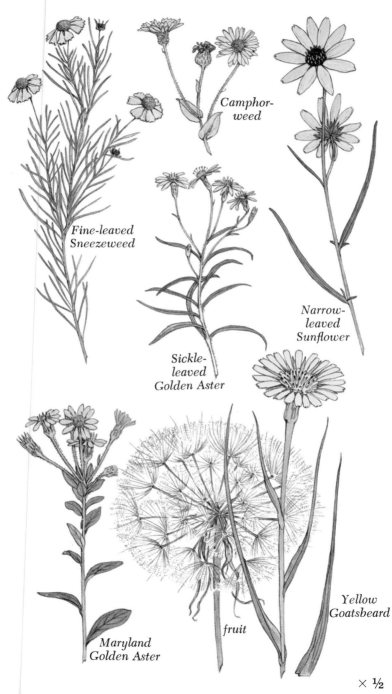

Fine-leaved
Sneezeweed

Camphor-
weed

Narrow-
leaved
Sunflower

Sickle-
leaved
Golden Aster

Maryland
Golden Aster

fruit

Yellow
Goatsbeard

× ½

Yellow, Dandelionlike Flowers (cont.)

Hawkweeds (*Hieracium*) Yellow flowers in heads ½–1″ wide, in a branching cluster. For other species, see pp. 360, 372. 1–5′ high. Dry soil. Spring to fall. Composite Family.

1. MAJORITY OF LEAVES BORNE ON THE STEM

Rough Hawkweed (*H. scabrum*) Usually without basal leaves; upper stem densely hairy. Stem stout, usually leafy to the flower cluster. Common.

Hairy Hawkweed (*H. gronovii*) Leaves at base of plant and mostly on the lower half of the stem; flower cluster two or more times longer than wide. Slender and stiffly erect. Mass. to s. Mich., Ill. and Kan. south.

2. MAJORITY OF LEAVES IN A BASAL ROSETTE (SEE P. 360)

White, Pink, Blue, Violet or Purple Flowers

*DAISYLIKE OR ASTERLIKE FLOWERS IN HEADS
½″ OR MORE WIDE*

Fleabanes (*Erigeron*) Flower rays more than 40; flower heads under 1″ wide (except 1 species with heads 1–1½″ wide that blooms in spring and early summer). See p. 382.

Asters (*Aster*) Flower rays less than 40 (except 1 species that has more than 40 rays, flower heads 1–2″ wide, and blooms in late summer and fall). See pp. 454–463.

FLOWERS OTHERWISE

Pearly Everlasting (*Anaphalis margaritacea*) Stem and underside of leaves white-woolly. Heads composed of several ranks of numerous, dry, pearly-white, petal-like bracts; the staminate heads have a yellow tuft in the center. Leaves narrow. 1–3′ high. Dry open places. Summer and fall. Composite Family.

Oyster Plant or **Salsify** (*Tragopogon porrifolius*) * Large, purple flower head, 2–4″ wide. The long-pointed bracts surrounding the head are longer than the flower rays. Leaves long and narrow. Flower closes at noon. 2–4′ high. Roadsides and fields. Spring and summer. Composite Family.

Hoary Alyssum (*Berteroa incana*) Stem and leaves grayish; tiny, white flowers with 8 parts, in racemes. See p. 130.

Sweet Coltsfoot (*Petasites palmatus*) Stem scaly; grows in wet places. See p. 358.

Horseweed (*Erigeron canadensis*) Whitish flowers in very small heads with numerous, minute rays. See p. 384.

Rough
Hawkweed
(yellow)

Hairy
Hawkweed
(yellow)

× 1½

Pearly
Everlasting
(white)

Oyster
Plant
(purple)

× ½

Yellow, Dandelionlike Flowers; Stem Leaves Clasping the Stem with a Heart- or Arrow-shaped Base

Wild Lettuce (*Lactuca*) Flower heads small (about ¼″ wide), as long as or longer than wide. Flower cluster loose and widely branched. Summer and fall. Composite Family.

Prickly Lettuce (*L. scariola*) * Leaves with numerous, spiny teeth; yellow flowers. The stem leaves have an arrow-shaped base and a bristly midrib beneath. Stem somewhat prickly at the base. 2–5′ high. Waste places.

Wild Lettuce (*L. canadensis*) Leaves not spiny-toothed; pale-yellow or reddish-yellow flowers. See p. 372.

Sow Thistles (*Sonchus*) Leaves with very numerous, spiny teeth; flower heads ½–2″ wide. Stem grooved. Weeds of fields and waste places. Summer and fall. Composite Family.

1. FLOWERS BRIGHT YELLOW; FLOWER HEADS 1¼–2″ WIDE

Field Sow Thistle (*S. arvensis*) * The heart-shaped base of the upper leaves clasps the stem; lower leaves deeply lobed. Base of flower head usually hairy. Spreads by creeping underground stems. 1½–4′ high.

2. FLOWERS PALER YELLOW; FLOWER HEADS ½–1¼″ WIDE

Spiny-leaved Sow Thistle (*S. asper*) * The heart-shaped base of the leaves clasps the stem, the lobes strongly recurved. Leaves often unlobed. 1–5′ high.

Common Sow Thistle (*S. oleraceus*) * The arrow-shaped base of the leaves clasps the stem; the lobes are not recurved. Lower leaves deeply lobed, usually with a large, triangular, terminal lobe. 1–8′ high.

Cynthia (*Krigia biflora*) Stem forked near the middle and bears a small, oblong, mostly entire, clasping leaf at the fork (stem occasionally forks more than once). Orange-yellow flowers in heads 1–1½″ wide. Basal leaves lobed, toothed or nearly entire. 8–24″ high. Open woods and meadows, s. N.Eng. to Man. south. Late spring and summer. Composite Family.

Smooth Hawksbeard (*Crepis capillaris*) * Stem leaves sparsely toothed, with an arrow-shaped base clasping the stem; flower heads ½–¾″ wide, in a branching cluster. Basal leaves toothed and cleft like those of the Dandelion. 1–2½′ high. Fields and waste places. Summer and fall. Composite Family.

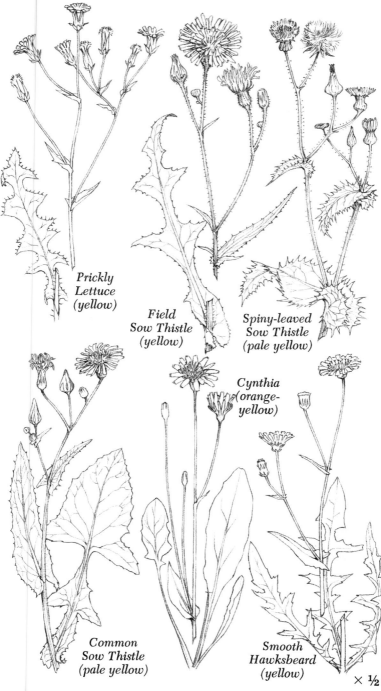

*Prickly
Lettuce
(yellow)*

*Field
Sow Thistle
(yellow)*

*Spiny-leaved
Sow Thistle
(pale yellow)*

*Cynthia
(orange-
yellow)*

*Common
Sow Thistle
(pale yellow)*

*Smooth
Hawksbeard
(yellow)*

× ½

Yellow, Dandelionlike Flowers; Stem Leaves Not Heart- or Arrow-shaped at the Base

Wild Lettuce (*Lactuca canadensis*) Pale-yellow or reddish-yellow flowers in small heads about ¼″ wide, the heads mostly longer than wide. Leaves very variable, ranging from deeply lobed on some plants to arrow-shaped, clasping and nearly entire on others. Stem smooth. 3–10′ high. Common in open places. Summer and fall. Composite Family.

Hawkweeds (*Hieracium*) Flower heads (when fully expanded) ½–1″ wide, with more than 12 rays; plants 1′ or more high. For other species, see pages 360 and 368. Summer and fall. Composite Family.

1. LARGER LEAVES BLUNT, NEARLY ENTIRE (SEE P. 368)

2. LARGER LEAVES POINTED

Common Hawkweed (*H. vulgatum*) * Flower heads 1–1½″ wide; basal leaves forming a rosette. Leaves tapering at both ends, with a few teeth, and often mottled with purple. The base of the flower head is covered with dark hairs. 1–3′ high. Fields and waste places, Que. to Mich., south to N.J. and Pa. Summer and fall.

Canada Hawkweed (*H. canadense*) Flower heads about 1″ wide; no basal rosette at flowering time. Leaves sharply toothed or cleft, the upper somewhat clasping the stem. 1–5′ high. Borders of woods and clearings.

Panicled Hawkweed (*H. paniculatum*) Flower heads about ½″ wide. The slender flowering branches are widely spreading or drooping. Leaves slightly toothed, smooth; no basal rosette. 1–4′ high. Dry woods.

Nipplewort (*Lapsana communis*) * Flower heads ¼–½″ wide, with 8–12 rays; stem slender; 1–3′ high. Heads in a loose, branched cluster. Lower leaves egg-shaped, shallowly toothed, often with several lobes at the base. Roadsides and waste places. Summer and fall. Composite Family.

Dwarf Dandelion (*Krigia virginica*) Low plant (under 1′ high) with basal leaves forming a rosette. See p. 362.

Wild Lettuce (pale or reddish yellow)

Common Hawkweed (yellow)

Canada Hawkweed (yellow)

Panicled Hawkweed (yellow)

Nipplewort (yellow)

× ½

Yellow or Orange Daisylike Flowers with a Dark Central Disk

Purple-headed Sneezeweed (*Helenium nudiflorum*) * Flower rays wedge-shaped, broadest at the tip, 3-lobed, drooping. Disk a purple or brown knob. Leaves with a few teeth or entire, their bases extending down the stem as wings. 1–3' high. Fields and roadsides; introduced from s. U.S. Summer and fall. Composite Family.

Coneflowers (*Rudbeckia*) Flower rays narrowed at the tip; disk a brown or purple cone or rounded knob, ½–¾" wide; larger leaves toothed or 3-lobed, not divided into leaflets. Rays yellow or orange, sometimes darker at the base. Dry to moist open places. Summer and fall. Composite Family.

1. FLOWER HEADS 2–4" WIDE

Black-eyed Susan (*R. serotina*) Stem leaves slightly toothed or entire; stem covered with bristly hairs. Disk blackish brown. 1–3' high. Very common.

Showy Coneflower (*R. speciosa*) Stem leaves coarsely toothed or cleft; stem slightly hairy. 1–4' high. N.Y. to Mich. south.

2. FLOWER HEADS 1–2" WIDE

Thin-leaved Coneflower (*R. triloba*) Some of the lower leaves 3-lobed. Rays proportionally wider than in the 3 other species. Stem branching. 2–5' high. N.Y. to Minn. south.

Orange Coneflower (*R. fulgida*) † Similar to Thin-leaved Coneflower but lower leaves toothed, not lobed; stem unbranched or slightly branched. 1–3' high. N.J. to Ind. south.

Gray-headed Coneflower (*Ratibida pinnata*) Flower rays long and narrow, strongly drooping; larger leaves pinnately divided into 3–7 lance-shaped, toothed leaflets. Disk a gray or brown knob, anise-scented when bruised and longer than wide. 3–5' high. Dry soil, s. Ont. and w. N.Y. to Minn. south. Summer and fall. Composite Family.

Common Sunflower (*Helianthus annuus*) * Disk nearly flat, 1–2" wide, purple or brown. Flower heads 3–6" wide (up to 10" wide in cultivated plants). Larger leaves broadly egg-shaped, toothed, long-stalked, rough on both sides. 3–10' high. Waste places and roadsides; native west of the Mississippi River. Summer and fall. Composite Family.

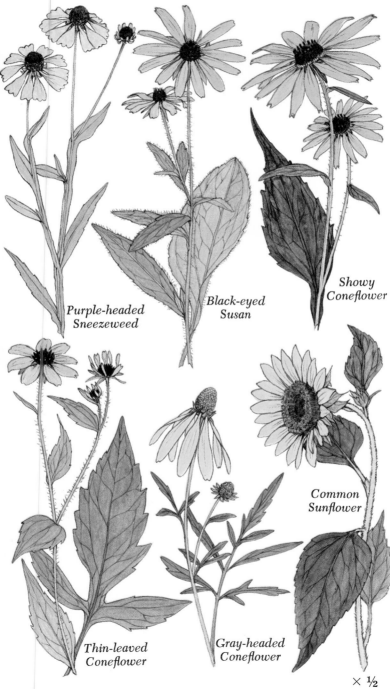

Purple-headed
Sneezeweed

Black-eyed
Susan

Showy
Coneflower

Thin-leaved
Coneflower

Gray-headed
Coneflower

Common
Sunflower

× ½

Yellow, Daisylike Flowers in Heads 1″ or More Wide, with a Yellow or Green Disk; or Flowers with Shining Petals

LOWER LEAVES TOOTHED, NOT DIVIDED

Elecampane (*Inula helenium*) * Flower rays very narrow, string-like, numerous, giving the 2–4″ flower head a disheveled appearance. Leaves large and rough, woolly beneath and finely toothed. 2–6′ high. Roadsides and pastures. Summer and fall. Composite Family.

Sneezeweed (*Helenium autumnale*) Flower rays wedge-shaped, broadest at the tip, 3-toothed, drooping. Disk knob-shaped. The bases of the leaves extend down the stem as wings. Leaves lance-shaped. 2–6′ high. Moist meadows and shores. Summer and fall. Composite Family.

Wingstem (*Actinomeris alternifolia*) Flower rays 10 or less, drooping, widest in the middle; upper part of stem usually winged (with thin ridges running down the stem below the leaves). Flower heads 1–2″ wide, with an untidy, moplike disk. Leaves lance-shaped or oblong, the lower leaves sometimes opposite. 3–8′ high. Rich soil, N.Y. and s. Ont. to Iowa south. Late summer and fall. Composite Family.

Gumweed or **Tarweed** (*Grindelia squarrosa*) * Bracts covering the base of the flower head are very sticky and bent downward. Flower heads about 1″ wide, with numerous rays. Leaves oblong, often clasping the stem. 6–36″ high. Dry soil, w. U.S.; widely naturalized in our area. Summer and fall. Composite Family.

Sunflowers (*Helianthus*) Flower rays widest in the middle, not noticeably drooping; flower heads not sticky; over 1′ high. Lowest leaves normally opposite. See p. 388.

Lesser Celandine (*Ranunculus ficaria*) Low plant with heart-shaped leaves and shining petals. See p. 364.

LOWER LEAVES DIVIDED

Tall or **Green-headed Coneflower** (*Rudbeckia laciniata*) Flower heads 2½–4″ wide, with 6–10 drooping rays. Disk a greenish-yellow knob. Lower leaves pinnately divided into 3–7 irregularly lobed leaflets. 3–10′ high. Swamps and moist thickets. Summer and fall. Composite Family.

Buttercups (*Ranunculus*) Flowers ½–1½″ wide, with shining petals. See p. 242.

Elecampane
(yellow)

Sneezeweed
(yellow)

Wingstem
(yellow)

Gumweed
(yellow)

Tall
Coneflower
(yellow)

× ½

Yellow, Daisylike or Asterlike Flowers in Head under 1″ Wide; or Flowers with Shining Petals

Ragworts or **Squaw Weeds** (*Senecio*) Flower heads ½–¾″ wide, on long (mostly over ½″) stalks; flower rays 8–15, long and narrow. The flower heads grow in a branched, terminal cluster. Stem leaves usually coarsely toothed or deeply cleft; basal leaves in most species merely toothed. Composite Family.

1. BASAL LEAVES LONG-STALKED, HEART-SHAPED OR ROUNDED AT THE BASE; FOUND IN WET OR MOIST PLACES

Golden Ragwort (*S. aureus*) Basal leaves egg-shaped or roundish, 1–1½ times as long as wide, blunt-toothed and blunt-tipped, with a heart-shaped base. 6–30″ high. Swamps and moist meadows; common. Spring and early summer.

Robbins' Ragwort (*S. robbinsii*) Basal leaves lance-shaped or narrowly egg-shaped, 2–2½ times longer than wide, sharply toothed and somewhat pointed at the tip, heart-shaped or rounded at the base. 12–30″ high. Wet meadows and shores, n. N.Eng. and n. N.Y. north; Roan Mt., N.C. Late spring and summer.

2. BASAL LEAVES TAPERING AT THE BASE; FOUND IN WOODS OR ON ROCKY BANKS

Round-leaved Ragwort (*S. obovatus*) Basal leaves egg-shaped, broadest above the middle, with very blunt ends. 6–24″ high. C. N.Eng. to Mich. south. Spring and early summer.

Balsam Ragwort (*S. pauperculus*) Basal leaves oblong or lance-shaped, bluntly toothed or sometimes lobed. 4–20″ high. Late spring and early summer.

3. BASAL LEAVES FINELY DIVIDED; FOUND IN WASTE PLACES

Tansy Ragwort (*S. jacobaea*) * Leaves finely divided, resembling those of the Tansy (p. 426). Coarse, leafy plant, 1–4′ high. Weed of roadsides and pastures. Common in e. Can. and locally established in ne. U.S. Summer and fall.

Seaside Crowfoot (*Ranunculus cymbalaria*) Low plant with roundish leaves; flowers about ¼″ wide; grows on sandy shores and in salt marshes. See p. 364.

Buttercups and **Crowfoots** (*Ranunculus*) Flowers with roundish, shining petals. See pp. 242 and 244.

Goldenrods (*Solidago*) Flower heads small and numerous, on short stalks. See pp. 446–453.

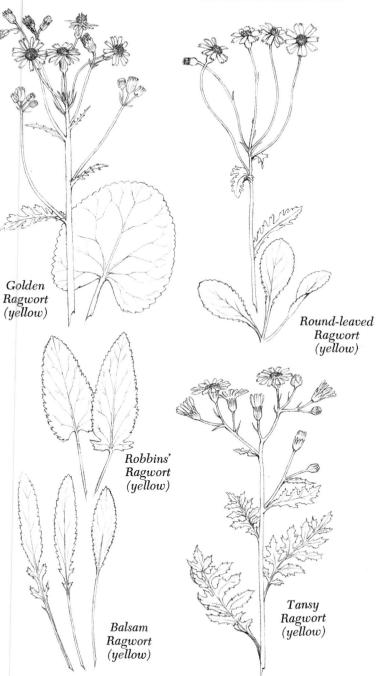

*Golden
Ragwort
(yellow)*

*Round-leaved
Ragwort
(yellow)*

*Robbins'
Ragwort
(yellow)*

*Balsam
Ragwort
(yellow)*

*Tansy
Ragwort
(yellow)*

× ½

White or Blue, Daisylike Flowers; Leaves Deeply Lobed or Divided

LEAVES FINELY DIVIDED INTO VERY NARROW SEGMENTS

Chamomiles (*Anthemis* and *Matricaria*) Weeds with white, daisylike flowers and finely divided foliage. 8–24″ high. Roadsides and waste places. Summer and fall. Composite Family.

Mayweed or **Stinking Chamomile** (*A. cotula*) * Foliage ill-scented. Flower heads ¾–1″ wide. Common.

Wild Chamomile (*M. chamomilla*) * Foliage with fragrance of pineapple; stem smooth. Flower heads ¾–1″ wide.

Field Chamomile (*A. arvensis*) * Foliage odorless; stems gray-downy. Flower heads 1–1½″ wide. Leaves less finely divided than the other three species.

Scentless Chamomile (*M. maritima*) *† Foliage odorless; stem smooth. Flower heads 1–1½″ wide.

*LEAVES DEEPLY CUT AND LOBED, BUT NOT
FINELY DIVIDED*

Oxeye Daisy (*Chrysanthemum leucanthemum*) * Long-stalked, white flower heads 1–2″ wide, with 15–30 slender rays. A familiar plant, usually bearing a single flower head. 1–3′ high. Very common in fields and meadows. Spring to fall. Composite Family.

Feverfew (*Chrysanthemum parthenium*) * White flowers in heads ½–¾″ wide, with 10–20 oblong rays; flower heads numerous, in clusters. Leaves divided into egg-shaped segments. 1–3′ high. Escaped from cultivation to roadsides and waste places. Summer. Composite Family.

Chicory (*Cichorium intybus*) Blue (occasionally white) flowers, in heads 1–1½″ wide, which are stalkless along the branches. See p. 382.

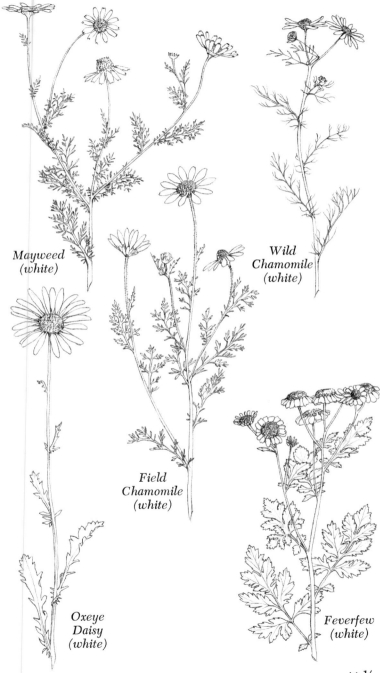

Mayweed
(white)

Wild
Chamomile
(white)

Field
Chamomile
(white)

Oxeye
Daisy
(white)

Feverfew
(white)

× ½

White, Pink, Blue, Violet or Purple, Daisylike or Asterlike Flowers; Leaves Toothed

FLOWER RAYS 7–40

Silverrod (*Solidago bicolor*) Rays 7–9, whitish; flower heads small, in long, cylindrical clusters. Our only white goldenrod. Lower leaves toothed, the upper often entire. 6–30″ high. Dry soil. Summer and fall. Composite Family.

Chicory (*Cichorium intybus*) * Rays blue (occasionally white), obviously toothed at the tip; flower heads large, 1–1½″ wide, stalk-less along the branches. Leaves partly clasping, toothed, lobed or entire. 1–4′ high. Roadsides, fields and waste places. Summer and fall. Composite Family.

Purple Coneflower (*Echinacea purpurea*) Rays reddish purple, drooping; flower heads very large (2½–4″ wide), with a bristly central disk. Lower leaves egg-shaped and long-stalked. 2–5′ high. North to Va., Ohio, Mich., Ill. and Iowa. Summer and fall. Composite Family.

Asters (*Aster*) Flower rays more than 9 (except 1 species with heart-shaped leaves), not obviously toothed at the tip or drooping. See pp. 454–463.

FLOWER RAYS MORE THAN 40

Fleabanes (*Erigeron*) Rays white, pink or purple, very narrow and numerous. Flower heads with a flat, yellow central disk. Lower leaves toothed. Composite Family.

Robin's Plantain (*E. pulchellus*) Flower heads 1–1½″ wide, violet or lilac (occasionally whitish). Leaves mostly at the base of the plant. Soft-hairy. 6–20″ high. Fields and open woods. Spring and early summer.

Common or **Philadelphia Fleabane** (*E. philadelphicus*) Flower heads ½–1″ wide, pinkish or whitish, with 100–150 rays; upper leaves clasp the stem. Soft-hairy. 6–30″ high. Open woods and fields. Spring and summer.

Daisy Fleabane or **Sweet Scabious** (*E. annuus*) Flower heads ½–¾″ wide, white or tinged with pink; rays 50–100; stem leaves toothed, not clasping; stem hairs stand out. 1–5′ high. Common in fields and waste places. Late spring to fall.

Lesser Daisy Fleabane (*E. strigosus*) † Similar to the Daisy Fleabane, but stem hairs lie closer to stem and stem leaves are mostly entire. 1–3′ high. Common.

Horseweed (*E. canadensis*) Rays minute. See p. 384.

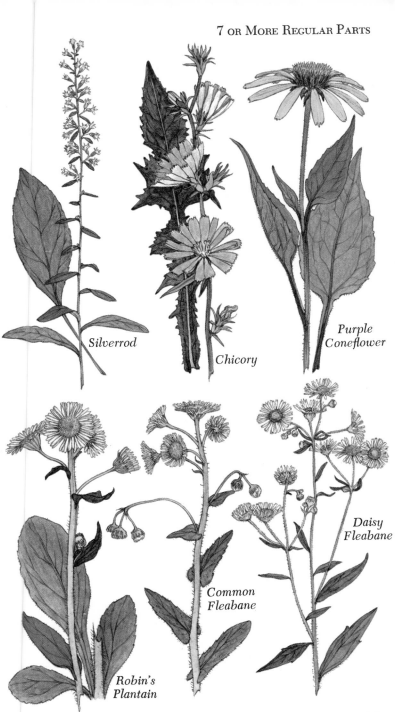

Silverrod

Chicory

Purple
Coneflower

Robin's
Plantain

Common
Fleabane

Daisy
Fleabane

× ½

Flowers Not Yellow or Orange and Not Daisylike or Asterlike

Rattlesnake Roots (*Prenanthes*) Flower heads about ½″ long, bell-shaped, usually nodding. Whitish, cream-colored or pinkish flowers. The leaves vary from divided to remotely toothed. Tall White Lettuce (p. 212) has 5 or 6 rays. Late summer and fall. Composite Family.

White Lettuce (*P. alba*) Stem and leaves with a whitish bloom; pappus (hairs beneath the bracts of the flower head) deep red-brown. Stem usually purplish. 2–5′ high. Woods and thickets.

Tall Rattlesnake Root or **Gall-of-the-earth** (*P. trifoliata*) Stem and leaves without bloom; lower leaves rather thin, usually in 3 segments, and with pointed lobes; pappus creamy-white. 2–6′ high. Woods and thickets, Nfld. to Ohio south; uncommon south of Pa. A dwarf form occurs on alpine summits.

Lion's Foot or **Gall-of-the-earth** (*P. serpentaria*) Similar to the Tall Rattlesnake Root, but the lower leaves are thickish and bluntly lobed. Flower cluster rather flat-topped. 1–4′ high. Dry woods and barrens, Mass. to Ohio south; uncommon north of Md.

Boott's Rattlesnake Root (*P. boottii*) A dwarf, alpine species with triangular or heart-shaped, almost entire, lower leaves. N. N.Eng. and n. N.Y.

Tall Blue Lettuce (*Lactuca biennis*) Blue flowers in small heads ¼″ wide. Flower heads very numerous, in a large, branched cluster. Leaves usually deeply lobed and coarsely toothed. 3–15′ high. Moist thickets and clearings. Summer and fall. Composite Family.

Horseweed (*Erigeron canadensis*) Whitish or greenish flowers in very small (⅛″ long) heads with minute, upright rays. Leaves lance-shaped or narrow, the lower toothed. Stem usually with bristly hairs. 3″–7′ high. Very common weed of fields and waste places. Summer and fall. Composite Family.

Spotted Knapweed (*Centaurea maculosa*) Pink, purple or whitish flowers in thistlelike heads; base of flower head covered with black-fringed bracts. See p. 234.

Baneberries (*Actaea*) White flowers in a short, dense raceme; leaves divided into numerous, toothed leaflets. See p. 424.

Goldenseal or **Orangeroot** (*Hydrastis canadensis*) Solitary, greenish-white flower about ½″ wide; leaves very broad and deeply lobed. See p. 420.

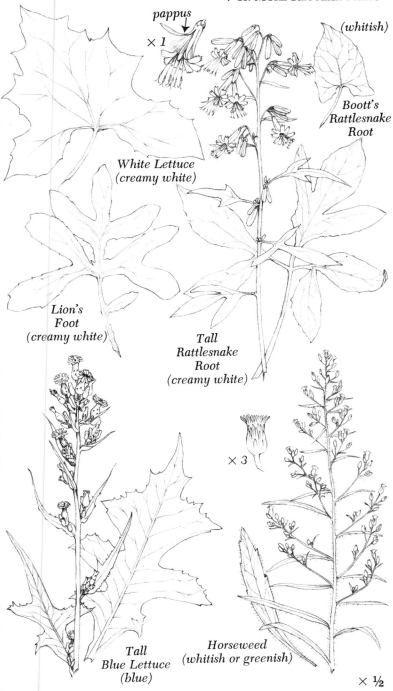

pappus

× 1

(whitish)

Boott's
Rattlesnake
Root

White Lettuce
(creamy white)

Lion's
Foot
(creamy white)

Tall
Rattlesnake
Root
(creamy white)

× 3

Tall
Blue Lettuce
(blue)

Horseweed
(whitish or greenish)

× ½

YELLOW FLOWERS

Coreopsis or **Tickseeds** (*Coreopsis*) Basal (or lowest) leaves lance-shaped. Composite Family.

1. FLOWER RAYS ENTIRE OR NEARLY SO (SEE P. 394)

2. FLOWER RAYS WITH 3–7 LOBES AT THE TIP

Lance-leaved Coreopsis (*C. lanceolata*) Flower heads 1½–2½" wide, with 6–10 bright-yellow rays. Leaves lance-shaped, 2–6" long, entire or with 1 or 2 lobes at the base. 10–24" high. Fields and roadsides; escaped from cultivation in the e. part of its range. Late spring and summer.

Leopard's Bane (*Arnica acaulis*) Basal leaves broad, with 5–7 ribs, in a rosette. See p. 390.

PINK OR ROSE (OCCASIONALLY WHITE) FLOWERS WITH A CONSPICUOUS YELLOW CENTER

Rose Coreopsis or **Pink Tickseed** (*Coreopsis rosea*) Leaves very narrow, almost threadlike; no basal leaves. Flowers daisylike, rose or white, with a yellow disk and 3-toothed rays; heads ½–1" wide. 6–24" high. Shores and bogs, along the coast. Summer and fall. Composite Family.

Large Marsh Pink (*Sabatia dodecandra*) Lower stem leaves and basal leaves lance-shaped. Flowers 1½–2½" wide, with 8–12 pink petals that are yellow at the base. 1–2' high. Brackish (rarely fresh) marshes and shores, s. Conn. south along the coast. **Plymouth Gentian** (*S. kennedyana*) has wider petals and a different habitat and range: shores of fresh ponds, N.S., se. Mass. and R.I. Summer and fall. Gentian Family.

WHITE, PINK OR ROSE FLOWERS WITHOUT A CONSPICUOUS YELLOW CENTER

Starflower (*Trientalis borealis*) Leaves in a single whorl of 5–10 leaves. The white flowers are star-shaped, with 5–9 (usually 7) pointed petals, and are about ½" wide. 3–9" high. Moist woods. Spring (summer on mountaintops). Primrose Family.

Bouncing Bet (*Saponaria officinalis*) Pink or white flowers, 1" wide; leaves with 3–5 prominent ribs. See p. 258.

Chickweeds (*Stellaria* and *Cerastium*) Leaves in pairs; white flowers, ¼–½" wide. See p. 274.

Ragged Robin (*Lychnis flos-cuculi*) Deep-pink or white flowers, ¾–1" wide, divided into narrow segments. See p. 260.

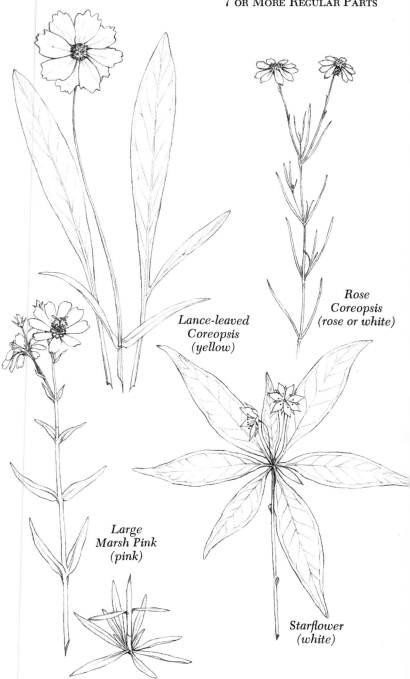

Lance-leaved
Coreopsis
(yellow)

Rose
Coreopsis
(rose or white)

Large
Marsh Pink
(pink)

Starflower
(white)

× ½

Yellow Flowers; Leaves with a Pair of Prominent Lower Veins Running Parallel to the Midrib

WITHOUT BASAL LEAVES

Sunflowers (*Helianthus*) Larger leaves unlobed and either with stalks under 1″ long or long-stalked; if the latter, the uppermost leaves are alternate. Flower rays neutral (see Oxeye, p. 390). A dozen additional species occur locally in our area. Summer and fall. Composite Family.

1. DISK BROWNISH OR PURPLE

Common Sunflower (*H. annuus*) Flower heads over 3″ wide; leaves egg-shaped. See p. 374.

Showy Sunflower (*H. laetiflorus*) Flower heads 1–3″ wide; leaves lance-shaped. See below.

2. DISK YELLOW; FLOWER HEADS 1½–4″ WIDE; RAYS 8–20

a. Stem smooth or slightly rough

Woodland Sunflower (*H. divaricatus*) Stalks of lower leaves very short (under ¼″ long). Leaves opposite, lance-shaped, tapering to the tip, rough on the upper surface. 2–6′ high. Dry woods.

Pale-leaved Sunflower (*H. strumosus*) Stalks of lower leaves at least ¼″ long; leaves thick and rough with conspicuous veins, pale beneath, shallowly toothed. Stem often with a whitish bloom. 3–8′ high. Dry woods and roadsides.

Thin-leaved Sunflower (*H. decapetalus*) Stalks of lower leaves at least ¼″ long; leaves thin, nearly smooth, green beneath, sharply toothed. Rays 8–15. 2–5′ high. Woods and thickets.

b. Stem hairy or very rough

Jerusalem Artichoke (*H. tuberosus*) Leaves egg-shaped, coarsely toothed, very rough and thick; bracts of flower head long-pointed. Heads 2–3½″ wide. 6–10′ high. Moist thickets and roadsides.

Tall or **Giant Sunflower** (*H. giganteus*) Leaves lance-shaped, shallowly toothed, mostly alternate; bracts of flower head long-pointed. Heads 1½–2½″ wide. Stem often purple. 5–10′ high. Swamps and damp thickets.

Showy Sunflower (*H. laetiflorus*) Bracts of flower head blunt or short-pointed. Disk yellow or purple. Leaves lance-shaped to narrowly egg-shaped. Stem rough. 2–8′ high. Dry soil, N.Y. to Sask. south; occasionally escaped in N.Eng.

Continued

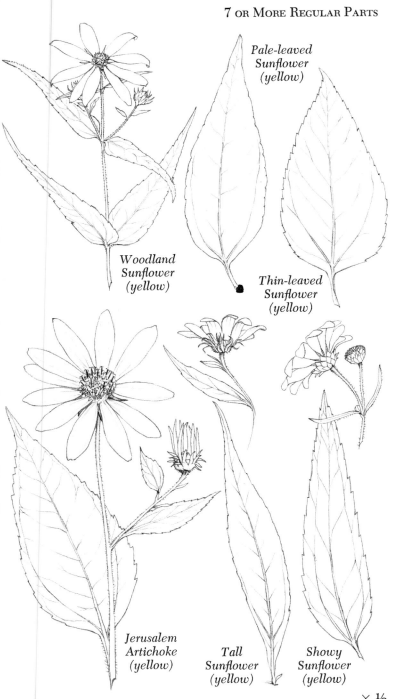

Pale-leaved
Sunflower
(yellow)

Woodland
Sunflower
(yellow)

Thin-leaved
Sunflower
(yellow)

Jerusalem
Artichoke
(yellow)

Tall
Sunflower
(yellow)

Showy
Sunflower
(yellow)

× ½

Yellow Flowers; Leaves with a Pair of Prominent Lower Veins Running Parallel to the Midrib (cont.)

WITHOUT BASAL LEAVES (CONT.)

Sunflowers (*Helianthus*) (cont.)

3. DISK YELLOW; FLOWER HEADS 1–1½″ WIDE; RAYS 5–8

Small Wood Sunflower (*H. microcephalus*) Leaves lance-shaped and tapering, rough above, short-stalked. Stem smooth. 3–6′ high. Moist thickets, Pa. to Ill. south.

Oxeye or **False Sunflower** (*Heliopsis helianthoides*) Larger leaves long-stalked (stalks 1″ or more long), coarsely and sharply toothed (but not lobed); even the uppermost are opposite. Flower heads 1½–2½″ wide; disk cone-shaped. Rays fertile, that is, they have a small, forked pistil at the base (not present in the true Sunflowers). Stem smooth (rough in 1 variety). 2–5′ high. Open woods and thickets. Summer and fall. Composite Family.

Large-flowered Leafcup (*Polymnia uvedalia*) Lower leaves broad, coarsely lobed, and abruptly narrowed at the base. Flower heads 1½–3″ wide, with 10–15 yellow rays. Coarse, large-leaved plant with a hairy stem. 3–10′ high. Small-flowered Leafcup (*P. canadensis*) has 5 rays or none (p. 278). Rich woods, N.Y. to Ill. south. Summer and fall. Composite Family.

BASAL LEAVES PRESENT

Hairy Arnica (*Arnica mollis*) Alpine plant of n. N.Eng. north. The flower heads are 1–2″ wide, and have 10–15 rays, each with 2 or 3 teeth. Stem leaves egg-shaped or broadly lance-shaped, the upper ones stalkless. Stem hairy. 6–24″ high. Mountain brooks and ravines. Summer. Composite Family.

Leopard's Bane (*Arnica acaulis*) Plant of sandy woodlands from s. Pa. and Del. south. The broad basal leaves have 3–7 prominent veins, are slightly toothed or entire, and form a rosette; stem leaves much smaller. Flower heads 1–1½″ wide with 12–15 rays. Stem hairy. 1–3′ high. Spring. Composite Family.

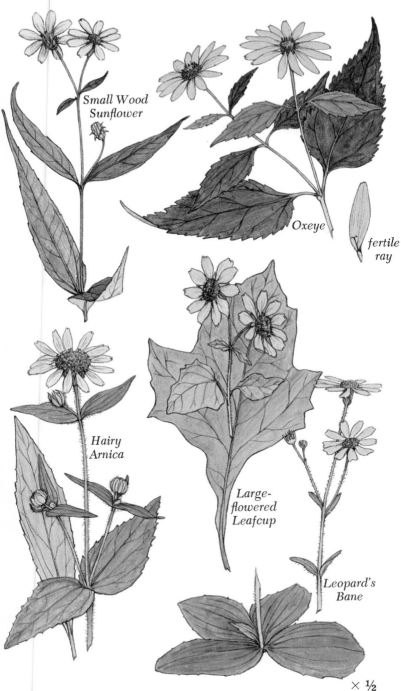

Small Wood
Sunflower

Oxeye

fertile
ray

Hairy
Arnica

Large-
flowered
Leafcup

Leopard's
Bane

× ½

Yellow Flowers; Leaves with Only the Midrib Prominent

Bur Marigolds or **Beggar Ticks** (*Bidens* and *Megalodonta*) Leaves lance-shaped, in pairs; plants not over 5' high and grow in wet places. Flowers in small heads, the rays conspicuous or quite small. For other species, see pp. 394 and 440. Late summer and fall. Composite Family.

1. AQUATIC PLANT WITH FINELY DIVIDED UNDERWATER LEAVES

Water Marigold (*M. beckii*) See p. 394.

2. NONE OF THE LEAVES FINELY DIVIDED

Larger Bur Marigold (*B. laevis*) Rays over ½" long, conspicuous. Flower heads 1½–2½" wide. 1–3' high. Swamps and shores, N.H. south; local inland.

Nodding Bur Marigold (*B. cernua*) Rays ¼–½" long, sometimes absent; leaves stalkless. Flower heads ½–1¼" wide, nodding in fruit. 6–36" high. Wet places.

Swamp Beggar Ticks (*B. connata*) Rays, if present, ⅓" long; leaves coarsely toothed, with definite stalks. See p. 440.

Cup Plant or **Indian Cup** (*Silphium perfoliatum*) Leaves egg-shaped, the pairs of upper leaves united at the base to form a cup. The flower heads are 2–3" wide, with numerous rays. Stem square, smooth. 4–8' high. Thickets and banks of streams, Ont. to S.D. south; introduced east to s. N.Eng. Summer and early fall. Composite Family.

Whorled Rosinweed (*Silphium trifoliatum*) Leaves lance-shaped, the middle leaves in whorls of 3 or 4, short-stalked. Flower heads 1½–2" wide, with 15–20 rays. Leaves rough. Stem smooth. 3–7' high. Woods and borders, Pa. to Ind. south. Summer and fall. Composite Family.

Tall or **Giant Sunflower** (*Helianthus giganteus*) Leaves lance-shaped, in pairs; 5–10' high; grows in wet or moist places. See p. 388.

White or Pink Flowers

Rue Anemone (*Anemonella thalictroides*) White or pinkish flowers, about ¾" wide, with 5–10 petallike sepals, in a small umbel. Leaves or leaflets, with 3 blunt lobes, grow in a whorl beneath the flower cluster, and in 3 groups of 3 on the long-stalked basal leaves. Delicate spring flower, 4–9" high. Open woods. Buttercup Family.

*Larger
Bur Marigold
(yellow)*

*Nodding
Bur Marigold
(yellow)*

*Rue
Anemone
(white
or pinkish)*

*Cup
Plant
(yellow)*

*Whorled
Rosinweed
(yellow)*

× ½

YELLOW FLOWERS

Water Marigold (*Megalodonta beckii*) Aquatic plant with finely divided underwater leaves. Flower heads 1–1½″ wide, held above the water. If the upper leaves grow above water, they are lance-shaped and toothed or deeply cleft. Ponds and quiet streams. Late summer and fall. Composite Family.

Bur Marigolds or **Beggar Ticks** (*Bidens*) Leaves divided into 3–7 sharply toothed leaflets. Composite Family.

1. FLOWERS INCONSPICUOUS (SEE P. 440)

2. FLOWERS SHOWY, THE HEADS 1½–2½″ WIDE

Tickseed Sunflower (*B. coronata*) The flower heads have 6–19 golden-yellow rays. Leaflets 5–7. 2–5′ high. Wet meadows and swamps, Mass. to Minn. south. Late summer and fall.

Coreopsis or **Tickseeds** (*Coreopsis*) Leaves with entire lobes or leaflets or leaves finely divided; not aquatic. Flower heads 1–2½″ wide. Composite Family.

1. FLOWER RAYS WITH 3–7 LOBES AT THE TIP

Lance-leaved Coreopsis (*C. lanceolata*) Leaves lance-shaped with 1 or 2 lobes at the base. See p. 386.

2. FLOWER RAYS ENTIRE OR NEARLY SO

Tall Coreopsis (*C. tripteris*) Lower leaves stalked, divided into 3–5 entire leaflets; plant 3–10′ high. Upper leaves lance-shaped, entire. Flowers anise-scented. Woods and thickets, Pa. and s. Ont. to Wis. south; escaped from cultivation east to Mass. Late summer and fall.

Whorled Coreopsis (*C. verticillata*) Leaves divided into narrow segments. 6–36″ high. Dry woods and clearings, Md. south. Summer.

Greater Coreopsis (*C. major*) Lower leaves stalkless, divided into 3 lance-shaped leaflets, and so appearing as whorls of 6 leaves; 18–36″ high. Open woods and clearings, s. Pa. and Ohio south. Summer.

WHITE, PINK OR ROSE FLOWERS

Rose Coreopsis (*Coreopsis rosea*) Leaf segments very narrow; rose (or white) flower of summer and fall. See p. 386.

Rue Anemone (*Anemonella thalictroides*) Spring flower; leaflets roundish, with 3 blunt lobes. See p. 392.

Anemones (*Anemone*) Leaflets sharply toothed or cleft; flowers long-stalked. See p. 288.

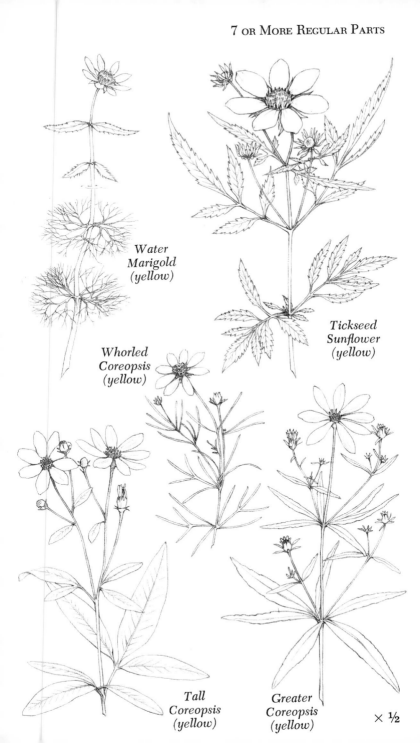

Water
Marigold
(yellow)

Tickseed
Sunflower
(yellow)

Whorled
Coreopsis
(yellow)

Tall
Coreopsis
(yellow)

Greater
Coreopsis
(yellow)

× ½

Sweet Bay (*Magnolia virginiana*) Showy, white flowers, 2–3″ wide. The leathery, entire leaves are dark green above, whitish beneath, blunt-tipped. Flowers with 6–9 petals, very fragrant. Fruit conelike, dark red. Large shrub or tree, 8–30′ high. Swamps and low woods, e. Mass. to Pa. south. Spring and early summer (occasionally fall). Magnolia Family.

Hollies (*Ilex*) Small, white or whitish flowers growing in the axils. Petals 6–8; staminate and pistillate flowers growing on separate plants. Mountain Winterberry (*I. montana*) has 4 or 5 petals (p. 168). Holly Family.

Winterberry or **Black Alder** (*I. verticillata*) Leaves sharply toothed, dull above, mostly egg-shaped and usually downy on the veins beneath, deciduous. Berries bright red. 6–15′ high. Swamps and damp thickets. Early summer.

Smooth Winterberry (*I. laevigata*) Leaves finely toothed along their entire margins, shining above, deciduous. Leaves mostly lance-shaped and smooth beneath. Berries red, larger than in the Winterberry. 4–10′ high. Wooded swamps, s. Me. to N.Y. south. Late spring and early summer.

Inkberry (*I. glabra*) Leaves having a few, obscure teeth near the tip, evergreen and shining. Berries black. 2–6′ high. Sandy soil along the coast. Early summer.

Witch Hazel (*Hamamelis virginiana*) Narrow, yellow petals; flowers in fall. See p. 168.

VINES

Passionflowers (*Passiflora*) Flowers ½–2″ wide, solitary or in pairs, and growing in the axils. Flowers with 5 petals and 5 sepals and conspicuously fringed in the center. Tendril-bearing. Thickets. Summer. Passionflower Family.

Passionflower or **Maypops** (*P. incarnata*) Whitish flowers with a pink or purple fringe, 1½–2″ wide. Flower solitary. Leaves with 3–5 deep, toothed lobes. Fruit a yellow, edible berry, about 2″ long. S. Pa. to s. Ill. south.

Yellow Passionflower (*P. lutea*) Greenish-yellow flowers, ½–1″ wide, usually in pairs. Leaves with 3–5 blunt, entire lobes. Fruit a blue-black berry, ½″ in diameter. S. Pa. to Kan. south.

Moonseed (*Menispermum canadense*) Very small, whitish flowers in clusters. See p. 356.

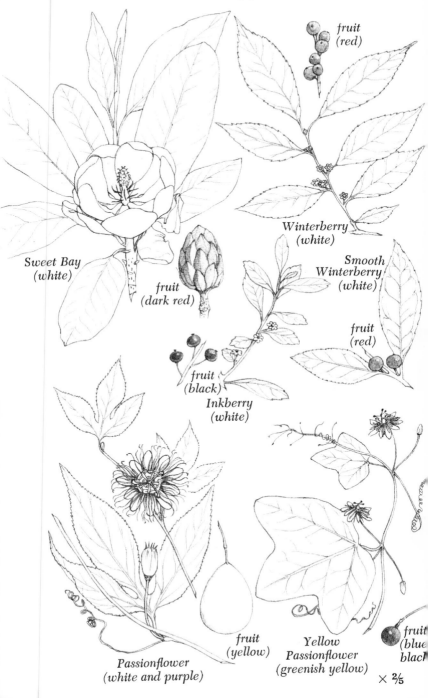

fruit
(red)

Winterberry
(white)

Sweet Bay
(white)

fruit
(dark red)

Smooth
Winterberry
(white)

fruit
(red)

fruit
(black)

Inkberry
(white)

fruit
(yellow)

Yellow
Passionflower
(greenish yellow)

Passionflower
(white and purple)

fruit
(blue
black)

× 2/5

WILDFLOWERS WITH NO APPARENT LEAVES AT FLOWERING TIME

Slender Glasswort or **Samphire** (*Salicornia europaea*) Fleshy, jointed plant of salt marshes and saline soil inland. Flowers green, tiny, in the upper joints. Joints longer than thick. **Dwarf Glasswort** (*S. bigelovii*) has joints thicker than long. **Woody Glasswort** (*S. virginica*) has creeping stems, forming mats. 2–15″ high. Late summer and fall. Goosefoot Family.

WILDFLOWERS WITH BASAL LEAVES ONLY

Common Pipewort (*Eriocaulon septangulare*) Plant of shallow water with whitish flowers in a button-shaped head at the top of a long, slender stalk. The leaves are grasslike, 1–3″ long. Summer. Pipewort Family.

Sweetflag or **Calamus** (*Acorus calamus*) Minute, greenish-yellow flowers in a dense spadix projecting from the side of a long, leaflike flowering stem, actually a spathe. The leaves are sword-shaped, 1–4′ long. Swamps and along streams. Spring and early summer. Arum Family.

Plantains (*Plantago*) Whitish, greenish or brownish flowers in a dense spike or head. Leaves entire or slightly toothed. Spring to fall. Plantain Family.

1. LEAVES LONG-STALKED, MOSTLY EGG-SHAPED; FLOWER SPIKE LONG AND SLENDER

Common Plantain (*P. major*) * Leaf stalks green at the base; spike rather blunt. Leaves prominently ribbed. Abundant weed of lawns, waste places and roadsides.

Red-stemmed or **Pale Plantain** (*P. rugelii*) † Very like the Common Plantain, but the leaf stalks are reddish at the base and the spike is narrowed at the tip.

2. LEAVES LANCE-SHAPED OR NARROW, STALKLESS OR SHORT-STALKED

English Plantain (*P. lanceolata*) * Leaves lance-shaped, with 3–5 ribs; spike short and dense. Very common and troublesome weed of lawns and fields.

Seaside Plantain (*P. juncoides*) Seaside plant with narrow, 1-ribbed, fleshy leaves; spike 1–5″ long. Salt marshes, sea cliffs and beaches, south to N.J.

Bracted Plantain (*P. aristata*) Leaves narrow, dark green, not fleshy; spike 1–6″ long with stiff bracts protruding from the flower cluster. 6–12″ high. Roadsides and waste places.

Continued

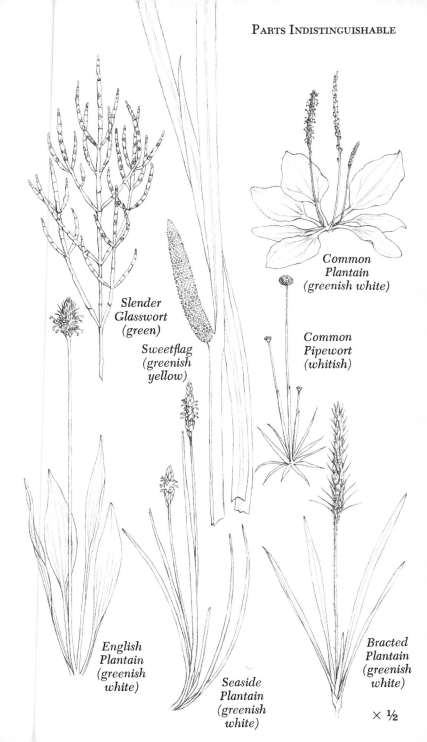

Slender
Glasswort
(green)

Sweetflag
(greenish
yellow)

Common
Plantain
(greenish white)

Common
Pipewort
(whitish)

English
Plantain
(greenish
white)

Seaside
Plantain
(greenish
white)

Bracted
Plantain
(greenish
white)

× ½

Golden Club (*Orontium aquaticum*) Aquatic plant with yellow flowers and oblong, long-stalked leaves. See p. 336.

Pussytoes or **Early Everlastings** (*Antennaria*) White-woolly plants of dry places. See below.

WILDFLOWERS WITH ALTERNATE LEAVES /
Leaves Entire

Stem and Underside of Leaves White-woolly

Pussytoes or **Early Everlastings** (*Antennaria*) Plants leafy at the base and usually forming dense mats. White flowers in small heads in a close cluster (solitary in 1 species) at the top of the stem. There are about a dozen species in our area, very similar in appearance and difficult to identify. Low plants of woods, fields and banks. Spring. 4–16″ high. Composite Family.

1. LARGEST LEAVES BROAD, 1½–3″ LONG BY ¾–1½″ WIDE, WITH 3 OR MORE MAIN VEINS BENEATH

    Plantain-leaved Pussytoes (*A. plantaginifolia*) Flower heads several; basal leaves dull green, woolly above.

    Smooth Pussytoes (*A parlinii*) † Flower heads several; basal leaves bright green and nearly smooth.

    Solitary Pussytoes (*A. solitaria*) Flower head solitary. Stem leaves small and very narrow. Rich woods, Md. and w. Pa. to Ind. south.

2. LARGEST LEAVES 1–2″ LONG BY ¼–½″ WIDE, WITH 1 PROMINENT VEIN

    Field Pussytoes (*A. neglecta*) Upper surface of leaves dull green and woolly; basal shoots very slender and prostrate, with small leaves that overlap only at the tip of the shoot. Common.

    Smaller Pussytoes (*A. neodioica*) Similar to the Field Pussytoes, but basal shoots short, with overlapping leaves, and turned upward at the tip. Lower leaves end in a tiny, abrupt point. Common.

    Canada Pussytoes (*A. canadensis*) † Similar to Smaller Pussytoes but upper surface of leaves bright green and smooth.

Pearly Everlasting (*Anaphalis margaritacea*) Leafy-stemmed plant with white flower heads ¼″ wide, composed of a yellow disk (turning brown) surrounded by numerous, pearly-white, petal-like bracts. See p. 368.

Continued

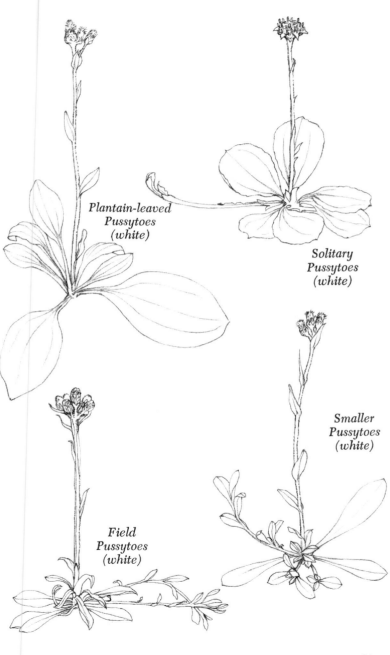

Plantain-leaved
Pussytoes
(white)

Solitary
Pussytoes
(white)

Smaller
Pussytoes
(white)

Field
Pussytoes
(white)

× ⅔

Stem and Underside of Leaves White-woolly (cont.)

Everlastings or **Cudweeds** (*Gnaphalium*) Leafy-stemmed plants; flower heads white, about ⅛″ wide, the bracts not petal-like. Leaves narrow or narrowly lance-shaped. Summer and fall. Composite Family.

Sweet Everlasting or **Catfoot** (*G. obtusifolium*) Flower heads in a branching cluster; leaves are narrowed at the base and do not clasp the stem. Mildly aromatic when bruised. Dry fields.

Clammy Everlasting (*G. macounii*) † Very like Sweet Everlasting but leaves are broad at the base and clasp the stem. 8–36″ high. Dry fields and borders.

Low Cudweed (*G. uliginosum*) Flower heads brownish in the center and growing in several compact clusters, closely surrounded by leaves. Homely, sprawling weed of gardens and waste places.

Stem Jointed; Leaves Arrow-shaped

Tearthumbs (*Polygonum*) Stems prickly. Weak-stemmed, sprawling plants of low thickets and wet places. The midrib of the leaves beneath and the 4-sided stems are armed with tiny, backward-pointing prickles. White or pink flowers in small, close clusters. Summer and fall. Buckwheat Family.

Arrow-leaved Tearthumb (*P. sagittatum*) Leaves narrowly arrow-shaped, 1–3″ long. The flowers have 5 lobes and usually 8 stamens. Common.

Halberd-leaved Tearthumb (*P. arifolium*) Leaves broadly arrow-shaped, 2–6″ long. The flowers have 4 lobes and 6 stamens.

Field Sorrel or **Sheep Sorrel** (*Rumex acetosella*) * Reddish or greenish flowers in branching, leafless racemes. Leaves usually arrow-shaped with flaring lobes. The flowers have 6 parts. 4–15″ high. Abundant and persistent weed of dry fields and gardens. Spring to fall. Buckwheat Family.

Stem Jointed; Leaves Not Arrow-shaped

Lizard's Tail (*Saururus cernuus*) White flowers in dense, nodding spikes 4–6″ long; leaves heart-shaped. The fragrant flowers have long, white stamens but are without petals or sepals. 2–4′ high. Swamps and along streams, R.I. to s. Mich. south. Summer. Lizard's Tail Family.

Continued

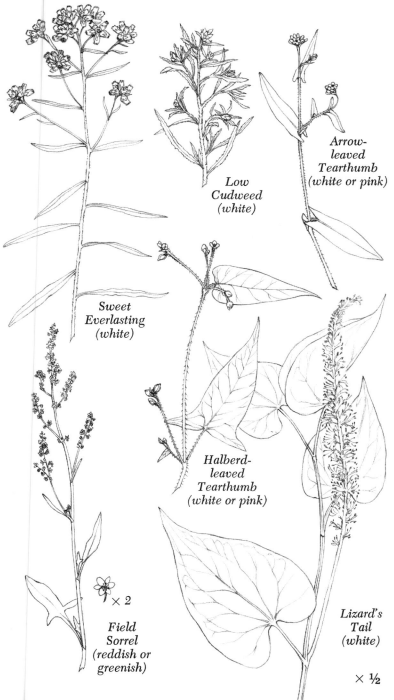

Low
Cudweed
(white)

Arrow-
leaved
Tearthumb
(white or pink)

Sweet
Everlasting
(white)

Halberd-
leaved
Tearthumb
(white or pink)

Lizard's
Tail
(white)

Field
Sorrel
*(reddish or
greenish)*

× 2

× ½

Stem Jointed; Leaves Not Arrow-shaped (cont.)

Docks (*Rumex*) Flowers distinctly stalked and growing in a series of whorls, which together form several branched racemes. Coarse, homely plants, often weeds, with numerous, small, drooping, green flowers. Fruit composed of 3 flat wings with one or more seedlike growths at the center. Stem grooved. 1–6' high. Late spring and summer. Buckwheat Family.

1. LEAF MARGINS WAVY

Bitter or **Broad-leaved Dock** (*R. obtusifolius*) * Lower leaves egg-shaped, mostly heart-shaped at the base, blunt, usually red-veined. Fruit with several spines on the edges of the wings. Waste places, roadsides, rich shade; common.

Curled Dock (*R. crispus*) * Lower leaves lance-shaped, pointed, with strongly curled margins; wings of fruit heart-shaped and entire or obscurely toothed. Weed of fields and waste places; common.

Golden Dock (*R. maritimus*) Lower leaves lance-shaped, often heart-shaped at the base; wings bearing several long bristles. Brackish marshes and shores, occasionally a weed in waste places.

2. LEAVES FLAT

White or **Seabeach Dock** (*R. pallidus*) Sprawling plant of brackish marshes and beaches; leaves with a whitish bloom, narrowly lance-shaped. Wings with wavy edges, narrow. South to Long I.

Swamp Dock (*R. verticillatus*) Plant of swamps and wet meadows; lower leaves lance-shaped, up to 1' long; wings of fruit entire, narrowed toward the tip.

Great Water Dock (*R. orbiculatus*) Plant of swamps and wet meadows; lower leaves 1–2' long; wings heart-shaped, entire or irregularly toothed. Stem stout. 3–6' high.

Jumpseed or **Virginia Knotweed** (*Tovara virginiana*) Flowers in slender, elongated spikes 4–12" long. See p. 130.

Knotweeds or **Smartweeds** (*Polygonum*) Flowers in spikes ½–4" long, or in the axils. See p. 190.

Bur Reeds (*Sparganium*) Whitish or greenish flowers in dense, round heads. See p. 410.

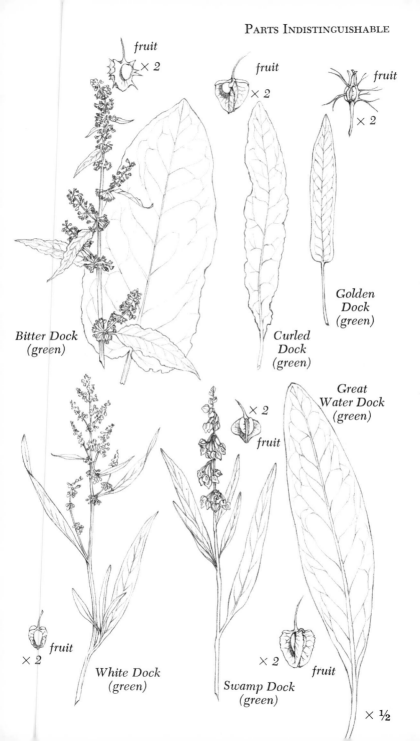

PARTS INDISTINGUISHABLE

fruit × 2

fruit × 2

fruit × 2

Bitter Dock (green)

Curled Dock (green)

Golden Dock (green)

Great Water Dock (green)

× 2
fruit

fruit × 2

× 2 *fruit*

White Dock (green)

Swamp Dock (green)

× 2 *fruit*

× ½

Stem neither White-woolly nor Jointed; Larger Leaves under 2″ Long; Flowers Growing Mostly in the Axils

PLANTS OF SALT MARSHES OR SEABEACHES

Seabeach Orach (*Atriplex arenaria*) Leaves oblong or oval, silvery-mealy. Green flowers. Fruit enclosed between two wedge-shaped, toothed bracts. Low and widely branched. Beaches along the coast, s. N.H. south. Late summer and fall. Goosefoot Family.

Common Saltwort (*Salsola kali*) Leaves prickly, thornlike. Green flowers. Loosely branched, 1–2′ high. A variety with less rigid and longer leaves, the Russian Thistle, is a troublesome weed of w. U.S., and is occasionally found in the East along roadsides and in waste places. Seabeaches. Summer and fall. Goosefoot Family.

Sea Blites (*Suaeda*) Leaves narrow, not prickly, flat on one surface, rounded on the other. Green flowers growing in the axils. Leaves fleshy. Salt marshes and seabeaches. Summer and fall. Goosefoot Family.

Low Sea Blite (*S. maritima*) Leaves pale green and usually whitened; plant low and spreading, rarely over 1′ high.

Tall Sea Blite (*S. linearis*) Leaves deep green, not whitened; plant erect or ascending, up to 3′ high. North to s. Me.

PLANTS OF WASTE PLACES, FIELDS OR ROCKS

Tumbleweed (*Amaranthus albus*) Weed of gardens and waste places. Leaves oblong or egg-shaped, rounded at the tip, the lower long-stalked. Flowers green and surrounded by bristly bracts. Stem whitish, bushy-branched, 6–30″ high. *A. graecizans*, a related species also called **Tumbleweed,** has a spreading, often prostrate, purplish stem. In the fall, the leafless plants of both species become uprooted and are tumbled about by the wind. Summer and fall. Amaranth Family.

Black Crowberry (*Empetrum nigrum*) Plant of rocky places and mountain summits; flowers purplish. See p. 126.

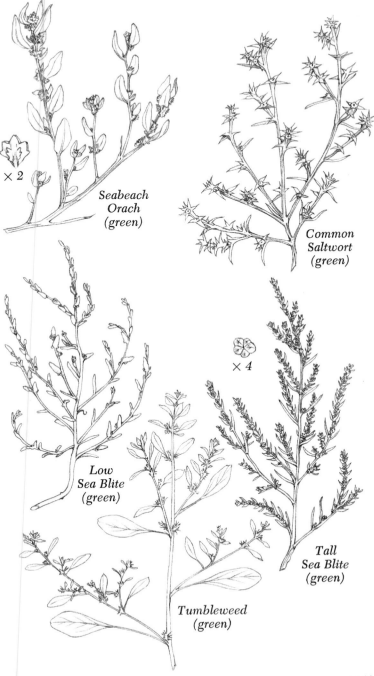

× 2

Seabeach
Orach
(green)

Common
Saltwort
(green)

× 4

Low
Sea Blite
(green)

Tall
Sea Blite
(green)

Tumbleweed
(green)

× ½

Stem neither White-woolly nor Jointed; Larger Leaves under 2″ Long; Flowers Mostly in Terminal Clusters

Spurges (*Euphorbia*) Plants with milky juice and yellowish or greenish flowers, mostly in a broad, terminal umbel. Uppermost leaves whorled or opposite. For other species, see pp. 202, 420 and 432. Weeds of roadsides and waste places. Spring to fall. Spurge Family.

> **Cypress Spurge** (*E. cyparissias*) * Leaves very narrow, numerous, under 1″ long. Flowers in an umbel. 6–12″ high. Especially common around old cemeteries.

> **Leafy Spurge** (*E. esula*) * Leaves narrowly lance-shaped or narrow, up to 3″ long, less crowded than in the previous species. 8–36″ high.

> **Petty Spurge** (*E. peplus*) * Larger leaves egg-shaped, with a blunt tip and short stalk. 6–12″ high.

Pinweeds (*Lechea*) Very small, greenish, reddish or brownish flowers in loose, branched clusters or short racemes; leaves narrow or oblong, ¼–1″ long. The flowers have 3 petals, but rarely open. In the fall, short, leafy shoots are developed from the base of the plant. Five other species occur in our area. Dry sandy or rocky soil in open places. Summer. Rockrose Family.

> **Narrow-leaved Pinweed** (*L. tenuifolia*) Leaves extremely narrow, both on the smoothish stem and along the basal shoots. 4–12″ high. S. Me. to Minn. south.

> **Hairy Pinweed** (*L. villosa*) Leaves oblong or lance-shaped on the stem, and smaller and broader on the basal shoots; stems hairy with spreading hairs. 6–30″ high. S. N.H. to Mich. south.

> **Intermediate Pinweed** (*L. intermedia*) Leaves narrowly lance-shaped on the stem and shoots, intermediate in size and shape between the two preceding species; hairs of the stem few and pressed against the stem. 8–24″ high.

Bearberry (*Arctostaphylos uva-ursi*) Trailing plant with white or pale-pink, bell-shaped flowers. See p. 198.

Milkworts (*Polygala*) Purple, greenish, white or orange flowers in dense heads or short spikes. See pp. 46, 48 and 72.

Horseweed (*Erigeron canadensis*) Whitish or greenish flowers in heads ⅛″ long; stem with bristly hairs. See p. 384.

Orach or **Spearscale** (*Atriplex patula*) Greenish flowers in interrupted spikes; leaves usually triangular. See p. 414.

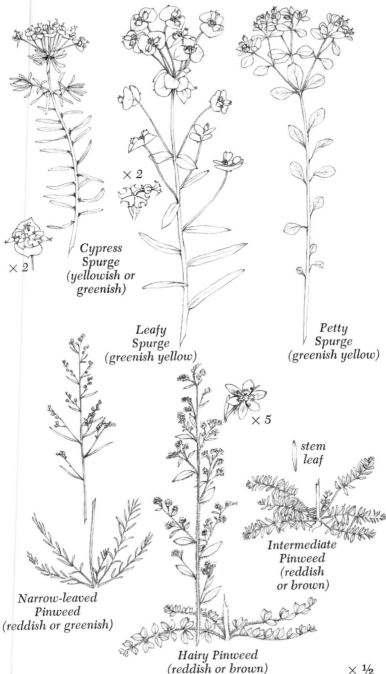

× 2

Cypress
Spurge
(yellowish or
greenish)

× 2

Leafy
Spurge
(greenish yellow)

Petty
Spurge
(greenish yellow)

× 5

stem
leaf

Intermediate
Pinweed
(reddish
or brown)

Narrow-leaved
Pinweed
(reddish or greenish)

Hairy Pinweed
(reddish or brown)

× ½

Leaves Very Narrow, the Larger Leaves over 1′ Long

Bur Reeds (*Sparganium*) Whitish or greenish flowers in dense, round heads. The upper heads bear the staminate flowers; the lower, pistillate heads develop into burlike fruits composed of numerous nutlets. Eight species occur in our area. 1–5′ high. Muddy shores and shallow water. Summer. Bur Reed Family.

1. LEAVES STRONGLY TRIANGULAR IN CROSS SECTION

Branching Bur Reed (*S. androcladum*) Leaves rather stiff and strongly ridged on the back, making them distinctly 3-sided. Nutlets taper on top and bear at the tip a pistil with 1 stigma. The branching of the flowering stalks occurs in all three species.

2. LEAVES FLAT OR ONLY SLIGHTLY TRIANGULAR IN CROSS SECTION

Great Bur Reed (*S. eurycarpum*) Frequently over 3′ high, with nearly flat, rather stiff leaves; nutlets broad and flat on top. Pistils with 2 stigmas.

Lesser Bur Reed (*S. americanum*) Usually under 3′ high; leaves flat and not stiff; nutlets tapering to both ends. Pistils with 1 stigma.

Cattails (*Typha*) Brownish flowers in dense, cylindrical spikes. The spike has two types of flowers — the upper half has staminate flowers, and the lower, pistillate flowers — and develops into the well-known cattail. 4–8′ high. Marshes. Summer. Cattail Family.

Common Cattail (*T. latifolia*) Leaves bluish- or grayish-green, nearly flat, up to 1″ wide. The upper and lower portions of the spike touch each other. Mature spike about 1″ in diameter. Common.

Narrow-leaved Cattail (*T. angustifolia*) Leaves green, rounded on the back, not over ½″ wide. The upper and lower parts of the spike are usually separated by a distinct gap. Mature spike about ½″ in diameter. Coastal species, less common inland.

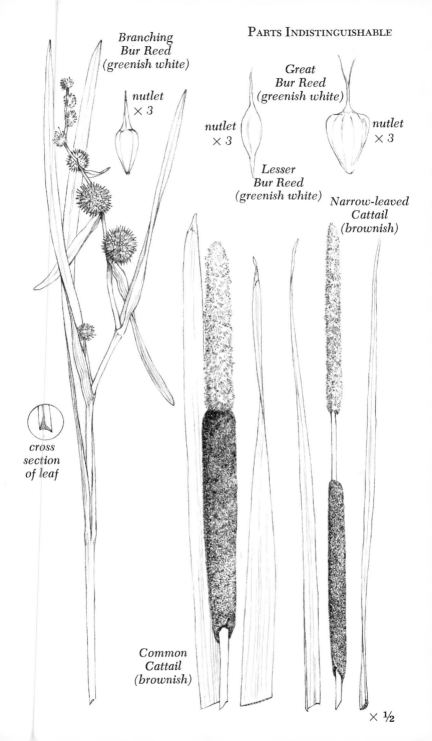

Branching
Bur Reed
(greenish white)

nutlet
× 3

PARTS INDISTINGUISHABLE

Great
Bur Reed
(greenish white)

nutlet
× 3

nutlet
× 3

Lesser
Bur Reed
(greenish white)

Narrow-leaved
Cattail
(brownish)

cross
section
of leaf

Common
Cattail
(brownish)

× ½

Stem neither White-woolly nor Jointed; Larger Leaves 2–12″ Long

PURPLE OR PINK FLOWERS

Burdocks (*Arctium*) Leaves egg-shaped, the lower ones usually heart-shaped, entire or somewhat toothed. Flowers in bristly heads, in fruit producing prickly, clinging burs. Coarse weeds of waste places. Summer and fall. Composite Family.

Common Burdock (*A. minus*) * Flower heads ½–1″ wide, stalkless or on short stalks. Leaf stalks hollow. 2–4′ high. Common.

Great Burdock (*A. lappa*) * Larger throughout, with flower heads 1–1½″ wide on long stalks. Leaf stalks solid and deeply grooved. 3–8′ high.

Blazing Stars (*Liatris*) Stem leaves narrow or lance-shaped; purple flowers in dense heads, arranged in a spikelike cluster (or sometimes solitary). There are 5–60 small, tubular, 5-lobed flowers in each head. Devil's Bit (p. 346) is also called Blazing Star. Summer and fall. Composite Family.

1. HEADS CYLINDRICAL, TWICE AS LONG AS WIDE

Spiked or **Dense Blazing Star** (*L. spicata*) Spikes dense, with the heads crowded and overlapping, rounded at base, mostly stalkless; lowest leaves usually over ½″ wide. Inside of flower tube smooth. 1–5′ high. Moist soil, N.J. to Mich. south.

Grass-leaved Blazing Star (*L. graminifolia*) Spike less dense than that of the Spiked Blazing Star; heads narrowed at the base, mostly stalked; lowest leaves under ½″ wide. Inside of flower tube soft-hairy. Very variable species. 1–3′ high. Dry soil, N.J. south.

2. HEADS BUTTON-SHAPED, NOT MORE THAN 1½ TIMES AS LONG AS WIDE

Northern Blazing Star (*L. borealis*) Upper bracts of flower head blunt, with narrow dark margin; heads noticeably stalked. 1–4′ high. Dry woods and clearings, sw. Me. to N.Y., south to N.J. and c. Pa.

Rough Blazing Star (*L. aspera*) Bracts of flower head broad, round, whitish-margined; heads short-stalked or stalkless. Stem stiffly erect. 1–4′ high. Dry open places, Ohio to N.D. south.

Scaly Blazing Star (*L. squarrosa*) Bracts of flower head pointed, spreading. 10–30″ high. Dry woods and fields, Del. to s. Ill. south.

Continued

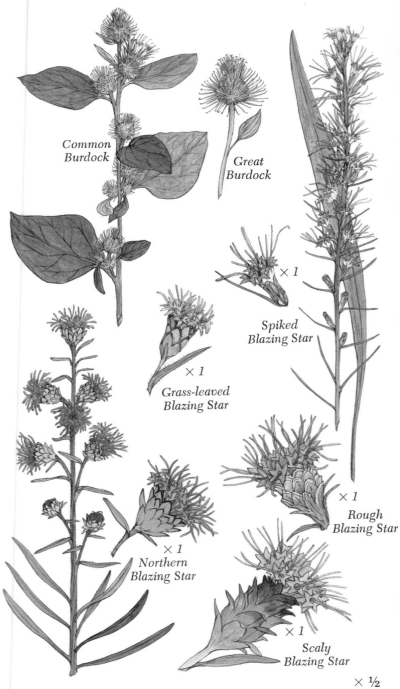

Common
Burdock

Great
Burdock

× 1

Spiked
Blazing Star

× 1

Grass-leaved
Blazing Star

× 1

Rough
Blazing Star

× 1

Northern
Blazing Star

× 1

Scaly
Blazing Star

× ½

Stem neither White-woolly nor Jointed; Larger Leaves
2–12″ Long (cont.)

GREEN, YELLOWISH OR YELLOW FLOWERS

Amaranths or **Pigweeds** (*Amaranthus*) Green flowers in bristly spikes. Leaves egg-shaped or lance-shaped, long-stalked, 2–6″ long. 1–6′ high. Weeds of gardens and waste places. For other species, see p. 406. Late summer and fall. Amaranth Family.

> **Green Amaranth** (*A. retroflexus*) * Flower spikes about ½″ wide, blunt, ½–2½″ long. Stem fine-hairy. Common.

> **Slender Amaranth** (*A. hybridus*) * Flower spikes about ⅜″ wide, the larger spikes more than 5 times longer than wide. Smoother and darker green than the Green Amaranth.

Orach or **Spearscale** (*Atriplex patula*) Green flowers in interrupted spikes; lower leaves usually opposite. Leaves most often triangular or broadly arrow-shaped, but may be lance-shaped or narrow, entire or slightly toothed. 1–3′ high. Commonly found in salt marshes, but also in waste places and inland in saline soil. Summer and fall. Goosefoot Family.

Salt-marsh Water Hemp (*Acnida cannabina*) Salt-marsh plant with green flowers in slender spikes; lower leaves alternate. Leaves lance-shaped, long-stalked. Spikes 1–5″ long. Stem fleshy. 1–10′ high. Salt marshes and tidal rivers, s. Me. south. Summer and fall. Amaranth Family.

Leafy Spurge (*Euphorbia esula*) Yellowish or greenish flowers, mostly in a terminal umbel; juice milky. See p. 408.

Goldenrods (*Solidago*) Numerous small yellow flowers in racemes or branching clusters. See pp. 446–453.

WHITE OR WHITISH FLOWERS

Tuberous Indian Plantain (*Cacalia tuberosa*) Heads of whitish flowers, ¼″ long, in a large, open, flattish, branching cluster. The basal and lower stem leaves are oval or egg-shaped, with 5–7 parallel veins, and taper to long stalks. 2–6′ high. Wet prairies and bogs, s. Ont. and Ohio to Minn. south. Summer. Composite Family.

Devil's Bit or **Blazing Star** (*Chamaelirium luteum*) Very small, white flowers in a slender, spikelike raceme. See p. 346.

False Solomon's Seal or **Wild Spikenard** (*Smilacina racemosa*) White flowers in a branched, pyramidal cluster. See p. 346.

Green
Amaranth
(green)

Slender
Amaranth
(green)

Orach
(green)

Salt-marsh
Water Hemp
(green)

Tuberous
Indian
Plantain
(whitish)

× ½

Flowers Growing Mostly in the Axils

Wood Nettle (*Laportea canadensis*) Coarse plant of wet or moist woods; stem bristly with *stinging* hairs. Leaves egg-shaped, coarsely toothed, 3–6″ long. The only nettle with alternate leaves. Flowers small and greenish, in loose, branching clusters. 1–4′ high. Summer. Nettle Family.

Three-seeded Mercury (*Acalypha rhomboidea*) Greenish flowers in tiny clusters, each cluster surrounded by a many-lobed, leaflike bract. Leaves long-stalked, egg-shaped, coarsely toothed, 1–3″ long. 3–24″ high. Fields, roadsides and waste places. Summer and fall. Spurge Family.

Clotburs or **Cockleburs** (*Xanthium*) Coarse plants of open places with rough stems and leaves. Greenish flowers of two kinds: the upper, staminate flowers in short spikes; the lower, pistillate flowers forming burs ½–¾″ long in the axils. Leaves long-stalked, broadly egg-shaped and coarsely toothed or lobed. About 15 species in our area, mainly differentiated by their burs. 1–3′ high. Summer and fall. Composite Family.

> **Beach Clotbur** (*X. echinatum*) Plant of seabeaches. The burs are hairy and have two stout beaks at the tip, which are strongly curved inward. Stem purple-blotched.

> **Common Clotbur** (*X. chinense*) Plant of farmlands, roadsides and waste places. The burs are nearly without hairs and the beaks are slender.

Water Pennywort (*Hydrocotyle americana*) Leaves roundly heart-shaped; a creeping plant of wet places. See p. 206.

Mermaid Weed (*Proserpinaca palustris*) Leaves lance-shaped, with numerous fine teeth or divided into narrow segments; grows in muddy places. See p. 122.

Goosefoots (*Chenopodium*) Flowers in small, dense clusters, forming interrupted spikes. See p. 422.

Yellow Flowers at the Ends of the Branches

Common Groundsel (*Senecio vulgaris*) * Golden-yellow flowers in heads ⅓–½″ long, clustered at the ends of the branches. Leaves deeply lobed. Black-tipped bracts cover the base of the flower heads. 4–20″ high. Weed of cultivated land and waste places. Spring to fall. Composite Family.

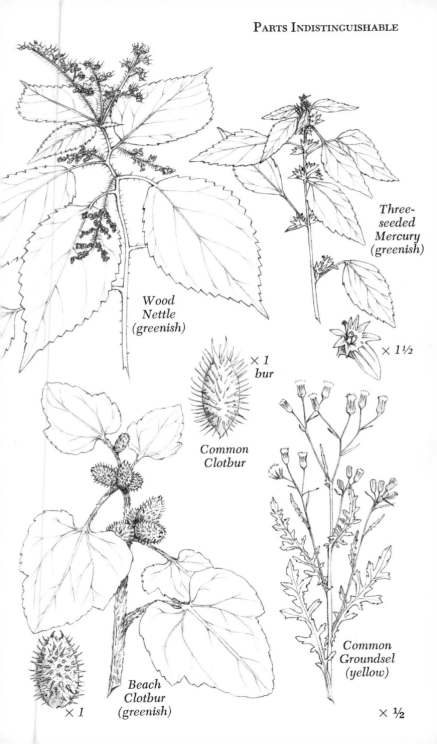

Wood
Nettle
(greenish)

Three-
seeded
Mercury
(greenish)

× 1½

× 1
bur

Common
Clotbur

Common
Groundsel
(yellow)

Beach
Clotbur
(greenish)

× 1

× ½

Purple or Pink Flowers in Heads

Thistles (*Cirsium* or *Carduus*) Leaves prickly. See p. 430.

Salt-marsh Fleabane (*Pluchea purpurascens*) Salt-marsh plant with purple or pink flowers in small heads about ¼″ long, growing in a flattish cluster. The leaves are lance-shaped or egg-shaped, sharply toothed. 1–4′ high. North to s. Me. Late summer and fall. Composite Family.

Knapweeds (*Centaurea*) Rose-purple flowers with fringed bracts covering the base of the flower head. See p. 210.

Ironweeds (*Vernonia*) Leaves lance-shaped, not prickly, with fine teeth; purple flowers in heads ½–¾″ wide. See p. 210.

Burdocks (*Arctium*) Leaves egg-shaped, the lower ones usually heart-shaped. See p. 412.

White or Greenish-white Flowers at the Ends of the Branches; Larger Leaves More Than Twice as Long as Wide

Pilewort or **Fireweed** (*Erechtites hieracifolia*) Greenish-white flowers in heads ½–¾″ long, swollen at the base and with a brush-like tip. A coarse, weedy plant with a smooth or hairy, grooved stem and shallowly or deeply toothed, lance-shaped or oblong leaves. 1–8′ high. Moist clearings and thickets, often on recently burned land. Summer and fall. Composite Family.

Rattlesnake Master or **Button Snakeroot** (*Eryngium yuccifolium*) White flowers in buttonlike heads ½–¾″ long. Lower leaves stiff, spiny-edged, parallel-veined, 6–36″ long, resembling the Yucca. *E. aquaticum* of bogs from N.J. south has feather-veined leaves and often bluish flowers. 2–5′ high. Woods and open places in wet or dry soil, s. Conn. to Minn. south. Summer. Parsley Family.

False Boneset (*Kuhnia eupatorioides*) White flowers in slender heads ⅓–½″ long, in a flattish cluster. Leaves slightly toothed or entire, and vary from narrow to broadly lance-shaped. 1–4′ high. Dry open woods and clearings, N.J. to Mont. south. Late summer and fall. Composite Family.

Horseweed (*Erigeron canadensis*) Flowers in very small heads ⅛″ long; stem usually with bristly hairs. See p. 384.

Mustard Family (Cruciferae) Tiny white flowers, mostly in racemes. See pp. 136 and 138.

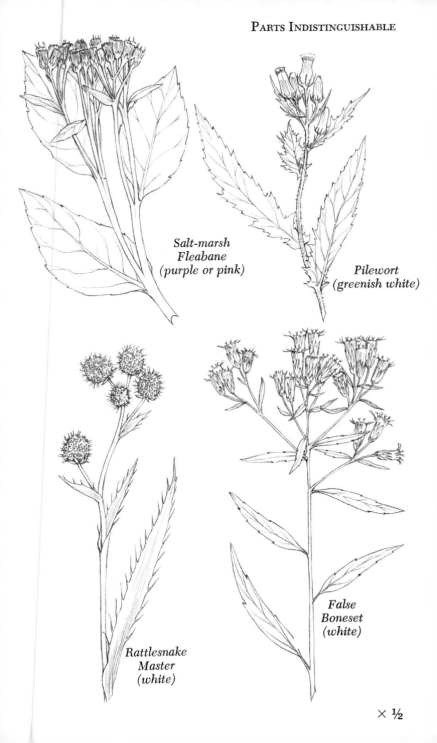

Salt-marsh
Fleabane
(purple or pink)

Pilewort
(greenish white)

Rattlesnake
Master
(white)

False
Boneset
(white)

× ½

White or Greenish-white Flowers at the Top of the Plant; Larger Leaves Broad, No More Than 1½ Times as Long as Wide

Goldenseal or **Orangeroot** (*Hydrastis canadensis*) Flower solitary, ½" wide, composed entirely of numerous, greenish-white stamens. Leaves 3, all deeply lobed; 2 stem leaves and 1 large basal leaf. Root yellow. 8–15" high. Rich woods, Vt. to Minn. south. Spring. Buttercup Family.

Tassel Rue or **False Bugbane** (*Trauvetteria carolinensis*) Flowers ½–¾" wide, with numerous, white stamens and in a flattish cluster. Basal leaves long-stalked, 6–8" broad, with 5–11 deep lobes. 2–3' high. Along streams, wooded hillsides, sw. Pa. to Mo. south. Early summer. Buttercup Family.

Indian Plantains (*Cacalia*) Erect whitish flowers in small heads, ¼–½" long, in flattish clusters. In each head are 5 or more 5-lobed flowers. Tuberous Indian Plantain (p. 414) has mostly entire leaves. Woods. Summer and fall. Composite Family.

Pale Indian Plantain (*C. atriplicifolia*) Basal leaves broad, lobed, pale beneath. Stem round, covered with a whitish bloom. 3–6' high. N.Y. to Minn. south.

Great Indian Plantain (*C. muhlenbergii*) Basal leaves roundish, coarsely toothed, green on both sides. Stem angled and grooved. 3–9' high. N.J. to Minn. south.

Sweet-scented Indian Plantain (*C. suaveolens*) Leaves triangular or broadly arrow-shaped, sharply toothed. Stem grooved. 3–5' high. Conn. to Iowa south.

Greenish or Reddish Flowers Mostly in Terminal Clusters

Wartweed or **Sun Spurge** (*Euphorbia helioscopia*) * Upper leaves opposite or whorled; juice milky. Below the many-branched cluster of green or tan flowers is a whorl of usually 5, finely-toothed, egg-shaped leaves with rounded tips. Lower leaves scattered along the stem. Stem smooth. 6–18" high. Waste places. Summer and fall. Spurge Family.

Orach or **Spearscale** (*Atriplex patula*) Leaves thick, fleshy, often triangular, the lower usually opposite. See p. 414.

Docks (*Rumex*) Stems jointed; leaves all alternate, unlobed. See p. 404.

Field Sorrel or **Sheep Sorrel** (*Rumex acetosella*) Stem jointed; leaves alternate, with 1 or 2 lobes at the base. See p. 402.

Continued

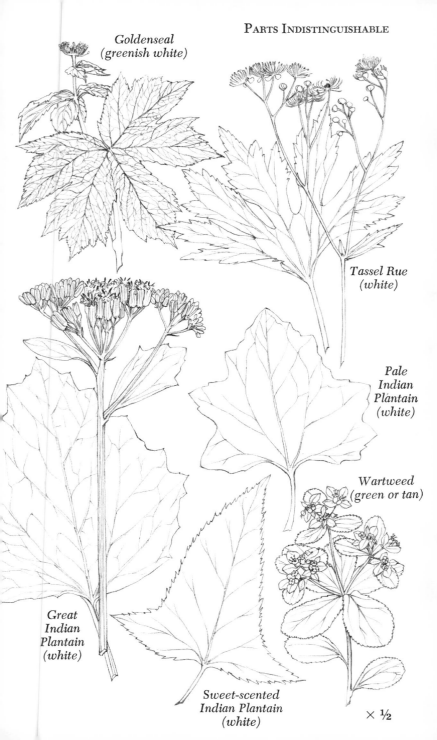

PARTS INDISTINGUISHABLE

Goldenseal
(greenish white)

Tassel Rue
(white)

*Pale
Indian
Plantain
(white)*

*Wartweed
(green or tan)*

*Great
Indian
Plantain
(white)*

*Sweet-scented
Indian Plantain
(white)*

× ½

Greenish or Reddish Flowers Mostly in Terminal Clusters (cont.)

Goosefoots (*Chenopodium*) Leaves all alternate; stems not jointed. Homely weeds with tiny flowers in many small, dense clusters or in interrupted spikes or in a branching terminal cluster. Summer and fall. Goosefoot Family.

1. LEAVES WHITISH OR GRAYISH BENEATH

Pigweed or **Lamb's Quarters** (*C. album*) * Larger leaves egg-shaped with a broad V-shaped base, irregularly toothed, 1–4″ long. Plant erect, ½–6′ high. Very common weed of gardens and waste places.

Oak-leaved Goosefoot (*C. glaucum*) * Larger leaves 1–2″ long, oblong with coarse, blunt teeth somewhat resembling those of an oak. Sprawling or prostrate weed of waste places, 6–18″ long.

2. LEAVES GREEN BOTH SIDES

a. Leaves aromatic

Mexican Tea (*C. ambrosioides*) * Larger leaves over 2″ long, lance-shaped, varying from wavy-toothed to deeply cut. Flower spikes leafy. 2–4′ high. Coarse, strong-scented weed of waste places.

Jerusalem Oak or **Feather Geranium** (*C. botrays*) * Leaves 1–2″ long, egg-shaped or oblong, deeply and irregularly lobed, the lobes having coarse, blunt teeth. Flower clusters nearly leafless. Sticky-hairy plant with odor of turpentine. 6–24″ high. Weed of roadsides and waste places.

b. Leaves not aromatic

Strawberry Blite (*C. capitatum*) Flowers in round heads ¼″ in diameter clustered along the upper stems. The heads become enlarged and bright red in fruit, resembling strawberries. Leaves somewhat triangular, with coarse teeth. 1–2′ high. Dry open soil.

Maple-leaved Goosefoot (*C. hybridum*) Flowers in a branching, nearly leafless, terminal cluster. Larger leaves broadly triangular with 2–6 large teeth and tapering tip. 1–5′ high. Woods and clearings.

Coast Blite (*C. rubrum*) Flowers in leafy, interrupted spikes, the spikes growing from the axils. Larger leaves egg-shaped, coarsely toothed. 12–30″ high. Plant of salt marshes south to N.J. and in saline places away from the coast.

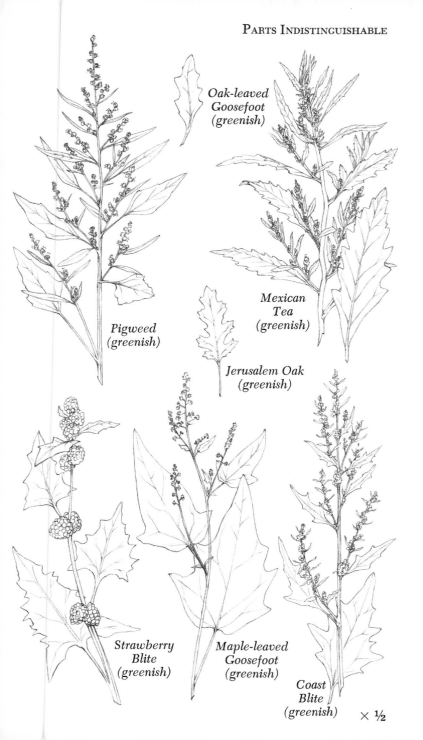

Oak-leaved
Goosefoot
(greenish)

Mexican
Tea
(greenish)

Pigweed
(greenish)

Jerusalem Oak
(greenish)

Strawberry
Blite
(greenish)

Maple-leaved
Goosefoot
(greenish)

Coast
Blite
(greenish) × ½

Leaves Divided into 3 or More Lance-shaped or Wider Leaflets; Flowers in Spikes, Racemes or Heads

LEAFLETS NUMEROUS

Baneberries (*Actaea*) Flowers in a single raceme 1–2″ long. Woodland plants notable for their showy berries. The 4–10 small, narrow, white petals are scarcely noticed due to the numerous, long, white stamens. Leaves wide-spreading and divided into many irregularly toothed, egg-shaped leaflets. 1–3 ft. high. Spring. Buttercup Family.

> **White Baneberry** or **Doll's Eyes** (*A. pachypoda*) Individual flower stalks rather thick and the raceme usually longer than wide. The berries are china-white with a conspicuous purplish eye and have thick, fleshy stalks. Occasionally red-berried forms with thick stalks are found.

> **Red Baneberry** (*A. rubra*) Flower stalks slender; raceme usually about as wide as long. The red (rarely white) berries are on slender stalks.

Bugbanes (*Cimicifuga*) Flowers in 1 or several racemes 6″ or more long; found in woods. Tall plants with large leaves divided into numerous egg-shaped or oblong, sharply toothed leaflets. The white flowers appear to be all stamens since the petals are tiny and the sepals fall quickly. 3–8′ high. Buttercup Family.

> **Black Snakeroot** or **Black Cohosh** (*C. racemosa*) Flowers ill-scented; blooms from late June to August. The single pistil has a broad stigma. W. Mass. to s. Ont. south.

> **American Bugbane** (*C. americana*) Flowers not ill-scented; flowering from late August into September. Pistils 3 or more, with practically no stigmas. Pa. south, in the mts.

Canadian Burnet (*Sanguisorba canadensis*) Flowers white, in dense spikes; grows in low meadows and bogs. See p. 146.

Goatsbeard (*Aruncus dioicus*) Flowers in numerous, 2–3″ spikes, which form a large, branched cluster. See p. 218.

LEAFLETS 3

Rabbit-foot Clover (*Trifolium arvense*) Flowers grayish-pink or grayish-white, in furry heads. See p. 60.

Black Medick (*Medicago lupulina*) Yellow flowers; leaflets tipped with a short bristle. See p. 58.

Hop or **Yellow Clovers** (*Trifolium*) Yellow flowers; leaflets not bristle-tipped. See p. 58.

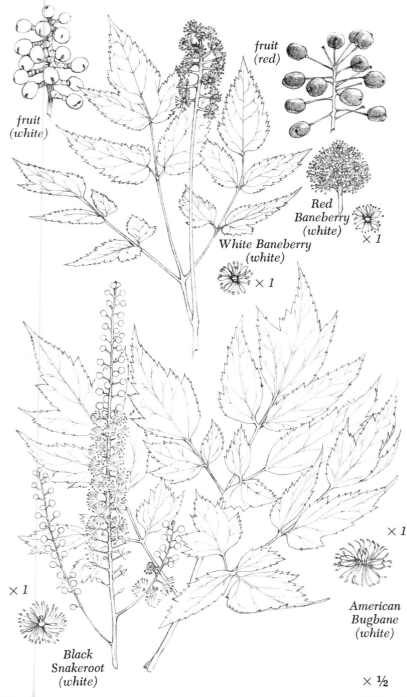

fruit
(white)

fruit
(red)

Red
Baneberry
(white)

× 1

White Baneberry
(white)

× 1

× 1

American
Bugbane
(white)

× 1

Black
Snakeroot
(white)

× ½

Leaves Divided into 3 or More Lance-shaped or Wider Leaflets; Flowers in Umbels or Branching Clusters

Sanicles or **Black Snakeroots** (*Sanicula*) Leaves palmately divided into 3–7 leaflets; uppermost leaves or bracts opposite. The fruits are small, bristly burs. 1–4' high. Dry or moist woods. Late spring and summer. Parsley Family.

1. GREENISH-YELLOW FLOWERS

Clustered Snakeroot (*S. gregaria*) Leaves with usually 5 leaflets. Fruit stalked. Rich woods.

2. GREENISH OR WHITISH FLOWERS

Sanicle or **Black Snakeroot** (*S. marilandica*) Larger leaves with 5 leaflets, the side leaflets so deeply cleft there seem to be 7. Fruit stalkless. The commonest species.

Short-styled Snakeroot (*S. canadensis*) Leaflets 3, two of them deeply cleft; staminate flowers no longer than the pistillate flowers (burs). Fruits roundish. Widely branched. S. and w. N.Eng. to Minn. south.

Long-fruited Snakeroot (*S. trifoliata*) Leaflets 3, uncleft or less deeply cleft and wider than those of *S. canadensis;* staminate flowers on long stalks above the pistillate flowers. Fruits longer than wide.

Meadow Rues (*Thalictrum*) Leaflets roundish, with 2–9 short, blunt lobes. See p. 146.

Spikenard (*Aralia racemosa*) Leaflets heart-shaped at the base; flower cluster longer than wide. See p. 224.

Parsley Family (Umbelliferae) Flowers in broad umbels or in few-flowered clusters. See pp. 218 and 222–226.

Leaves Deeply and Irregularly Lobed or Divided into Narrow Segments; Leaves Not Prickly

YELLOW, YELLOWISH OR GREEN FLOWERS

Tansy (*Tanacetum vulgare*) * Yellow flowers in a broad, flat-topped cluster of buttonlike heads. An old-fashioned garden flower that is now a common weed of roadsides and vacant city lots. Leaves deeply cut into fine divisions and strongly aromatic. 1–4' high. Summer and fall. Composite Family.

Pineapple Weed (*Matricaria matricarioides*) * Yellow flowers in heads ¼" wide; low sprawling plant with pineapple odor when bruised. Flower heads at ends of branches. Barnyards, roadsides and fields. Summer and fall. Composite Family. Continued

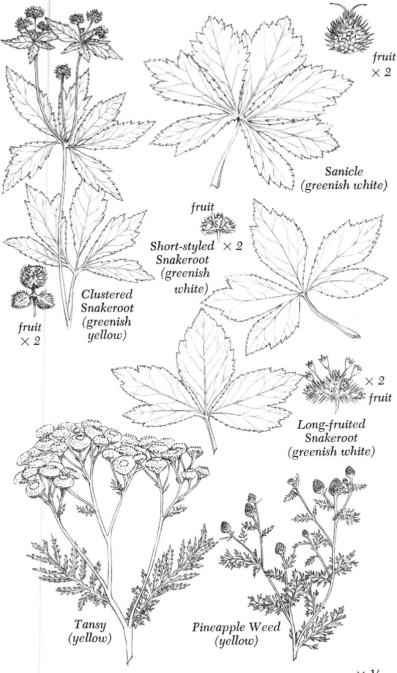

fruit
× 2

Sanicle
(greenish white)

fruit

Short-styled × 2
Snakeroot
(greenish
white)

Clustered
Snakeroot
(greenish
yellow)

fruit
× 2

× 2
fruit

Long-fruited
Snakeroot
(greenish white)

Tansy
(yellow)

Pineapple Weed
(yellow)

× ½

Leaves Deeply and Irregularly Lobed or Divided into Narrow Segments; Leaves Not Prickly (cont.)

YELLOW, YELLOWISH OR GREEN FLOWERS (CONT.)

Common Ragweed (*Ambrosia artemisiifolia*) Green flowers, the small flower heads growing in leafless racemes; lower stem leaves usually opposite. See p. 438.

Wormwoods (*Artemisia*) Green or yellowish flowers, the flower heads in leafy spikes or clusters. Plants with deeply lobed or finely divided, aromatic leaves found in dry soil. 1–8′ high. At least 10 other species are found locally in our area. Summer and fall. Composite Family.

1. LEAVES DENSELY WHITE-WOOLLY, AT LEAST BENEATH

Beach Wormwood or **Dusty Miller** (*A. stelleriana*) * Flower heads ¼″ wide; leaves bluntly lobed, white-woolly on both sides. Often cultivated for its white foliage; now escaped to sandy beaches and dunes along the coast and on large inland lakes. 1–2½′ high.

Common Mugwort (*A. vulgaris*) * Flower heads about ⅛″ wide; leaves with pointed lobes, white-woolly beneath. Waste places.

2. LEAVES NOT WHITE-WOOLLY

Tall Wormwood (*A. caudata*) Flower heads very small, mostly nodding, in long clusters that extend beyond the surrounding leaves. Leaf divisions very narrow. Biennial, forming an overwintering rosette of basal leaves. Dry sandy soil, especially on seabeaches.

Biennial Wormwood (*A. biennis*) * Flower heads erect, in axillary clusters or spikes shorter than the surrounding leaves. Roadsides and waste places.

WHITE, PURPLE OR PINK FLOWERS

Spotted Knapweed (*Centaurea maculosa*) White, purple or pink flowers in thistlelike heads; the bases of the flower heads are covered with black-fringed bracts. See p. 234.

Pilewort or **Fireweed** (*Erechtites hieracifolia*) Whitish flowers in heads, the bracts of the heads green. See p. 418.

Parsley Family (Umbelliferae) Very small, white flowers in broad umbels. See p. 220.

Mustard Family (Cruciferae) Tiny white flowers, mostly in racemes. See p. 150.

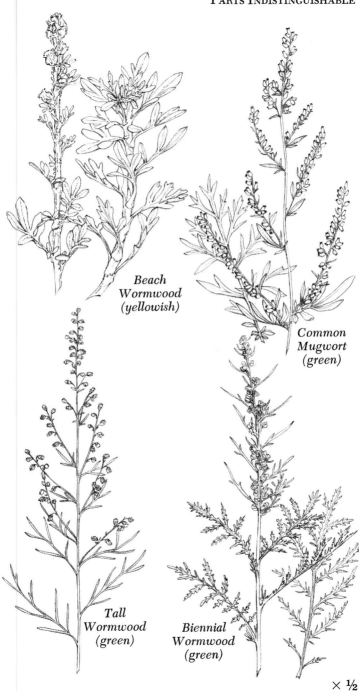

*Beach
Wormwood
(yellowish)*

*Common
Mugwort
(green)*

*Tall
Wormwood
(green)*

*Biennial
Wormwood
(green)*

$\times$ 1/2

Plants with Prickly, Deeply Lobed Leaves; Flowers in Large Heads

Thistles (*Cirsium* or *Carduus*) A group of plants well known because of their spiny leaves and large flower heads of purple (rarely white), or in one species yellow, flowers. Most of our species are biennials, forming a rosette of prickly leaves that overwinter the first year. Summer and fall. Composite Family.

1. FLOWER HEADS 1″ OR LESS HIGH

Canada Thistle (*Cirsium arvense*) * A bad weed of pastures and waste places, difficult to eradicate because of its creeping underground stems. The small, numerous flower heads are purple or occasionally white. 1–3′ high.

2. FLOWER HEADS 1½–2″ HIGH; LEAVES WHITE-WOOLLY BENEATH

Tall Thistle (*Cirsium altissimum*) Most of the leaves merely toothed, only a few of the lowest leaves sometimes deeply lobed like those of the other thistles. Tall plant (3–10′) of thickets and rich soil, s. N.Y. to Minn. south.

Field Thistle (*Cirsium discolor*) Leaves deeply cut, their undersides covered with a white felt. 3–7′ high. Fields and roadsides.

3. FLOWER HEADS 1½–2½″ HIGH; LEAVES NOT WHITE-WOOLLY BENEATH

a. *Stems prickly below the leaves*

Bull Thistle (*Cirsium vulgare*) * Heads at the ends of prickly branches. A very prickly, common thistle of pastures and waste places. 3–6′ high.

Musk or **Nodding Thistle** (*Carduus nutans*) *† Similar to Bull Thistle but heads nodding, on long, mostly naked stalks. 1–6′ high. Roadsides and waste places.

b. *Stems not prickly; flowers purple or yellow*

Pasture Thistle (*Cirsium pumilum*) Flower heads large and fragrant; grows in dry pastures and fields. Flowers purple. Stem hairy. 1–3′ high. Me. to Ohio, south to Del. and Md. and inland to N.C.

Swamp Thistle (*Cirsium muticum*) Base of flower head cobwebby with fine white hairs; grows in wet swampy places. Flowers purple. 3–9′ high. Common.

Yellow Thistle (*Cirsium horridulum*) Base of flower head closely surrounded by erect, spiny leaves; yellow (rarely purple) flowers. Fields, meadows, borders of salt marshes, s. Me. south along the coast.

Canada
Thistle

Tall
Thistle

Field
Thistle

Pasture
Thistle

Yellow
Thistle

Bull
Thistle

Swamp
Thistle

× 2/5

PLANTS WITH MILKY JUICE

Spotted Spurges (*Euphorbia*) Flowers growing mostly in the axils. Unattractive plants with often red-blotched leaves and stems, and insignificant whitish, green or reddish flowers scattered in the upper axils or at the ends of the branches. Leaves entire or very finely toothed, ¼–1½" long. Summer and fall. Spurge Family.

> **Milk Purslane** (*E. supina*) Prostrate weed of gardens and waste places, often growing out of cracks in concrete sidewalks. Stems hairy, spreading on the ground in several directions. Common.

> **Seaside Spurge** (*E. polygonifolia*) Sprawling plant of sandy beaches. Stem smooth, often red. Atlantic coast and Great Lakes.

> **Eyebane** or **Upright Spotted Spurge** (*E. maculata*) Plant more or less erect with a stem up to 2½' high. Dry fields and roadsides.

Spurges (*Euphorbia*) Flowers in terminal clusters; lower leaves alternate. See p. 408.

JUICE NOT MILKY

Knawel (*Scleranthus annuus*) * Low, spreading plant with tiny green flowers at the ends of the branches and in the upper axils; even the upper leaves are opposite. The cup-shaped calyx has 5 green lobes with narrow white margins; petals absent. Leaves very narrow, pointed, ¼–1" long. 1–5" high. Dry sandy soil, waste places. Spring to fall. Pink Family.

Hyssop-leaved Boneset (*Eupatorium hyssopifolium*) White flowers in a flattish-topped terminal cluster. The leaves are narrow, sometimes slightly toothed, and mostly occur in whorls of 3 or 4, with clusters of smaller leaves growing in the axils. 1–3' high. Dry sandy fields and open woods, Mass. to Pa. and s. Ohio south. Late summer and fall. Composite Family.

Milkworts (*Polygala*) Flowers in dense heads or spikes. See p. 72.

Pinweeds (*Lechea*) Tiny, reddish, brownish or greenish flowers in loose clusters or short racemes; upper leaves alternate; leaves under 1" long. See p. 408.

Orach or **Spearscale** (*Atriplex patula*) Greenish flowers in interrupted spikes; upper leaves usually alternate; larger leaves over 1" long. See p. 414.

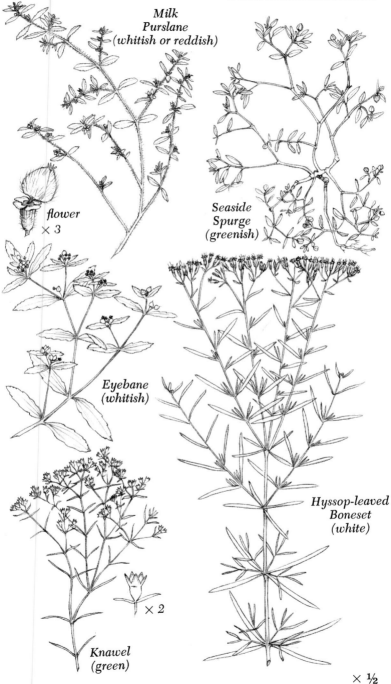

Milk
Purslane
(whitish or reddish)

flower
× 3

Seaside
Spurge
(greenish)

Eyebane
(whitish)

Hyssop-leaved
Boneset
(white)

× 2

Knawel
(green)

× ½

White Flowers in Broad, Branching Clusters

Bonesets or **Thoroughworts** (*Eupatorium*) Mostly tall, erect plants, branching at the top of the stem. The flowers are in small heads, together forming a broad, often flat cluster. The species described below are the most widely distributed. Summer and fall. Composite Family.

1. LOWER LEAVES BROADEST AT THE BASE AND UNITED
   TOGETHER TO FORM A SINGLE LEAF

   Boneset or **Thoroughwort** (*E. perfoliatum*) A common plant of low ground, readily recognized by its distinctive pierced leaves. Stem hairy. 2–5′ high. Flowers grayish-white. Leaves taper-pointed.

2. LOWER LEAVES STALKLESS OR NEARLY SO

a. Leaves bearing a few small teeth

   Tall Boneset (*E. altissimum*) Leaves 2–5″ long, lance-shaped and tapering at both ends, and with 3 prominent veins. Stem leafy. 2½–6′ high. Open woods and prairies, Pa. to Minn. south.

   White-bracted Boneset (*E. leucolepis*) Leaves 1–3″ long, in pairs, narrowly lance-shaped, with 3 obscure veins. Wet sandy or peaty soil near the coast, Mass. south.

   Hyssop-leaved Boneset (*E. hyssopifolium*) Leaves very narrow, mostly in whorls of 3 or 4. See p. 432.

b. Leaves coarsely toothed or with numerous small teeth

   Upland Boneset (*E. sessilifolium*) Stem and leaves smooth; leaves lance-shaped, tapering to a long point and finely toothed. 2–6′ high. Rich woods, s. N.H. to s. Minn. south.

   Rough Boneset (*E. pilosum*) Stem hairy; larger leaves oblong, bluntish, with 3–12 coarse teeth on each margin. Upper leaves nearly entire. 3–5′ high. Wet or moist open places, s. N.Eng. south.

   Hairy Boneset (*E. pubescens*) Stem hairy; larger leaves egg-shaped or oblong, more pointed than those of Rough Boneset, with 12–25 sharp teeth on each margin. Upper leaves toothed. 2–5′ high. Dry open woods and clearings, s. Me. to s. Ohio south.

   Round-leaved Boneset (*E. rotundifolium*) Like Hairy Boneset, but leaves smaller, teeth fewer and blunt.

   White Boneset (*E. album*) Stem hairy or downy; leaves lance-shaped, rather coarsely toothed. 1–3′ high. Dry sandy woods, Long I. to s. Ohio south.

Continued

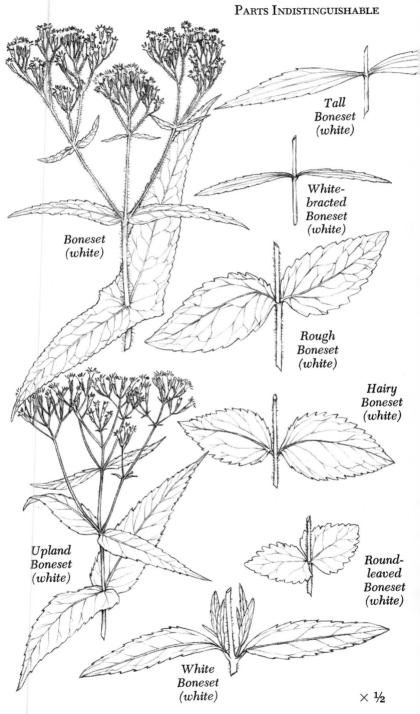

Tall
Boneset
(white)

White-
bracted
Boneset
(white)

Boneset
(white)

Rough
Boneset
(white)

Hairy
Boneset
(white)

Upland
Boneset
(white)

Round-
leaved
Boneset
(white)

White
Boneset
(white)

× ½

White Flowers in Broad, Branching Clusters (cont.)

Bonesets or **Thoroughworts** (*Eupatorium*) (cont.)

3. LOWER LEAVES DEFINITELY STALKED

White Snakeroot (*E. rugosum*) Lower leaves broadly egg-shaped, long-pointed, with stalks ¾" or more long. Flowers bright white, in heads about as broad as high. 1–5' high. Rich woods.

Smaller White Snakeroot (*E. aromaticum*) Like the White Snakeroot but leaves shorter-stalked, short-pointed and thickish. Open woods, Mass. to s. Ohio south.

Late-flowering Boneset (*E. serotinum*) Lower leaves broadly lance-shaped; uppermost leaves usually alternate. Flower heads longer than wide. Thickets and clearings, N.J. to Wis. south; occasionally north to Mass.

Pink, Blue, Violet or Purple Flowers, in Broad Clusters

Joe-Pye Weeds (*Eupatorium*) Leaves in whorls of 3–7. Tall, robust plants with purple or pink flowers in a large branching cluster of small cylindrical heads. 3–10' high. Summer and fall. Composite Family.

1. FLOWER CLUSTER FLATTISH ON TOP

Spotted Joe-Pye Weed (*E. maculatum*) Stem deep purple or purple-spotted; leaves with a single main vein and tapering gradually to the base. Common inland in damp meadows and thickets.

2. FLOWER CLUSTER ROUNDED OR DOMED ON TOP

Eastern Joe-Pye Weed (*E. dubium*) Stem finely spotted with purple; leaves with 3 main veins (the lower pair extending halfway up the leaf), narrowed abruptly at the base. Swamps and thickets, near the coast.

Trumpetweed (*E. fistulosum*) Stem very tall, hollow and covered with a whitish bloom. Leaves with a single main vein, and teeth blunter than the other species of Joe-Pye Weeds. Moist open places.

Sweet-scented Joe-Pye Weed (*E. purpureum*) Stem solid, purple at joints; rich woods. Vanilla-scented when bruised. Flowers pale pink. S. N.H. to Minn. south.

Mistflower (*Eupatorium coelestinum*) Leaves in pairs. Flowers blue or violet, resembling the garden Ageratum. Leaves triangular, long-stalked. 1–3' high. Moist woods, thickets, N.J. to Ill. south. Late summer to fall. Composite Family.

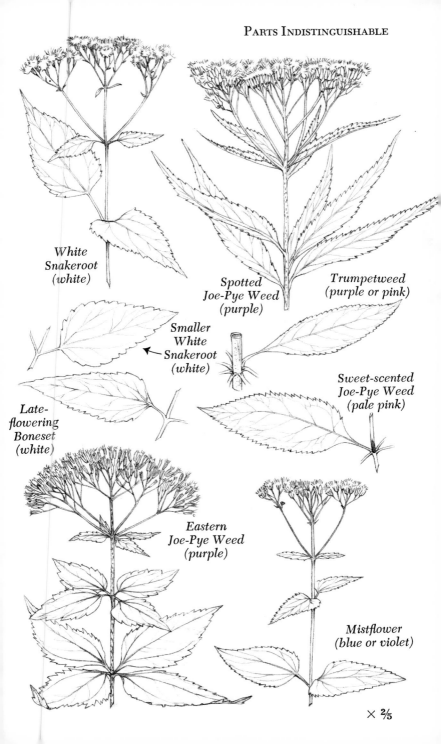

White
Snakeroot
(white)

Spotted
Joe-Pye Weed
(purple)

Trumpetweed
(purple or pink)

Smaller
White
Snakeroot
(white)

Late-
flowering
Boneset
(white)

Sweet-scented
Joe-Pye Weed
(pale pink)

Eastern
Joe-Pye Weed
(purple)

Mistflower
(blue or violet)

× 2/5

Flowers Mostly in Terminal Racemes or Spikes

Ragweeds (*Ambrosia*) Green flowers in racemes. Leaves with 3–5 deep lobes or divided into narrow segments (rarely entire). Unattractive weeds whose pollen is a principal cause of hay fever. Summer and fall. Composite Family.

Common Ragweed (*A. artemisiifolia*) Leaves opposite or alternate, divided into narrow segments, the segments irregularly toothed or lobed. Staminate flower heads in racemes 1–6″ long; pistillate in small clusters. 1–6′ high. Very common weed of cultivated ground and roadsides.

Great Ragweed (*A. trifida*) Leaves with 3–5 deep lobes or rarely entire. 3–15′ high. Moist open grounds. Common, except in N.Eng.

Dwarf Enchanter's Nightshade (*Circaea alpina*) Small, white flowers in racemes; plant under 1′ high. See p. 116.

Flowers Growing Mostly in the Axils

Nettles (*Urtica*) Greenish flowers in slender, spreading or drooping clusters; stem bearing a few to many bristly, *stinging* hairs. Coarse weeds of thickets and waste places. Summer and fall. Nettle Family.

Stinging Nettle (*U. dioica*) * Stem densely covered with stiff, bristly, stinging hairs. Leaves egg-shaped, with a heart-shaped base, coarsely toothed. 1–3′ high.

Tall Nettle (*U. procera*) Stem with only a few bristly, stinging hairs. Leaves lance-shaped or narrowly egg-shaped, rounded or slightly heart-shaped at the base. 2–9′ high.

Clearweed or **Richweed** (*Pilea pumila*) Flowers in branching clusters; stem fleshy and translucent, very smooth, usually under 1′ high. Leaves long-stalked, egg-shaped and coarsely toothed. A low plant with whitish or greenish flowers. Moist shady places. Summer and fall. Nettle Family.

False Nettle (*Boehmeria cylindrica*) Flowers in stiff, unbranched, continuous or interrupted spikes; stem neither bristly nor translucent; 1–3′ high. Does not have stinging hairs like the true nettles. The spikes of greenish flowers are often leafy at the tip. Leaves egg-shaped, coarsely toothed. Moist or boggy places. Summer and fall. Nettle Family.

Continued

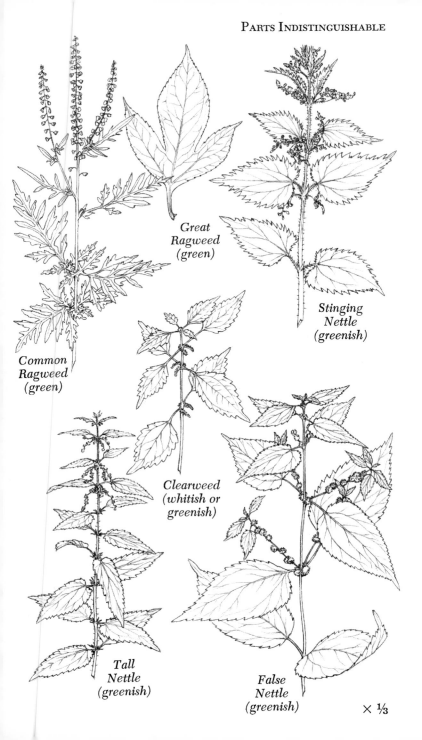

Great
Ragweed
(green)

Stinging
Nettle
(greenish)

Common
Ragweed
(green)

Clearweed
(whitish or
greenish)

Tall
Nettle
(greenish)

False
Nettle
(greenish)

× ⅓

Flowers Growing Mostly in the Axils (cont.)

Mint Family (Labiatae) White, pink or purplish flowers in dense whorls around the main stem; stem square. See p. 90.

Spotted Spurges (*Euphorbia*) Insignificant whitish, greenish or reddish flowers, 1 to few in a cluster; leaves very finely or obscurely toothed; juice milky. See p. 432.

Flowers in Heads, Not in Broad Clusters

Bur Marigolds or **Beggar Ticks** (*Bidens*) Yellowish, orange or greenish flowers in small heads; leaves or leaflets lance-shaped. Weedy plants with 2–4-pronged barbed fruits (achenes) that cling to clothing. Heads sometimes with a few, small, yellow rays. For other species, see pp. 392 and 394. Late summer and fall. Composite Family.

1. LEAVES TOOTHED, NOT DIVIDED INTO LEAFLETS

Nodding Bur Marigold (*B. cernua*) Leaves without stalks; heads nodding in fruit. See p. 392.

Swamp Beggar Ticks (*B. connata*) Leaves stalked, lance-shaped, coarsely toothed, sometimes lobed at the base; heads erect in fruit. 1–4′ high. Wet places.

2. LEAVES DIVIDED INTO 3–5 LEAFLETS, WHICH ARE REGULARLY TOOTHED, NOT LOBED

Beggar Ticks or **Sticktight** (*B. frondosa*) Each flower head surrounded by 5–9 narrow, leaflike bracts; center of flower head orange. Wet or dry waste places.

Tall Beggar Ticks (*B. vulgata*) † Very similar to the Beggar Ticks, but 10–20 bracts surround the pale-yellow flower head. 1–4′ high.

3. LEAVES DIVIDED INTO LEAFLETS, THE LEAFLETS IRREGULARLY TOOTHED AND LOBED

Spanish Needles (*B. bipinnata*) Flower head longer and slenderer than the other species. Stem square. 1–3′ high. In dry or rocky situations or as a weed in cultivated fields. Mass. to Ill. south.

Small-flowered Leafcup (*Polymnia canadensis*) Yellowish or whitish flowers in small heads; leaves large, angularly lobed. See p. 278.

Teasel (*Dipsacus sylvestris*) Lilac flowers in a large, thistlelike head. See p. 160.

Swamp
Beggar Ticks
(greenish yellow)

fruit
× 2

Spanish
Needles
(greenish yellow)

fruit
× 2

Beggar Ticks
(greenish yellow)

fruit
× 2

× ½

FLOWERING IN EARLY SPRING

Leatherwood or **Wicopy** (*Dirca palustris*) Pale-yellow, funnel- or bell-shaped flowers, about ⅓″ long, the stamens protruding. Blooms in early spring before the alternate, egg-shaped or oval leaves develop. Bark very tough, used by the Indians for thongs. Fruit oval, red, about ½″ long. 2–6′ high. Rich or damp woods. Mezereum Family.

Spicebush (*Lindera benzoin*) Yellow flowers about ⅛″ wide with 6-parted calyx and no petals. Blooms in early spring before the leaves appear. Leaves alternate, entire and egg-shaped or oval. Twigs fragrant when bruised. Fruit bright red. 3–15′ high. Damp woods and along streams. Laurel Family.

Broom Crowberry (*Corema conradii*) Flowers in small, terminal heads with conspicuous purple stamens when in bloom. Leaves very narrow, about ¼″ long, evergreen. Low, branching shrub, 6–24″ high. Sandy or rocky soil along the coast, N.S. to Mass.; N.J. pine barrens; Shawangunk Mts., N.Y. Spring. Crowberry Family.

FLOWERING IN SUMMER AND FALL

Groundsel Tree (*Baccharis halimifolia*) Whitish flowers in small heads; blooms in the fall. Staminate and pistillate flowers on separate plants. Leaves are alternate, egg-shaped, and usually coarsely toothed, but sometimes the upper ones are entire. 3–10′ high. Conspicuous in late fall by the silky-white hairs appearing when the pistillate heads mature. Open woods and thickets, Mass. south along the coast. Composite Family.

Marsh Elder or **Highwater Shrub** (*Iva frutescens*) Greenish, nodding flower heads in leafy spikes. The leaves are opposite, toothed and somewhat fleshy. 2–10′ high. Coastal salt marshes and seashores, N.S. south. Late summer and fall. Composite Family.

New Jersey Tea (*Ceanothus americanus*) Small, white flowers in short, dense clusters; leaves alternate; blooms in summer. See p. 310.

Black Crowberry (*Empetrum nigrum*) Purplish flowers in the axils. See p. 126.

Wild Hydrangea (*Hydrangea arborescens*) White flowers in broad, branching clusters; leaves opposite; blooms in early summer. See p. 302.

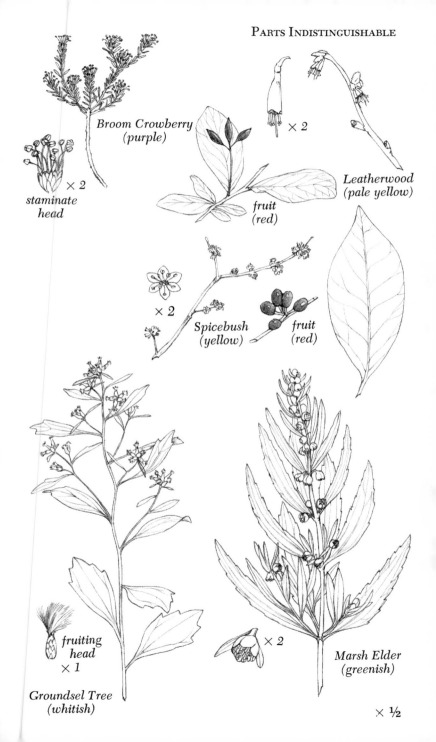

Broom Crowberry
(purple)

× 2
staminate
head

fruit
(red)

× 2

Leatherwood
(pale yellow)

× 2

Spicebush
(yellow)

fruit
(red)

fruiting
head
× 1

Groundsel Tree
(whitish)

× 2

Marsh Elder
(greenish)

× ½

WOODY VINES CLINGING BY TENDRILS

Grapes (*Vitis*) Leaves broad and deeply heart-shaped at the base. Stems high-climbing; flowers small, greenish, in branched clusters. Late spring and early summer. Grape Family.

1. UNDERSIDE OF LEAVES HAIRY, COVERED WITH MATTED WOOL OR WHITENED BENEATH

Fox Grape (*V. labrusca*) A tendril or flower cluster opposite most of the leaves (unlike the next species, which usually has nothing opposite every third leaf). Leaves with low teeth and usually with 3 shallow lobes. Fruit purplish, musky, about ¾" in diameter. Dry or moist thickets, s. Me. to Mich. south.

Summer Grape (*V. aestivalis*) No tendril or flower cluster opposite every third leaf. Most leaves with 3–5 lobes. Fruit black, acid, ¼–½" in diameter. Dry woods and thickets, N.H. to s. Minn. south.

2. UNDERSIDE OF LEAVES GREEN, AND SMOOTH OR NEARLY SO

Riverbank Grape (*V. riparia*) Leaves sharply 3-lobed, coarsely and sharply toothed. Fruit bluish-black, with bloom, sweet after frost. Riverbanks and bottomlands.

Frost Grape (*V. vulpina*) Like the Riverbank Grape, but leaves unlobed or slightly 3-lobed. Fruit black and shining, sweet after frost. S. N.Y. to Ill. south.

Virginia Creeper or **Woodbine** (*Parthenocissus quinquefolia*) Leaves divided into 5 coarsely toothed leaflets. Small whitish or greenish flowers in branching clusters. Fruit a bluish-black berry. Tendrils ending in disks. The similar *P. inserta* has tendrils without disks. Summer. Grape Family.

VINES WITHOUT TENDRILS

Climbing Hempweed or **Climbing Boneset** (*Mikania scandens*) White or pink flower heads in branching clusters; leaves opposite. The leaves are triangular or heart-shaped, slightly toothed. Wet thickets and swamps, s. Me. to s. Ont. south. Summer and fall. Composite Family.

False Buckwheats or **Bindweeds** (*Polygonum*) White or greenish flowers in racemes or axillary clusters; leaves heart- or arrow-shaped at the base; stems jointed. See p. 322.

Common Hop (*Humulus lupulus*) Leaves with 3–5 deep lobes, sharply toothed. See p. 326.

Moonseed (*Menispermum canadense*) Leaves roundish, entire or shallowly lobed. See p. 356.

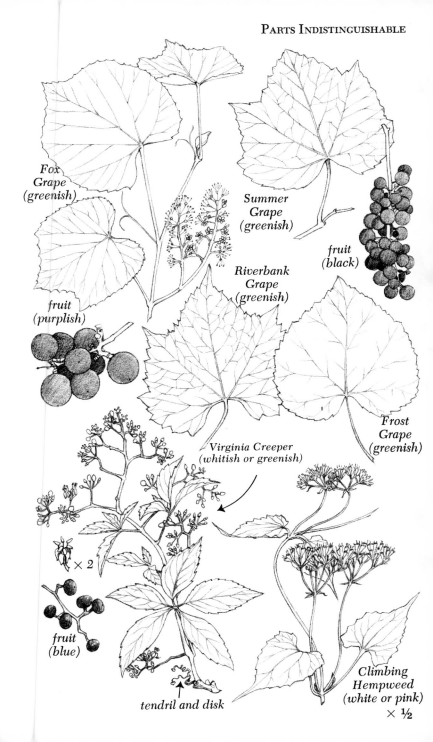

Fox Grape (greenish)

fruit (purplish)

Summer Grape (greenish)

fruit (black)

Riverbank Grape (greenish)

Frost Grape (greenish)

Virginia Creeper (whitish or greenish)

× 2

fruit (blue)

tendril and disk

Climbing Hempweed (white or pink) × ½

Flowers in Curved, One-sided Clusters, Together Forming a Large Terminal Cluster

BASAL LEAVES AND LOWEST STEM LEAVES CONSPICUOUSLY LARGER THAN THE REST OF THE LEAVES; STEM LEAVES DECREASING RAPIDLY IN SIZE UPWARDS

1. LEAVES THICK AND FLESHY, ENTIRE

Seaside Goldenrod (*S. sempervirens*) Plant of salt marshes and sandy soil near the sea. The showy flowers have 8–10 rays. Leaves oblong or lance-shaped, smooth. 1–8' high.

2. AT LEAST THE BASAL LEAVES TOOTHED

a. In dry soil of woods, thickets and fields

Gray Goldenrod (*S. nemoralis*) Basal leaves bluntly or obscurely toothed; stem and leaves grayish and fine-hairy. Larger leaves lance-shaped, tapering to the base. Flower cluster more or less 1-sided. 6–36″ high. Dry fields and open woods; common.

Sharp-leaved Goldenrod (*S. arguta*) Basal leaves sharply double-toothed, broadly egg-shaped, abruptly narrowed to a slender point; middle stem leaves sharply toothed; racemes horizontally spreading. Rays 5–8. Stem smooth. 2–4' high. Dry open woods, s. Me. to s. Ont. south.

Early Goldenrod (*S. juncea*) Basal leaves sharply toothed, lance-shaped and tapering gradually to the base; middle stem leaves nearly entire; stem smooth, green. Rays 8–12. Fields and borders; common.

Elm-leaved Goldenrod (*S. ulmifolia*) Basal leaves (often absent) and middle stem leaves sharply toothed; racemes few, arching upward; rays 3–5. 2–4' high. Dry soil, Mass. and Vt. to Minn. south.

b. In bogs and swamps

Rough-leaved Goldenrod (*S. patula*) Upper surface of leaves very rough; stem 4-sided. Basal leaves large (up to 16″ long), elliptical, tapering abruptly to the leaf stalk. Stem stout. 2–7' high. Swamps and wet meadows, usually in limestone regions, Vt. to Minn. south.

Swamp Goldenrod (*S. uliginosa*) Upper surface of leaves smooth; stem smooth, not 4-sided. Basal leaves lance-shaped, finely toothed, gradually tapering to the base, up to 12″ long. Disk flowers 4–8. 2–5' high. Swamps and wet thickets.

Continued

Gray
Goldenrod

Elm-
leaved
Goldenrod

Seaside
Goldenrod

Early
Goldenrod

Swamp
Goldenrod

Sharp-
leaved
Goldenrod

Rough-
leaved
Goldenrod

× 2/5

Flowers in Curved, One-sided Clusters, Together Forming a Large, Terminal Cluster (cont.)

ALL THE LEAVES MORE OR LESS UNIFORM OR VERY GRADUALLY REDUCED IN SIZE

1. LEAVES 3-VEINED, WITH 2 PROMINENT VEINS PARALLEL TO THE MIDRIB

Late Goldenrod (*S. gigantea*) Main stem smooth, usually covered with a whitish bloom; flower heads about ³⁄₁₆″ long. Leaves lance-shaped, sharply toothed. 2–7′ high. Moist or dry open places.

Tall Goldenrod (*S. altissima*) Main stem grayish-downy; flower heads about ³⁄₁₆″ long. Leaves remotely toothed, rough above, downy beneath. 2–7′ high. Dry open places.

Canada Goldenrod (*S. canadensis*) Main stem smooth near the base, downy above; flower heads under ⅛″ long. Leaves narrowly lance-shaped, sharply toothed. Flower rays very small. 1–5′ high. Fields and roadsides.

2. LEAVES NOT NOTICEABLY 3-VEINED

a. Leaves entire

Sweet Goldenrod (*S. odora*) Leaves narrowly lance-shaped, 2–4″ long, and usually anise-scented when bruised, although some plants have no odor. Flower rays 3–4. 2–4′ high. Dry open woods and clearings, s. N.H. to Ohio south.

b. Leaves toothed

Rough-stemmed Goldenrod (*S. rugosa*) Stem hairy or rough. A variable species, usually with rough and deeply veined leaves and a very hairy stem. Flower rays 6–10. 1–7′ high. Fields and thickets; common.

Elliott's Goldenrod (*S. elliottii*) Stem smooth; lower and middle leaves similar in size; flower rays 6–10. The leaves are smooth and elliptical or lance-shaped. 2–6′ high. Swamps and meadows, N.S. and e. Mass. south near the coast.

Elm-leaved Goldenrod (*S. ulmifolia*) Main stem smooth; the lower leaves distinctly larger than the middle leaves. Rays 3–5. See p. 446.

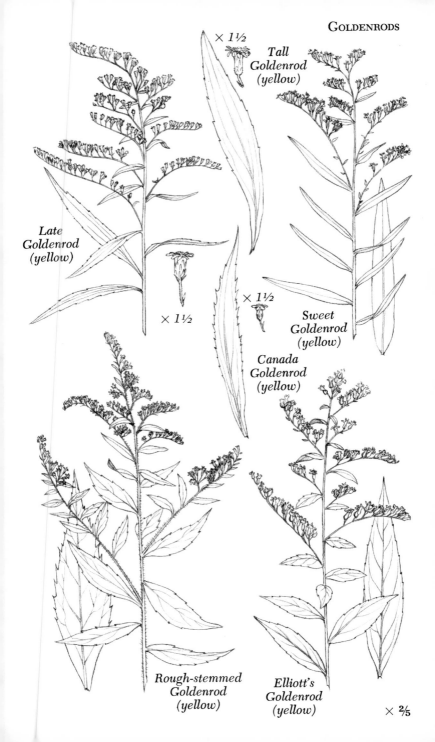

× 1½

Tall
Goldenrod
(yellow)

Late
Goldenrod
(yellow)

× 1½

× 1½

Sweet
Goldenrod
(yellow)

Canada
Goldenrod
(yellow)

Rough-stemmed
Goldenrod
(yellow)

Elliott's
Goldenrod
(yellow)

× ⅖

Stem Branched at the Top, Forming a Flattish Flower Cluster

LEAVES NARROW, WITHOUT LONG-STALKED BASAL LEAVES

Lance-leaved or **Grass-leaved Goldenrod** (*S. graminifolia*) Largest leaves about ¼″ wide, narrowly lance-shaped, entire, with 3–5 veins. 2–4′ high. Moist to dry open soil; common.

Slender-leaved Goldenrod (*S. tenuifolia*) Largest leaves very narrow (about ⅛″ wide), with either a single vein or 3 indistinct veins. There are often tufts of smaller leaves in the axils. 1–2½′ high. Sandy soil, N.S. and s. Me. south along the coast.

BASAL LEAVES LONG-STALKED, MUCH LARGER THAN THE UPPER LEAVES

Stiff or **Hard-leaved Goldenrod** (*S. rigida*) Leaves oval or oblong, rough. Lower leaves obscurely toothed or entire. Flower heads large for a goldenrod. Stem downy, 1–5′ high. Sandy or gravelly woods, Mass. to Sask. south.

Ohio Goldenrod (*S. ohioensis*) Leaves lance-shaped, smooth. The stem leaves point upward. Stem smooth, 2–3′ high. Bogs, wet meadows and sandy shores, w. N.Y. and e. Ont. to Wis. and Ill.

Flowers Principally in Axillary Clusters; Flower Rays Few (Mostly 3 or 4)

Zigzag or **Broad-leaved Goldenrod** (*S. flexicaulis*) Leaves egg-shaped, sharply toothed, abruptly narrowed at the base to a short stalk. Flowers grow in short clusters in the axils or in a terminal cluster. Stem zigzags and is somewhat angled. 1–3′ high. Rich woods.

Blue-stemmed or **Wreath Goldenrod** (*S. caesia*) Leaves lance-shaped, sharply toothed; stem arching, bluish. Flowers grow in the axils. 1–3′ high. Rich, open woods and clearings.

Flowers in a Terminal Cluster Longer Than Broad; Individual Flower Clusters neither Curving nor One-sided

BASAL LEAVES DENSELY HAIRY

Hairy Goldenrod (*S. hispida*) Stem and leaves densely hairy. Flowers orange-yellow, otherwise similar to Silverrod (p. 382). 1–3′ high. Dry open woods or rocky slopes, mostly in limestone regions.

Continued

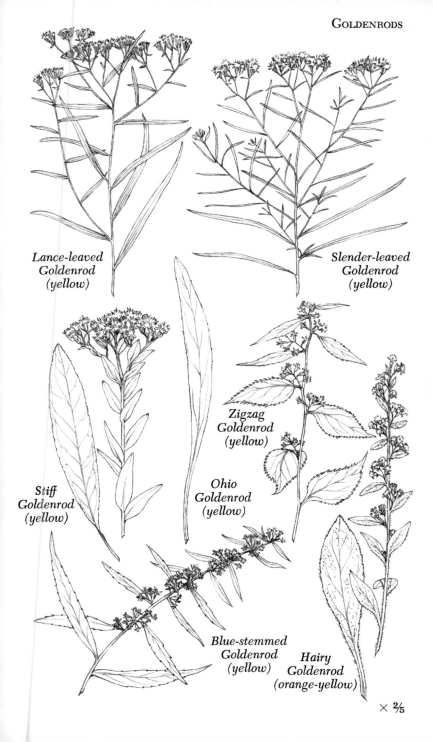

Lance-leaved
Goldenrod
(yellow)

Slender-leaved
Goldenrod
(yellow)

Stiff
Goldenrod
(yellow)

Ohio
Goldenrod
(yellow)

Zigzag
Goldenrod
(yellow)

Blue-stemmed
Goldenrod
(yellow)

Hairy
Goldenrod
(orange-yellow)

× ²⁄₅

Flowers in a Terminal Cluster Longer Than Broad; Individual Flower Clusters neither Curving nor One-sided (cont.)

BASAL OR LOWEST LEAVES SMOOTH OR NEARLY SO

1. PLANT OF SWAMPS AND BOGS

Bog Goldenrod (*S. purshii*) Lower leaves lance-shaped, long-stalked, slightly toothed or entire. Rays 4–6; disk flowers 9–16. Flowering branches stiffly erect. 1–4′ high. Bogs, more frequent in limestone areas.

2. NORTHERN PLANTS OF LEDGES, MOUNTAIN WOODS AND SUMMITS

Large-leaved Goldenrod (*S. macrophylla*) Basal leaves large, egg-shaped, abruptly narrowed to the stalk. Flower heads large, ¼–½″ high. 6–48″ high. Cool woods and mountain slopes, Mt. Greylock, Mass., and Catskill Mts. north.

Alpine Goldenrod (*S. cutleri*) Basal leaves tapering to the stalk; alpine summits. Middle leaves not much smaller than basal. 3–12″ high. N. N.Eng. and n. N.Y.

Rand's Goldenrod (*S. randii*) † Basal leaves tapering to the stalk; open ledges, but not alpine. Middle leaves much smaller than basal leaves. 6–24″ high. N. N.Eng. and n. N.Y. north.

3. PLANTS OF OPEN WOODS, FIELDS, ROADSIDES, PINE BARRENS

a. Bracts of flower heads with green, spreading tips

Stout Goldenrod (*S. squarrosa*) Flowers in a long cluster. Leaves egg-shaped. Stem stout. 2–5′ high. Dry open woods and clearings.

b. Bracts of flower heads not spreading

Showy Goldenrod (*S. speciosa*) Lower leaves large, egg-shaped or oval, toothed; middle leaves much smaller; rays 5–8, large. Flower cluster usually large and branching. Stem reddish. 2–6′ high. Woods and fields, Mass. to s. Minn. south.

Downy Goldenrod (*S. puberula*) Lower leaves lance-shaped or oblong, toothed; stem minutely hairy; floral bracts narrow; rays about 10, bright yellow. Flower cluster long and slender. 1½–3′ high. Open woods, sandy roadsides, mostly along coast.

Slender or **Erect Goldenrod** (*S. erecta*) Leaves and cluster similar to the Downy Goldenrod; stem smooth; floral bracts broad, blunt; rays 6–9, light yellow. 2–3′ high. Dry open woods, s. N.Eng. to Ind. south.

Wandlike Goldenrod (*S. stricta*) Lower leaves lance-shaped, entire; upper leaves very small and numerous, erect. Flower cluster very long and slender. 2–8′ high. Damp sands, N.J. south.

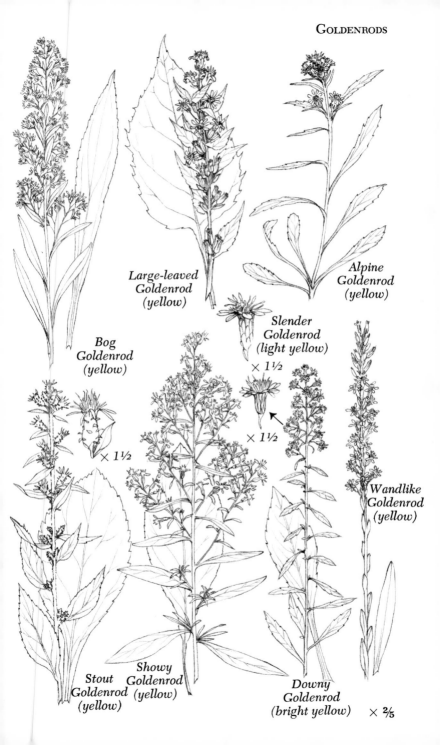

Large-leaved
Goldenrod
(yellow)

Alpine
Goldenrod
(yellow)

Slender
Goldenrod
(light yellow)
× 1½

Bog
Goldenrod
(yellow)

× 1½

Wandlike
Goldenrod
(yellow)

Stout Showy
Goldenrod Goldenrod
(yellow) *(yellow)*

Downy
Goldenrod
(bright yellow) × ⅖

Basal Leaves and Lower Stem Leaves Heart- or Arrow-shaped and Long-stalked

LARGER LEAVES ENTIRE OR SLIGHTLY TOOTHED

Wavy-leaved Aster (*A. undulatus*) Stalks of the larger stem leaves enlarged at the base and clasping the stem. Rays light blue-violet, 8–15; heads ¾–1″ wide. Leaves rough, wavy-margined or slightly toothed. Stem stiff and rough. 1–4′ high. Dry open woods, clearings.

Short's Aster (*A. shortii*) Lower stem leaves narrowly heart-shaped, entire or nearly so, the stalks slender, without wings, not clasping. Pale-violet flowers; heads about 1″ wide. 1–4′ high. Woods and rocky slopes, s. Pa. to Wis. south.

LARGER LEAVES OBVIOUSLY TOOTHED

1. BASAL LEAVES HEART-SHAPED, 3″ OR MORE WIDE

Large-leaved Aster (*A. macrophyllus*) Violet or lavender flowers (rarely white); the stalks of the flower cluster bearing minute glands. Basal leaves often harsh and thick. 1–4′ high. Dry woods; common.

Schreber's Aster (*A. schreberi*) † White flowers; stalks of flower cluster glandless. Basal leaves thinner and smoother than in the Large-leaved Aster. 1–4′ high. Rich woods and borders, N.Eng. to Ill. south.

2. BASAL LEAVES LESS THAN 3″ WIDE OR NONE

White Wood Aster (*A. divaricatus*) White flowers; heads ¾–1″ wide, in a flattish cluster; lower stem leaves heart-shaped, with coarse and sharp teeth. 1–3′ high. Dry woods and clearings, s. Me. to Ohio south; common.

Heart-leaved Aster (*A. cordifolius*) Blue-violet to rose (rarely white) flowers; heads ½–⅝″ wide; middle stem leaves sharply and conspicuously toothed and slender-stalked; bracts of flower heads with dark-green tips. 1–5′ high. Woods and thickets; common.

Lowrie's Aster (*A. lowrieanus*) Flowers and bracts like those of the Heart-leaved Aster; middle stem leaves shallowly toothed, with winged stalks and a very smooth (almost greasy) surface. Conn. to Mich. south.

Arrow-leaved Aster (*A. sagittifolius*) Blue, pinkish or white flowers; heads ½–¾″ wide; middle stem leaves shallowly toothed, narrowly egg-shaped, somewhat heart- or arrow-shaped at the base, the stalks winged; the bracts of the flower heads narrow, with a central green stripe. 2–5′ high. Dry woods, w. Vt. to N.D. south.

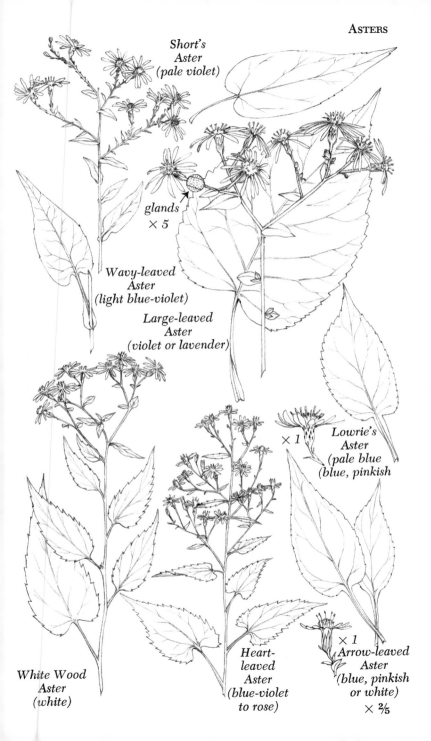

Short's
Aster
(pale violet)

glands
× 5

Wavy-leaved
Aster
(light blue-violet)

Large-leaved
Aster
(violet or lavender)

× 1

Lowrie's
Aster
(pale blue
(blue, pinkish

White Wood
Aster
(white)

Heart-
leaved
Aster
(blue-violet
to rose)

× 1
Arrow-leaved
Aster
(blue, pinkish
or white)

× ⅖

Larger Leaves Noticeably Toothed, Not Both Heart-shaped and Long-stalked

LARGER LEAVES WITH A BROAD BASE, WHICH OBVIOUSLY CLASPS THE STEM

Crooked-stem Aster (*A. prenanthoides*) The lower third of the leaf narrow and entire, noticeably enlarged where it clasps the stem. Blue-violet flowers; heads 1–1½" wide. Stem zigzags, much branched. 1–3′ high. Moist thickets, w. Mass. to Minn. south.

Purple-stemmed Aster (*A. puniceus*) Leaves gradually tapering to the clasping base; stem usually stout, reddish and hairy. Blue-violet, pale-violet or lilac, rarely white, flowers; heads 1–1½" wide. 2–8′ high. Swamps and low thickets; common.

LEAVES CLASPING THE STEM ONLY SLIGHTLY, IF AT ALL

1. FLOWER HEADS OVER ½" WIDE

Sharp-leaved, Mountain or **Whorled Aster** (*A. acuminatus*) Upper leaves larger than the lower leaves and appearing to be whorled. Leaves coarsely toothed, long-pointed. White or purple-tinged flowers; heads 1–1½" wide. 8–36" high. Moist or dry woods, Nfld. to e. Ont. south.

Rough-leaved Aster (*A. radula*) Leaves broadly lance-shaped, sharply toothed, rough on both sides and prominently veined. Violet flowers; heads 1–1½" wide. 8–40" high. Wet woods and bogs, Nfld. south to Md., inland to W.Va.

Panicled Aster (*A. simplex*) Leaves narrowly lance-shaped, toothed or entire; flowers white or tinged with violet; heads ¾–1" wide. 2–6′ high. Meadows and shores.

New York Aster (*A. novi-belgii*) Leaves narrowly lance-shaped, slightly toothed; flowers violet; bracts of flower head with out-ward-curving tips. See p. 460.

2. FLOWER HEADS ¼–½" WIDE

Calico or **Starved Aster** (*A. lateriflorus*) Flower heads with 9–15 rays; leaves lance-shaped, usually with a few, sharp teeth near the middle. Flowers white or purple-tinged, often with a purple disk. 1–4′ high. Fields and borders; common.

Small White Aster (*A. vimineus*) Flower heads with 15–30 rays; leaves narrowly lance-shaped, slightly toothed. See p. 458.

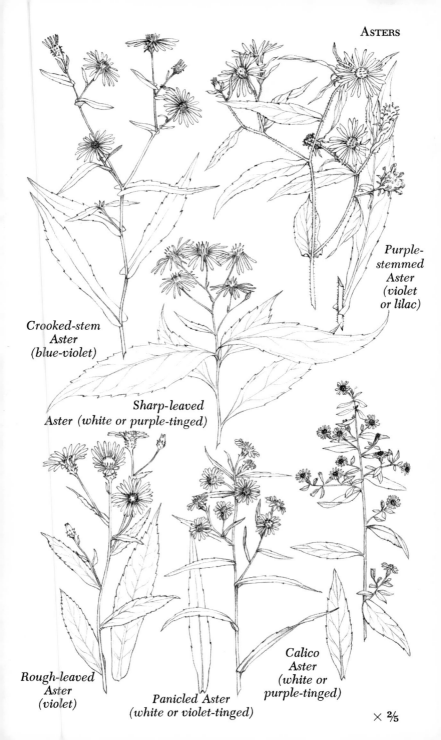

Purple-stemmed Aster (violet or lilac)

Crooked-stem Aster (blue-violet)

Sharp-leaved Aster (white or purple-tinged)

Rough-leaved Aster (violet)

Panicled Aster (white or violet-tinged)

Calico Aster (white or purple-tinged)

× 2/5

Larger Leaves Narrow or Narrowly Lance-shaped (7 or More Times Longer Than Wide); Flower Heads ¼–¾″ Wide

1. PLANTS OF SALT MARSHES

Small or **Annual Salt-marsh Aster** (*A. subulatus*) Flower heads under ½″ wide; rays purplish, very short. Leaves narrowly lance-shaped, 2–10″ long. 1–3′ high. Along the coast; rare inland.

Large or **Perennial Salt-marsh Aster** (*A. tenuifolius*) Flower heads ½″ or more wide. See p. 460.

2. PLANTS OF FIELDS, MEADOWS OR ROADSIDES

Many-flowered Aster (*A. ericoides*) Bracts (at base of flower head) with broad, green, spreading tips. Flowers white. Leaves narrow, with rough edges, ½–1½″ long. 1–6′ high. Me. to B.C. south.

Heath Aster (*A. pilosus*) Bracts of flower head stiff, long-pointed and often spreading; uppermost leaves sharply pointed. Flowers white. Stem stiffly branched. 1–5′ high. C. Me. to Minn. south.

Small White Aster (*A. vimineus*) Bracts of flower heads narrow, neither stiff nor wide-spreading; flowers white; heads under ½″ wide. Larger leaves narrowly lance-shaped, usually obscurely toothed. Flowers numerous. Stem often arching. 1–5′ high. S. Me. and sw. Que. to Mich. south.

Bushy Aster (*A. dumosus*) Bracts of flower heads narrow, not spreading; flowers pale lavender, bluish, or sometimes white; heads ½–¾″ wide; leaves bluntly pointed. The flowering branches bear numerous, very small leaves. 1–3′ high. Dry to moist sandy soil, s. N.Eng. to Mich. south, mostly along the coast.

Larger Leaves Narrow or Narrowly Lance-shaped (7 or More Times Longer Than Wide); Flower Heads ¾–1½″ Wide

1. LOW PLANTS (6–24″HIGH) OF DRY, ROCKY OR SANDY SOIL

Stiff Aster (*A. linariifolius*) Violet flowers; heads about 1″ wide; leaves ¾–1½″ long, stiff and numerous. Stems stiff, growing in tussocks. 6–24″ high. Dry sandy or rocky soil.

Upland White Aster (*A. ptarmicoides*) Snowy-white flowers; heads about ¾″ wide, in a flattish cluster. Leaves stiff, 3–6″ long. 1–2′ high. Dry, rocky places, w. Que. south to Conn., N.Y., Ohio and Mo., and in mts. to Ga., usually in limestone areas.

Continued

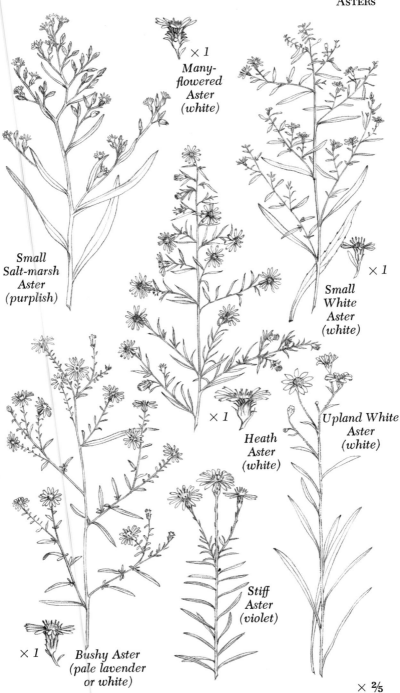

× 1
Many-
flowered
Aster
(white)

Small
Salt-marsh
Aster
(purplish)

× 1

Small
White
Aster
(white)

× 1

Heath
Aster
(white)

Upland White
Aster
(white)

× 1   Bushy Aster
(pale lavender
or white)

Stiff
Aster
(violet)

× 2/5

Larger Leaves Narrow or Narrowly Lance-shaped (7 or More Times Longer Than Wide); Heads ¾–1½" Wide (cont.)

2. PLANTS OF DAMP TO WET SITUATIONS WITH SLENDER STEMS; USUALLY UNDER 3' HIGH

Bog Aster (*A. nemoralis*) Leaves very numerous, ½–2½" long, with the rough margins turned slightly inward. Light violet-purple rays; heads 1–1½" wide. 6–24" high. Bogs and shores, N.J., N.Y. and Mich. north.

New York Aster (*A. novi-belgii*) Leaves narrowly lance-shaped, slightly clasping the stem, the larger over 3" long; bracts of the flower heads with outward-curving tips. Violet rays; heads ¾–1¼" wide. 1–4' high. Damp thickets and swamps, along the coast.

Large or **Perennial Salt-marsh Aster** (*A. tenuifolius*) Plant of salt marshes with a few fleshy, long, narrow leaves; bracts not spreading. Flower heads ½–1" wide; pale-purple to white rays. 6–24" high. N.H. south.

Rush Aster (*A. junciformis*) Larger leaves very narrow, 2–6" long, rough-edged; bracts not spreading. Flower heads about 1" wide; violet, rose or white rays. 1–3' high. Bogs and swamps, n. N.J. to Iowa north.

3. PLANT WITH STOUT STEMS, USUALLY OVER 3' HIGH

Panicled Aster (*A. simplex*) Flower heads ¾–1" wide; rays white or faintly tinged with violet. See p. 456.

Larger Leaves Lance-shaped or Wider (2–6 Times Longer Than Wide), Obscurely Toothed or Entire, Not Both Heart-shaped and Long-stalked

MIDDLE AND UPPER LEAVES WITH A HEART-SHAPED BASE, WHICH DEFINITELY CLASPS THE STEM

New England Aster (*A. novae-angliae*) Stem stout, bristly-hairy; 2–8' high. Flower heads 1–2" wide, with numerous (40–50) violet-purple rays (occasionally rose-colored or white). Leaves lance-shaped, clasping. Fields, damp meadows and shores.

Late Purple or **Spreading Aster** (*A. patens*) Stem rough, slender; 1–3' high. Leaves oval or oblong, blunt or short-pointed, clasping. Flower heads 1" wide; rays deep violet. Dry woods and fields, c. Me. to Minn. south.

Smooth Aster (*A. laevis*) Stem smooth, with a whitish bloom. Leaves thick, very smooth to the touch, mostly entire. Flower heads ¾–1" wide; blue or violet rays. 1–4' high. Dry fields and open woods, Me. to Sask. south. Continued

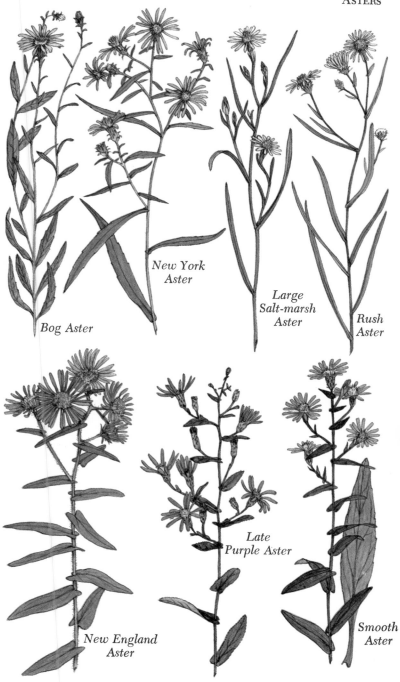

Bog Aster

New York
Aster

Large
Salt-marsh
Aster

Rush
Aster

New England
Aster

Late
Purple Aster

Smooth
Aster

× **2/5**

Larger Leaves Lance-shaped or Wider (2–6 Times Longer Than Wide), Obscurely Toothed or Entire, Not Both Heart-shaped and Long-Stalked (cont.)

LEAVES NOT OBVIOUSLY CLASPING THE STEM

1. FLOWERS WHITE OR FAINTLY TINGED WITH VIOLET

Flat-topped Aster (*A. umbellatus*) Flower heads ½–¾″ wide, in a flattish cluster; grows in moist places; rays 7–15. Leaves lance-shaped or elliptical. 2–8′ high. Moist thickets and borders of swamps.

Cornel-leaved Aster (*A. infirmus*) Flower heads about 1″ wide; grows in dry woods and on slopes; rays 7–12. Leaves egg-shaped or elliptical, entire, the lower leaves smaller than the middle leaves. 1½–3′ high. Mass. to Ohio south, mostly inland.

Panicled Aster (*A. simplex*) Flower heads ¾–1″ wide; rays 20–40; 2–6′ high. See p. 456.

Calico or **Starved Aster** (*A. lateriflorus*) Flower heads ¼–½″ wide, with 9–15 rays. See p. 456.

2. FLOWERS VIOLET, LILAC OR PURPLE

Showy Aster (*A. spectabilis*) Showy, bright-violet flowers; heads 1–1½″ wide; grows in dry sandy soil. Basal leaves long-stalked, lance-shaped or narrowly egg-shaped, obscurely toothed or entire, 3–5″ long. Bracts of flower head usually spreading. 1–2′ high. E. Mass. south along the coast.

Eastern Silvery Aster (*A. concolor*) Lilac flowers; heads about ¾″ wide, in a long raceme, sometimes with a few short branches. Leaves oblong, 1½–2″ long, silky-hairy on both sides. Sandy soil along the coast, s. Mass. south.

Bog Aster (*A. nemoralis*) Light violet-purple flowers; heads 1–1½″ wide; bogs and shores, See p. 460.

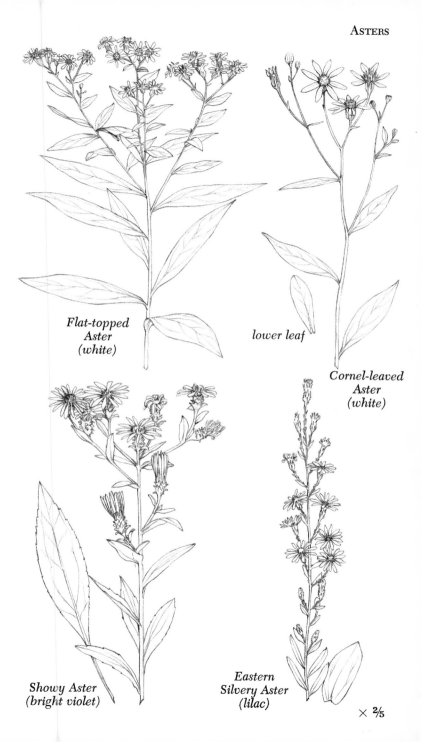

Flat-topped
Aster
(white)

lower leaf

Cornel-leaved
Aster
(white)

Showy Aster
(bright violet)

Eastern
Silvery Aster
(lilac)

× ⅖

Index

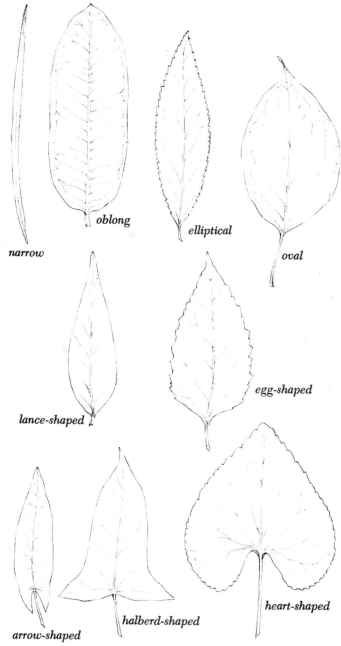

narrow

oblong

elliptical

oval

lance-shaped

egg-shaped

arrow-shaped

halberd-shaped

heart-shaped